More Critical Praise for *Trade Options Online*

"*Trade Options Online* serves as a superb resource for the current and future online options traders, who must negotiate the mountain of information on the Web."

—Bernie Schaeffer, Chairman,
Schaeffer's Investment Research, Inc.

"As the first book on the subject, *Trade Options Online* is a valuable addition to any option trader's library. George has been an eSignal user for many years and we enjoy working with him to help educate our users. We are continually impressed with the way he leads the industry with his new ideas on trading. In this book, George clearly relays to the reader the information every option trader needs to make money on the Internet."

—Julie Craig, Data Broadcasting Corporation
(www.esignal.com)

"George Fontanills has written the first book for option traders who want to trade online. This is a practical how to get started guide equally applicable for a beginner or an advanced option trader. It covers not only option strategies but also introduces the resources necessary for a trader to become successful. I especially liked the Appendixes where he ranked the leading option web sites and online option brokers—'this alone is worth the price of the book'!"

—Kris Skrinak, General Manager
ClearStation, Inc.

"With the tremendous growth of online trading, option traders rely upon guidance tailored to their individual needs. Fontanills' *Trade Options Online* is an invaluable resource for both the new and the experienced option trader."

—Alan Suslow, CEO, Mr. Stock

"George Fontanills has written the definitive guide for all option traders and investors who want to trade online. The book makes it easy to understand the building blocks of successful options trading by clearly explaining how to identify the potential risk and profitability of an option trade. This book is yet another fine example of why Quote.com selected George Fontanills to provide options education to its subscribers on the "Butterfly Corner" (http://butterfly.quote.com). *Trade Options Online*, and especially its Appendixes, will become an invaluable tool for the twenty-first century option trader. I am grateful that George has taken the time to pass his experience and ideas on to option traders all over the world. Tres beau travail, George!"

—Francis Gagnon
Derivatives Site Producer, Quote.com

wiley online trading for a living

Electronic Day Trading to Win / Bob Baird and Craig McBurney

Day Trade Online / Christopher A. Farrell

Trade Options Online / George A. Fontanills

Electronic Day Trading 101 / Sunny J. Harris

How I Trade for a Living / Gary Smith

trade options online

GEORGE A. FONTANILLS

John Wiley & Sons, Inc.
New York • Chichester • Weinheim • Brisbane • Singapore • Toronto

Library of Congress Cataloging-in-Publication Data:
Fontanills, George.
    Trade options online / George A. Fontanills.
      p. cm.—(Wiley online trading for a living)
    Includes index.
    ISBN 0-471-35938-6 (alk. paper)
    1. Options (Finance)—Computer network resources.   2. Investments—
Computer network resources.   3. Internet (Computer network)
   I. Title.   II. Series.
   HG6024.A3F663   2000
   025.06'33263228—dc21   99-16342

Printed in the United States of America

10 9 8 7 6 5 4 3 2 1

contents

acknowledgments

Napoleon Hill, a motivational speaker, wrote, "Man alone has the power to transform his thoughts into physical reality; man alone can dream and make his dreams come true." I have always lived my life by making my dreams come true. One of my greatest secrets to success is to surround myself with talented people who want to be a part of assisting my dreams to become reality.

My mission is to develop, teach, and trade high profit/low risk trading strategies for people who want to learn how to become successful options traders. I would like to take this opportunity to acknowledge the dedication of all our staff who continually contribute to my success and that of our companies. The staff of our education and research division, called "Optionetics" and Global Investment Research Corp., are totally committed to the welfare of our students by teaching them how to make high profits while managing the risks of trading. Additionally, our Boston-based money management business, Pinnacle Investments of America, Inc., has an equally dedicated staff who concentrate on helping me to maximize returns for our investors. I am grateful to them all and take this opportunity to mention some of the essential people in my life who inspire and support me. In particular, and in no order of importance, I would like to especially thank the following:

My contributing writer, Tom Gentile, who is my coinstructor at Optionetics Seminars and our chief options strategist. Tom is responsible for the trading models that we create to test our theories for our money management and also acts as a publisher of our research. He has been quoted in *Barron's* and in the *Wall Street Journal*. Tom is a guru at spread trading, and the art of the straddle.

Kym Trippsmith, my senior editor of this book, whose dedication to the completion of this project was simply amazing. Kym has worked with me for the past four years organizing my thoughts into articles and published materials. Her hard work and attention to detail have enabled me to concentrate on what I enjoy and do best— trade and make money. Thank you, Kym. Without you this book would never have been completed.

My partner, Tony Clemendor, whom I met at Harvard Business

School in 1984, has been my loyal friend ever since. After he had led a successful business career in his own right, I managed to persuade him to join our team several years ago. It was one of our best decisions to entrust him with the business development of our companies.

Special thanks go to the CEO of our companies, my partner and friend, Richard Cawood, who drives me on to the next level of success. I leave Richard to organize the details of our businesses and my life so I can concentrate on my trading.

I also want to thank Andrew Neyens for his expert work on the final edit of the manuscript. As always he is a trading wizard with an excellent eye for details that may have been otherwise overlooked.

As always, my deepest thanks go to my trading family and friends. I am very grateful to my friends who have supported and believed in me for the past 10 years. An amazing part of business is the diverse people that you meet. Thankfully, I have had many more good experiences than bad. My good experiences represent times spent with highly talented individuals who give without expectation of reward or self-promotion. Their kind deeds and actions have helped to raise my performance to higher levels.

Each day I thank God for giving me a second lease on life after my bout with cancer as a young man. I am blessed to be able to do what I enjoy every day for a living, to travel when and where I want, and to be with my family. I have so much to be thankful for, especially my marvelous family who have always been there for me with their unconditional support and love.

I have dedicated this book to our wives. Without their support we would not have been able to attain the success we have. They understand why we get up at 2 A.M. to check the markets, they tolerate us having access to real-time quotes at all times, they endure our hectic travel schedules, and they always encourage us to climb to new heights.

Finally, I would like to thank my students, who inspire me to publish my ideas and continue to teach. Since I started educating the public in 1993, I have always let students reattend my seminars for free so they can keep up with new trading discoveries. In six years of teaching, we have developed a loyal following of successful traders and they, too, provide me with new ideas for trading. If you have any trading ideas, please feel free to contact me. I hope to meet you someday at one of my many speaking engagements or at an Optionetics seminar. As an online trader, I believe that you are the future of trading.

Good luck and great trading!

George Fontanills
President
Pinnacle Investments of America, Inc.
Boston, MA
george@piafunds.com

introduction

the online trading revolution

There is a revolution going on! Every day the Internet is changing the way human beings live, work, and play. Never before has information been so readily available. But we are infants in this new medium, constantly testing the limits of our postmodern playground. In the end, the far-reaching effects of living online will be a momentous testament to human evolution.

You may be wondering how this revolution began. In 1969 the U.S. Department of Defense developed a labyrinth of networked computers to enable the exchange of information to and from anywhere in the world. In its early stages, the Internet was little more than a basic text. But in 1989, an interconnected information network called the World Wide Web introduced a multimedia format with text, graphics, sound, and video. The Internet has since become a global communications system for commerce, research, entertainment, and investing. We are witnessing the birth of a new age.

Every 100 days, one million new users start surfing the Net the world over. This astonishing rate of growth has given birth to a new investing medium the like of which has never been seen before: online trading. The advent of online trading is changing the very nature of the investment game. Online brokers now handle 14% of all stock trades and this number is rising dramatically. As millions of independent traders gain access to information that used to be available only to investment professionals, computerized trading is quickly becoming the wave of the future—and the future is now. To compete in the markets of the third millennium, traders have to learn how to ride the crest of the cyberwave right into the heart of Wall Street.

Integrating online trading practices into your daily investment experience can be a painstakingly arduous process. Even if you have the time to keep abreast of the latest technological advances, the highest-tech gadgets and software programs of today are outdated as soon as you remove them from the packing box. The general public is adrift in a sea of soon-to-be-obsolete computers, out-of-date programs, and software that takes up way too much hard drive space. This tide will not turn anytime soon. Computer technologies are evolving at a seemingly exponential pace, advancing online trading to the vanguard of the economic front.

Keeping up with the increased demands of online trading maintenance is a double-edged sword. On the one hand, you have more independence than ever before; but on the other hand there's a huge commitment of time involved. Suddenly there's the constant barrage of e-mails to read, portfolio trackers to monitor, stocks that need to be researched, and daily news clips to be digested. After countless hours spent sitting in front of my computer, I realize I can't live without it. Computers increase my ability to analyze thousands of trades in a matter of seconds and make researching a company as simple as a few strokes on the keyboard. My computer also allows me to move faster than ever before. I can reach decisions that make or lose large sums of money without discussing my decisions with anyone. Therein lies the work. An online trader has to assume complete responsibility for understanding the intricacies of the marketplace and making good trading decisions. The computer can help in many ways; but comprehensive market knowledge and experience are vital to making money. Point-and-click investors cannot invest as though they are playing video games. There is real money at stake and the stakes are high if you enter the potentially lucrative world of the markets as an online trader.

As traders and investors, we are currently living in between two

---

portfolio trackers
a portfolio tracker is an online service provided by a financial web site or an online brokerage that enables an investor to keep track of the daily price movement, breaking news, and investor sentiment of a chosen list of stocks and indexes.

worlds. In the first world, telephones and newspapers remain the mainstay of an investor's necessary equipment. Every morning, millions of investors hungrily scan newspapers for clues to profitable trading opportunities while phones remain the primary means of placing a trade through a broker. I must admit that I personally revel in my ability to still talk to a real person. But these traditions are slowly giving way to the new world order of megabytes and modems, search engines and online brokerages. At the present time, online trading is an anomalous entity with a life all its own. Until the rules of this cyberworld solidify, investors will remain precariously balanced—one hand on the cellular phone and the other on the keyboard.

---

investing newspapers

Wall Street Journal   With worldwide distribution and an extensive readership, the *Wall Street Journal* is packed with financial information and has the ability to significantly influence the makets. If a company gets in the *Wall Street Journal*, it is news! (interactive.wsj.com).

Investor's Business Daily (IBD)   Founded by William J. O'Neil, the *IBD* was originally developed to add a new dimension of crucial information for the investment community. The *IBD* focuses on concise investment news information, sophisticated charts, tables, and analytical tools while adding valuable information that the *Wall Street Journal* may not provide (www.investors.com).

In two years (1997–1998), seven million new online trading accounts were opened. Online trading is currently responsible for 40% of the volume on Nasdaq. The phenomenal infiltration of millions of new online investors into the markets is unprecedented. Many online brokerages are stretched beyond their capacity, resulting in widespread growing pains. Massive bottlenecks on a number of high-volume Internet stocks as well as periodic access difficulties have triggered a variety of problems and losses for traders across the board. Buy and sell orders have been delayed or not processed at all. Online brokerage servers have experienced system failures and traders have been denied access to their accounts. The chat rooms are filled to the brim with complaints. Even the Securities and Exchange Commission (SEC) and other governmental regulators have been warning investors to exercise caution. But the record number of investors signing up with online brokerages speaks for itself.

There are some horror stories of entire systems shutting down totally for hours on end, and of online brokerages not being able to execute orders or handle the volume of calls. This has become the online trader's nightmare. Your money is locked up, you're stuck on hold for hours, and you can't access your account. Meanwhile the market is moving against you and you are unable to react. This time, it's not because of indecision but because of the inefficiency of your online broker's systems. The SEC is actively addressing this issue with aggressive requirements for all Internet brokers and random audits to ensure compliance. As online brokerage firms learn to forecast demand and set up the appropriate systems for support of a parabolic growth in the number of customers, these problems should become less apparent.

Nasdaq
the National Association of Securities Dealers automated quotations system is a computerized exchange that provides brokers and dealers with price quotations for securities traded over-the-counter as well as for many New York Stock Exchange–listed securities (www.nasdaq.com).

Securities and Exchange Commission (SEC)
commission created by Congress to regulate the securities markets and protect investors. It is composed of five commissioners appointed by the President of the United States and approved by the Senate (www.sec.gov).

Will online trading replace traditional investment methods altogether? It is conceivable that it will. There may always be a group of investors who never use online trading systems due to fear of the computer or fear of lost orders, but these individuals in the future will likely become the minority. In order to be prepared for this massive shift, investors need to become cyber-friendly. This is an uphill battle at best, as electronic investing parameters seem to be in a state of constant revision. The profusion of financial resource web sites and online brokerages can be overwhelming and confusing. Too much information can be crippling. What about the long-range services provided by a full-service brokerage? In order to reap the advantages and avoid growing pains currently afflicting the online trading industry, serious investors need to develop a systematic approach to cyber-investing.

People are attracted to online trading because it is an empowering situation. For the first time in history, anyone has access to the kind of information that used to be the sole domain of powerful brokers and market analysts. Online trading has finally bridged the information gap by affording off-floor traders a new level of autonomy. This newly found independence can be satisfying as well as addictive.

For an options investor, the battle is even more complex. Although options augment the diversity of an investor's portfolio, they also increase the number of choices that have to be made. Just finding an online brokerage with the right combination of variables could take weeks of investigative research. There are a myriad of factors that require review (including commission costs, customer support, option services, timely executions and exits, and the ease of access to accounts especially during high-volume sessions). Many investors simply don't know where to start or whom to trust. Others simply don't have time for this kind of in-depth research.

But that's just the tip of the iceberg. Although there is an abundance of online brokerages that handle options, very few offer cross margining or handle complex options combinations and spread orders efficiently. In most cases, spreads must still be entered manually by phone to a live broker. That's because online systems tend to process a spread as two separate orders—a dangerous game, especially if one of the options is short. Unfortunately, nothing short of widespread restructuring will solve these problems. As this book goes to press, online brokerages are attempting to find solutions that will make online trading, especially options trading, safer and easier for off-floor investors. In addition, as more and more online brokers move from a correspondence clearing process to a self-clearing mechanism, we may see a giant step toward increasing the efficiency of online options trading.

---

options
a trading instrument that represents the right to buy or sell a specified amount of an underlying stock at a predetermined price within a specified time. The option purchaser has the right, but not the obligation, to exercise the specifics of the contract. The option seller assumes a legal obligation to fulfill the specifics of the contract if the option is assigned to an option buyer.

---

spread orders
the simultaneous purchase and sale of at least two different option contracts of the same underlying stock.

To become adept at options cyber-trading, you have to have a working knowledge of options strategies, enough computer savvy to give you a competitive edge, and an online brokerage that can handle complex options strategies. This book is designed to provide you with the means to develop your skills as an online options trader. The journey into this new world awaits. Let's get started.

why trade options online

Options are a relatively new trading instrument. Options were traded over-the-counter (OTC) by a limited number of put/call dealers up until 1973 when the Chicago Board Options Exchange (CBOE) formally established a standardized list of recognized options. Currently the CBOE lists options on 680 stocks with more than 700,000 option contracts traded daily. The CBOE is an auction market system that employs floor brokers and market makers to execute customer orders and inspire additional competition in the markets. The three other domestic exchanges that trade options are the Pacific Stock Exchange (PCX) in San Francisco, the American Stock Exchange (AMEX), and the Philadelphia Stock Exchange (PHLX).

Chicago Board Options Exchange (CBOE)
the CBOE is the largest options exchange in the United States. Its web site offers new option listings, information on equities, options, and LEAPS, and tutorials. Specialization includes calls and puts on NYSE stocks, the S&P 500, U.S. Treasury bonds, and other indexes (www.cboe.com).

Pacific Stock Exchange (PCX)
the Pacific Stock Exchange is the third most active stock exchange in the country and the third largest stock options exchange in the world. More than 2,600 stocks, bonds, and other securities issued by publicly traded companies, as well as options on more than 550 stocks are traded on the PCX, along with a variety of indexes (www.pacificex.com).

Prior to the advent of online trading, investors had limited information resources and often needed a broker to perform company research or assess option volatility. But computer technology has changed all that. Software has also changed the nature of the game by enabling traders to sort through thousands of possible option positions in mere seconds to find trading opportunities with the greatest chance of making money. However, finding and learning how to use the most suitable program for your needs can be very time-consuming. Luckily, most programs come with a 30-day trial period giving you the chance to play before you pay. (See Appendix C.)

American Stock Exchange (AMEX)
the American Stock Exchange is comprised of companies that were too small to be listed on the New York Stock Exchange. The AMEX web site united with Nasdaq's site to offer quotes, news, and exchange information as well as excellent educational materials (www.amex.com).

Philadelphia Stock Exchange (PHLX)
founded in 1790, the Philadelphia Stock Exchange was the first organized stock exchange in the United States. Trading more than 2,800 stocks, 700 equity options, 12 index options, and 100 currency options, the PHLX web site offers 15-minute-delayed quotes along with volatility charts, news, research, and daily market analysis (www.phlx.com).

As a professional, I could not trade options without the use of electronic investing technologies. Millions of investors and traders seem to agree. Prestigious full-service brokers are losing ground to on-line brokerages that offer 24-hour access and cheaper commissions. Although you still need a broker who is reliable and easily accessible, your scope of interest needs to go beyond the person at the other end of the phone line. You are forging a new relationship and your ability to prosper primarily relies on how well you can use the tools the Internet offers. This places new demands on you as a trader, increasing the scope of details you have to keep track of tenfold. You are no longer dependent on the whims of your broker. You are self-reliant, and this self-sufficiency requires you to balance independence with increased responsibilities (i.e., your ability to respond). Increased autonomy is one of the main reasons that trading options online is growing at such a phenomenal rate.

online pros and cons

Online trading offers options traders an assortment of advantages over traditional full-service and discount brokerages. The foremost advantage is that online brokerages have severely reduced their commission costs from the lofty levels set by traditional brokers. All brokers get paid a commission fee each time an order is placed or exited. The amount of this commission depends on what kind of service the broker provides. Each transaction is called a round turn and costs as little as $5 at an online brokerage and over $100 at a full-service brokerage.

Three main kinds of traditional brokers have dominated the playing field: full-service, discount, and deep-discount brokers. Full-service brokers require higher commissions because they research markets in order to advise clients. Discount brokers offer lower commissions because they limit their services to placing orders and facilitating exits. Deep-discount brokers offer even lower commission rates as they primarily trade large blocks for big investors. Online brokerages have broken the mold completely by offering the lowest commission costs ever via easy computer access. Although their services differ, timely executions and good fills are still the most important part of a brokerage's services. Since a one-tick difference in execution can cost you a bundle, look for an online brokerage that balances low cost with reliable service and good fills.

Another major improvement comes in the form of information. Online brokerages offer real-time quotes, charts, news, and analysis as well as the ability to customize this information to fit your portfolio. Now you have the means to research stock tips immediately, read up-to-the-minute news almost as it happens, monitor the mood of markets throughout the day, and access option premiums for price fluctuations and volatility. You no longer have to sit on hold waiting for your broker to say, "I'll get back to you on that." The marketplace is alive and you're right there with it.

In the old days, one of the best ways to find a good broker was through the recommendation of other traders. This hasn't changed much. For your convenience, reviews of more than 60 online brokerages have been included in Appendix E of this book. Since the Internet is in a constant state of evolution, this information will be updated at www.optionetics.com. You should also take a look at Gomez Advisors (www.gomez.com) or Online Investment Services (www.sonic.net/donaldj), two of the most comprehensive web sites that specifically rate and review online brokerages. If you want to know what your fellow investors have to say, there are a variety of online message boards and chat rooms that specifically post individual rants and raves; check out Yahoo!'s chats and forums directory (dir.yahoo.com/Business_and _Economy/Finance_and_Investment/Chats_and_Forums).

Gomez Advisors
founded by Juan Gomez, a senior analyst from Forrester Research, this well-researched site has become an Internet favorite and is widely referenced as the premiere online brokerage watchdog. Cyberfinance scorecards for bankers and brokerages are ranked by overall score, categories, and consumer profiles (www.gomez.com).

Online Investment Services
this free site is dedicated to researching and collecting comments on online brokerages. Compare high, middle, and deep discount brokerages by service, commission rates, and customer service. If you have an experience with a brokerage that you want to share with the public at large, this is the place to post it (www.sonic.net/donaldj).

Computerized trading also offers traders the chance to engage powerful software programs. Various analyses can be performed that directly access real-time and/or delayed quotes. One of the most popular functions is called screening. Screening enables a trader to choose a specific set of criteria—market outlook, strike spread, maximum risk, and volatility assumptions—in order to search for trades that meet those requirements. In the blink of an eye, you have a list of viable trades that can be further explored for signs of profitability.

real-time quotes
streaming quotes that are received as the prices change at the exchanges.

delayed quotes
quotes that are delayed up to 20 minutes from the actual price changes at the exchanges.

Finally, although commission fees are not tax deductible, online investors can deduct computer-related costs. Monthly Internet service provider fees, online subscriptions, and computer costs can be listed under "miscellaneous itemized deductions" (although you are limited to writing off only any amount over 2% of your adjusted gross income). When it comes to taxes, it's best to seek professional help; but it doesn't hurt to save those receipts!

The disadvantages of online trading are primarily for new investors. Trading options requires a broker that can handle the intricate nature of complex spreads and delta neutral strategies. If you are just starting out in your trading career, you need a broker who is going to help you, not harm you. If your broker is little more than an order taker, then you are 100% responsible for every little detail—a precarious position for a new trader. If you are a novice trader, you need to find a broker that understands options trading and can give you the support you need to become a successful trader.

how to get the most from this book

The text of this book concentrates on two main areas of focus: option strategies and online disciplines. The first two chapters focus on introducing online trading practices into your everyday life as a trader. Since there is an overabundance of financial web sites, the sites, brokerages, and products selected for review are those that I believe to be most useful to options investors. Each chapter includes personal tips and insights designed to enhance your online experience and act as building blocks for your investment approach.

Chapter 3 takes you step-by-step through stock and options basics (experienced traders may wish to skip this chapter). Chapters 4 through 8 provide a detailed analysis of 15 managed risk option strategies that are designed to take advantage of everyday market opportunities using online resources. In order to enhance your ability to understand each strategy, I have included a hypothetical trade that details how to compute each strategy's maximum risk, maximum profit, breakevens, and exit alternatives. A great deal of effort has been expended to test these strategies and to develop off-floor techniques that enable traders to consistently build up their trading accounts.

By focusing on clear explanations of how to really make money in the markets using options, this book refrains from exposing readers to information that is overly theoretical or technically complicated. In fact, technical analysis has been intentionally avoided. I want to help you integrate these options-based trading techniques into a comprehensive strategic trading plan that fits your own personal profile.

Chapter 9 attempts to pull everything together by walking you step-by-step through a series of web sites in search of a profitable trade. Chapter 10 offers concrete information regarding online brokerages and their ability to cater to the unique needs of the option trader. After an in-depth review of every available online brokerage (as of July 1999), I have made my choice for the top 10 online brokerages for options traders. Chapter 11 delves into placing a trade online and although each online brokerage has its own unique design format, we'll take a walk through the online trading process using Mr. Stock as our prototype brokerage.

The final chapter presents a view of the big picture. I have included a brief account of information concerning the Internet's current legal battles, introduced electronic communication networks (ECNs), and interviewed two heavyweight online financial journalists to get their take on the future of online trading and its effect on the investment world. I also do a little forecasting of my own.

Several Appendixes offer a variety of information geared to helping investors find what they need to maintain a competitive online edge. Appendix A contains a summary of key investment strategies; reviews profit, risk, and breakeven calculations; and supplies easy-access decimal conversions for quick referencing and other need-to-know material. Appendix B contains a glossary of fundamental and technical analysis methodologies. This handy reference guide is designed to help you define some of the more complex techniques that may be referenced over the Internet as clues to forecasting market price movements. Appendix C contains a list of options trading software and the Internet sites where they can be reviewed. Appendix D features reviews of almost 250 financial resource sites broken down into the following categories: Supersites, News, Research, Education, Technical Analysis, Options, Webzines, High Technology, Exchanges, Advisory Sites, Specialty Sites, and Fun & Games. This exhaustive list of resource sites and reviews is the most comprehensive list I've ever run across and I'm proud to be able to share this wealth of knowledge in this book. Finally, Appendix E surveys about 65 online brokerages as they compare to one another in services, commissions, and resources.

This book is designed as an instructional guide to help you unleash the unlimited power of your computer and take advantage of what the Internet has to offer you as an options trader. It is also an instructional manual with the lowdown on managed risk option strategies to enable you to make the most out of today's volatile markets. If you're ready, it's time to join the new breed of online investors who are forging a new path with a wealth of resources at their fingertips. It is my deepest hope that this book may inspire you to become as passionate about online trading as I am. It's time to seize hold of your financial destiny—mouse in hand—and venture forth into cyberspace in search of the great American trade.

chapter 1

online investing 101

cyberspace—the final frontier

In 20 short years, the Internet has gone from an abstract concept to a global information network with endless applications in everyday life. In 1999, 40 million households in the United States alone are surfing the Net. Online entertainment is giving television a run for its money. E-commerce is altering the way people spend their hard-earned dollars. As this immense shift changes the nature of the human adventure, entire new industries are blooming. I'm afraid the Age of Aquarius is over. This is the dawning of the Age of the Microchip and our new currency is information.

The success of the Internet has created a maelstrom in the investment world. Conventional brokers, the traditional intermediaries of an investor's game plan, are losing ground as more than seven million investors move to online brokers instead. Reduced commissions and lightning-fast information access have enabled online brokerages to redefine the role of a broker. With a keystroke, traders can access real-time quotes, annual reports, breaking financial news, technical and fundamental analytical data, and investing tips from a multitude of insightful (and not so insightful) market analysts. In seconds you can find out which stocks are hitting new highs or new lows or review an option's volatility. News sites compete for readers by offering daily market analyses, economic reports, and shrewd investment commentary. Market research firms maximize the investment community's ability to track ever-changing fundamentals and technical indicators. Even exchanges offer a variety of free services geared to educate and inform the Net-surfing masses. In fact, there is so much information available on the Internet that it can be overwhelming. The key is to develop a comprehensive game plan that enables you to systematically trade to win.

Competing in today's marketplace requires constant Net awareness. You have to pay attention to various sources of information to keep abreast of what's happening. To diffuse the inherent frustration of searching the Net for useful information, a trader has to implement a master plan. Developing such a plan is a process of evolution; new sites are integrated into the daily routine as other sites are abandoned. The hardest part of this process lies in defining your starting point and destination. You may never arrive, but it's crucial to have goals to work toward. Once these goals have been defined—college for the kids, retirement by age 50, or a house in the country—it is essential to assess where your starting point is. How much money can you afford to place in a trading account? What kind of returns will enable you to attain your goals? How much money can you afford to lose? To determine your financial capabilities, take a discerning look at how much cash you have readily available and the value of assets that could be converted into cash. Once you come up with the total amount of your capabilities, you need to assess your real needs. Do not invest your rent payment, monthly food budget, or any funds critical to your family's future. Do not mortgage the house in order to start trading. Use funds that are readily available and can be traded without attachment. If you don't have enough to get started, start a nest egg, earmark it for your new trading career, and start to learn all you can about trading. When you finally have enough money to open an account, you'll be that much further ahead of the game.

Time is another important consideration. To determine the trading style that best fits your needs, you have to accurately assess your time constraints. In the beginning, you have to allot the time you have available to learning about trading as well as monitoring your trades. To become a full-time trader, you have to monitor the markets more aggressively. If you have only 15 minutes in the morning and evening to track your positions, short-term trading is simply out of the question. You need to structure a trading program that will let you trade in your spare time until you have the resources to make trading a full-time profession.

The next step is to determine the level of risk you find tolerable. Maybe it is naive to think that anyone should find any risk tolerable;

however, the reality of investing is that risk exists no matter what you do. Yes, you can limit risk and you can manage risk; however, *risk is an inherent element of investing*. This refers to financial risk and opportunity risk. To be a successful investor, you have to get the highest return for the amount of available capital you own. To reach this goal, always calculate the maximum risk a trade presents before placing it. If you are buying options, you risk the money paid to purchase the options. If you are selling options, your risk is unlimited depending on the price of the underlying stock. Unlimited risk is a dangerous endeavor. Hedging risk by using option spreads and delta neutral strategies is a viable way to create trades that leverage your resources and maximize profit potentials.

> **risk**
> the potential financial loss inherent in an investment.

Since a love affair with anything you do increases your chances of success, you have to make your daily online routine fun. The excitement of surfing the Net drives your performance. To make your journey smooth, your entire computer system must be aligned to support your master plan. Everything from the software you use to the access provider that serves as your gateway to the Internet is an important part of the process. Choose carefully. The road you travel will be much less bumpy if you love the road you have chosen.

getting the right stuff

To the uninitiated, getting hooked up to the Internet is a confusing prospect. Since everything you buy is outdated practically as soon as it's paid for, choosing the right computer and additional high-tech gadgets can be overwhelming. But regardless of all the potential frustrations, getting online is not that difficult. There are four essential products/services that you need: a working computer, a high-speed modem, an Internet service provider (ISP), and a browser. Get ready to blast off into cyberspace by taking a look at each of these components.

computers

The most important part of your system is a personal computer. The next question then becomes PCs (IBM or IBM-compatible) versus the Apple family of computers. Unfortunately, trading software for Apple computers is practically nonexistent. Although this significantly limits a trader to PC use, choosing the right one is still a complex and personal decision. I'm certainly not an expert, but I am aware of certain criteria that can help determine which computer is best suited to a trader's needs. These criteria are processors, random access memory (RAM), hard drive space, and portable convenience.

processors   As I write this (July 1999) the microprocessor chip market presents a rather odd situation. Intel recently released the Pentium 3 processor, but few trading programs can take advantage of the additional features it offers. The chips made by Advanced Micro Devices and Cyrix that compete with Intel's Pentium 2 processor run fast enough and do more than most traders will ever need. Until the clock speeds double from their current speeds and trading software comes to market that effectively uses those higher speeds, I feel that some of the older (introduced about 9 to 12 months ago), less expensive chips represent the best values right now. On the other hand, if you can get a faster chip for only a slight price increase, why not go for it and wait for the industry to catch up with you?

> **chip**
> a microelectronic device that can store copious amounts of information. A chip is comprised of miniature transistors on a very thin silicon or sapphire rectangle. The type of chip you use contributes to a computer's speed.

random access memory (RAM)   Random access memory (RAM) is the operating memory that your computer uses when it's running to open programs, save material and transfer clipboards. If you are running out of RAM, your computer's speed will slow down and make opening several programs at the same time impossible. Adding RAM may increase the speed of your computer more than upgrading the computer chip. Since the price of RAM has been slowly dropping to about

> **random access memory (RAM)**
> RAM is the memory available for use while you are working (or playing) on your computer. RAM memory controls just how many software applications you can open simultaneously and stores information before it is saved to a disk or the hard drive. Once a computer is turned off, RAM memory shuts off as well and any material not saved is lost into the great beyond.

$2 per Meg, I suggest putting as much RAM into your computer as you can afford—at least 64 megabytes.

---

meg
short for megabyte, which means one million bytes or information units, each consisting of eight bits apiece.

---

hard drives (storage memory)   A hard drive stores all the information on your computer even when the computer is shut down. As the prices of hard drives continue to fall, the memory has been steadily increasing. Most new computers come with 2 to 10 gigabytes of storage memory. You may wonder just how much room you need; that depends on how many programs you want to run. Comprehensive trading programs may need as much as 350 Megs of hard drive space for real-time or delayed data collection. Since 1,000 Megs equals 1 gigabyte, one trading program needs 15% of a 2-gigabyte hard drive. Given all the wonderful programs available that like to eat up hard drive space, the smallest hard drive you're likely to be comfortable with is a 2-gigabyte hard drive, and you may prefer at least a 4-gigabyte hard drive in order to run multiple programs.

---

hard drive (HD)
the hard drive is a disk permanently installed inside a computer that acts as a permanent storage area for large amounts of information including programs, files, and graphics. Hard disks are measured by how many megabytes of information they can store.

---

monitors   A good monitor is an essential part of your computer setup. A 17-inch monitor is fairly standard and does the job reasonably well. A 21-inch monitor is the next step but at a very steep price increase. One alternative to buying a 21-inch monitor is to buy a video card (a part that will go inside your computer with one edge of the card showing on the outside) that will allow you to use two monitors on the same computer. The two-screen approach will give you about 30% more screen than a 21-inch monitor and cost about 75% of the 21-inch monitor price. The two monitors together give you the same picture that you get on one monitor; it will just be stretched over two screens. If you are a heavy trader, consider two 17-inch monitors or a single 21-inch monitor. Either way, monitors take up a lot of room. You may want to consider a flat-screen monitor because its footprint is much smaller, but keep in mind that the price of a flat-screen monitor currently exceeds the cost of a 21-inch monitor by a large margin.

---

monitor
the visual device that displays the text and graphics generated by a computer.

---

modems

A modem is a small communication device that connects your computer with the outside world. Modems basically come in two varieties, internal and external. Almost all of the newer computers come with an internal modem, which costs a little less and attaches to the inside of the computer box with one edge on the outside of the computer. However, if you have an older computer and need to buy a modem, go ahead and pay the extra bucks for a top-of-the-line modem—U.S. Robotics, Global Village, or Motorola—with 28.8K to 56K bits per second (bps). An external modem attaches to one of the ports on your computer. It gets its electricity straight from an electric outlet, so you will need to allocate a spot on your surge protector for it. Make sure you get a cable with the modem—there's nothing more frustrating that not being able to find the right cable to make your dial-up networking happen. If you want something even more efficient, you may want to check out a cable access modem. They are a little more expensive but extremely fast and dependable. Call your local cable company for details on modem services in your area.

---

modem
an electronic device that connects computers to telephone lines. The modem takes the digital output of a computer and transforms it into an analog signal of the telephone lines and vice versa, enabling connection to the Internet.

---

compact disc—read only memory (CD-ROM) players (CD players)

Since most data providers and computer software companies use CDs to distribute their information and programs, a CD player has become an integral part of any computer. Among CD players, the speed of the player is the only factor I think is important. Some programs require a CD player with a certain minimum speed, while others don't. If you are looking at a particular program, find out if it requires a minimum CD player speed; if it does, make sure your CD player runs at least that fast. For a program that does not specify a minimum speed, get at least a "24×" speed CD player. Since most new computers come with a built-in CD player with much higher speeds, this should not pose much of a problem.

CD-ROM (Compact Disc—Read-Only Memory)
a thin, five-inch-diameter metal disk that provides storage of computerized data. Software applications are usually stored on CD-ROMs.

---

telephone lines

Now that we know what kind of computer to look for, let's start surveying access providers to the Internet. First, let's consider what type of phone line to use. There are three main kinds: analog, digital, and T1 lines. An analog line is the most common and probably runs into your house to your phones. Most telephone companies provide analog lines that work reasonably well. A digital line costs more, but is more efficient than an analog line (how much more efficient depends on your local telephone company). Finally, a T1 line costs more than a digital line—a lot more. T1 lines are the most efficient of the three because they connect you directly to the Internet. Most people will do just fine with an analog line direct from the phone company. Consider a digital line if you need a slightly faster response time or enjoy playing online computer games. Don't worry about a T1 line unless you plan to trade every stock on every market in the world every three minutes and you start your trading account with $50,000,000.

---

analog
information that is in a state of continuous flow, such as sound waves, electrical current, and telephone lines.

---

digital
information that is transmitted and stored in a binary form of 1s and 0s. Computers store all text, graphics, and sound in digital form.

T1
a telephone line that utilizes digital transmission in order to handle intense telephone use and computer networks.

internet service providers (ISPs)

An ISP allows you to access the Internet through its Internet server. You will want to consider two different types: (1) direct ISPs and (2) indirect ISPs. A direct ISP will hook you directly to the Internet without organizing much material for you to look at. It opens the door and then lets you wander around inside trying to find what you want. If you know where to find what you want, the direct ISP will get you there fastest. Most direct ISPs are local entities that provide local access telephone numbers to only limited geographic areas. Some United States direct ISPs now cover large parts of the country and also provide local access in certain overseas cities.

Internet service provider (ISP)
company that provides a connection between individual computer systems and the Internet.

An indirect ISP gives you access to the Internet and provides a large amount of information, search engines, and links to both financial and nonrelated topics. The best-known indirect ISPs are America Online and Prodigy. They provide local telephone access numbers across almost all of the United States and many overseas cities. Direct ISPs and indirect ISPs cost about the same for unlimited access (approximately $19.95 per month, although a few providers are beginning to drop that rate to attract new users). If you don't consider yourself Internet literate, you may want to subscribe to an indirect ISP because they are more user-friendly. I prefer a direct ISP because they tend to have less advertising, which helps the screens move faster. However, the most important part of choosing a server provider is to find one that offers a local dial-up number, or you'll have to pay long-distance costs for every minute that you stay connected to the Internet. Reliability is also extremely important. Don't wait to get online before finding out how often the server fails. Call up a few ISPs and ask them how much mail can be received before your mailbox is full. Does the server disconnect after 30 minutes of inactivity? Is there an extra charge for a personal web page? Make sure you keep track of how long you had to sit on hold waiting for a live customer service representative.

internet browsers

If you use a direct ISP, you will need to purchase an Internet browser. A browser is a software program that hosts your Internet journeys. The two most popular browsers are Netscape Navigator and Microsoft

Internet Explorer. While some people swear by one, both are well designed and will help you surf the Net efficiently. If you don't have a
preference, then choose whichever one you can get for free (Microsoft
Internet Explorer is part of the Microsoft Windows 98 setup). All
browsers enable you to send and receive e-mail, bookmark your favorite sites, and easily backtrack your current session.

---

browser
a client program that allows users to read hypertext documents on
the World Wide Web, and navigate between them. Examples are
Netscape Navigator, Lynx, and Microsoft Internet Explorer. Browsers
can be text-based or graphic.

---

data providers

Serious traders need to subscribe to a data provider for real-time, delayed, or end-of-day price quotes. To determine which service fits
your trading style best, you need to identify several factors. Do you
want to pursue long- or short-term investments? What specific markets do you want to trade? How much money can you commit to your
trading account? Table 1.1 is designed to help you decide which kind
of data reception is best suited to your needs. Bottom line: If you're
going to trade and compete with commercial and professional traders,
you need to have the same data they do. Although the siren's song of
real-time data feeds and day trading is very seductive, if you are just
starting out delayed feed is more than enough to help you get your
feet wet. It has everything you'll need to learn and practice trading
systems as well as find, place, and exit trades.

---

data provider
a source of information that provides you with current price data on
stocks, futures, and options, as well as up-to-the-minute news and
market analyses. This information can be accessed in a variety of
ways including online, cable, FM, satellite, and wireless networks.

Lastly, you need to take a look at price. Trading is a business. If
you sign up for real-time data feed, expect to pay (including exchange fees) anywhere from $150 to over $1,000 a month depending
on the markets you want to trade. This monthly expense almost im-

table 1.1 types of quotes

Type of Quote	Description	Advantages	Disadvantages
End-of-day	Anything from paper charts to Internet remote quotes and chart retrieval or a dial-up download of end-of-day data directly to your computer for analysis.	1. Cheapest form of data available. Much of it is even free, if you can find it. Overall, it's a great way to start. 2. Many part-time traders can use end-of-day data to find opportunities after the market closes and place trades before the market opens the next day.	If you are an intraday trader, end-of-day data is of little use to you.
Delayed	Real-time streaming data that is delayed by 15 to 20 minutes.	1. A great way to collect tick-by-tick data at a cost less than real-time data. 2. Can be used by many trading software analysis programs to find longer-term investment opportunities.	Comes at least 15 minutes after the actual event. So, if you are trying to trade during the day using delayed data, you will not enjoy as much success as you would with real-time data because by the time you see a big move in a stock with delayed data, the big move is over.
Real-time	Tick-by-tick streaming data received from a quote service as the prices at the exchange change.	1. Cable receivers are easy to install. Online collection data is continuous feed, which will be collected and stored at your PC for review and analysis. 2. Receive real-time quotes directly over the Internet from vendors that resell data in real-time format. Check out eSignal (www.dbc.com). 3. Can be used by many trading software analysis programs to find various investment opportunities.	1. Can be expensive depending on the level of service you need. 2. If you want to set up an FM receiver, the cost for the reception equipment will be billed in advance by the data vendor. You have to make room for a three-foot satellite dish, complete with stand, which needs concrete blocks to secure to the ground.

mediately forces you to make trades to generate profits to cover your data cost. Forced trades are seldom profitable. To become a successful trader, you have to learn to walk before running. That's why conservation of capital through controlled expenses is a must. As your experience level increases, you can always increase your data speed.

one computer or two? laptop or desktop?

Many people may never think of owning more than one computer, but it can be a real asset for a trader. Trading involves collecting real-time, delayed, or end-of-day data; displaying, formatting, and analyzing trading data; doing online research; and basic spreadsheet and word processing. The first two tasks can take a major bite out of the computer's memory resources. If you try to do all four tasks at the same time, your computer may freeze up and you run the risk of damaging files or your whole system in the process. Two computers when trading are not essential, but otherwise you have to make sure that your computer uses a fast processor and holds a lot of RAM and hard drive memory.

laptop computer
a portable personal computer that is small enough to fit in a person's lap. Weighing less than eight pounds, laptop computers usually have a flat screen and LCD display, and are powered by a rechargeable battery. They can be connected to a larger monitor or other peripherals when back at the office.

desktop computer
a stationary computer with a full-size monitor and hard drive.

You may want to consider getting a laptop as a second computer. Laptops are extremely convenient if you need to keep track of your portfolio while you're on the road. Unfortunately, most laptops are not equipped with the fastest processors and usually do not contain as much RAM as a desktop computer. Those that do can be quite expensive. If you choose to buy a laptop as your primary computer, you may want to purchase a 17-inch monitor and a keyboard with a mouse to plug into the back of the laptop when you are not on the road.

search engines

Once you're on the Net, the most basic way to find what you're look-ing for is to use one of the many search engines (Excite, Yahoo!, Lycos, AltaVista, etc.). Simply type in a keyword and the search engine will find sites or topics that match your subject. You can then scroll down the list and by double clicking on a URL (uniform resource locator) be directly transported to that site's home page. A URL usually begins with "http://" (omitted in this book because the newest browsers au-tomatically add this prefix) and has a variety of endings including "com" (the most popular) or "net" (if it's a business), "org" (short for nonprofit organization), or "edu" (denoting school). The first main screen of a site is referred to as a home page. Links are then provided to alternate screens on that site for further viewing.

---

search engines
Internet portals that enable users to search for web sites that have a connection to the specific word used in the search.

---

links
a pointer in an HTML document that leads to another World Wide Web site, or to another place within the same document; also called a hyperlink. Linked text is usually underlined or shown in a different color from the surrounding text. Sometimes graphics are links or contain links. A link is activated by clicking on it.

Once you've made your purchases and hooked everything up, you're ready to go online and take your first steps toward financial inde-pendence. But don't jump the gun. There are still a number of decisions to be made. You have to choose an online brokerage, pick out trading software, and determine which resource sites (if any) are worth the price of subscription. This process can be quite time-consuming, espe-cially when you're champing at the bit to start trading. A word to the wise: Take your time. Don't worry about missing some trend or losing out on the next winning initial public offering (IPO). There's always an-other great trade on the horizon. Take the time to arm yourself well; it'll pay off down the road.

online research

The rise of online trading has added a whole new dimension to the investment ball game. The Internet is literally overflowing with financial investment sites and online brokerages. To lend order to the seemingly infinite nature of available information, it is important to forge consistent investigative patterns while leaving a little room for spontaneous forays into uncharted territory. Online trading is a balancing act. You have to determine what information is important, find out where it can be easily located, and decide how you want to keep track of it. There are very few shortcuts in this process. Finding the optimum combination of resource sites as well as the best online brokerage is a process of evolution. You just have to surf from site to site until you develop a daily ritual that works for you. This process will take its own sweet time and it's important to enjoy each part of the process. As Rumi, a renowned thirteenth-century philosopher, said, "A good traveler is not intent upon arrival."

Likewise, to enjoy online trading you have to delight in cultivating your own resources, investigating specific industry sectors, developing a watch list and a portfolio, and keeping track of your positions. Finding a potentially profitable trading opportunity is only the beginning. There is plenty of research that needs to be done to verify the stock's capacity for price movement. Once you have established the trend within the market, you may want to analyze the industry group it belongs to as well as any psychological market indications of the bearish or bullish nature of the marketplace. If a company continues to look promising, there are software programs that can help you to find the most profitable strategy to employ. However, it is important to remember that the marketplace is an uncontrollable force. Your ability to respond to the market's seemingly random impulsiveness will determine how much money you make or lose. If you have already developed a system for studying the markets, you may find the next section a bit redundant. Feel free to skip ahead, as this section is devoted to those who are getting their feet wet for the first time and need to know how to get started.

---

bearish
a declining market, especially over a prolonged period of time. Often caused by the mass conviction that a weak economy depresses corporate profits.

> **bullish**
> a rising stock market, especially over a long period of time—at least
> six months. Often caused by the mass conviction that a strong
> economy produces increased corporate profits.

analyzing the market

Currently, there are more than 9,300 available stocks to trade. A
stock is an extremely sensitive trading instrument. Its price is the result of the unanimous consent by all market participants as to the
value of that stock. At any moment, the mass psychology of the trading public can shift, triggering trend reversals that often defy the
odds. Perhaps that's why trying to analyze a stock in order to forecast price movement has a seemingly infinite number of variables
and methodologies. To take advantage of trading software or financial research sites, it is vital to develop a healthy understanding of
fundamental market data, technical indicators, and the effect that
news, commentary, and analysts have on market opinion. The public's subsequent reaction to this information guides the mass psychology that drives investors to buy or sell, ultimately determining
stock and option prices. You may wonder how we can ever hope to
forecast price movement when human unpredictability controls our
financial future.

> **stock**
> a stock, also called a share, is a unit of ownership in a company. The
> value of each share is based upon a wide variety of factors including
> the total number of outstanding shares, the value of the company, its
> earnings and debts, what the company produces now and is
> expected to produce in the future, and the overall demand for the
> stock.

In general, traders analyze stock prices by comparing the present to past performance, while expectations are based on future
events. Current events change prices by changing the way investors
forecast the future of a company and the general economy. If a future
move is anticipated, when it happens it won't change the price all that
much because investors have already paid for the future. (There's a
scary concept!) This area of trading can be overwhelming to a novice
trader. There seems to be no end to the details that need to be taken

into account. To become adept, you have to be willing to persistently reconnoiter the markets on a day-to-day basis. In the beginning, you may feel buried by an avalanche of numbers, statistics, and indicators. Just keep reading and watching how the markets react to such things as earnings estimates, analyst upgrades and downgrades, the release of new products, management changes, and the threat of interest rate adjustments.

As a small investor, you have to carefully select your analysis tools because you are competing with traders who have access to scores of analysts studying a wide array of price variables daily. In order to help you, I have divided the complex realm of market research and price forecasting into three basic fields: individual stock assessment, broad market analysis, and psychological market criteria. The first category—individual stock assessment—can further be broken down into fundamental and technical analysis. Let's take a closer look at these research and analysis fields.

individual stock assessment

For the beginner, picking the right stock is what trading is all about. In the past, finding a profitable stock has been an arduous task. You had to manually take into account a variety of fundamental and technical variables which is why professional analysts got paid big bucks for their services. But times have changed. Stock screening programs act as online data research engines enabling traders to find stocks with the click of a mouse. Just choose which parameters are important and your computer will instantaneously generate a list of stocks that fit these criteria.

A multitude of software programs and online sites offer stock screening functions and options position searches. Some of the online sites are free and others require a monthly subscription fee for more advanced searches. INVESTools (www.investools.com) is an excellent site with two different stock screening services available—one free and one that costs $9.95 per month. The free screen lets you choose from nine preset search screens (Growth and Value Screen, Strong Growth Screen, Stock Winners Screen, Low Price-to-Book Screen, Blue Chip Stocks Screen, Small Cap Screen, Low P/E Ratio Screen, High Dividend Yield Screen, Insider Ownership Screen). The subscription service allows you to customize your search by choosing among 68 variables in 12 key categories. Although the free screening can offer some great insights into possible hot markets, the lists tend to be long. For a narrower search, try the 30-day free trial subscription service.

Another excellent web site, Wall Street City (www.wallstreetcity .com), also has a screening service that can be found by clicking "Search for an Investment" on the left-hand sidebar. It has a host of preselected screens including analyst rankings, pattern breakouts, and quarterly earnings surprises. The premium subscription service includes options searches as well.

Hoover's Online (www.hoovers.com) also features an excellent free stock screening using up to 20 performance criteria. This screening service requires the input of specific detailed parameters. You can select everything from the type of industry you prefer to company size, rates of return, and volatility.

Stock screening yields some very useful information but to be able to use it effectively you must understand the inner workings of specific fundamental parameters. Understanding the value of individual stock indicators is a complex process. Let's take a look at a few of the more important fundamental and technical analysis indicators in order to get a basic sense of how search engines can be programmed. A comprehensive list can be found in Appendix B.

fundamental analysis
Fundamental analysis forecasts price movement by focusing on economic and production data. Corporations have miles of paper trails that review every contributing factor of a company's strength including product development and reception, targeted customer identification, consumption, profit outlook, management strength, and supply and demand for products. Economic data includes income statements, past records of earnings, sales records, present assets, annual reports, and new product consumption rates. Fundamental analysts use this data to determine whether a stock's current market price is overvalued or undervalued and to anticipate stock price trends and the future success or failure of the company.

---

fundamental analysis
an approach to trading research that seeks to predict stock price movements using a variety of indisputable basic facts including income statements, past records of earnings, sales, assets, management changes, and products and services.

In its most refined state, fundamental analysis produces two basic theories that affect market perception: If a stock's fundamentals are bullish, the stock's price should rise; if a stock's fundamentals are bearish, the stock's price should fall. Low prices relative to the company's real value increase demand, which in turn drives up the price of the stock. Higher prices reduce the demand for shares and the increase in the supply of shares leads to lower prices. This cycle feeds on itself, deftly creating market dynamics.

Traders must also pay attention to the competition among different companies in the same industry sector. For example, there is extreme competition among high-tech corporations where breakthroughs in technology spawn dramatic market movement. Trying to stay on the cutting edge of these markets is a full-time job. Studying the entire industry is vital to being able to forecast a company's success. And that's where the money is!

Most of the information you gain from television or newspapers is fundamental analysis. Perhaps a company's product is selling like hotcakes, or a management change is altering the direction in which a corporation is going. Perhaps a disaster occurred triggering the selling of a corporation's stock shares. Fundamental analysis ranges from the mundane to data that is so economically complicated it may require a degree in business to understand it. As you progress as a trader, you will learn to gauge what data is important enough to take notice of and what can be filtered out. There are no right or wrong answers. Anything that helps you to get a feel for a market is valid. It simply takes time and energy to develop a discerning ear for fundamental information and practice to know how to apply it correctly.

Almost every web site is capable of downloading basic fundamental information. Just type in the stock's symbol and you'll instantly receive a "snapshot" of a company's fundamentals, which reveals information that is valid for a specific period of time. I pay close attention to the 52-week high and low because this indicates where the current price is in relation to where it's been. Volume is another important factor. I look for volume spikes and tend to avoid stocks with less than 300,000 shares trading daily.

A stock's quarterly earnings growth is another key to assessing its profitability. The earnings per share value (EPS) is calculated by dividing the net income of the company in one quarter by the number of outstanding common shares. A comparison between the current EPS and one from the same quarter of the previous year can be used to determine earnings growth. In addition, analysts project a company's earnings and the price of the stock often reflects that projection. However, as the end of the quarter approaches, there is much speculation as to whether a company can live up to its EPS projection. This speculation often inspires volatility and that means market movement, which is one of the keys to finding profitable option trades.

Price-earnings ratio (P/E) is another important value because it compares a company's stock price to the earnings per share. Computed by simply dividing a stock's price by the annual earnings, it tells you how many times the earnings a stock is trading at. The P/E of individual stocks is then compared to the P/E for all stocks of a given industrial sector. Be aware that many Internet-related stocks do not have valid P/E ratios because they are operating at a net loss and still enjoying unparalleled success when it comes to demand for shares of stock. The sales-to-price per share ratio is a much more accurate benchmark for evaluating emerging-growth companies.

Accumulation-distribution reflects a stock's daily long shares compared to short stock shares. This rating is one of the most important indicators of a stock's strength or weakness. In general, a stock with an A rating means there is plenty of demand for the stock (high volume) and the price will probably continue to rise. A stock with an E rating means that the supply for a stock is greater than the demand and could trigger a drop in price. I like to focus on A's only for buying and E's for a bearish approach.

A company's fundamental data also include the closing price, the change from previous day's close, the day's high and low, the 52-week high and low, and volatility. This area of analysis enables traders to make educated comparisons, but it may take a little time to get comfortable with all those imposing little numbers. For your convenience, a list of fundamental analysis tools can be found in Appendix B.

Although there are many web sites that you can consult for fundamental data, Hoover's Online (www.hoovers.com) is definitely one of the best. It offers a cache of fundamental analysis tools, SEC filings, and company reports. You can also sign up for e-mails that make timely investment recommendations.

I also highly recommend VectorVest (www.vectorvest.com). Although the majority of this site is subscription-based, it does provide free fundamental stock analysis. VectorVest has developed a unique system for evaluating a stock's actual value by analyzing a variety of fundamental indicators including earnings, earnings growth rate, dividend payments, dividend growth rate, financial performance, current interest, and inflation. It also provides additional indicators including relative value, relative timing, and VST-Vector. Its subscription services are comprehensive including extensive historical data, recommendations, and the inherent values of call and put options.

If you want to see what a company has to say for itself, check out Companies Online (www.companies.online.com). This comprehensive site is the brainchild of business experts Dun & Bradstreet and the search engine moguls at Lycos. Before trading hit the Net, Dun & Bradstreet specialized in obtaining credit data directly from commercial firms and combining this information with data solicited from their creditors. This information was eventually made available to subscribers in reports and a ratings directory. Companies Online hosts a comprehensive business database for report requests and links to more than 100,000 corporations' web sites. You can browse by company and industrial sector, check out the company of the week, or link to Dun & Bradstreet's home site to request a company report.

technical analysis

Technical analysis is built on the theory that market prices display repetitive patterns that can be tracked and used to forecast future price movement. It evaluates price movement by creating charts that study market strength and gauge weakness by analyzing statistics generated by past prices and volume. Although understanding market behavior can be challenging for novice traders, a good technical analyst can review a variety of factors and forecast future price action with a certain degree of confidence. To understand how to identify trends and reversals, you have to learn how to look at a chart. There are three main kinds of trends: major, intermediate, and minor. A major trend is one that lasts more than six months. An intermediate trend lasts from one to six months, and a minor trend lasts less than a month.

---

technical analysis
technical analysis uses historical price movement and volume to predict a market's future strength or weakness. Since price is the bottom line, technical analysts look primarily at price movement to determine price patterns. From these patterns they try to extrapolate future price movements.

---

trends
a market that is increasing steadily to the upside or decreasing steadily to the downside is said to be a trending market. Catching the trend is one of the keys to successful trading—"the trend is your friend."

There are an abundance of technical analysis techniques including Bollinger bands, chi-squares, the Elliott Wave theory, candlestick charts, Kagi charts, and the maximum entropy method. Most of these technical methods are very complicated and require computer programs to view. It is definitely worthwhile to become familiar with a few of these techniques even if it's just to know what the competition is using. However, do not feel compelled to buy every technical analysis book you can find—it will only lead to analysis paralysis.

Since trading is a game of timing, charts were devised to speed up the process of information gathering. Charting techniques show a stock's price movement over time. Charts can be constructed to represent specific time perspectives—intraday, daily, weekly, or monthly. The vertical axis represents price fluctuation and the horizontal axis denotes time.

There are three basic kinds of charting techniques: bar charts, line charts, and candlestick charts. A bar chart uses vertical lines, each with two small horizontal bars at 90-degree angles. The vertical line itself represents the stock's price range for a specific period of time (hourly, daily, etc.). The horizontal bar to the left indicates the opening price; the one to the right, the closing price. Line charts are less complex. They just show a stock's closing price from day to day, week to week, and month to month like some kind of join-the-dots game. Candlestick charts are a little more elaborate. Like bar charts, they show a stock's daily price range. But they are also color coded to reveal the relationship between a stock's open and close. If a stock closed higher than it opened, the body of the candlestick is white, indicating a bullish market. If the candlestick is dark, then the stock closed lower than it opened, indicating a bearish market. (Figures 1.1, 1.2, and 1.3 show each of these basic charting techniques.)

As an options trader, you are looking at markets over the longer term. To assess a market's movement, you have to look at annual charts, paying close attention to the most recent few weeks. Online technical sites are geared to provide you with various charts that show price movement over various time spans. You can easily check out a stock's daily movement for the past year at one stroke of the keyboard. However, it's one thing to gauge a market's movements by looking at a chart and another to be able to insightfully analyze what you see. Technical analysts have a broad range of analysis patterns that can be used to try to forecast price movement. Price patterns are signposts, not laws; but these signposts help to create the mass psychology of the marketplace. A pattern has influence only if people believe it to be true. Therefore, although it is helpful to be able to know the difference between a head and shoulders pattern and a double top and bottom (see Appendix B for pattern definitions), it is not as essential to the process as many technical analysts would have us think. But since many investors look to pattern analysis, it doesn't hurt to know what they're thinking.

Volume is another important element of chart pattern analysis that helps traders to assess a trend's strength or weakness. Volume bars can usually be found at the bottom of price charts. Each bar corresponds to the number of shares traded—the higher the bar, the heavier the volume. Strong uptrends are usually accompanied by heavy volume. When an uptrend starts to lose momentum, volume decreases. A divergence occurs when price and volume start to move in

figure 1.1   basic charting techniques: bar charts—30-day dell computer bar and volume chart

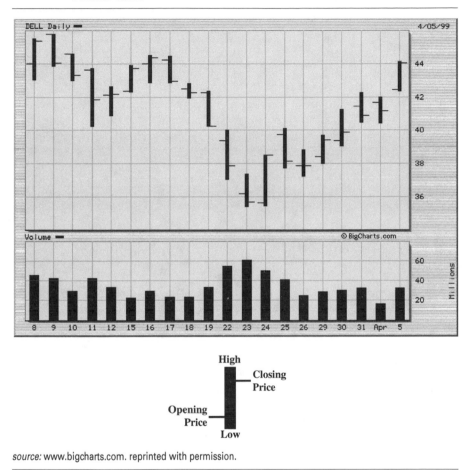

source: www.bigcharts.com. reprinted with permission.

opposite directions, signaling an end to the trend. I look for dramatic volume increases to catch a trend as it takes off.

You can also use indicators to track existing trends. There are two basic kinds of indicators: lagging indicators and oscillators. Lagging indicators are techniques that confirm a trend divergence after it has happened. Oscillators forecast a market as overbought or oversold by assessing when a market has reached a high to the upside or a low to the downside. When a market reaches a peak in either direction, it is ripe for a reversal, and managed risk strategies can be applied to take advantage of this movement.

figure 1.2 basic charting techniques: line charts—30-day dell computer line and volume chart

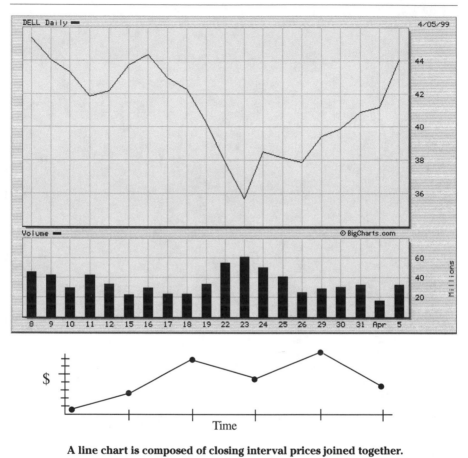

A line chart is composed of closing interval prices joined together.

source: www.bigcharts.com. reprinted with permission.

A moving average—the analysis of price action over a specified period of time on an average basis—is one of the most popular lagging indicators. A moving average adds together the closing prices of a market over a period of time—50 or 200 days is standard—and then divides the sum by the number of days used. Each day a new number is added and the oldest is dropped, creating a slightly different average. You can either look at one moving average line at a time or check out more than one at a time to look for crossovers. For example, you may look at the price of IBM trading right now and how that price compares to the average of the past 50 days and the aver-

figure 1.3   basic charting techniques: candlestick charts—30-day dell computer candlestick and volume chart

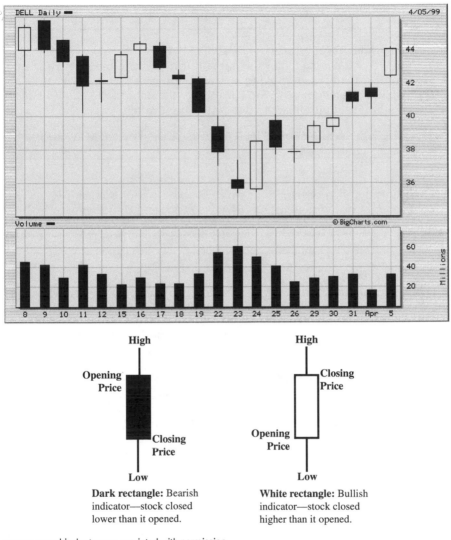

Dark rectangle: Bearish indicator—stock closed lower than it opened.

White rectangle: Bullish indicator—stock closed higher than it opened.

source: www.bigcharts.com. reprinted with permission.

age price over the past 200 days. When the 50-day average goes below the 200-day average, you sell; and conversely when the 50-day average goes above the 200-day average, you buy. This is a very simplistic explanation. Technicians go to great lengths to fine-tune which time spans and averages to use. Although you can play around with this technique studying a variety of time spans, it is advisable to use a 50-day or 200-day average as a base because they are the most commonly used.

---

lagging indicators
a method of technical analysis that confirms a trend divergence after it has happened (like a moving average) and gives clues to where it is headed, or an economic indicator that lags behind the overall pace of economic activity (like the unemployment rate)

---

oscillator
a technical indicator used to identify stocks and options with overbought or oversold prices that may trigger a trend reversal.

---

moving average
a moving average—probably the best known, and most versatile, technical indicator—is a chart used for judging a market's current trend. The moving average uses a simple mathematical procedure to smooth or eliminate the fluctuations in data and to assist in determining when to buy and sell.

Oscillators are indicators that help traders to predict a market's momentum by focusing on the rate at which a market is moving. Utilizing price and volume statistics, oscillators are used to predict the strength or weakness of a current market, determine overbought or oversold conditions, and locate turning points within the market. Momentum charts and rate of change (ROC) oscillators can help you initiate momentum investing in order to trade with or against the momentum of the market in hope of profiting from it. Geologists study volcanoes looking for indications of impending movements that may lead to eruptions. It's the same with momentum investors. They study the markets watching for pressure to start building, followed by an explosion and a calm thereafter. You might catch the first move, place the appropriate strategy, and then get off when the momentum fizzles. A slowdown follows the eruption, often triggering a reversal. If you miss the eruption, you can still make a profitable trade by using a contrarian approach—a practice in which you trade against the majority view, fading the trend. In general, fast moves up lead to fast moves down and vice versa.

momentum
when a market continues in the same direction for a certain time frame, the market is said to have momentum. A momentum indicator is a technical indicator that utilizes price and volume statistics for predicting the strength or weakness of a current market. Momentum trading exists when a trader invests with (or against) the momentum of the market in hopes of profiting from it.

contrarian approach
a contrarian is said to fade the trend by going against the majority view of the marketplace.

There are many web sites dedicated to providing technical analysis tools and data for the online investor. BigCharts.com (www.bigcharts .com) is one of the best technical analysis sites on the Net. It's a quick and easy site that offers a wide variety of technical charts and graphs absolutely free. Just type in a stock's ticker symbol and single click on "Interactive Chart" and the next screen will provide you with an abundance of charting choices, from moving averages to stochastics. You can also save your favorite charts for easy reference.

Barchart.com (www.barchart.com) is another excellent free site that serves up technical charts per your parameters. Created by Market Research, Inc. (MRI), Barchart.com is well stocked with all kinds of technical charts, quote screens, and custom portfolios, and will even send you end-of-day data on the stocks of your choice directly to your e-mail address absolutely free.

broad market analysis

There are three distinct ways for the marketplace as a whole to move: up, down, or sideways. If the market moves up, it is a bullish market. If it declines, it is a bearish market. If it stays in the same place, it is a neutral market. Discerning this distinction is the fundamental issue of a broad market indicator.

One of the primary methods of assessing stock market activity is to review the performance of indexes. An index is a group of stocks that make up a portfolio in which performance can be monitored based on one calculation. Broad market indicators use indexes as the basis for several analyses since they represent significant cross sections of the marketplace.

The Dow Jones Industrial Average (DJIA) is probably the best-known index. It is widely quoted as the quintessential economic indicator of market direction. Everyone has heard the Dow mentioned on the evening news as a key indicator of the day's trading performance. The closing prices of the DJIA stocks are averaged to determine if the overall mood of the marketplace was bearish or bullish. But what is the Dow and how did it get started? In 1884, Charles Dow surveyed the average closing prices of nine railroad stocks and two manufacturing companies that in his opinion represented the general trends in the national economy. He printed the results in his newspaper, a forerunner of today's *Wall Street Journal.* Over the next 12 years, he honed that list until settling on 12 industrial stocks. In 1896, Charles Dow began to publish this list and the overall average every day. Today's Dow Jones Industrial Average reflects the performance of 30 major companies representing key manufacturing and energy industries worth approximately 25% of the total value of all stocks listed on the New York Stock Exchange (NYSE).

In today's highly unpredictable markets, there are seven other indexes that track market movement in an attempt to forecast stock performance and direction. The New York Composite Index represents all stocks traded on the NYSE. Likewise, the AMEX Market Value Index and the Nasdaq Composite Index monitor all of the stocks traded at their respective exchanges. In a completely different vein, the Standard & Poor's 500 Index is considered the milestone for large investors. As its name implies, the S&P 500 examines the performance of 500 major stocks and is widely traded as a futures index.

Value Line is an independent investment service that tracks the performance of more than 1,800 stocks. It also has an excellent subscription-based web site (www.valueline.com) that offers free quotes, graphs and charts, featured articles, and a plethora of research information on mutual funds, stocks, and options. The Russell 2000 index tracks 2,000 smaller U.S. companies, especially up-and-coming stocks that hit the market most recently as initial public offerings (IPOs). The Wilshire 5000 is the largest index. It keeps track of all the American-based stocks traded over-the-counter (OTC) and in the exchanges—currently more than 7,000 stocks.

Each index can be reviewed in terms of unique time frames. The first place to start is by looking at the closing price. Next, check out the previous day's close as well as the percentage change between the two. Then take a look at the shift in price since the previous year and the overall change for the year to date. These four time frames can help you to understand the index's current trend. Trends in the indexes tend to be similar and often reflect the general mood of the economy.

Keeping tabs on industry group leadership is another important key to analyzing the marketplace. Almost 200 industrial groups ranging from restaurants to chemicals and plastics are ranked on the price performance of their respective stocks. This confirms which group has been experiencing the highest percentage of price movement fluctuation. Many investors believe that almost half of a stock's price performance can be attributed to its respective industrial group.

The advance-decline line (A/D line) is calculated by taking the percentage of stocks advancing and subtracting the percentage of stocks declining on a daily or weekly basis. This total is then plotted on top of the Industry Index to create the advance-decline line. The A/D line moves upward when a greater percentage of stocks in the group are advancing and moves downward when a majority of companies are declining in price.

The stock market acts like a pendulum, swinging back into balance until another economic hurricane hits. Once again, check out BigCharts.com. Its welcoming format can help you to analyze the general conditions of the marketplace by clicking on "Broad Market Overview." Start by scrutinizing "Advancing, Declining, and Unchanged" lists to determine the bull-to-bear ratio. Review price and volume charts for the major indexes and compare the number of stocks with new highs to those with new lows.

a quick course in macroeconomics

The Federal Reserve System essentially controls the flow of money in the United States. The Fed is a conglomerate of 12 separate district banks governed by a seven-member Board of Governors. In many ways, the Fed works more like a government agency than a corporation. It handles everything from the U.S. government's daily banking to receiving unemployment, withholding, and workers' compensation taxes. The Fed is also responsible for fulfilling the financial obligations of the U.S. government including providing Social Security and Medicare payments.

Federal Reserve System
established by Congress in 1913, the Federal Reserve System regulates the U.S. monetary and banking system by supervising, among other things, the quantity of new bills printed, and interest rates; it keeps a watchful eye over member banks, and acts as the government's bank.

The Fed also controls the release of new money. Every six weeks, the Fed's Open Market Committee meets to regulate monetary policy by balancing the amount of money in circulation without creating inflation. It typically takes about six months for the economy to react to changes in monetary volume control. This delay causes the economy to have a life of its own, especially because many decisions do not trigger the originally intended impact. To further control the money supply, the Fed adjusts interest rates to balance out the rate of inflation while attempting to inspire national growth.

The Federal Reserve discount rate is the interest rate banks must pay to borrow money from the Federal Reserve. This rate is extremely important because it is directly related to the flow of money in the economy. An interest rate is the annual percentage rate charged for the privilege of borrowing money. A change in interest rates can affect anything from bonds to the adjustable interest rate on your monthly mortgage payment. Subsequently, a relationship exists between interest rates, the prices of bonds, and the stock market. The dynamic among the three can be used as a guide to understanding market movement—bearish or bullish. Table 1.2 illustrates the typical interaction among interest rates, bonds, and stocks. When interest rates rise the stock market usually declines. However, there will be times when the interest rates may increase and the stock market advances, or vice versa. This is referred to as a divergence.

A bond is a debt instrument issued by a government or corporation that promises to pay its bondholders periodic interest at a fixed rate (the coupon), and to repay the principal of the loan at maturity (a specified future date). Bonds are usually issued with a par or face value of $1,000, representing the principal or amount of money borrowed. The interest payment is stated on the face of the bond at issue. A bond's interest rate stays the same for the duration of the bond's maturity. That's why bonds have an inverse relationship to national interest rates. If interest rates rise, the value of a bond usually drops; if interest rates drop, the value of a bond usually rises in comparison.

table 1.2   typical economic interrelationships

Interest Rates	Bonds	Stocks
Up	Down	Down
Down	Up	Up
Sideways	Sideways	Up

For example, let's say that you decide you are going to lend me $1,000 for a five-year period of time. I agree to pay you interest at a rate of 8% each year, which happens to be the market rate for interest charges. Therefore, I will pay you $80 per year interest. The very next day, interest rates jump to 10% (I am exaggerating to make a point); you now could have lent the same $1,000 and received 10% interest. This would give you $100 per year. Did the value of the first loan go up or down with the interest rate rising? The value of the 8% loan went down because you do not have the opportunity to lend it out at the higher rate of interest. Therefore, when interest rates go up, bond (loan) prices fall.

When interest rates go down, bond prices rise. If interest rates drop to 5%, an investor would receive only $50 on the same $1,000 investment. If you are already receiving $80, the value of your loan increases. That's how bonds are traded. As interest rates fluctuate, the value of a bond rises and falls in opposition. If a market is interest rate–driven, this refers to a point in the business cycle when interest rates are declining and bond prices are rising. This is often enough to inspire a stock market rally as money shifts from interest rate instruments to equity-based instruments.

---

interest rates
the charge for the privilege of borrowing money, usually expressed as an annual percentage rate.

In general terms, this inverse relationship also holds for the stock market and interest rates. Hence, bond prices and the stock market move in tandem. Why? Let's assume your company has to buy $10,000 worth of equipment. You don't want to pay cash for the equipment; therefore, you finance the purchase. To finance anything, you pay interest. In this case, you pay 8% interest—$800 per year. Interest is an expense that gets subtracted from what you earn. Therefore, if you earn $20,000 before interest expenses, you will have earned $19,200 after interest is paid ($20,000 – $800 = $19,200). However, if interest rates are 10%, the same $10,000 loan costs $1,000 annually. Now your earnings are reduced to $19,000 ($20,000 – $1,000 = $19,000). In this way, the value of a stock is inversely linked to interest rates—the higher your interest rate, the less money flows to your earnings. Since paying higher interest rates reduces earnings, a company's value will also decrease. This can seriously affect stock prices. Therefore, an increase in interest rates (or a fall in bond prices) should trigger a decrease in stock prices. This inverse relationship does not always hold. There are periods when a divergence will occur and a company's earnings will increase regardless of interest rates' direction. However, these divergences are generally short-term in nature.

Another voice to be listened to is that of the Federal Reserve chairman, currently Alan Greenspan. Whenever he speaks, the stock market hums with volatility. Twice a year, the Federal Reserve chairman officially speaks to Congress (Humphrey-Hawkins Testimony) and stocks rally or descend in anticipation of what he'll say. In the wake of his testimony, the rising or lowering of interest rates may realign the course of the economy. This kind of information has a powerful effect on the markets.

The releases of several government reports also influence the economics of the country and thereby the markets as well. The employment report is released on the first Friday of the month. It contains the current unemployment rate. A high unemployment rate speaks of more people looking for fewer jobs. This can lead to a decrease in wages because of increased competition. Less money for employment leads to lower production costs, tempering inflation. Ultimately this may lead to lower interest rates and turn the market from bearish to bullish.

The consumer price index (CPI) is another important report for an avid investor to review. The CPI directly measures inflation by studying the change in the cost of a standardized quantity of goods and services paid by consumers. A general increase in the CPI may lead to an increase in interest rates and that can have a bearish effect on the markets. A retail sales report released monthly by the Commerce Department has a similar message. An increase in retail sales shows a strong economy, as does a significant increase in new housing in the housing start report. Prolonged increases may lead to higher interest rates to discourage inflation. A report on the gross national product (GNP) acts as a litmus test for the economy by taking everything into account.

If you want to be alerted as to when these reports will be released, go to InfoBeat (www.infobeat.com) and sign up as a subscriber. InfoBeat will e-mail daily newsletters that include a calendar of report releases as well as news, commentary, and portfolio updates.

psychological market indicators

Psychological market indicators can be thought of as criteria that analyze the subconscious of the marketplace. These indicators can be obtained by analyzing current market conditions. However, they are psychological by nature because their utilization depends on your interpretation of the facts. Keep in mind that some scenarios may inspire contrarian interpretations of the findings.

You can start by comparing the number of bullish investment advisers to the number of bearish investment advisers. Although this information is relatively straightforward, this percentage can be interpreted to be contrarian in nature since a vast number of advisers are wrong a lot of the time. Therefore, more bulls than bears may indicate that the market is topping out, getting ready for a fall.

Another way to gauge investment sentiment is to analyze options trading volume. Since buying puts is a bearish move and purchasing calls is a bullish move, the ratio between the two is supposed to reveal how many investors are bullish and how many are bearish. However, since the majority of investors are wrong, investors often insist that this ratio actually indicates yet another contrarian point of view. You can also study the ratio between put premiums and call premiums with a similar contrarian view. If put premiums are more expensive than call premiums, they must be experiencing higher volatility which leads to an increase in put prices—a bearish indicator.

One of the most inclusive subscription sites that report this kind of information can be found at Daily Graphs Online (www.dailygraphs .com). Developed by William O'Neil, the founder of *Investor's Business Daily (IBD)*, this comprehensive site features 70 key technical and fundamental interactive factors on more than 11,000 stocks traded on the NYSE, AMEX, and Nasdaq. Additional data is available on 2,800 companies that have met a stringent set of financial criteria designed by the *IBD*. To access the service, you have to download and install special software directly onto your hard drive and pay a subscription fee. Psychological market indicators can be accessed from the "Market Indicators" screen.

conclusion

Whether you actually execute your trades online or just use the Internet to research and select the companies you want to pursue, the Internet is an invaluable resource for traders. This chapter was designed to get you up and running. In addition, we covered some of the more popular approaches to selecting stocks from fundamental and technical analysis to trading on market sentiment. There is a trading methodology that suits just about everyone's temperament; it's just a matter of finding that method through trial and error. Once you decide what kind of information is necessary to your trading process, it can easily be found on the Internet at either a free site or one that charges a small subscription fee.

As a fundamental analyst, you will need to access all of the data that gives you a picture of a company's current status and future prospects. Unless you have a strong business background or are very familiar with a particular industry, this method of trading will probably take some time to master. To determine the true growth prospects for a company, you need to gather a number of fundamental criteria and review the firm's competitors, as well as how the company's products are received by consumers. This kind of information can be found at www.hoover.com, www.zacks.com, and www.edgar.gov. If you work in an industry and are familiar with all of the players, you are just that much ahead of the game.

As a technical analyst, you need to understand how to interpret sophisticated charting technology. There are literally hundreds of sites that will instantly create a daily chart with historical prices. Some of the best sites—such as www.stockpoint.com, www. bigcharts.com, and www.clearstation.com—will also give you the ability to choose which technical indicators you want to include. The best way to learn how to use charts is to visit these sites and experiment with the technical indicators. By looking at the graphs with the indicators overlaid, you can start to get a sense for what types of indicators are useful.

The debate on fundamental versus technical trading is an old one. Some traders swear by one and hold great disdain for the other. Other traders successfully integrate both methods. For example, fundamental analysis can be used to forecast market direction while technical analysis can trigger appropriate entrances and exits. Determining what works best for you will probably entail a period of experimentation. Ultimately, it depends on what kind of trading you wish to pursue. Perhaps you just want to buy stock and hold it until it makes a profit. Then you are looking for methods that help you to determine when a stock is undervalued and on the move up. My own preference is for nondirectional options strategies that capitalize on volatility swings.

Whichever market analysis techniques you choose to employ, make sure you test them over a sufficient period of time. You can do this by using current prices and watching market movement or by back-testing using trading software. Inevitably, as the markets change, suitable methods of analysis will change also. The key is to remain open-minded and flexible so that you can take advantage of whatever works. Although each of these trading methods deserves a chapter of its own, my purpose has been to briefly introduce them and inspire you to investigate them further by visiting sites that offer the best selection of trading tools.

The road to online investing prosperity is an individual experience. On your journey, you will undoubtedly encounter certain obstacles that block your path. Although no one can really tell you how to navigate around these impediments, you can try to learn as much as you can from other people's mistakes. Since my own journey has been filled with major victories and devastating losses, I hope you can use what I've learned to avoid making a few of your own mistakes.

chapter 2

online trading resources

ready, set, surf!

So, you're all hooked up and ready to surf. A double click on your dial-up networking service and suddenly you are assaulted by the alien sound of the computer uplinking to the Internet. These unmistakable tones and beeps always remind me of some kind of space age communication device. "Onscreen," you say, double clicking your Internet browser. In the blink of an eye, your default home page appears and suddenly it's just you and your mouse against the forces of the marketplace. But before you shift into warp speed, you'll save a lot of time by prioritizing the web sites you visit to retrieve important market information.

Efficiency is the key to successful online trading. The three basic fields of market research—broad market indicators, psychological market criteria, and individual stock assessment—can also be thought of as comparison, gossip, and screening. On a typical trading morning, I'll review the day's movers and shakers, compare them to the overall economic factors of the day, and then listen to what the street has to say about those companies. Once I locate a few stocks that look promising, I spend some time researching their price and volume potentials. If everything looks good, it's time to review their option premiums in search of a strategically sound profit opportunity.

During the past decade I have slowly developed a daily online ritual that collects investment information from a variety of sites. My research for this book has involved exploring more than 300 investment sites and online brokerages. To simplify the investigative process for you, the sites are divided into 13 categories: Supersites, News, Research, Education, Technical Analysis, Options, Webzines, High Technology, Exchanges, Advisory Sites, Specialty Sites, Fun & Games, and Search Engines. The following informal guide to the kinds of investment sites that are out there should help you get the lay of the virtual landscape. A comprehensive list of 229 sites can be found in Appendix D. For the latest update to the website rankings contained in this book, go to www.optionetics.com.

kinds of sites

The number of financial resource sites on the Internet seems infinite. Sites come and go, redesigning their formats and upgrading their services as they strive to attract users in this highly competitive field. Financial resource sites offer a broad array of informational services. You'll find stock and option quotes, news and commentary, fundamental and technical data, chat rooms and message boards, live interactive sessions, advisory e-mail services, and an endless assortment of investment ideas. The sites are actually a testament to human creativity made possible through advertising and subscriptions.

Although many sites are free, many others charge a fee for additional services like real-time quotes, portfolio tracking, e-mailed news, and advisory alerts. Since the best way to decide if you like a site's services is to check it out, free trial subscriptions are common. Trial subscriptions can help you to decide whether the services you're considering paying for actually enhance your profit-making ability. So don't be surprised if you are constantly being asked to register or subscribe, even when sites are free. There are also the obligatory disclaimers that have to be formally acknowledged to complete registration. I have yet to read the legalese in any of these documents, but they basically want to make sure that subscribers absolve the sites of any wrongdoing. This process can become annoying, especially when the subscription form is less than user-friendly. As you skip from site to site, you will be asked to choose a user name and password. It's a good idea to establish a consistent online identity so that no matter which site you visit, you can remember how to log on.

Since there is an abundance of investment-oriented sites, after a while, they may all start to look alike. One way to stay organized is to take notes as you go and bookmark sites that you find useful so that you can find your way back. It can be helpful to go to a site that specializes in providing links to financial web sites. This kind of convenient one-stop shopping can help you to easily peruse a variety of sites. I highly recommend the following investment link sites: www.cyberinvest.com, the webinvestor.com, www.investorama.com, and www.investorlinks.com.

supersites

These comprehensive megasites have just about everything—from real-time quotes and interactive charts to news, commentary, and stock research capabilities. Most sites have a free area as well as subscription-based services. Subscriptions often include real-time or delayed quotes, recommendations, and daily e-mail newsletters containing quotes and news items on stocks in your portfolio. This kind of personal attention can be very helpful—but get ready for the number of e-mails you receive to soar. It's a matter of personal choice. Although what works for me may not be quite what interests you, I highly recommend Signal Online (www.dbc.com), Microsoft Investor (www.investor.msn.com), Motley Fool (www.fool.com), and Wall Street City (www.wallstreetcity.com).

news

Most news services are spin-offs from the major news services, including television and print news media. ABC, NBC, CBS, Fox, CNN, Forbes, and Bloomberg all have web sites offering comprehensive investment coverage. Online news is often available with video and audio accompaniment, but you have to download the right software. The beauty of online news services is that they continuously update their information, unlike their print media cousins. Timely news is of utmost importance to the online trader, especially to option traders looking for volatile markets. My favorite news sites include Barron's (www.barrons.com), Bloomberg (www.bloomberg.com), CBS MarketWatch (www.cbsmarket watch.com), CNNfn (www.cnnfn.com), Reuters MoneyNet (www. moneynet.com), and TheStreet.com (www.thestreet.com).

research

Sites that specialize in market research provide a variety of analysis tools. Researching a company entails reviewing finances and management abilities and making sure operations are creating high cash flow, healthy earnings, and a strong balance sheet. Specifically, look for a low debt level, which translates into more operating cash for reinvestment in the business. Annual reports, company profiles, earnings estimates, and insider reports are available. To help you figure out which stocks are really moving, many sites include a section on price percentage winners and losers. Some of my favorite research sites include Hoover's Online (www.hoovers.com), Market Guide Investor (www.marketguide.com), and StockSmart Pro (www.stocksmartpro.com).

education

Educational sites help traders to get up to speed by providing innovative investment education through virtual stock exchanges, one-on-one online educational workshops, and investment games. This is also a good place to go to brush up on any technical analysis techniques that have you shaking your head and rolling your eyes. These sites are excellent for the novice trader putting in his or her first order. My favorites include Cassandra's Revenge (www.stockscape.com/news letters/cassandra), Equity Analytics (www.e-analytics.com), and Motley Fool (www.fool.com).

technical analysis

Sites that focus on technical analysis tools provide a variety of charts and graphs for the avid technical trader. This is where you can go to create charts with moving averages, stochastics, and momentum indicators. Some also offer chat rooms if you feel like discussing the ramifications of your research with the masses. Check out BigCharts.com (www.bigcharts.com), ClearStation (www.clearstation.com), and Daily Graphs Online (www.dailygraphs.com).

options

Some sites are completely dedicated to helping option traders get the customized information they need. Although a number of option services are advisory in nature, others offer real-time and delayed quotes, options calculators, historical option premiums and volumes, intraday and weekly charts, volatility and other Greek variables, and technical charts. The best option sites that I use include, OptionInvestor.com (www.optioninvestor.com), OptionsAnalysis.com (www.options analysis.com), OptionSource.com (www.optionsource.com), and Strike price.com (www.strikeprice.com).

webzines

Webzines are an extremely new concept that is really starting to take off. Although newspapers and magazines have jumped onto the cyber-bandwagon by developing online subscription services that mirror their newsstand issues, some webzines can only be found online. The rise of this form of publication, although still in its infancy, has an impressive track record and an obvious upside potential for growth. Two of the best webzines are Kiplinger Online (www.kiplinger.com) and Red Herring Online (www.herring.com).

high technology

Recent surges in Internet stocks have created a niche for sites that focus on high-technology stocks. These sites monitor the latest high-tech news, movers and shakers in the industry, product development and releases, research and development tools, and chat rooms. Check out CMPnet (www.cmp.net) and Good Morning Silicon Valley (www.mercurycenter.com/gmsv). If you want to take the temperature of a tech stock's volatility then surf over to Silicon Investor (www.siliconinvestor.com). It features one of the most popular chat rooms on the Net where you can dial in any tech stock and find investors from all over the country voicing their opinions and asking questions.

exchanges

These days every exchange has a web site. A tremendous amount of information about new and previously listed company data, annual reports, research, publications, and news and quotes is readily available along with daily market analysis. Check out the New York Stock Exchange (www.nyse.com), the Chicago Board Options Exchange (www.cboe.com), the Nasdaq AMEX (www.nasdaq-amex.com), the Pacific Stock Exchange (www.pacificex.com), and the Philadelphia Stock Exchange (www.phlx.com).

advisory sites

Investment analysts are continually upgrading and downgrading stocks to strong buys, holds, or sells. Analysts can now download their recommendations through advisory sites. As this information leaks out into the public's domain, it becomes the noise on the street and it makes dollars and sense to pay attention to who is upgrading what and why. This is increasingly true as more and more financial sites use e-mail services to broadcast their picks and pans. Two of the best advisory sites include Avid Trading (www.avidtrader.com) and Daily Picks (www.dailypicks.com).

specialty sites

There are a number of sites that target a particular audience or focus on a specific kind of market. Sites that target specific audiences include the Green Money Online Guide (www.greenmoney.com), which specializes in social and environmentally responsible companies, and Women's Wire (womenswire.com/money), an investment site from a woman's point of view. Information-specific sites include those that focus on credit ratings at Moody's Investors Service (www.moodys.com), mutual funds (www.morningstar.net), and small cap stocks (www.smallcapinvestor.com).

fun & games

Who says investing has to be all work and no play? The originators of these sites offer trading simulations, participatory games, and educational guides that enable kids and adults alike to venture forth into the investment arena. These sites are a welcome relief after too many hours of number crunching and corporate research. Get out of the rat race and into the virtual sandbox with Hey Idiot.com (www.heyidiot.com), StockTrack (www.stocktrak.com), and Wall Street Sports (www.wall streetsports.com).

search engines

If you can't find what you're looking for, you've probably used a search engine to probe the Internet for appropriate sites. All search engines have their own site and most offer a business and finance section. Check out Lycos (www.lycos.com/business) or Yahoo! Finance (quote.yahoo.com).

e-mail newsletters

If you don't have time to go looking for the latest news updates and analysts' reports, you might want to check out e-mail newsletters. Yet another component of a diverse online trading experience, e-mail newsletters are available from a variety of web sites, professional analysts, and financial advisers. These convenient alerts are filled with intraday summaries, customized portfolio news clippings, and controversial counsel from numerous advisers who are more than happy to deliver their advice right to your e-mail address. Some newsletters are free and filled with distracting advertisements. Others require a subscription fee. You can also set up a portfolio and receive daily updates and news alerts concerning the stocks you are watching. Some services have room for multiple portfolios while others may limit subscribers to five at a time. To keep track of things, it may be helpful to create two distinct portfolios: stocks you are watching and stocks you are trading.

---

e-mail newsletters
publications seeking to provide financial advice including trade recommendations and market commentary to their subscribers.

When it comes to advice, you should know that impartiality is not guaranteed. There are those advisory services that accept compensation or have a financial interest in the companies that they mention. It's a good idea to read the fine print (which can be tedious) or search the chat rooms for any consternation concerning newsletters with conflict of interest disorders.

A great way to get started is to visit InfoBeat (www.infobeat. com), a web site that lists a wide variety of e-newsletters. Onetime free registration enables you to subscribe to as many newsletters as you wish to receive. There are some very good subscriptions available, including TheStreet.com's Midday Musings, Notes from a Fool, Red Herring's Catch of the Day, Silicon Alley Daily, Wired News Daily, and The Internet Stock Report® with Steve Harmon. You can sign up for any of these reputable newsletters absolutely free. While you're at InfoBeat, go ahead and enter a portfolio. The site has an excellent array of products and services including morning, midday, and closing highlights as well as news and weekend reports on the stocks of your choice.

rules of net surfing

There is one concern that online traders share: efficiency. System delay or shutdown is unavoidable as you careen from site to site. These errors can be triggered by an infinite array of technological breakdowns and human fallibilities. How many times have I sat staring at my computer, waiting for the next screen for what seemed like an eternity as my blood pressure rose off the Richter scale? In many cases, a network error had severed my connection completely and I'd actually been off-line the whole time and didn't even know it.

Wasting time on the Net is a constant frustration that can really up your stress level. Murphy's Law seems to have been tailor-made for computers. Internet servers always go down at the most inopportune moments. Not being able to access your trading account can be nerve-racking, especially during times of high volatility. These kinds of system errors can increase your anxiety to dangerous levels—not exactly the ideal frame of mind to be in when looking for a good trade.

Many of us have been trained to finish one project at a time in order to give each one undivided attention. Certainly one of the keys to higher self-esteem comes from learning to appreciate the feeling of accomplishment that accompanies the completion of a task. But the Internet is not like real life. In the virtual land of the Net, you have to learn to multitask in order to relax while surfing from site to site. You have to learn how to wait patiently for market research and price movement to present worthwhile trading opportunities.

These days it has become perfectly normal for me to cruise the Net reviewing prices and graphs while composing e-mail, reading a document, talking on the phone, editing a manuscript, and placing a trade. After all, this is the new millennium and I'm living online now. But if you are new to computers, this kind of multitasking can be hard going at first. The following rules may help put you in the right frame of mind.

1. Get a fast modem and a fast computer. Nothing is more frustrating than waiting for the next connection to come into view. Computer speed is an essential part of being able to make money in the markets.

2. Don't subscribe to more than three e-mail services at a time. You'll be overwhelmed with e-mail alerts.

3. Bookmark the sites that strike you as useful immediately so that you don't lose them.

4. Have an off-line master list of all portfolios (real or paper). Always have a Plan B. You can call an online broker if your server shuts down, but you still need to know what's in which account.

5. Paper trade any recommendations from an advisory source before putting your money on the line. That way you can verify the value of the information prior to risking any hard-earned cash.

6. Try not to print out research materials. Information gets old so fast that hard copies are usually a waste of paper (and trees).

7. Keep your fingers on the pulse of the mass psychology of the markets by checking out a variety of resource sites and analyst commentaries.

8. Don't be afraid to subscribe to new services every once in a while to get differing perspectives.

9. Get to know the "E. F. Huttons" of the Net. If Zacks Investment Research is talking, you can bet that a lot of people are listening.

Zacks Investment Research

Zacks Investment Research is a very popular financial site that offers a variety of free and subscription services. It provides access to research produced by over 3,000 analysts at the more than 240 brokerage firms as well as a vast array of brokerage and equity research, screening, and advisory tools (www.zacks.com).

---

10. Get in the habit of surfing a few select message boards or chat rooms to see what individual traders and analysts have to say concerning stocks you are interested in trading. You can also create a portfolio at Company Sleuth (www.companysleuth.com) and receive by e-mail a daily

account of all new chat room postings on the stocks of your choice.

11. Take all investment advice with a grain of salt. Always do your homework before allowing something that sounds too good to be true to rob you blind.

engage

In order to help you get the most out of your online experience, the following section details possible online rituals. Your online workout will probably vary from day to day depending on your time availability and market dynamics.

The first thing you want to do is take a look at the day's news headlines to see what's happening that could affect a possible or current investment. Although news of all kinds can affect the behavior of the marketplace, bad news (as a rule) travels faster than good news. Therefore, you're looking for bad news opportunities and good news trends. If nothing jumps out at you, it's time to search for stocks that are up or down 30% (minimum) since yesterday's close. This task can be accomplished—as can most online research—at an abundance of web sites. I like to start by going to CBS MarketWatch and clicking on "Market Data" at the top of the page to access "Percent Gainers and Losers" and "Volume Leaders." You can choose from lists directly from the New York Stock Exchange (NYSE), American Stock Exchange (AMEX), and Nasdaq. Look for companies that appear on both lists or new stocks that just made the list and may be beginning to make a move. In addition, you might want to review the "Volume Alerts" column, which lists NYSE and Nasdaq "Volume % Change Leaders."

---

volume
the number of shares bought and sold for a specific stock or option.

This initial process gives you the lay of the land. To find a serious contender, look for stocks (or options) with plenty of liquidity. A large number of buyers and sellers creates a high volume of trading activity that translates into high liquidity. Liquidity is imperative because it gives a trader the opportunity to move in and out of a market with ease. I look for stocks that have a trading volume of at least 300,000 shares a day and preferably a million. Almost any site with fundamental data or delayed price quotes will show a stock's volume. I like

BigCharts.com (www.bigcharts.com) because while I'm there I can also create a 12-month price and volume chart.

If a stock passes the liquidity test, then I have to find out if the stock has options available. Checking for options involves searching for an option chain. You can accomplish this by surfing over to StrikePrice.com (www.strikeprice.com) and entering a stock symbol in the "Option Chain" box. If a page of option quotes comes up, then you're in business. You can also get very accurate quotes at the Chicago Board Options Exchange (www.cboe.com).

Then it's time to go to OptionsAnalysis.com (www.optionsanalysis. com) to scan for volatility skews by analyzing which stock options are ranked the most and least expensive. Once my list is complete, I may have a few stocks that show promise as well as a few stock options that are worth the time it takes to review the performance of the underlying stock.

---

volatility skew
volatility skews measure and account for the limitation found in most options pricing models and can be used to estimate an option's real worth. High volatility increases the price of a trading instrument. A volatility skew exists when higher strike options are overpriced in comparison to the lower strike options and vice versa. Specific option strategies take advantage of various kinds of volatility scenarios.

Once you find a few stocks or options that fit these criteria, it's time to do some in-depth research. Surf over to www.clearstation.com and enter a stock symbol in the box that says "Get Graph." A market snapshot will appear along with several charts including price, volume, stochastics, and MACD graphs. ClearStation also provides a list of current news articles and community messages.

MACD
moving average convergence/divergence or MACD refers to the crossing of two moving averages *or* the failure of two moving averages to confirm a trend.

Yahoo! Finance (quote.yahoo.com) is another site that offers a multitude of research tools. Enter a stock symbol and then click on

"Research" to monitor everything from earnings to broker recommendations. If you want to do a little creative research, click on "SEC" to read the last quarterly report filed to the Securities and Exchange Commission, or go to "Profile" to find the link to the company's web site. You can also check the stock's insider trading (select "Insider") or check the message board to see what other investors have to say.

TheStreet.com (www.thestreet.com) is another excellent site that provides financial reports and informative commentaries throughout the day as the market moves. Published exclusively online, TheStreet.com has a reputation for objectivity and timeliness. As a first-time user, I was pleased to find that a free initial 30-day subscription enabled me to check out the site in its entirety. I started by clicking on "Today" to review the up-to-the-minute stories regarding today's market movements. I then clicked on "Stock News" to get a bird's-eye view of the movers and shakers of the day. TheStreet.com also has a section that covers "Tech Stock" movements. If any of the articles motivate me to do additional investigation regarding specific stocks, I click on "Portfolio" and add them to my list so I don't forget to watch them closely for future trading opportunities. Finally, I click on the "Commentary" section to review columnist Herb Greenberg or money manager James J. Cramer's opinions. There's also a chat room if I feel like comparing notes on my favorite watch list contenders.

If that's not enough, you can also sign up for a free two-week membership to Zacks Investment Research services (www.zacks.com). Zacks is an important site because it has earned the ear of the street and therefore is quite an influence on the mass psychology of the marketplace. This site summarizes the current stock recommendations of 3,000 analysts employed by 230 U.S. brokerage firms for more than 6,000 companies. These recommendations are translated into a number of subscription and free services geared for the avid investor. Start by checking out the "Stock Pick of the Month" as well as "Timely Buys." If any of these stocks look interesting, click on them and you'll have a choice of what kind of data you want to see. I usually go for "The Whole Enchilada," which gives me more information than I need. I also like Zacks's "Earnings per Share Surprise Service," which reveals the top 10 positive and negative surprises—stocks with above estimated earnings tend to go up, while stocks that report a negative surprise tend to fall.

Perhaps one of the best ways to follow a stock is to see what other people have to say about it. One of my favorite places to check out the high-technology stock buzz is to surf over to the Silicon Investor member home page (www.techstocks.com). Sign up for a two-week trial membership and then enter a particular word or stock symbol, or review "Stock Talk" subjects by category (software, communications, biotechnology, etc.). Corporate profiles and forums are also available.

Once I've discovered a stock that looks good, I surf over to www.cboe.pcquote.com to check the delayed option prices directly from the Chicago Board Options Exchange. I plug in the stock symbol and flag "list all options" in order to be able to review today's options and their respective premiums. I usually print this out and then switch my focus to determining the right strategy to take advantage of the stock's position. But let the trader beware! Some stocks have hundreds of options—Yahoo! and Amazon.com, for example—and selecting "list all options" can result in a 20-minute delay. If you plan on printing it out, make sure your printer has plenty of paper, because these lists are huge.

If I can find a potentially profitable trade using the delayed option prices, I move to www.strikeprice.com, scroll down to "Historical Option Data," and enter the option symbols I am considering trading. By this time, I also need to review the options' volatilities so it's back to OptionsAnalysis.com to enter the option symbol to check out the option Greeks. If everything looks promising and the risk-to-reward ratio is acceptable, I'm ready to place the trade.

This process may seem quite long and involved, but don't get discouraged. I wrote this section with the intention of mentioning an array of sites that can be used to track down a profitable options trade. Your own process may be much simpler. It just depends on the kind of analysis you like to do before making a trade. Developing your online trading procedure is an adventure—do it with gusto!

online quotes

Almost every investing site I've researched provides traders with the opportunity to get a snapshot quote on a specific stock. Some of these quotes are real-time, but many more are delayed by at least 15 minutes. If you want to receive streaming real-time data on a portfolio of stocks, you must be willing to pay for it.

To receive quotes free of charge, you have to be willing to register at a web site and then take the time to set up a portfolio of companies. Most sites will send you daily e-mails updating you on closing prices of the day as well as any breaking news that involves companies on your portfolio list. You can also access the sites throughout the day to get current quotes.

Wall Street City (www.wallstreetcity.com) provides free real-time quotes from Telescan Direct, a premier provider of wireless news and stock quotes, if you register as a subscriber. (Be careful. If you don't supply the exact information required, you will be asked to use your browser's "Back" toggle, which erases everything you already input. It took me five tries to get everything right!) To use the free service, just input a stock symbol, and the stock's real-time price will be displayed along with an intraday price chart, a list of the stock's 10 most recent trades, news and commentary, various alerts, and technical breakouts. Unfortunately, if you want more information than that, you have to join up as a paid subscriber. A 30-day free trial period is available, but you must be willing to supply a valid credit card number to back it up.

Quote.com (www.quote.com) is another site dedicated to providing real-time financial information for serious investors. This service requires that you download its software to receive live, updated charts, quote sheets, hot lists, and historical data. A built-in web browser also provides access to fundamental information and up-to-the-minute news. Overall rates are relatively low and direct payment is charged to receive data from a specific exchange.

My favorite online data service is eSignal (www.dbc.com). This subscription-based service provides an exhaustive list of services and trading tools, including real-time streaming data and live interval charts. It is also compatible with a number of software programs such as OptionStation and SuperCharts. The Portfolio and Quote windows provide extremely versatile spreadsheets for keeping up with movements of multiple stocks. A right-hand click on any stock symbol provides access to news, fundamental data, technical charts, and Nasdaq Level II screens, as well as an easy-to-read options chain.

Nasdaq Level II
a Nasdaq Level II color-coded screen provides real-time information concerning who is buying and selling a specific stock and the volume of shares they are trading. Color-coding assists traders to determine which way the market should go: Yellow indicates the best quote or first tier of buyers, followed by green, then dark blue, and finally light blue.

---

trading software

The development of trading software enables traders to search through thousands of positions to find optimal trading opportunities in a blink of an eye. Perhaps the only drawback comes from the fact that having access to a myriad of technical indicators doesn't necessarily mean you know how to use them. Grasping the concepts underlying technical analysis methodologies can be extremely difficult. To gain an idea of just how big this area of expertise is, see the list of technical analysis systems in Appendix B.

To find out which program best fits your needs, you can use a selection system I developed that will help you make your own assessment. This system is the result of many years of investigation and has enabled me to find extremely useful applications. Before looking at your first program, you should create a comprehensive spreadsheet of preferred features—no matter how remote they may seem. Then, weight how important each of your listed items is on a scale of 1 to 10 using 10 as the highest or most important rating. Next, decide on a scoring guide for each factor you review. I generally use a scale of 1 to 4 with 4 as the highest score. Finally, make sure you have everything on the list that interests you so that you can live with the selection even if it's not the program you originally wanted. You are now ready to review various software programs.

Some software companies will let you download the software directly from the Internet to review a beta version for free for a few weeks. Others will send you the program with a 30-day money-back guarantee. You'll have to pay for it up front, but if you don't like it you can send it back and ask for a refund. Others will make you pay for it up front with no refunds. Always read the fine print before ordering a product.

beta version software
software that is distributed to select users for testing before it is officially released to the public. Many software manufacturers will allow you to download beta version software directly over the Internet to try out a program before buying it.

How you gather your information is up to you. Once you have scored all of the factors, multiply the score by the weight and record that as the net score. Finally, add up the net scores to come up with the total score for each software program. Table 2.1 provides a demonstration on my selection process. Once you have the facts, you can decide whether to purchase the one with the highest score or the one that you simply enjoyed using the most.

In my opinion, OptionStation 2000 by Omega Research is one of the best options software programs on the market. I use it in combination with the other Omega Research products, TradeStation 2000 and Radar Screen 2000. Together, these interdisciplinary software applications enable me to fully analyze potential trading opportunities with great charting and technical analysis tools as well as the best back-testing programs available. Perhaps the greatest compliment I can give Omega is that I grew up as a trader using Omega products.

table 2.1 software scoring example

Factors	Weight (1–10)	Scoring Guide	Score (1–4)	Net Score (Weight × Score)
1. Graphing	8	1 = one type 2 = two types 3 = three types 4 = four types	3	24
2. Number of data vendors supported	5	1 = one vendor 2 = two vendors 3 = three vendors 4 = four vendors	4	20
3. Ability to test own strategies	2	0 = No 4 = Yes	4	8
4. Price	10	1 = <$500 2 = <$750 3 = <$1,000 4 = >$1,000	2	20
Total score				72

Omega Research
one of the best financial software designers in the investment industry, Omega Research has created TradeStation, OptionStation 2000, Radarscreen, and SuperCharts (www.omegaresearch.com).

conclusion

The two main approaches to analyzing stocks—fundamental and technical analysis—were discussed in Chapter 1. Regardless of the primary method you decide to use, there are certain common analysis methods that all traders should pay close attention to, such as moving averages, volume spikes, and new highs and lows. Success as a trader depends on maintaining an awareness of what is going on in the marketplace and what the street thinks is going on.

Finding profitable stocks is a matter of personal taste, combined with professional insights, hobbies, and interests. For some traders, finding the right stocks may be as easy as asking their 10-year-old child what the hottest games are on the market. For others, it's a matter of looking at television to decide who has the most compelling product and advertisements. Others simply look at which stocks are moving and have the ear of the marketplace.

This last category is where the online traders can really save some time. With the click of a few keys, you can instantly find out which stocks have had a sudden increase in price, a sharp rise in volume, or even major growth in insider buying activity. Most of the financial sites noted in this book can easily supply you with a quick list of the top 10 and bottom 10 stocks in any category. Some of the more specialized stock screening programs will give you a list of companies that meet your personal movement criteria.

The Internet's community nature also gives you the unprecedented opportunity to "chat" with other traders from around the world to hear what they think about specific stocks or stocks in a particular sector. There is a chat room for virtually every major stock, index, and market sector imaginable. Always keep in mind, however, that some people who post opinions in chat rooms have their own agenda in building up or tearing apart a stock, so be discriminating.

chat rooms
interactive online message boards where individual investors can post their own opinions on a multitude of subjects from online brokerages to specific stocks.

Once you figure out how you are going to pick your stocks, you need a way to stay on top of their activity. There are literally hundreds of sites that can give you the capability to track stocks through the use of portfolios. However, only a handful of online portfolios give you the ability to track option prices and positions. That's one of the reasons I prefer to use eSignal. This top-notch service is well worth the subscription fee.

Online trading is a bastion for independent thinkers. You have a wealth of resources at your fingertips that will engage your imagination and challenge your mental capacity. I look for sites that offer reliability and efficiency with as few screens as possible between me and my final destination. Most traders will do anything to speed things up. Luckily, technology has all kinds of gadgets and programs that can help you to do so. I even know a few traders who use two modems at one time to increase their speed.

Another part of the game is keeping track of everything. E-mail alerts can help, but you need to develop a system for organizing stocks into portfolios and watch lists. I often use electronic flags to remind myself of things that need to be reviewed or sites that had some interesting tidbits of information. Utilize sites that help you to make informed decisions and increase your understanding of the markets. If you stumble on a few techniques that seem to work, keep testing them for a while. Over time, you'll find the right combination of sites to help you become a successful online trader.

chapter 3

a primer for trading stocks and options

stock basics

In its most basic form, stock market trading involves the buying and selling of stocks and stock options. A stock, also called a share, is a unit of ownership in a company. The value of each share is based on a wide variety of factors, including the total number of outstanding shares, the value of the company, its earnings and debts, what the company produces now and is expected to produce in the future, and the overall demand for the stock.

The main motivating force behind the company's initial selling of shares is for a company to raise capital to grow the business. When a buyer purchases stock, he or she actually owns part of the company and stands to profit when the company's earnings increase. How much is owned depends on how many shares of stock are purchased. Holders of common stock are the last to be paid any profits from the company and the first to profit from company growth.

Stock exchanges in the United States offer investors and traders the opportunity to buy and sell stocks and stock options. If there are more buyers than sellers, prices will rise. If there are more sellers than buyers, prices will fall. There are three ways to describe market movement: bullish, bearish, and neutral. A market is bullish if the prices are rising. To make money in a bullish market, traditional investors buy stock. A bearish market is falling in price and can be profited on by selling stock. A neutral market continuously fluctuates between two prices: support (low) and resistance (high). Several combination option strategies can be employed to take advantage of a sideways-moving market.

There are scores of analysts that study certain industries and companies in order to forecast market movement. They typically issue earnings estimates and reports that assess a company's value. Prior to the release of a report, street expectation of market movement drives the market prices. If investors feel a report will beat the street expectations, there will be more buyers compared to sellers and the price of the shares will be bid up. If the majority of the investors feel that the company's earnings will disappoint the street, then the prices will decline.

The size of a company can be a major determinant of price and risk. There are three unofficial size classifications: blue-chip, mid-cap, and small-cap. Blue-chip is a term derived from poker where blue chips hold the most value. Hence, blue-chip stocks symbolize stocks with the highest capitalization in the marketplace. Typically they enjoy solid value and good security, with a record of continuous dividend payments and other desirable investment attributes. Mid-cap stocks usually have a bigger growth potential than blue-chip stocks but they are not as heavily capitalized. Small-cap stocks can be potentially difficult to trade because they do not have the benefit of high liquidity. However, these stocks, although quite risky, are usually relatively inexpensive and big gains are possible. Some traders like to trade riskier stocks that have the potential for big price moves while others prefer the longer-term stability of blue-chip stocks. In general, the stocks you choose to trade depend on your time availability, stress threshold, and account size.

Officially, there are two kinds of stocks, common stocks and preferred stocks. A company initially sells shares of common stock to help raise capital for expansion. Investors make money by purchasing stock at a lower price and selling it at a higher price. This profit is called capital gains. However, if the company falters, the price of the stock may plummet and shareholders may end up holding stock that is practically worthless. Usually only large, fully established companies can afford to pay dividends to their shareholders and hence holders of common stock may or may not earn quarterly dividend payments. Holders of preferred stock receive guaranteed dividends prior to common stock holders, but the amount never changes even if the company triples its earnings. Also, the price of preferred stock increases at a slower rate than that of common stock. However, if the company loses money, holders of preferred stock have a better chance of receiving some of their investment back. All in all, common stocks are riskier than preferred stocks, but offer greater rewards if the company does well.

There is also a classification for stocks based on what they do with their profits. If a company reinvests its profits to promote further growth, then it is known as a growth stock. If it pays regular dividends to its shareholders, then it is an income stock. Growth stocks are more risky than income stocks but have a greater potential for big price moves.

If the price of a stock gets too high, a corporation may choose to split the stock. For example, if you own 1,000 shares at $100 each and a two-for-one stock split is announced, you will now own 2,000 shares at $50 each. The value is the same, but the shares now cost much less; this makes it easier for additional investors to enter the market, driving the price back up. If a stock's price drops too low, a reverse stock split may occur. A one-for-two reverse stock split would mean that 1,000 shares at $100 apiece are reduced to 500 shares at $200 each. Splitting stocks often triggers heavy volatility.

It is also important to determine whether a stock is cyclical in nature. Cyclical stocks closely reflect the general state of the economy. For example, if the economy is experiencing a slump, recreation and travel stocks are usually the first to feel the consumer pinch. Seasonal factors or events drive other stocks. Traders practically need to grow antennas to keep up with all of the possible factors that contribute to price fluctuation.

exchanges

Stocks are traded on various organized exchanges all over the world 24 hours a day. There are three major exchanges in the United States: the New York Stock Exchange (NYSE), the American Stock Exchange (AMEX), and Nasdaq. The first stock exchange was organized in Philadelphia in 1790. However, by 1817, the New York Stock Exchange was established on Wall Street and quickly became the most powerful center of financial exchange in the world. The original American Stock Exchange—originally called the New York Curb Exchange—was founded in 1842 and trading took place in the street until 1921. In contrast, the National Association of Securities Dealers automated quotations system, or Nasdaq, is an electronic stock market. It facilitates the trading of stocks using a vast telecommunications network linking brokers all over the country. Nasdaq currently lists over 5,540 foreign and domestic companies—more listings than any other exchange— and handles more than 45% of all shares traded.

These three exchanges handle the majority of the large and mid-size companies. In most cases, companies are traded on only one of the three major exchanges, although they may also be listed in various regional exchanges such as Los Angeles, Philadelphia, Chicago, Cincinnati, and Boston. Smaller companies with limited share volume are traded on the over-the-counter (OTC) market. The OTC market is a negotiated rather than auction-style market that lists more than 30,000 stocks. Brokers who trade these smaller companies receive daily price updates called the Pink Sheets by fax or computer.

In 1973, the Chicago Board Options Exchange (CBOE) formally established options trading by creating a standardized list of recognized options. Up until that time, options has been traded over-the-counter by a limited number of put/call dealers. Currently the CBOE lists options on 680 stocks with more than 700,000 option contracts traded daily. That's approximately 65% of the options traded nationwide. The CBOE is an auction market system employing floor brokers and market makers to execute customers' orders and inspire competition in the markets. The three other domestic exchanges that trade options are the Pacific Stock Exchange in San Francisco, the American Stock Exchange, and the Philadelphia Stock Exchange.

option basics

An option is a versatile trading instrument that provides high leverage and can significantly limit the overall risk of a trade. Options serve as a contract between two parties—a buyer and a seller—for a specified period of time after which the contract expires and the option holder loses the right to buy or sell the underlying shares of stock. Buying an option is done at a debit to the buyer and gives you the right, but not the obligation, to buy or sell a stock at a specified strike price. In contrast, selling an option brings in an immediate credit, but comes with an obligation to buy or sell the underlying stock if the option is assigned and exercised. Not all stocks offer options. If you find a stock that interests you, there are plenty of web sites that can verify a stock's option availability.

There are two kinds of options: calls and puts. Calls give you the right to buy the underlying asset and puts give you the right to sell the underlying asset. The cost of an option is referred to as the option premium. All the options of one type (put or call) that have the same underlying stock are called a class of options. For example, all the calls on IBM constitute an option class. All the options in one class with the same strike price are called an option series. For example, the IBM 105 calls with various expiration dates constitute an option series.

Options are available with various strike prices depending on the current price of the underlying stock. For example, if IBM is currently trading at $105 per share, you may choose to buy a call option at 95, 100, 105, 110, or 115. If you decide to buy an August IBM 105 call, you would have the option to buy IBM at $105 per share until the third Friday in August. If the price of IBM rises to 120, you can profit from the 105 call either by exercising the option and buying IBM at the lower price or by selling the option for a higher premium. If the price of IBM falls below 105, your option's premium will also decrease.

Strikes are available in the current month, the following month, and several months throughout the year and beyond. There are three expiration cycles with four months in each cycle: (1) January, April, July, and October; (2) February, May, August, and November; and (3) March, June, September, and December.

LEAPS options (Long-term Equity AnticiPation Securities) are long-term options that don't expire for at least nine months. Once an option's expiration gets closer than nine months, it becomes a plain option again with an entirely new ticker symbol. Be this as it may, LEAPS are in every way an option. Their expirations are a long way off, which makes them prime candidates for long-term plays and relatively secure bets for shorter-term trades.

Option pricing is a complex process with seven main components that affect the premium of an option:

1. The current price of the underlying financial stock.
2. The strike price of the option in comparison to the current market price (intrinsic value).
3. The type of option (put or call).
4. The amount of time remaining until expiration (time value).
5. The current risk-free interest rate.
6. The volatility of the underlying financial stock.
7. The dividend rate, if any, of the underlying financial stock.

Each of these factors plays a unique part in the price of an option. The first four are easily deduced from the option itself. The last three are more complex. For example, higher interest rates can increase option premiums, while lower interest rates can lead to a decrease in option premiums. Dividends act in a similar way, increasing and decreasing an option premium as they increase or decrease the price of the underlying asset. Volatility not only contributes to an option's price, but it also helps to define which strategy can best be used to take advantage of specific market movement. High-volatility stocks usually have higher-priced options while low-volatility stocks offer lower-priced options. There are options strategies that can be applied to take advantage of either scenario.

call options

A call option gives you the right to purchase 100 shares of the underlying stock at a specified strike price until the third Friday of the expiration month. You may choose to buy (go long) or sell (go short) a call option. If you go long a call option, you are purchasing the right (but under no obligation) to buy the underlying stock at the option's strike price until the expiration date. The premium of the long call option will show up as a debit in your trading account and is the maximum loss you risk by purchasing the call. In contrast, the maximum profit of a long call option is unlimited, depending on how high the underlying stock rises in price (the upside). In general, you want to buy calls in bullish markets and sell calls in bearish markets.

Purchasing a call option is one of the simplest forms of options trading. A bullish trader purchases a call because he or she expects the underlying asset to increase in price. The trader will most likely make a profit if the market price of the underlying asset increases fast enough to overcome the call option's time decay. Profits can be realized two ways. If the underlying stock increases in price before the option expires, the holder can exercise the call and purchase the underlying stock at the lower strike price. In addition, a rise in the price of the underlying asset increases the value of the call option, which can then be sold at a profit.

If you choose to sell or go short one call option, you are selling the right to buy 100 shares of the underlying stock at a specific strike price until the expiration date. A short call offers a limited profit—the price of the premium—and unlimited risk depending on how high the price of the underlying rises. In most cases, you are anticipating that the strike price of the short call will remain above the price of the underlying stock and will therefore expire worthless and you can keep the premium received. If the price of the underlying stock rises above the strike price, your short call may be assigned to an option buyer who exercises it. You are then obligated to deliver 100 shares of the underlying stock to the option buyer at the call's strike price. This entails buying the stock at the current (higher) price and selling it back to the option holder at the (lower) call strike price, thereby creating a loss. This process can be expensive, which is why I never recommend selling naked or unprotected options.

Call options give you the right to buy something at a specific price for a specific time. If the current market price is more than the strike price, the call option is in-the-money (ITM). If the current market price is less than the strike price, the call option is out-of-the-money (OTM). Call options that are OTM by their expiration date expire worthless. If the current market price is the same as the strike price, the call option is at-the-money (ATM). In general, I prefer to work with ATM options because they have the most liquidity. However, the strike price rarely equals the stock's market price exactly. Near-the-money may be a more accurate description.

Call options are available at various strike prices. Just pick up the financial pages of a good newspaper or surf the Net to www.cboe.com and look at the options for IBM. Strikes for stocks priced above $25 per share usually come in multiples of 5 while strikes for stocks less than $25 come in $2\frac{1}{2}$ dollar intervals. In addition, you normally have a choice of several different expiration dates for each strike price. Table 3.1 shows a hypothetical variety of strike prices, expiration months, and call premiums for IBM, the underlying stock, priced at $106 per share. The first column's numbers represent the strike prices of the IBM calls. The months across the top are the expiration months. The numbers inside the table are the option premiums. For example, the price of an IBM January 105 call is $2. Since each $1 in premium for a stock option is equal to $100 per contract, a price of $2 indicates that one contract would trade for $200 (2 × $100) plus commissions. If the price of IBM rises above $105 per share, a 105 option will move into-the-money and can most likely be sold or exercised at a profit.

put options

Put options give the buyer the right to sell shares of stock. Just like call options, put options come in various strike prices with a variety of expiration dates. However, unlike call options, if you are bearish (expect market prices to fall), you might consider going long a put option. If you are bullish (expect the market to rise), you might decide to go short a put option.

If you choose to go long one put option, you are purchasing the right to sell 100 shares of the underlying stock at whatever strike price you choose until the third Friday of the expiration month. The premium of the long put shows up as a debit in your trading account and the cost of the premium is the maximum loss you risk. The maximum

table 3.1 IBM call option premiums

Price of IBM = 106

Call Strike Price	January	April	July
100	$6\frac{3}{8}$	$7\frac{1}{2}$	$8\frac{1}{4}$
105	2	$3\frac{7}{8}$	$4\frac{3}{4}$
110	$\frac{3}{8}$	$1\frac{9}{16}$	$2\frac{3}{4}$

profit is virtually unlimited as the stock falls toward zero. As the underlying stock falls, the long put becomes more valuable because it gives you (or the person you sell it to) the right to sell the underlying stock at the higher strike price.

If you choose to go short one put option, you are selling the right to sell 100 shares of the underlying stock at a specific strike price until the expiration date. The premium is the maximum profit you can receive by selling a call option. It shows up as a credit in your trading account. However, the maximum loss is virtually unlimited depending on the price of the underlying stock as it falls toward zero. In most cases, you are anticipating that the underlying stock price will remain above the put strike price until expiration, leaving the put to expire worthless (so that you can keep the premium received). If, however, the underlying stock falls below the put's strike price, the option might be assigned to a put buyer and he or she may choose to exercise it. You are then obligated to buy 100 shares of the underlying stock at the higher strike price from the option holder.

A put option is in-the-money (ITM) when its strike price is higher than the market price of the underlying stock. A put option is at-the-money (ATM) when the price of the underlying stock is equal or close to its strike price. A put option is out-of-the-money (OTM) when the price of the underlying stock is greater than the strike price. Put options that are out-of-the-money by their expiration date expire worthless.

Purchasing put options is generally a bearish move. An option holder who has purchased a put option benefits when there is a decrease in the price of the underlying asset. This enables the holder to exercise the option and sell the underlying asset at the higher price on the open market. A decrease in the price of the underlying asset also promotes an increase in the value of the long put's premium so that it can be sold for a higher price than was originally paid to purchase it. The purchase of a put option provides unlimited profit potential and limited risk based on the put option's premium and commissions. The sale of a put option provides limited risk as the underlying stock falls to zero; the maximum profit is limited to the credit received from the premium.

intrinsic value and time value

Intrinsic value and time value are two of the primary determinants of an option's price. Intrinsic value can be defined as the amount by which the strike price of an option is in-the-money. It is actually the portion of an option's price that is not lost due to the passage of time. The following equations will allow you to calculate the intrinsic value of call and put options:

Call Options: Intrinsic value = Underlying stock's current price – Call strike price

Put Options: Intrinsic value = Put strike price – Underlying stock's current price

Neither ATM nor OTM options have any intrinsic value because they have no real value. You are simply buying time value, which decreases as an option approaches expiration. The intrinsic value of an option is not dependent on the time left until expiration. Time value is the amount by which the price of an option exceeds its intrinsic value and is directly related to how much time the option has until expiration. For example, if a call option costs $5 and its intrinsic value is $1, the time value would be $4 ($5 – $1 = $4).

Let's use Table 3.1 on page 69 to calculate the intrinsic value and time value of a few call options (with expiration in April).

1. **Strike Price = 100**

   Intrinsic value = Underlying price – Strike price = $106 – $100 = $6

   Time value = Premium – Intrinsic value = $7\frac{1}{2}$ – $6 = $1\frac{1}{2}$

2. **Strike Price = 105**

   Intrinsic value = Underlying price – Strike price = $106 – $105 = $1

   Time value = Premium – Intrinsic value = $3\frac{7}{8}$ – $1 = $2\frac{7}{8}$

3. **Strike Price = 110**

   Intrinsic value = Underlying price – Strike price = $106 – $110 = –$4 = Zero intrinsic value

   Time value = Premium – Intrinsic value = $1\frac{9}{16}$ – $0 = $1\frac{9}{16}$ = All time value

An option's intrinsic value tells you the minimum amount the option should be selling for and is therefore also called the minimum value—the cheaper the option, the less real value you are buying. The intrinsic value of an option is solely dependent on the price of the underlying stock and remains the same regardless of how much time is left until expiration. However, since theoretically an option with three months left till expiration has a better chance of ending up in-the-money than an option expiring in the present month, it is worth more.

Time value has a snowball effect. If you have ever bought options, you might have noticed that at a certain point close to expiration, the market stopped moving anywhere. That's because option prices are exponential—the closer you get to expiration, the more money you're going to lose if the market doesn't move. On the expiration day, all an option is worth is its intrinsic value. It's either in-the-money or it isn't. An option has less time value and more intrinsic value as it becomes deeper in-the-money and the option starts to move more like the underlying asset.

liquidity

Most of the strategies in this book have very specific market conditions that empower them to make money. Liquidity is one of these market conditions. Liquidity is the ease with which a market can be traded. A plentiful number of buyers and sellers usually boosts the volume of trading in a market, which, in turn, creates frenetic trading activity. Lots of activity produces a liquid market. Liquidity is an important factor in trading because it allows traders to get their orders filled easily as well as to quickly exit a position.

The best way to discover which markets have liquidity is actually to visit an exchange. The pits where you see absolute chaos are markets with liquidity. As long as there are plenty of floor traders screaming and yelling out orders as if their lives depended on it, you probably won't have a problem getting in and out of a trade. However, I tend to avoid the pits where the floor traders are falling asleep as they read the newspapers. These are obviously illiquid markets and it would not be a wise move to place an options-based trade there.

If you don't have the ability to actually visit an exchange, you can still check out the liquidity of a market by reviewing the market's volume to see how many shares have been bought and sold in one day. Volume is a basic attribute that can easily be found by accessing a snapshot quote from most online financial sites. You can also assess a market's momentum by monitoring the change in volume to see if it is increasing or decreasing. Many traders use momentum to locate a market's turning points that may trigger significant price moves.

It's hard to quantify just how much volume is enough to qualify a market as one with liquidity. However, as a rule of thumb, I prefer to look for markets that are trading at least 300,000 shares every day. Since there are no absolutes, there are situations when this rule can be tossed out the window in exchange for common sense. But until you have enough experience, this may be a good rule of thumb to follow.

offsetting versus exercising

To exit a long option position, you can either exercise or offset it. If you want to exercise a long call option, you simply notify your broker, who will then notify the margin department. By the next day, you will own the corresponding underlying position. If you exercise a long put option, you will end up short the underlying stock, American options can be exercised at any time prior to expiration.

The more popular route is to offset a long or short option. Most traders offset an option when they decide they have made enough profit on the trade, or have lost as much as they can bear to lose. Offsetting an option involves reversing the original transaction prior to the exercise date. Many brokerages automatically offset an option prior to expiration if it is at least $3/4$ point in-the-money. Offsetting can be applied through the following procedures:

1. If you bought a call, you have to sell the call.
2. If you sold a call, you have to buy the call.
3. If you bought a put, you have to sell the put.
4. If you sold a put, you have to buy the put.

Buyers of options are the only ones who have the choice to exercise the option and purchase (call) or sell (put) the underlying stock at the strike price. Although 95% of all options with value are offset, there are various reasons why a trader might choose to exercise an option instead. Of the 5% that are exercised, 95% are exercised at expiration. Neglecting to offset your option means that you have not exited your position. In this way, your option expires worthless. If you are shorting an option, this may be your strategy. But if you have purchased an option, you will lose the premium by letting it expire. Also, the closer you get to expiration, the less time value an option has, which can be a factor in the price of the premium.

trading accounts

Determining how much money you need in order to start trading can be very tricky. There are generally two types of transactions: cash and margin. Cash trades require you to put up 100% of the money in cash. All costs of the trade have to be in the account before the trade is placed. For example, if you wanted to buy 100 shares of IBM at 100, you would have to pay $10,000 plus commissions up front. If IBM were to rise to 110, the account would show an open position profit of $1,000, or a 10% rise in the account.

In contrast, margin trades allow you to put up a percentage of the total cost of the trade amount in cash and the rest is "on account." The brokerage company lends you an amount of money against the security of the investment you buy. The actual amount of money you are required to put on deposit with your clearing firm to secure the integrity of the trade is the margin amount. This amount changes depending on the market and size of the trade you are placing. Most traders prefer margin accounts because these accounts allow them to leverage assets in order to produce higher returns. If the price of the stock goes against your position, you will be required to post additional money into your margin account to keep the position open. If you cannot provide the extra cash needed to fulfill the new margin requirements, you lose your position. This is one of the reasons that shorting the market is so dangerous.

Of course, brokers don't lend money for free. They charge a fixed rate of interest on the loan amount as well as the usual commission on the trade. The interest rate and commissions are paid regardless of what happens to the price of the stock. The rate is usually broker call rate plus the firm's add-on points. The rate is cheaper than most loans due to the fact that it is a secure loan.

Based on the SEC's rules, the margin on most stock purchases equals 50% of the amount of the trade. For example, 100 shares of IBM at $100 a share costs a total of $10,000. You would be required to have a minimum of $5,000 on deposit in your margin account. However, recent volatility explosions in many Internet stocks have triggered some brokerages to up their margin amounts and in some cases deny margin trades completely.

If you choose to sell short, you are actually borrowing the stock shares from your broker at one price in anticipation of a drop in the market price. If the market price falls, you can buy back the shares at the lower price to repay the loan from your broker and pocket the difference. If the stock price rises, you eventually have to buy back the stock to cover your position at a higher price than you received for selling it. This can be a very expensive process, especially if a stock has been heavily shorted, because as the price starts to rise, a buying flurry among short sellers may drive the price sky-high. Margin on short selling is extremely expensive. You have to be able to cover the entire cost of the stock plus 50% more. This value will change as the market price fluctuates. At some brokerages, investors must have a minimum of $50,000 in their margin accounts plus the margin amount for the trade in order to short the market.

Long options do not require margins. They must be paid for up front, but at a fraction of the cost of buying the underlying stock. For example, since each premium point in stock options costs $100, a stock option at $3^{1}/_{2}$ will cost you $350 regardless of the underlying asset's current market price. However, if you choose to short sell the same option, you would have to have a certain amount of margin in your account. If you were short selling the option without a corresponding hedge, many brokers would require at least $50,000 in your account to place a short option trade. If you are hedging the short option, then the margin amount is subject to your broker's discretion.

Combining the buying and selling of options and stocks may create a more complex margin calculation; however, these strategies usually have reduced margin requirements in comparison to just buying or shorting stocks alone. In general, since every trade is unique, margin will depend on the strategy you employ and your broker's requirements. If you're worried about the margin at the outset of the trade, you probably shouldn't place the trade. This rule can keep you from putting on positions that are larger than you can really handle.

conclusion

In this chapter, I tried to impart a basic understanding of the main trading instruments that I use: stocks and stock options. If the information seems a little confusing to those of you who are just starting out, the following review may help you get in the swing of things.

- *Call Options.* Call options give traders the right to buy the underlying stock. A call option is in-the-money (ITM) if its strike price is below the current price of the underlying stock. A call option is out-of-the-money (OTM) if its strike price is above the current price of the underlying stock. A call option is at-the-money (ATM) if its strike price is the same as (or very close to) the current price of the underlying stock.

- *Buying Calls.* If bullish (you believe the market will rise), buy (go long) calls. Buyers have rights. A call buyer has the right, but not the obligation, to buy the underlying stock at the strike price until the expiration date. If you buy a call option, your maximum risk is the money paid for the option—the debit. The maximum profit is unlimited depending on the rise in the price of the underlying asset. To offset a long call, you have to sell a call with the same strike price and expiration to close out the position. By exercising your long call, you are choosing to purchase the underlying stock at the strike price of the call option.

- *Selling Calls.* If bearish (you believe the market will fall), sell (go short) calls. Sellers have obligations. A call seller has the obligation to deliver the underlying stock at the strike price to the person to whom the option was assigned, if that person chooses to exercise the call. If you sell a call option, your risk is unlimited to the upside. The profit is limited to the credit received from the sale of the call. When selling calls, make sure to choose options with little time left until expiration. Call sellers want the call to expire worthless so that they can keep the whole premium. To offset a short call, you have to buy a call with the same strike price and expiration to close out the position.

- *Intrinsic Value and Time Value of Calls.* The intrinsic value of a call option is calculated by subtracting the call strike price from the current price of the underlying stock. The time value for a call option is calculated by subtracting the intrinsic value from the call premium.

- *Put Options.* Put options give traders the right to sell the underlying stock. A put option is in-the-money (ITM) if its strike price is above the current price of the underlying stock. A put option is out-of-the-money (OTM) if its strike price is below the current price of the underlying stock. A put option is at-the-money (ATM) if its strike price is the same as (or very close to) the current price of the underlying stock.

- *Buying Puts.* If bearish (you believe the market will fall), buy (go long) puts. Buyers have rights. A put buyer has the right, but not the obligation, to sell the underlying stock at the strike price until the expiration date. If you buy a put option, your risk is the money paid for the option, the debit. The profit is unlimited depending on the decrease in the price of the underlying asset. To offset a long put, you have to sell a put with the same strike price and expiration to close out the position. By exercising your long put, you are choosing to go short the underlying stock at the strike price of the put option.

- *Selling Puts.* If bullish (you believe the market will rise), sell (go short) puts. Sellers have obligations. A put seller has the obligation to buy the underlying stock at the strike price from the person to whom the option was assigned, if that person chooses to exercise the put option. If you sell a put option, your risk is limited as the underlying falls to zero. The profit is limited to the credit received from the sale of the put. When selling puts, make sure to choose options with little time left until expiration. Put sellers want a put to expire worthless so that they can keep the whole premium. To offset a short put, you have to buy a put with the same strike and expiration price to close out the position.

- *Intrinsic Value and Time Value of Puts.* The intrinsic value of a put option is calculated by subtracting the current price of the underlying stock from the put strike price. The time value for a put option is calculated by subtracting the intrinsic value from the put premium.

chapter 4

basic option trading strategies

the greatest show on earth

Those of us who make a living on Wall Street live on the edge of our seats, not to mention our sanity. The past few years have borne witness to record-breaking volatility. Markets have exploded, while the economies of several foreign countries have collapsed. Forecasting market direction has become more complex than ever before. Yet one thought rings true: There is nothing like the excitement and spontaneity of the marketplace.

In many ways, your first trade is a rite of passage. To place it with confidence, you have to know how to play the game by cultivating your own resources in order to exploit market movement. Perhaps the attainment of effectual market knowledge is the biggest creative challenge a trader has to face. In this way, the stock market is the greatest equalizer of our times. It doesn't matter how many degrees or how much money you have in your trading account. The Internet has leveled the playing field once and for all. The accumulation of profits depends on a trader's ability to place consistent winning trades while mitigating losses through the practice of risk management.

If you're going to enter the field of trading, you're going to become acquainted with risk. Trading stocks and options has large potential rewards, but also large risks. You must be aware of these risks and be willing to accept them in order to invest in the markets. As a rule, never trade with money you cannot afford to lose. There are no guarantees; as a trader, you'll have to settle for probabilities and potentials. However, by predefining the risk you can afford to sustain, you can avoid making mistakes that jeopardize your whole trading career. But do not be fooled—investment risk is as inevitable as taxes. Traders are constantly trying to locate new investments that offer healthy returns with minimal risks. The more trading experience you have, the easier it becomes to assess the risk of a particular market and use it to your advantage. However, one rule of thumb remains an essential key to successful trading: Never take the risk unless it's worth the return.

Risk comes in two varieties: the known and the unknown. Each time you make an investment, you are putting the cost of that investment on the line. This is a known risk because it involves a specific amount of money. The threat of unseen risk takes many forms. Unknown outside forces can exert relentless influence beyond anything market research may be able to decipher. Everything from changing interest rates to inflation and natural disasters has an effect on the markets.

It is also beneficial to think of evaluating risk in two ways: macroeconomic and microeconomic. Macroeconomic risks consist of uncertainties that affect entire groups of investment instruments. Interest rates, inflation, governmental regulations, and industry trends are all examples of macroeconomic risks. Microeconomic risks consist of fundamental and technical indicators that affect a specific company. Future earnings, management changes, P/E ratios, and the company's competitive position are all examples of microeconomic risks. Although macro- and microeconomic risks are subjective, they can provide a rudimentary perspective from which informed investment decisions can be made.

Trading is an art and a science. The art of trading requires intuition, discipline, and imagination. A trader who incorporates acquired knowledge with previous experience gradually develops trading intuition. Systematically attacking the markets each day creates a disciplined approach. Imagination is the soul of successful trading; it cannot be taught, but it can be enhanced. Eventually, these three variables form the basis of a trader's uniquely personal style. Don't allow fear and doubt to stand in your way. Simply keep your eyes on the higher goal: to forge a new career as an online trader. At first, you will have to be satisfied with learning what may seem to be a series of abstract concepts and factual details. In time, these smaller units of information will merge together and you'll start to get a sense of the big picture. Learning to trade is a cumulative process;

each piece of the puzzle may or may not have its place in your trading style.

riding the roller coaster

The global economy is a living, breathing entity. To understand it, you have to get to know it personally; and that takes time. Experience is earned, literally. If your experience culminates in effectual market knowledge, it's because you've found a way to tie all the loose ends together. You have to think about the markets as a dynamic environment where market sentiment and economic forces synergistically interact to make a whole.

As cyber-traders armed to the nines with technology's latest and greatest, we've chosen to shed the protection of the more conventional full-service brokerages in order to pull ourselves up to the top—by our virtual bootstraps. But even with all that technology has to offer, the financial future of the markets is still greatly affected by the whim of human emotion; this makes the business of forecasting market movement a subjective discipline. Human emotional reaction to market movement is a main motivating factor behind volatility. High volatility in a market triggers mass confusion and anxiety—emotions that tend to move a market even more erratically.

As market instability continues to intensify worldwide, there is an even greater need for managed-risk options strategies. In recent times, this kind of activity has bordered on frenzy as a handful of Internet-related stocks soar out of control at inflated prices. These markets are the kind that options traders like me love to trade. Offering unparalleled flexibility, options offer rights and confer obligations. They can be used alone or combined with one another to take advantage of specific market conditions. They can be used to hedge positions, offset the net cost of a trade, and limit the overall risk of the combined position. Options strategies take advantage of as well as curtail the losses associated with high volatility and provide traders with straightforward mathematical equations to calculate a trade's maximum risk and reward. From there, it's easy to determine a trade's risk to reward ratio. You can also assess a trade's profit range by computing the trade's breakevens. Once this information has been determined, an informed decision can be made as to a trade's probability of profitability. The potential reward is either worth the risk or it's not.

In order to master complex options strategies, it is essential to have a thorough understanding of basic long and short stock and options strategies. There are six basic strategies: long stock, short stock, long call, short call, long put, and short put. These six strategies generate more than 20 advanced techniques that take advantage of a wide variety of market scenarios. Following an explanation of risk profiles, the remainder of this chapter is designed to teach you how to perform these six basic trading methods.

risk profiles

A risk profile is one of the most helpful tools to assess a a trade's overall probability of profitability by visually graphing a trade's profit and loss potentials in relation to the price of the underlying market. As the underlying market experiences price fluctuations, the profit and loss of the trade varies accordingly. A risk profile uses three calculated variables—maximum risk, maximum profit, and breakevens—to create a graph of a trade's risks and rewards. The maximum risk of a trade estimates how much money can be lost if the worst-case scenario occurs. The maximum profit is the most you can ever hope to make on a trade. By comparing these two values, you can set up a risk to reward ratio that reveals whether the trade is worth placing. A breakeven point is the market price the underlying stock has to reach for the trade to break even (thus the name). Some trades have an upside breakeven because they offer unlimited profit to the upside. Others may have only a downside breakeven because they offer unlimited profit to the downside. A number of strategies require traders to calculate both the upside and downside breakevens to determine the profit range of the trade.

---

risk profile
a graphic determination of the risk and reward on a given trade at any given price. The vertical axis represents a trade's profit and loss and the horizontal axis represents a range of prices for the underlying asset.

---

maximum risk
the maximum loss a trade has the potential of incurring.

---

maximum profit
the maximum amount of profit that a trade has the potential to make.

breakeven
the stock price at which a trade breaks even. For example, a stock must reach a certain price for an option to avoid loss. For a call, the breakeven equals the strike price plus the premium paid. For a put, the breakeven equals the strike price minus the premium paid.

Knowledgeable traders can spot a good trade just by looking at its risk profile. One way you can become familiar with the nature of these graphs is to find a software program that generates risk profiles. Learning what to look for just takes time and experience. To understand the basics, take a look at Figure 4.1. This graph details the risk curve of a long September IBM call option with a strike price of 130 and a premium of $4^3/_8$. The horizontal row of numbers at the bottom of the chart represents the market price of the underlying asset. The vertical row of numbers at the side of the chart represents the trade's potential profit and loss. The horizontal line in the middle of the graph establishes a profit/loss of zero. These three lines represent a risk graph's basic format. The meat of a risk profile lies in the diagonal line that represents the actual profit and loss of the trade. This diagonal line plots the corresponding profit or loss value as it relates to the underlying asset's price. In addition, wherever the diagonal profit/loss line crosses the horizontal zero line, a breakeven point occurs.

Looking at the risk graph, it is easy to see that the risk on this trade is limited to the price paid for the call option. The point where the profit/loss line crosses the horizontal zero line is the breakeven. The breakeven of a long call is derived by adding the premium of the call option to its strike price. In this example, the breakeven is $134^3/_8$ ($130 + 4^3/_8 = 134^3/_8$). The underlying asset has to rise to $134.38 in order for the trade to start making a profit. Beyond this point, the profit line continues to climb indefinitely as the price of the underlying stock rises—a graphic representation of the trade's unlimited profit potential. If IBM falls below $134^3/_8$, the maximum risk is limited to the cost of the call premium—$437.50.

The rest of this chapter introduces six basic trading strategies and their corresponding risk profiles. These examples are provided to teach you about the strategies and do not represent actual trades. The six basic strategies are comprised of the following:

1. Long stock—unlimited profit/limited risk
2. Short stock—limited profit/unlimited risk

figure 4.1   risk profile basics (long 1 September IBM 130 call @ 4³/₈—IBM @ 128¹/₄)

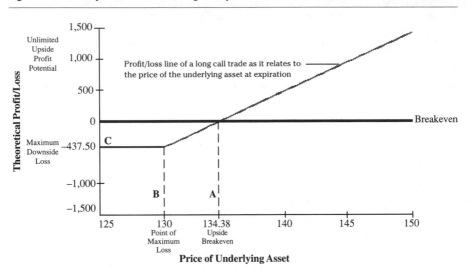

Price of Underlying Asset

- The horizontal axis represents the price of the underlying asset.
- The vertical axis represents the theoretical profit or loss of the trade.
- The diagonal line represents the actual profit or loss of the trade depending on the price of the underlying asset. By looking at any price on the bottom axis, you can figure out the corresponding profit or loss the trade makes when the underlying asset expires at a certain price.
- Line A tracks the upside breakeven ($134.38) of the trade to the corresponding price of the underlying asset. If the price of the underlying asset rises above this point, the trade starts to make a profit that is unlimited in nature (the profit/loss line continues to move upward and to the right as the price of the underlying asset rises).
- Line B shows the price of the underlying asset at the point of maximum loss ($130—the strike price of the long call option).
- Line C shows the maximum loss amount (–$437.50).

3. Long call—unlimited profit/limited risk
4. Short call—limited profit/unlimited risk
5. Long put—unlimited profit/limited risk
6. Short put—limited profit/limited risk (as the stock falls to zero)

All subsequent options strategies are combinations of these six strategies. Likewise, the risk graphs of more complicated strategies are just combinations of the risk curves of these six basic strategies. These basic strategies are the fundamental building blocks of the more complex strategies explored in subsequent chapters.

long stock

Traditional investors still regard the buy-and-hold strategy of stock investing as the number one trading approach. Although going long the market is fraught with risk, understanding the risks involved is a rudimentary lesson for anyone serious about investing. In its most basic format, investors buy stocks in order to profit from a rise in the price of the stock. An increase in the price of the stock obviously adds value to the investment. A profit is derived from the difference between the cost of the initial investment and the closing price received when the stock shares are sold.

---

going long the market
buying stocks, options, or futures contracts in order to profit from a directional move in the market price is referred to as going long.

Timing is the key to making money in buy-and-hold investments. To make a profit, investors must be able to identify a low and forecast an upcoming rise in price. Once a stock has been purchased, traders must watch for signs of a decline in price in order to sell off the shares before the decline hits. Developing a methodology that assesses a stock's fair value and determines price trends is the crux of making money as a traditional investor. Generally speaking, buy and sell decision making may be approached from two differing perspectives: assessing the overall mood of the market and analyzing characteristics of each individual stock.

According to *Investor's Business Daily*, a leading investment newspaper, three out of four stocks follow the general mood of the market. This means that if the market is experiencing a sharp decline, three out of four stocks will depreciate in value; and if the markets are rising, three out of four stocks will go along for the ride. Many investors use this generalization to anticipate the buying of undervalued stocks or the selling of overvalued stocks. However, although many traders may follow the herd, one should never underestimate an individual stock's propensity to march to a different drummer. To successfully navigate the limitless sea of investment possibilities, an investor has to gradually develop a unique methodology that encompasses both fundamental and technical analysis. Once a contender has been located, it's important to create a risk profile to assess the trade's profit and loss potential. As an example,

table 4.1 GTE fundamentals	
GTE Corporation	
Last price	$60^{15}/_{16}$
Volume	3,333,800
52-week range	$44^{5}/_{16}$ to $64^{3}/_{8}$
P/E ratio	24.97

source: www.bigcharts.com 11/16/98

let's create a hypothetical trade by tracking the purchase of 100 shares of GTE (Table 4.1).

The maximum risk for a long stock trade is limited to the price paid for the shares. The maximum profit is unlimited as the price of the stock rises. If GTE is trading at $60^{15}/_{16}$, 100 shares would cost $6,093.75. Using a margin account, this trade would require 50% of the total price as a margin deposit or $3,046.88. The breakeven on this trade is the exact price of the stock when the trade is initiated—$60^{15}/_{16}$. The risk profile for this example is shown in Figure 4.2. Notice how the profit/loss line slopes upward from left to right, visually graphing the trade's ability to make a profit as the price of the GTE stock rises. If the price of the stock falls, money is lost on a dollar-for-dollar basis and a larger margin deposit may be required to stay in the trade.

After 43 days, GTE rises to $70^{13}/_{16}$. If we sell our 100 shares at this price we will have made a profit of $987.50 (not including commission costs). This translates into a 16% return on investment—a modest profit (Table 4.2).

> **rule of thumb**
> look for stocks that have hit their low and look poised to trend up again.

short stock

If an investor believes the price of a stock is heading into a bearish decline, it may be profitable to sell short. This technique has a limited profit potential (as the price falls to zero) and unlimited upside risk. To short a stock, an investor borrows the stock shares from his or her brokerage firm to be sold at an exchange. The investor's account

figure 4.2   long stock (long 100 shares of GTE stock @ 60¹⁵/₁₆)

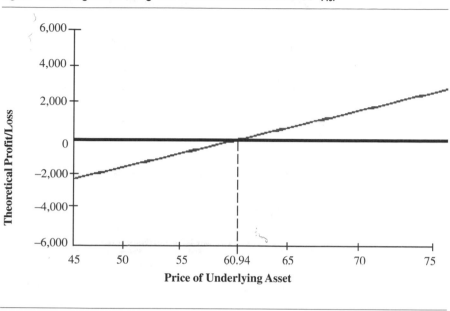

table 4.2   long stock strategy results

		Long 100 Shares of GTE		
Price at Initiation	Price at Exit	Days in Trade	Profit/Loss	Return on Investment
$6,093.75	$7,081.25	43	$987.50	16%

receives a credit for the total selling price of the stock. If the stock price declines, the investor can buy the stock back at the lower price and pocket the difference as profit. If the stock price rises, the investor may be required to place an additional margin deposit to stay in the trade. Buying the stock back is known as covering the short.

selling short
selling stocks, options, or futures in order to profit from a directional move in the market price is referred to as selling short.

If you are interested in shorting stock as a means of investing, consider these important points before jumping in headfirst:

- Margin requirements for shorting stocks differ from long stock positions. Most brokerage firms require the full price of the stock plus 50% or more as margin on a short stock trade. Additional margin may be required if the stock price rises dramatically.
- If the stock were to pay a dividend, the short seller is responsible for the payment.

---

dividend
a sum of money paid out to a shareholder from a stock's profits at the behest of the company's board of directors.

- Holding a short position in the stock for over one year does not constitute a long-term capital gain. Capital gain tax shelters are for long stockholders, not short sellers.

---

capital gain
the profit received when a trade makes money, minus any commission costs. Capital gains are subject to being taxed.

To illustrate this strategy, we have to find a company that is in a bearish trend. After searching the Internet for clues, I stumbled on Philip Morris (MO), one of America's leading tobacco companies. Once I get the itch to check out a company, there are innumerable factors that may or may not have a bearing on whether a stock holds promise. I usually start by taking a basic look at a contender's fundamentals and historical prices by going online to www.bigcharts.com. In this case, I find Philip Morris trading at $57 per share, almost at the top of its 52-week range (Table 4.3). Since Philip Morris is currently involved in several legal battles and is also facing newly imposed taxes on many of its tobacco products, I smell a bearish market ready to fall.

In this example, we'll go short 100 shares of Philip Morris (MO) stock selling for $57 per share (December 1). Therefore, an investor would receive $5,700 upon placing the trade. The maximum reward is

table 4.3   philip morris fundamentals

Philip Morris (MO)	
Last price	57
Volume	8,832,600
52-week range	$34^{3}/_{4}$ to $59^{1}/_{2}$
P/E ratio	17.93

source: www.bigcharts.com 12/1/98

limited to the price of the stock at initiation or $5,700. The price of
Philip Morris must decline below $57 for the investor to make a profit.
The maximum risk of a short stock strategy is unlimited as the price of
the stock rises. So as the price of Philip Morris rises, the investor
starts to lose money on a dollar-for-dollar basis. Once again the investor can break even on the trade by exiting the trade when the
stock is at the same price as it was when the trade was initiated. The
risk profile for this trade (Figure 4.3) shows a profit/loss line that
slants downward from left to right, revealing the trade's propensity to
lose money as the price of the stock rises.

figure 4.3   short stock (short 100 shares of MO stock @ 57)

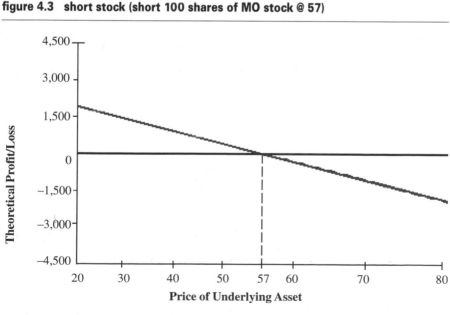

table 4.4   short stock strategy results

Short 100 Shares of MO @ 57				
Price at Initiation	Price at Exit	Days in Trade	Profit/Loss	Return on Investment
$5,700	$4,037.50	73	$1,662.50	29%

After 73 days, I suspect the market may be growing bullish again. So when Philip Morris declines to $40\frac{3}{8}$, we buy the shares back for $4,037.50, leaving a tidy profit of $1,662.50—a 29% profit on investment (Table 4.4). Not bad, but never forget that short selling has its pros and cons.

I recommend short selling as a means of hedging risk, preferring to mitigate the unlimited risk associated with going short by combining short shares with options. I do not recommend trading naked short options, either. Even if you have a large trading account, putting yourself in a position of unlimited risk is simply not advisable when there are so many limited-risk alternatives.

---

rule of thumb
look for a bearish market that is ready to make a sharp move down. This strategy is best used in tandem with an option to limit risk.

---

long call

A long call option offers limited risk and unlimited profit potential at a fraction of the cost of buying the underlying stock. A call option, when purchased, gives the holder the right, but not the obligation, to buy 100 shares of the underlying stock at the option's strike price at any time until the option's expiration date. The holder pays a specific price or premium for the call option, which is the maximum risk of the trade. A profit is made when the price of the underlying stock rises above the breakeven.

Traders may exercise their right to buy the underlying stock at the lower strike price and then sell it at the higher current price, pocketing the difference as profit. However, most traders are not interested in owning the stock. They prefer to simply sell a call option at a higher

---

long call strategy
the purchase of a call option with the expectation that the underlying asset's price will rise—a bullish strategy with limited risk and unlimited reward.

---

strike price
all options have strike prices. The strike price represents the price at which the underlying stock can be purchased (call) or sold (put) at any time prior to the option's expiration date if the option is exercised.

---

expiration date
the last day on which an option may be exercised. American-style options can be exercised at any time before the expiration date. European-style options can be exercised only on the expiration date.

---

premium. The value of the premium increases due to a rise in price of the underlying stock, as well as a handful of other important market factors. If the price of the underlying stock declines in value, the premium of the option also falls. In this case, the option may expire worthless and the holder loses the premium paid for the call.

Using our previous GTE scenario from the long stock example, let's create an example of a long call trade. The bid and ask dynamic is common to all stocks and options and is offered by most quote services. The bid is the highest price a prospective buyer is prepared to pay for a specified time for a trading unit of a specified security. The ask is the lowest price acceptable to a prospective seller of the same security. Together, the bid and ask prices constitute a quote, and the difference between the two prices is the bid-ask spread. If there is a high demand for the underlying asset, the prices are bid up to a higher level. In contrast, a low demand for a stock translates to the market being "offer down" to the lowest price at which a person is willing to sell. As an off-floor trader, you will typically buy at the ask and sell at the bid. Meanwhile, the floor trader typically makes his or her money by purchasing from off-floor traders at the bid and selling to someone else at the ask. Since we are talking about buying a call option, Table 4.5 shows the bid prices of GTE call options with various strike prices and expiration dates.

---

table 4.5   various GTE call option premiums

Price of GTE = $60^{15}/_{16}$ (11/16/98)

Call Strike Price	December	January	March
45	$16^{1}/_{8}$	$16^{1}/_{8}$	$16^{1}/_{2}$
50	$11^{1}/_{8}$	$11^{1}/_{4}$	$11^{7}/_{8}$
55	$6^{1}/_{4}$	$6^{3}/_{4}$	$7^{7}/_{8}$
60	$2^{3}/_{8}$	$3^{1}/_{4}$	$4^{1}/_{4}$
65	$^{1}/_{2}$	$1^{1}/_{8}$	$2^{1}/_{4}$

Using these prices, let's buy one GTE call with a strike price of 60 and a March expiration date. The premium for this call is $4^{1}/_{4}$ or $425 ($100 \times 4^{1}/_{4}$ = $425). The maximum loss of this trade is the premium paid, or $425. The maximum potential reward is unlimited depending on the rise in the price of GTE. To derive the price at which the trade breaks even, simply add the premium to the option strike price. In this example, the breakeven is $64^{1}/_{4}$ ($60 + 4^{1}/_{4}$ = $64^{1}/_{4}$). For this trade to make money, the price of GTE has to rise above $64^{1}/_{4}$. Figure 4.4 shows the risk profile of this trade.

After 44 days, GTE rises to $70^{13}/_{16}$ and this increases the premium for the long 60 call option to $11^{1}/_{8}$ for a profit of $687.50—a 162% return on investment (Table 4.6). Although the profit on a long call is not as high as the profit on the long stock (on a dollar basis) using the same market, the risk on the long call is significantly less. This demonstrates an option's ability to increase the leverage of the funds in your trading account.

Traders can use the long call strategy to make a profit in two scenarios. The more basic technique is to buy a call in a rising market and sell it when the premium increases. The other scenario entails buying a call to protect profits on a short stock. If you sell a stock short and then the price of the stock declines, there is a chance that the stock may reverse direction and wipe out the profit. For example, if you sell XYZ for $100 a share and it then falls in price to $80, you can protect your $20 profit by purchasing an XYZ 80 strike call option. If the price of XYZ starts to rise, you can exercise the 80 call and use the shares to cover the short stock. If XYZ continues to fall, the premium on the long call will decrease, but at a slower rate than the short stock will be gaining.

figure 4.4   long call (long 1 March GTE 60 call @ 4¹/₄)

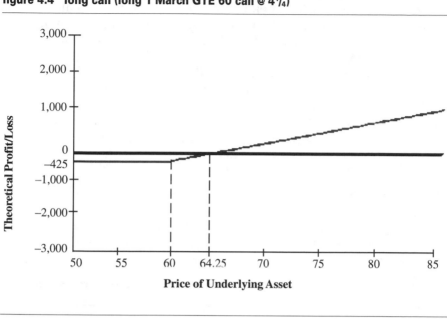

table 4.6   long call results

<table>
<tr><th colspan="5">Long 1 March GTE Call</th></tr>
<tr><th>Price at Initiation</th><th>Price
at Exit</th><th>Days in
Trade</th><th>Profit/Loss</th><th>Return on
Investment</th></tr>
<tr><td>$425</td><td>$1,112.50</td><td>44</td><td>$687.50</td><td>162%</td></tr>
</table>

> **rule of thumb**
> buy call options in a bullish market with at least 45 days until
> expiration.

short call

Selling a call option—commonly known as writing a call option—is a
bearish strategy that offers limited profit potential and unlimited risk.
When a short call is placed, the writer receives a credit in his or her

account in the amount of the option premium. As long as the price of the underlying stock falls below the strike price of the call, the call writer may keep the credit received. If the price of the underlying stock rises above the call strike price, then the short call option is in danger of being assigned to an option holder and subsequently exercised. If the option is exercised, the writer of the short call is obligated to deliver the underlying stock to the assigned option holder at the strike price of the short call. This entails buying the underlying stock at the current market price and delivering it to the option holder at the strike price. The difference between the current market price and the strike price comprises the loss on the trade.

---

short call strategy
the sale of a call option with the expectation that the underlying asset's price will fall—a bearish strategy with unlimited risk and limited reward.

---

assignment
the decision by an option holder to exercise a long option results in an assignment to an option seller. In the case of the assignment of a call, the option seller must deliver the underlying stock to the option holder at the short call option's strike price regardless of the current price of the underlying asset. In the case of an assignment of a put, the option seller must purchase the underlying asset from the option holder at the short put option's strike price regardless of the current price of the underlying asset.

Let's explore what Philip Morris has to offer us in the way of short call prices. Table 4.7 shows the call premiums at the ask price for various Philip Morris (MO) options. Since the profit on a short call option depends on the option expiring worthless, less time until expiration increases a trader's chance of keeping the short option's premium. I prefer to sell options with less than 45 days until expiration. However, if you are selling a call, it is essential to find a balance between the time till expiration and the premium received from the sale. Never risk unlimited loss unless the reward is worth it.

Using the prices in Table 4.7, let's create an example by going short one January MO 60 call at $3\frac{1}{4}$. Upon initiation of the trade, the option writer receives a credit of $325. This is the maximum profit

table 4.7   philip morris call option premiums

Call Strike Price	December	January	March
50	4	$5^1/_8$	7
55	$2^7/_8$	4	$5^1/_8$
60	$2^1/_4$	$3^1/_4$	$4^1/_4$
65	$1^7/_8$	$2^3/_4$	$3^1/_2$

figure 4.5   short call (short 1 January MO 60 call @ $3^1/_4$)

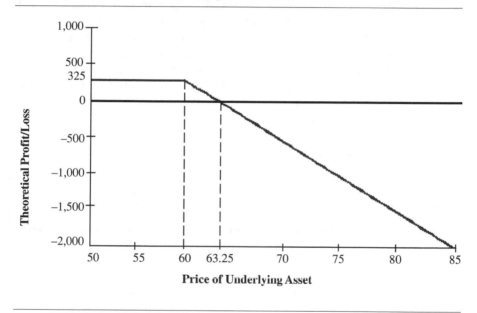

available on this trade. The maximum loss is unlimited as the price of the underlying stock rises above the breakeven, which is derived by adding the call premium to the strike price of the option. This trade breaks even when the price of MO falls below $63^1/_4$ ($60 + 3^1/_4 = 63^1/_4$). Figure 4.5 shows this trade's risk profile. Notice how the profit line rises as the price of the underlying stock declines.

After 45 days, the short call expires worthless. Since Philip Morris did not rise above 60, the short call was never in danger of being exercised when Philip Morris was selling for $52^1/_4$ (Table 4.8). Therefore, we get to keep the premium of $325 and only had to pay the commission for placing the trade. The margin to place naked calls is very

table 4.8 short call results			
Short 1 January MO Call			
Price at Initiation	Price at Exit	Days in Trade	Profit/Loss
$325	0	45	$325

expensive—or sometimes not even allowed by certain brokerages. Other brokerages require at least $50,000 in your account if you want to place a naked option position—a high opportunity cost in that you cannot touch the margin amount until the trade is closed.

Traders can write calls to profit from a declining market or to protect profits on a long stock position. In the latter scenario, called a covered call strategy, a purchase of underlying stock is offset by selling a call option against it. A covered call strategy is best implemented in a bullish to neutral market where a slow rise in the market price of the underlying asset is anticipated.

rule of thumb
sell a call option with less than 45 days until expiration in a bearish market and monitor the market carefully for signs of a reversal.

long put

A long put option offers limited risk and limited profit potential as the stock falls to zero. A put option, when purchased, gives the holder the right, but not the obligation, to sell 100 shares of the underlying stock at the option's strike price at any time until the option's expiration date. Profit is achieved when the underlying stock falls below the breakeven. Risk is limited to the price paid for the option premium—an amount substantially less than the unlimited risk that accompanies shorting a stock.

long put strategy
the purchase of a put option with the expectation that the underlying stock's price will fall—a bearish strategy with limited risk and unlimited reward.

Traders have two basic methods of collecting a profit on a long put in a declining market. If the price of the underlying stock falls, traders may choose to exercise their right to short the underlying stock at the higher strike price and then buy back the shares at the lower market price, pocketing the difference as profit. Most traders, however, prefer to offset the position by selling a put option at a higher premium. If the price of the underlying stock rises in value, the premium of the put option decreases and may expire worthless, leaving the buyer out the money paid for the put.

Since a long put strategy works best in a bearish market, let's find a trade using Philip Morris (MO). When purchasing options, it is important to buy enough time so that the option has a better chance of being in-the-money by expiration. Using the bid quotes in Table 4.9, let's buy one March MO 60 put at $5^1/_8$. The maximum loss of this trade is the premium paid, or $512.50 (100 × $5^1/_8$ = $512.50). The maximum reward is potentially unlimited, depending on the fall in the price of MO all the way to zero. To compute the price at which the trade breaks even, simply subtract the premium from the option strike price. In this example, the breakeven is $54^7/_8$ (60 − $5^1/_8$ = $54^7/_8$). For this trade to make money, the price of MO has to fall below $54^7/_8$. The risk profile of this trade is shown in Figure 4.6.

After 49 days, Philip Morris has fallen to $40^3/_8$ and the long put has shot up to $19^5/_8$ for a whopping profit of $1,450—a 283% return on investment (Table 4.10). This scenario demonstrates how an option strategy can be used to leverage trading funds in order to consistently build your account. If you had gone short 100 shares of Philip Morris, you could have made a profit of $1,662.50. But a short stock trade would have required a hefty margin whereas a long put strategy does not require any margin beyond the debit of the put option's premium.

---

table 4.9   philip morris put option premiums

Price of MO = 57 (12/1/98)

Put Strike Price	December	January	March
45	$^1/_8$	$^1/_4$	$1^1/_4$
50	$^3/_8$	$^1/_2$	$1^{13}/_{16}$
55	$^3/_4$	$1^3/_{16}$	$3^1/_8$
60	$1^7/_8$	$2^3/_4$	$5^1/_8$
65	4	$6^1/_2$	7

figure 4.6   long put (long 1 March MO 60 put @ 5¹/₈)

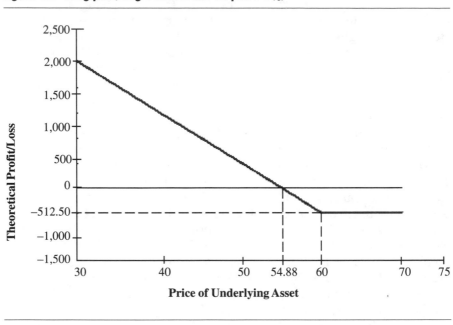

table 4.10   long put results

	Long 1 March MO Put			
Price at Initiation	Price at Exit	Days in Trade	Profit/Loss	Return on Investment
$512.50	$1,962.50	49	$1,450	283%

There are two basic ways to make money by purchasing puts. Traders can simply buy a put in a declining market and follow the previous example or buy puts to lock in profits on a long stock position. The latter technique is a form of hedging. If the price of the stock continues to rise, then the trader may lose the put premium. However, if the price of the stock starts to fall, the money lost on the long stock position is offset by the rise in the put premium. In addition, long puts are used in a variety of spreads and delta neutral trading strategies.

> **rule of thumb**
> buy puts with at least 45 days until expiration in a bearish market.

short put

Selling a put option—also known as writing a put option—offers limited profit potential and limited risk as the stock falls to zero. When a short put trade is placed, the writer receives a credit in his or her account in the amount of the option premium. As long as the price of the underlying stock rises above the put strike price, the put writer may keep the credit received. If the price of the underlying stock falls below the put strike price, then the short put option is in danger of being assigned to an option holder. If the option holder exercises the option, the writer of the short put is obligated to buy the underlying stock from the assigned put holder at the strike price of the put option. The put writer then owns the stock at a higher price than it can be sold for at the current market price.

> **short put strategy**
> the sale of a put option with the expectation that the underlying stock's price will rise—a bullish strategy with limited risk (as the underlying asset falls all the way to zero) and limited reward.

In a short put strategy, profit occurs if the option expires worthless. Therefore, it is best to sell options with 45 days or less until expiration. With this in mind, let's create an example by using Table 4.11 to go short one January GTE 60 put at $2^3/_4$. Upon initiation of the trade, the option writer receives a credit of $275—the maximum profit available on this trade. The maximum loss is limited as the price of the underlying stock falls below the strike price of the option to a price of zero. To derive the breakeven of a short put, simply subtract the put premium from the strike price of the option. This trade breaks even when the price of GTE rises to $57^1/_4$ ($60 - 2^3/_4 = 57^1/_4$). Figure 4.7 features the risk profile of this example.

If the market continues to rise, the short put will not be assigned and exercised by expiration. In this example, GTE remains above the $60 strike price until the put option expires worthless and

---

table 4.11   GTE put option premiums

Price of GTE = $60^{15}/_{16}$ (11/16/98)

Put Strike Price	December	January	March
45	$^1/_8$	$^1/_4$	$1^1/_4$
50	$^3/_8$	$^1/_2$	$^{13}/_{16}$
55	$^3/_4$	$1^3/_{16}$	$2^1/_8$
60	$1^7/_8$	$2^3/_4$	$3^1/_4$
65	4	$6^1/_2$	7

---

we get to keep the $275 credit we received upon entering the trade (Table 4.12).

Traders can profit from a short put position in two basic ways. They can simply sell an uncovered put in a rising market. Technically this strategy comes with limited risk as the underlying asset can only fall as far as zero. But the term "limited" is misleading in this context. A significant loss can occur if the underlying asset falls heavily. That's why a short put strategy should be used with extreme caution. The other technique is to write a covered put by selling the underlying

---

figure 4.7   short put (short 1 January GTE 60 put @ $2^3/_4$)

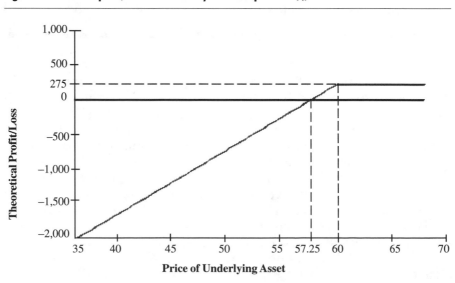

---

table 4.12   short put results

Short 1 January GTE 60 Put @ $2^3/_4$

Price at Initiation	Price at Exit	Days in Trade	Profit/Loss
$275	0	41	$275

---

stock and selling a put option against it—a strategy best implemented in a bearish to neutral market where a slow fall in the market price of the underlying stock is anticipated. If the underlying stock rises, the put will be assigned and when it is exercised the resulting shares that are purchased from the option buyer can be used to cover the losing short.

rule of thumb
sell puts in bullish markets with less than 45 days until expiration.

conclusion

This chapter takes a look at the six most basic trading strategies—three bullish and three bearish (Table 4.13). Looking at the three bullish strategies using GTE, the long stock garnered the highest profit ($987.50), followed by the long call ($687.50), and finally the short put ($275). Of the three, the short put produced the lowest profit and had the highest risk. Although the long stock offered the highest profit, it also required a much higher initial investment to produce a lower return on investment than the long call strategy. Since leveraging your money is an important part of playing the markets, long options usually offer traders the chance to get the biggest bang for their buck.

leveraging
the utilization of available funds in order to increase the quantity or magnitude of investments and thereby magnify investment returns.

table 4.13 basic option strategy results

Position	Trade Entry		Exit Price	Maximum Risk	Profit/Loss	Return on Investment (ROI)
	Debit	Credit				
Bullish						
Long Stock	Long 100 shares of GTE stock @ $60^{15}/_{16}$	$6,093.75	—	$7,081.25	$6,093.75	$987.50	16%
Long Call	Long 1 March GTE 60 Call @ $4^1/_4$	$425.00	—	$1,112.50	$425.00	$687.50	162%
Short Put	Short 1 January GTE 60 Put @ $2^3/_4$	—	$275.00	0	Limited to stock price of zero	$275.00	Depends on margin
Bearish						
Short Stock	Short 100 shares of MO stock @ 57	—	$5,700.00	$4,037.50	Unlimited	$1,662.50	29%
Short Call	Short 1 January MO 60 Call @ $3^1/_4$	—	$325.00	0	Unlimited	$325.00	Depends on margin
Long Put	Long 1 March MO 60 Put @ $5^1/_8$	$512.50	—	$1,962.50	$512.50	$1,450.00	283%

The three bearish positions offer a similar scenario. The profit on the long put position is only $212.50 less than the profit on the short stock using the same market entry and exit days. However, the risk on the short stock is unlimited while the risk on the long put position is limited to the price paid for the put. Although the long put strategy garnered a slightly smaller profit, it did so with a whopping 283% return on investment. The short call position garnered a limited profit and exposed us to significant risk.

chapter 5

vertical spreads

introduction

This chapter reviews two kinds of vertical spreads: debit spreads and credit spreads. Both techniques stand to make a profit when a directional change in the price of an underlying asset occurs. Correctly forecasting the nature of a directional trend is the key to making a profit on these strategies. Trending directional markets can often be located by observing increases in volatility. Vertical spreads offer limited risks and limited rewards. Low risk makes these strategies inviting, especially for beginners.

> **vertical spread**
> a spread in which one option is bought and one option is sold, where the options have the same underlying asset expiration date, but have different strike prices.

There are two kinds of debit spreads: the bull call spread and the bear put spread. As their names announce, a bull call spread is placed in a bullish market using calls and a bear put spread is placed in a bearish market using puts. Debit spreads use options with more than 45 days till expiration. The maximum risk of a debit spread is limited to the net debit of the trade—far less than what it would cost to trade the underlying instrument.

> **debit spreads**
> an options spread in which the difference between the long and short options' premiums results in a net debit—the maximum risk on the spread.

In contrast, the maximum profit of a credit spread is limited to the net credit of the trade. There are two kinds of credit spreads: the bull put spread and the bear call spread. The bull put spread is placed in a bullish market using puts and a bear call spread is placed in a bearish market using calls. In general, credit spreads have lower commission costs than debit spreads because additional commissions are avoided by simply allowing the options to expire worthless.

> **credit spreads**
> an options spread in which the difference between the short and long options' premiums results in a net credit—the maximum profit on the spread.

In general, vertical spreads combine long and short options with the same expiration date but different strike prices. The key is to find a market with option premiums that create a spread with high potential reward and low risk. They enable traders to take advantage of the way option premiums respond to changes in the price of the underlying asset. Traders should decide on an exit strategy in advance. I usually look for a 50% profit or I'll exit the position before a 50% loss. I also recommend doing two contracts at once. Try to exit one of the spreads with enough profit to cover the cost of the double contracts. The other trade will become a virtually free trade, allowing you to take more of a risk and accumulate a bigger profit.

bull call spread

A bull call spread consists of buying a lower strike call and selling a higher strike call in a proportion of one to one with the same expiration date. This strategy is best implemented in a bullish market. It provides high leverage over a limited range of stock prices and the total investment is usually far less than the amount required to buy the stock outright.

---

bull call spread
a debit spread involving the purchase of a lower strike call and the sale of a higher strike call—a bullish strategy with limited profit and limited risk.

A bull call spread offers limited profit potential and limited downside risk. No matter how high the underlying climbs, a bull call spread offers a limited reward. Conversely, no matter how low the underlying falls, this strategy offers a limited loss. The maximum risk is limited to the net debit paid for the spread and occurs when the underlying stock closes at or below the strike price of the long call. The maximum reward is limited to the difference in strike prices multiplied by the value per point minus the net debit. The maximum reward occurs when the price of the underlying stock closes at or above the strike price of the short call. The breakeven of a bull call spread is calculated by adding the net debit to the lower call strike price. Always check resistance and support levels before placing a bull call spread to make sure the breakeven is within the stock's normal price range.

A bull call spread is best used when you are moderately bullish. If you were extremely optimistic about a major move in the market, you may want to use a bullish strategy that offers an unlimited reward. As an example, let's create a hypothetical bull call spread using Dell Computer Corporation stock (DELL). (Table 5.1.)

Looking at the prices in Table 5.2, there are a number of possible bull call spreads that can be created. Since bull call spreads involve a net debit, it is best to use options with 45 days or more until expiration to give the trade enough time to make a profit. Therefore, let's create a bull call spread by going long 1 May DELL 65 Call @ $11^1/_4$ and short 1 May DELL 80 Call @ $6^1/_4$ (Table 5.3).

The maximum loss on this trade is limited to the net debit, which

---

table 5.1   dell computer fundamentals

Dell Computer Corporation (DELL)

Last price	$65^{15}/_{16}$
Volume	20,591,100
52-week range	$18^{13}/_{16}$ to $73^{1}/_{2}$
P/E ratio	64.09

---

source: www.bigcharts.com 12/2/98

---

table 5.2   dell computer call option premiums

Price of DELL = $65^{15}/_{16}$ (12/2/98)

Call Strike Price	January	February	May
55	$12^{3}/_{4}$	$13^{1}/_{2}$	$18^{1}/_{4}$
60	$8^{7}/_{8}$	$9^{1}/_{4}$	$13^{1}/_{2}$
65	$5^{7}/_{8}$	$7^{1}/_{2}$	$11^{1}/_{4}$
70	$3^{1}/_{2}$	$5^{1}/_{4}$	$9^{7}/_{8}$
75	$2^{1}/_{4}$	$4^{3}/_{8}$	$7^{1}/_{4}$
80	1	3	$6^{1}/_{4}$

---

table 5.3   bull call spread trade calculations

Bull Call Spread Using Dell Computer @ $65^{15}/_{16}$

Maximum Risk = Net debit	$500
Maximum Reward = (Strike difference × 100) – net debit	$1,000
Breakeven = Long strike price + (net debit ÷ 100)	70
Return on Investment = Reward / risk	200%

---

is $500 [$(11^{1}/_{4} - 6^{1}/_{4})$ × 100 = $500]. To calculate the maximum profit, multiply the difference in strike prices by the value per point and then subtract the net debit. In this trade, the maximum profit is $1,000 {[(80 – 65) × 100] – 500 = $1,000}. This trade risks $500 to make a maximum profit of $1,000—that's a 200% return on investment. The breakeven is derived by adding the net debit divided by 100 to the long call strike

figure 5.1   bull call spread (long 1 May DELL 65 call @ 11¹/₄, short 1 May DELL 80 call @ 6¹/₄)

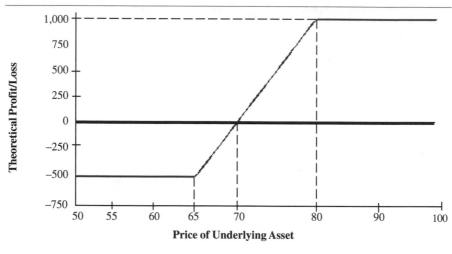

price. In this example, the breakeven is 70 [65 + (500 ÷ 100) = 70]. Dell has to rise $4^{1}/_{16}$ points to reach 70 in order to start making a profit and doesn't max out until Dell reaches 80. Luckily, the May expiration gives the trade six months to get there. Figure 5.1 shows the risk profile of this example.

By tracking this trade, we find that after 44 days, the price of Dell peaks out at $85^{5}/_{16}$. You can then exercise the 65 call and then sell those shares to the assigned option holder for $80 a share for the maximum profit of $1,000 (Table 5.4).

To find a market that is appropriate for placing a bull call spread, look for stocks that are trending up nicely or have reached their support level and are poised for a rebound. Your intention is for the market to rise as high as the strike price of the short

---

rule of thumb
buy the ATM options and sell the OTM options. Look for markets that are trending up and then use options with 45 days or greater until expiration. The greater the strike spread, the higher the profit potential.

table 5.4 bull call spread results

Long 1 May DELL 65 Call @ 11¼, Short 1 May DELL 80 Call @ 6¼

Debit at Initiation	Exercise 65 Call	Assignment of 80 Call	Profit/ Loss	Return on Investment
$500	–($6,500)	$8,000	$1,000	200%

call. That way, if it's exercised early, you can make the maximum return on the trade by exercising the long call and pocketing the difference.

bear put spread

A bear put spread is a debit spread created by purchasing a higher strike put and selling a lower strike put on a one to one basis with the same expiration date. This strategy is best implemented in a bearish market. It provides high leverage over a limited range of stock prices. The profit on this strategy can increase by as much as 1 point for each 1-point decrease in the price of the underlying asset. However, the total investment is usually far less than the amount required to buy the stock. The strategy has both limited profit potential and limited downside risk.

---

bear put spread
the sale of a lower strike put and the purchase of a higher strike put—a bearish strategy with limited risk and limited reward.

Let's create an example using Sears, Roebuck and Company (S). (Table 5.5.) Using the premiums in Table 5.6, there are a number of possible bear put spreads that can be created. Since bear put spreads involve buying options, it is best to use options with 45 days or more until expiration to give the trade enough time to make a profit. Therefore, let's create a bear put spread by going long 1 July Sears 45 Put @ 5⅝ and short 1 July Sears 35 Put @ 3. (Table 5.7.) The maximum risk of a bear put spread is limited to the net debit of the spread. In this example, the maximum risk is $262.50 [(5⅝ – 3) × 100 = $262.50]. The maximum profit of a bear call spread is calculated by multiplying

---

table 5.5 sears fundamentals

Sears, Roebuck and Company (S)

Last price	43
Volume	3,887,200
52-week range	$39^1/_{16}$ to 65
P/E ratio	15.64

---

source: www.bigcharts.com 12/2/99

---

table 5.6 sears put option premiums

Price of Sears = 43 (12/2/99)

Put Strike Price	January	April	July
35	$^1/_4$	$1^1/_4$	3
40	$1^1/_4$	$2^7/_8$	4
45	$3^3/_8$	5	$5^5/_8$
50	7	$7^5/_8$	$8^5/_8$
55	10	$12^1/_8$	$12^1/_2$

---

table 5.7 bear put spread trade calculations

Bear Put Spread Using Sears @ 43

Maximum Risk = Net debit	$262.50
Maxiumum Reward = (Strike difference × 100) – net debit	$737.50
Breakeven = Long strike price – (net debt ÷ 100)	$42^3/_8$
Return on Investment = Reward / risk	281%

---

the difference in strike prices by the value per point and then subtracting the net debit. This trade offers a maximum profit of $737.50—
a 281% return on investment {[(45 – 35) × 100] – $262.50 = $737.50}. To
calculate the breakeven for a bear put spread, you simply subtract the
net debit divided by 100 from the higher strike price. The breakeven
for this trade is $42^3/_8$ [45 – (262.50 ÷ 100) = $42^3/_8$]. Sears has to drop below $42^3/_8$ to start making a profit—just slightly lower than the current

market price at the trade's initiation. This trade has seven and a half months until expiration—plenty of time for the trade to move in-the-money. The risk profile for this example is shown in Figure 5.2.

Before placing the trade, it is important to dig up some fundamental data that supports our view that Sears will continue to drop, thereby making this trade profitable. The easiest way to get the big picture is to check out a few online sites for newsworthy information. I usually start by going online to eSignal's "Trader's Toolbox" to browse the latest news. In this case, Sears shows up on the "Movers and Shakers" list of "U.S. Decliners." I also found an article that further supports my position—not only did Sears report lower-than-expected earnings, but same-store revenue also decreased. I then move on to check some basic fundamentals, which provide enough proof to believe that this trade has a good chance of being successful.

The best way to exit a bear put spread is for the underlying market to move below the strike price of the short option in hopes that the short put will be assigned. You will then have to purchase the underlying stock from the option holder at the lower short put strike price and by exercising your long put sell it at the higher price to garner the maximum profit. In this example, Sears has been moving slowly and has dropped only to $39^{1}/_{2}$ after 71 days. Since it looks poised for a rebound, it's a good idea to take the available profit by selling the long option and buying back the short option. The price of the long 45 put has risen to $7^{7}/_{8}$ and the price of the 35 put has fallen to $1^{1}/_{2}$ for a profit of \$375 $[(7^{7}/_{8} - 1^{1}/_{2} - 2^{5}/_{8}) \times 100 = \$375]$. (Table 5.8.)

figure 5.2   bear put spread (long 1 July 45 put @ $5^{5}/_{8}$, short 1 July 35 put @ 3)

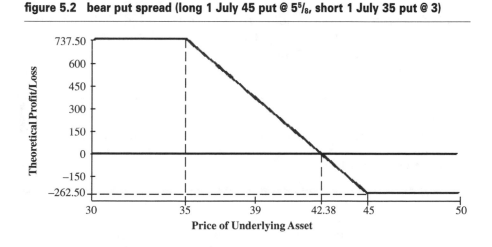

table 5.8 bear put spread results

	Long 1 July 45 Put @ 5⅝, Short 1 July 35 Put @ 3				
Debit at Initiation	45 Put at Exit	35 Put at Exit	Days in Trade	Profit/ Loss	Return on Investment
$262.50	71	$787.50	$150	$375	143%

---

rule of thumb
buy the ATM puts and sell the OTM puts. Look for markets that are
trending down or have reached 52-week lows; and then check the
fundamentals (look a little deeper; when a company goes down it
happens quickly). Make sure you have at least 45 days or more until
expiration.

---

bull put spread

A bull put spread is a credit spread created by purchasing a lower
strike put and selling a higher strike put on a one to one basis. Both
options must have the same expiration date. This strategy is best implemented in a bullish market. It provides limited profit potential and
limited downside risk. The profit on this strategy can increase by as
much as 1 point for each 1-point increase in the price of the underlying asset. However, the total investment is usually far less than the
amount required to buy the stock outright.

---

bull put spread
a credit spread involving the sale of a higher strike put and the
purchase of a lower strike put—a bullish strategy with limited risk
and limited reward.

Since a bull put spread makes the maximum profit when the
short put expires worthless, options with 45 days or less give the un-

derlying stock less time to move into a position where the short put will be assigned. In the best scenario, the underlying stock moves and stays above the higher strike price by expiration.

Let's devise a bull put spread using Xerox as our underlying stock (Table 5.9). Using the option premiums in Table 5.10, let's create a bull put spread by going long 1 January XRX 90 Put @ 1 and short 1 January XRX 105 Put @ 8. In this example, the long put is out-of-the-money and the short put is at-the-money. The profit on this trade relies on the short put expiring worthless by expiration. To exit this trade profitably, you need XRX to move above the strike of the short option and stay there until expiration so that the options will expire worthless. (Table 5.11.) The maximum profit is limited to the net credit received on the trade, or $700 [(8 − 1) × 100 = $700]. The maximum risk is calculated by multiplying the difference in strikes times the value per point and then subtracting the net credit. The maximum risk of this trade is {[(105 − 90) × 100] − $700 = $800}. The breakeven of a bull put spread is calculated by subtract-

---

table 5.9   xerox corporation fundamentals

Xerox Corporation (XRX)

Last price	$104^1/_2$
Volume	837,300
52-week range	$66^3/_{16}$ to $116^1/_2$
P/E ratio	75.77

source: www.bigcharts.com 12/3/98

---

table 5.10   xerox corporation put option premiums

Price of XRX = $104^1/_2$ (12/3/98)

Put Strike Price	December	January	April
90	$^1/_2$	1	$3^3/_8$
95	1	$2^1/_8$	$4^1/_2$
100	3	$5^1/_8$	$6^1/_2$
105	$6^5/_8$	8	$11^3/_8$
110	$10^1/_4$	$11^3/_4$	$14^5/_8$
115	13	$15^1/_8$	$17^3/_8$

table 5.11   bull put spread trade calculations

Bull Put Spread Using Xerox @ 104$^1/_2$

Maximum Risk = (Strike difference × 100) – net credit	$800
Maximum Reward = Net credit	$700
Breakeven = Short strike price – (net credit ÷ 100)	98
Return on Investment = Reward / risk	88%

figure 5.3   bull put spread (long 1 January XRX 90 put @ 1, short 1 January XRX 105 put @ 8)

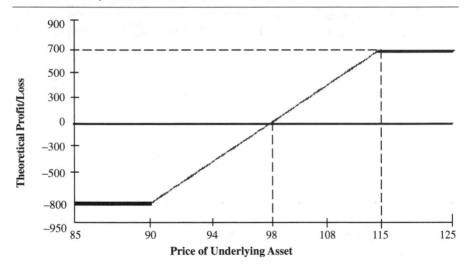

ing the net credit divided by 100 from the higher strike put. In this example, the breakeven is 98 [105 – (700 ÷ 100) = 98]. This trade makes a profit when Xerox stays above 98. Its risk profile is shown in Figure 5.3.

After 43 days, XRX did not slip beneath the short put's strike and assignment did not occur. This bullish run makes this trade a winner and both options expire worthless. We get to keep the $700 net credit received at the trade's initiation (Table 5.12).

table 5.12 bull put spread results

Long 1 January XRX 90 Put @ 1, Short 1 January XRX 105 Put @ 8

Credit at Initiation	Stock Price at Initiation	Stock Price at Exit	Days in Trade	Profit/ Loss
$700	$104^1/_2$	$116^3/_8$	43	$700

rule of thumb
a bull put spread is a credit spread in which the profit depends on the underlying stock remaining above the strike of the short put so that the options expire worthless. Look for a wide range between premiums and use options with fewer than 45 days until expiration.

bear call spread

A bear call spread is a credit spread created by purchasing a higher strike call and selling a lower strike call on a one to one basis. Once again, both options must have the same expiration date. As the name implies, this strategy is best implemented in a bearish market. It has both limited profit potential and limited downside risk. Profit increases as the underlying stock falls below the strike price of the lower strike short call.

bear call spread
a credit spread involving the sale of a lower strike call and the purchase of a higher strike call—a bearish strategy with limited risk and limited reward.

While fishing for a bearish market, I stumbled on At Home Corporation (ATHM), which was rapidly approaching its 52-week high. Table 5.13 features a few of At Home's fundamentals, and Table 5.14 details various call option premiums.

---

table 5.13 at home corporation fundamentals

At Home Corporation (ATHM)

Last price	$119^7/_8$
Volume	3,386,400
52-week range	$23^1/_2$ to 125

---

source: www.bigcharts.com 1/11/99

---

table 5.14 at home corporation call option premiums

Price of ATHM = $119^7/_8$ (1/11/99)

Put Strike Price	February	April
105	$21^1/_8$	$26^3/_4$
110	$16^5/_8$	$22^1/_8$
115	$15^1/_2$	$18^1/_8$
120	$12^1/_4$	$15^3/_4$
125	8	$11^5/_8$
130	$5^7/_8$	$8^1/_4$
135	$2^1/_8$	$5^3/_8$

A credit spread relies on the short option expiring worthless to be successful. Therefore, it is best to use options with less than 45 days till expiration. Since the short call has to expire worthless, it's best to choose a short strike price that the underlying stock has a low probability of reaching. Therefore, let's create a bull call spread by going long 1 February ATHM 135 Call @ $2^1/_8$ and short 1 February ATHM 120 Call @ $12^1/_4$. The maximum profit on a bear call spread is limited to the net credit received on the trade. In this example, the maximum profit is $1,012.50 [($12^1/_4 - 2^1/_8$) × 100 = $1,012.50]. (Table 5.15.) The maximum risk is calculated by multiplying the difference in strikes by the value per point and then subtracting the net credit. This trade's maximum risk is $487.50 {[(135 − 120) × 100] − $1,012.50 = $487.50}. The breakeven for a bear call spread is calculated by adding the net credit divided by 100 to the lower strike call. This trade breaks even at $130^1/_8$ [120 + (1,012.50 ÷ 100) = $130^1/_8$]. For this trade to make the maximum profit, ATHM has to stay below 120 so that the short call will expire worthless. Figure 5.4 shows the risk profile for this example.

table 5.15 bear call spread trade calculations

Bear Call Spread Using ATHM @ 119^7/$_8$

Maximum Risk = (Strike difference × 100) – net credit	$487.50
Maximum Reward = Net credit	$1,012.50
Breakeven = Short strike price + (net credit ÷ 100)	130^1/$_8$
Return on Investment = Reward / risk	208%

figure 5.4 bear call spread (long 1 February ATHM 135 call @ 2^1/$_8$, short 1 February ATHM 120 call @ 12^1/$_4$)

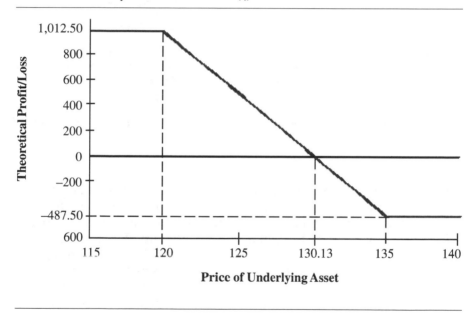

Price of Underlying Asset

When the options expire on the third Friday of February, ATHM is trading at 101^3/$_{16}$, well below the breakeven of 130^1/$_8$. Letting the options expire worthless enables the trade to keep the maximum profit of $1,012.50 received at the trade's initiation. (Table 5.16.) Since ATHM dropped below the short strike and stayed there until expiration, the short 120 option was not in danger of being exercised. If ATHM had risen above 120 and the short option had received notice of exercise, you would have to deliver 100 shares of ATHM to the option holder at $120 per share by purchasing the shares at the current market price. If ATHM was priced above the

---

table 5.16   bear call spread results

Long 1 February ATHM 135 Call @ $2^{1}/_{8}$, Short 1 February ATHM 120 Call @ $12^{1}/_{4}$

Credit at Initiation	Stock Price at Initiation	Stock Price at Exit	Days in Trade	Profit/ Loss
$1,012.50	$119^{7}/_{8}$	$101^{3}/_{16}$	39	$1,012.50

---

strike price of the long option (135), you could have exercised the long option to mitigate your losses.

---

rule of thumb
look for a moderately bearish market. The smaller the spread, the less the risk. Use options with fewer than 45 days until expiration with a wide premium range to enhance limited profits.

---

conclusion

Vertical spreads are best used when moderate price action is forecast. Once you have discovered a directional trend, play around with a couple of strategies and various strike prices and expiration dates to find the trade with the best probability of profitability. Since the bid and ask prices of option premiums fluctuate daily, vertical spreads are best placed as limit orders to maintain the desired point spread between the options. In addition, as you are learning these strategies, try to keep the difference between strikes relatively small. You may want to place two contracts at a time and then exit one contract when you reach 50% of the maximum reward. The other contract becomes a free trade and you can try to make a higher profit by letting it ride.

You can practice this strategy by studying market movement and paper trading markets that seem appropriate. A paper trade is a hypothetical position using real prices for the benefit of learning how a strategy works. Once you have initiated a paper trade, you can learn how the passage of time and price movement affect the trade firsthand. Many online financial research sites and brokerages offer portfolio services to make this process of paper trading easier than ever before. Many of them will e-mail you automatic updates using end-of-day prices. In addition, pay close attention to how you exit these strategies and keep notes on your successes and failures. Any fictitious losses can be chalked up to experience rather than costing out-of-pocket cash, and all winning trades will inspire confidence. As you become familiar with these strategies, knowing how to use a computer to help you make your next decision will become second nature. "Let your fingers do the walking," as they say.

chapter 6

delta neutral strategies

introduction to delta neutral trading

Two basic human emotions propel the mass psychology that supports traditional trading methodologies: greed and fear. These emotions spread like wildfire as markets soar to new highs or dwindle into obscurity. Catching the trend is a natural obsession for traditional buy-and-hold investors. But when a trend reverses in midstream, traders who simply buy stocks hoping prices will rise can be washed up in an instant. To avoid being part of the herd mentality, traders may want to exchange the hype and complexity of directional investing for an entirely new game altogether—delta neutral trading.

Delta neutral trading is a powerful approach to creating spread positions with the potential to make money regardless of which way the underlying asset moves. Delta is one of several option Greeks that are used to describe option price fluctuations. Technically, delta measures the price sensitivity of an option's premium with respect to a $1 change in the price of the underlying stock. For example, a call option with a delta of plus 50 would have risen 50 cents as a result of a $1 rise in the price of the underlying stock.

A delta neutral trade is composed of trading instruments with an overall position delta of zero (i.e., the sum of all the deltas in the strategy has a net position of zero). The delta neutral approach takes advantage of the difference between fixed and variable deltas. A stock has a fixed delta; no matter how the price of the stock fluctuates, a stock's delta never changes. For example, buying 100 shares of stock has a fixed delta of plus 100. In contrast, a variable delta changes as the price of the underlying stock moves. All options have variable deltas. The combination of fixed and variable deltas can create trades that offer traders profit potentials in both directions.

---

option Greeks
a set of measurements that explore the risk exposures of a specific trade. Options and other trading instruments have a variety of risk exposures that can vary dramatically over time or as markets move. Each risk measurement is named after a different letter in the Greek alphabet, thus the name.

---

delta
the change in the price of an option relative to the change of the underlying security.

---

delta neutral
a combination option/options or option/stock trade in which the sum of all the deltas equals zero. Delta neutral trades have the capacity to make money regardless of market direction.

Another way to think of an option delta is the degree of probability that an option will close in-the-money (ITM) by expiration. An at-the-money (ATM) option has a 50–50 chance of closing in-the-money. Therefore, an ATM option has a delta of plus or minus 50. An out-of-the-money (OTM) option has a lower probability of closing in-the-money; therefore, OTM options have delta values lower than 50. An in-the-money (ITM) option has a greater than 50% chance of closing in-the-money and therefore boasts a delta greater than 50. As options go deeper and deeper in-the-money, their deltas approach 100 and they begin to act more like the underlying stock.

To facilitate delta neutral trading, it is essential to be well acquainted with the deltas of options and how they change. In general, the following rules always apply to delta neutral trading: Buying stock or calls creates a positive delta; selling stock or calls creates a negative delta; buying puts creates a negative delta; and selling puts creates a positive delta.

---

at-the-money
when the strike price of an option is the same as the current price of the underlying instrument.

---

out-of-the-money
a call option is out-of-the-money when its strike price is above the current market price of the underlying asset. A put option is out-of-the-money when its strike price is below the current market price of the underlying asset. An out-of-the-money option has no intrinsic value and expires worthless.

---

in-the-money
a call option is in-the-money when its strike price is less than the current market price of the underlying asset. A put option is in-the-money when its strike price is greater than the market price of the underlying asset. If you were to exercise an in-the-money option, it would generate a profit.

Delta neutral trades are best suited for people who have limited time availability. They offer traders a longer-term approach than the second-to-second perspective a day trader enjoys. Delta neutral trades are intentionally devised to take a couple of days to a few months to ripen.

Delta neutral trading involves combining stocks with options, or options with options, in such a way that the sum of all the deltas in the trade equals zero. A zero position delta enables a trade to make money within a certain range of prices regardless of market direction. As the price of the underlying stock moves, the overall delta changes. Before placing a trade, the upside and downside breakevens must be calculated to gauge the trade's profit range. A trader also needs to calculate the maximum potential profit and loss in order to assess the viability of the trade. In some cases, additional profits can be made by adjusting the trade back to delta neutral through buying or selling more options or shares of stock.

> **zero position delta**
> the sum total of all deltas in a combination trade equal zero—the trade is delta neutral.

Delta neutral strategies have been devised to scientifically take advantage of specific market conditions. Matching the right strategy to the right set of circumstances takes training, skill, and practical experience. The strategies examined in this chapter are based on the more basic option strategies previously explored. By studying them closely, you will be well on your way to a successful delta neutral trading career.

volatility

Volatility is a complex and often misunderstood trading concept. In its most basic form, volatility is defined as a statistical measurement of a stock's price change (regardless of direction) represented by a percentage. I prefer to think of it as the speed of change in a market. A stable market moves slowly and a volatile market moves quickly. An option has a better chance of ending up in-the-money in a high-volatility market. High volatility often leads to the overpricing of options while low volatility may contribute to the undervaluing of options.

> **volatility**
> the amount by which an underlying instrument is expected to fluctuate in a given period of time. Options often increase in price when there is a rise in volatility even if the price of the underlying doesn't move anywhere.

To further complicate the issue, there are two kinds of volatility: historical volatility and implied volatility. Historical volatility (also known as statistical volatility) is based on a stock's past price action during a specific time period. It can be calculated by using the standard deviation of a stock's price changes from close to close of trading going back 21 to 23 days. Implied volatility is a computed value that measures an option's volatility, rather than that of the underlying asset. The fair value of an option is calculated by entering the historical volatility of the underlying asset into an option pricing model. The computed fair value may differ from the actual market price of the option. Implied volatility is the volatility needed to achieve the option's actual market price. In basic terms, historical volatility gauges price movement in terms of past performance and implied volatility approximates how much the marketplace thinks prices will move.

Both kinds of volatility are valuable tools for finding profitable trading opportunities. A stock's historical volatility is often significantly impacted by scheduled and breaking news, including unexpected earnings, management reorganizations, newly released products and services, and news regarding industry competitors. Implied volatility, on the other hand, is very cyclical. It tends to move back and forth within a given range. It can also act as a guide to avoiding the purchase of overpriced options and the sale of underpriced options. Many of my best trades have been found online as I searched for an abnormality in the price of an option compared to the movement of the underlying stock. An abnormality is created when the market price of an option increases without a change in the price of the underlying stock. This situation triggers an increase in the implied volatility of these options. When the theoretical option price and the current market price significantly differ, an abnormality occurs, causing the overpricing or undervaluing of an option's premium.

To determine whether an option is undervalued or overpriced, you can calculate 20-day or 90-day volatility ratios. The 20-day volatility ratio is calculated by dividing 1-day implied volatility by 20-day statistical volatility. The 90-day volatility ratio is calculated by dividing 1-day implied volatility by 90-day statistical volatility. If the implied volatility of a stock's options moves below or above the actual statistical volatility of the stock, it may create a volatility crush.

When implied volatility moves above statistical volatility, a high volatility ratio is created. If this condition arises in a stock you are tracking, it is safe to assume that the options are overvalued. In this scenario, if the price of a stock increases, but the implied volatility of the option decreases, you may lose money even though the stock moved in your favor. This is a sign to sell options. If implied volatility falls below statistical volatility, the volatility ratios are low and the options are likewise undervalued. If the price of the stock falls and the implied volatility increases, option premiums will increase. This is a good time to buy options.

Option traders must learn to integrate the use of implied and statistical volatility ratios into finding optimal trading opportunities. If you locate a stock with underpriced options, you may want to try placing a long straddle. In contrast, a stock with overvalued options may be ripe for a short straddle. Specific volatility scenarios can also be used to implement ratio spread and ratio backspread strategies (see Chapter 7). At first, volatility may seem complex, but it's well worth your while to get comfortable using because it can alert you to profitable markets.

There are many web sites and software programs that provide traders with volatility information including www.optionsanalysis.com.

> **rule of thumb**
> buy underpriced options during periods of low volatility; sell overpriced options during periods of high volatility.

long straddle

A long straddle is a nondirectional trading strategy that involves buying both a call and a put with identical strike prices and expiration dates. It is best placed in a market with low volatility where a sharp volatility increase is anticipated. Buying a straddle can be quite expensive because you have to pay both option premiums. However, your maximum risk is limited to the net debit of the double premiums and you don't have to worry about margin requirements. Since you have to make enough profit to cover the double premiums, this strategy requires the underlying stock price to move sharply in either direction beyond the breakevens by anticipating a period of increased volatility.

> **long straddle strategy**
> a delta neutral options strategy best placed in a highly volatile market that involves the simultaneous purchase of equal numbers of ATM puts and calls with the same expiration date.

Let's create a long straddle using Amazon.com, a leading online bookstore (Table 6.1), using the premiums in Table 6.2. Since a long straddle involves buying options, it is best to use options with 60 days or more until expiration to give the trade enough time to move into the trade's profit range. Let's create a long straddle position by going long 1 January AMZN 190 Call @ $26^7/_8$, and long 1 January AMZN 190 Put @ 32. This is a delta neutral trade because a long ATM call has a delta of +50 and a long ATM put has a delta of –50, thereby creating a net delta of zero.

The maximum risk of a long straddle is the equal to net debit of the trade (Table 6.3). In this example, the maximum risk is the net debit of $5,887.50 [$(26^7/_8 + 32) \times 100$ = $5,887.50]. Since the maximum profit is unlimited in both directions, a long straddle's range of profitability is

---

table 6.1   amazon.com fundamentals

Amazon.com (AMZN)

Last price	$188^{1}/_{2}$
Volume	3,709,600
52-week range	$24^{7}/_{8}$ to $214^{1}/_{2}$
P/E ratio	0

---

source: www.bigcharts.com 12/4/98

---

table 6.2   amazon.com option premiums

Price of AMZN = $188^{1}/_{2}$ (12/4/98)

Expiration Date	Call Premium	Put Premium
January 190	$26^{7}/_{8}$	32
April 190	$49^{7}/_{8}$	47

---

table 6.3   long straddle trade calculations

Long Straddle Using Amazon.com @ $188^{1}/_{2}$

Maximum Risk = Net debit	\$5,887.50
Maximum Reward = Unlimited above and below breakeven	Unlimited
Downside Breakeven = Strike price – (net debit ÷ 100)	$131^{1}/_{8}$
Upside Breakeven = Strike price + (net debit ÷ 100)	$248^{7}/_{8}$

---

determined by deriving the upside and the downside breakevens. The upside breakeven occurs when the underlying asset's price equals the strike price plus the net debit divided by 100. In this example, the upside breakeven is $248^{7}/_{8}$ [190 + (5,887.50 ÷ 100) = $248^{7}/_{8}$]. The downside breakeven occurs when the underlying asset's price equals the strike price minus the net debit divided by 100. In this case, the downside breakeven is $131^{1}/_{8}$ [190 – (5,887.50 ÷ 100) = $131^{1}/_{8}$]. Therefore, Amazon.com has to move above $248^{7}/_{8}$ or below $131^{1}/_{8}$ for this trade to make a profit.

Figure 6.1 shows the risk profile of this trade. As previously defined, a long straddle is the purchase of a call and a put with the same strike price and the same expiration date. Since risk profiles are combinations of other risk curves, a long straddle's risk profile is the combina-

figure 6.1   long straddle (long 1 January AMZN 190 call @ 26⁷/₈, long 1 January AMZN 190 put @ 32)

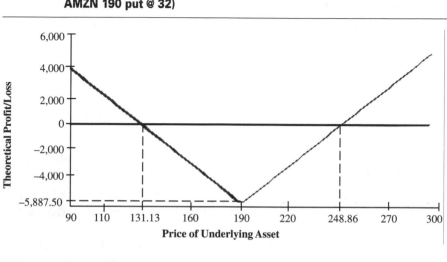

tion of a call and a put risk curve. Together they create a U-shaped curve, which signals limited risk and unlimited profit potentials beyond the breakevens.

By tracking this trade, we find that after 10 days, Amazon.com makes a phenomenal $46\frac{1}{4}$ leap in only one day (it happens, folks). By the following week, Amazon.com has climbed to $314\frac{15}{16}$. In 24 days it has climbed to $351\frac{15}{16}$ (an increase of $163\frac{7}{16}$ points). If we exit the trade at that price, we can sell the call for $146\frac{1}{2}$ (an increase of $119\frac{5}{8}$ points), and sell the put for $1\frac{1}{8}$ (a decrease of $30\frac{7}{8}$ points). This leaves a net profit of \$8,875 [$(146\frac{1}{2} - 26\frac{7}{8}) - (32 - 1\frac{1}{8}) \times 100 = \$8,875$]. (Table 6.4.)

To find a market that is appropriate for placing a long straddle, it is imperative to find markets with the capacity to make big moves. Look for stocks that are listed in the "Price Percentage Winners" columns (eSignal's "Movers and Shakers" list or ClearStation's "Tag and Bag"). Most likely you'll find the press will be talking them up as well as the chat rooms. Then check the fundamentals and find out what's going on with the company. You can also scan for undervalued options in a volatile market.

---

rule of thumb
look for markets that have the capacity to make large moves in either direction with 60 days or more until expiration.

table 6.4 long straddle results

Long 1 January AMZN 190 Call @ $26^7/_8$, Long 1 January AMZN 190 Put @ 32

Debit at Initiation	Call Price at Exit	Put Price at Exit	Days in Trade	Profit/ Loss	Return on Investment
$5,887.50	$14,650	$112.50	24	$8,875	151%

short straddle

A short straddle involves selling a put and a call with identical ATM strike prices and expiration months. This strategy is attractive to the aggressive strategist who is interested in selling large amounts of time premium in hopes of collecting all or most of this premium as profit if the underlying stock remains fairly stable. This is a higher-risk strategy than the long straddle because both options are uncovered. I do not suggest to any trader to ever place a short straddle that is uncovered, but there are methods that can be utilized to substantially reduce the risks associated with this strategy.

---

short straddle strategy
a delta neutral options strategy best placed in a stable market that involves the simultaneous sale of the same number of ATM puts and calls with the same expiration date.

For example, let's create a short straddle using Microsoft Corporation, a leading high technology stock. Table 6.5 shows Microsoft's fundamental information. Since a short straddle involves the selling of options, it is best to use options with less than 45 days till expiration. Using the values in Table 6.6, let's create a short straddle by going short 1 January MSFT 135 Call @ $6^3/_4$ and short 1 January MSFT 135 Put @ $8^1/_4$. The maximum reward for this trade is limited to the net credit, or $1,500. The maximum risk is unlimited to the upside and downside beyond the breakevens, which makes this trade potentially dangerous. This trade will require a substantial margin deposit to place.

The risk profile for a short straddle combines a short call and a short put to create an upside-down U-shaped curve. This clues us into

table 6.5	microsoft corporation fundamentals

Microsoft Corporation (MSFT)	
Last price	$133^9/_{16}$
Volume	22,452,300
52-week range	59 to $133^3/_4$
P/E ratio	59.63

source: www.bigcharts.com 12/7/98

table 6.6   microsoft corporation option premiums

Price of MSFT = $133^9/_{16}$ (12/7/98)

Expiration Date	Call Premium	Put Premium
December 135	$2^3/_4$	4
January 135	$6^3/_4$	$8^1/_4$

the fact that short straddles have limited profit potential and unlimited risk. The risk profile for this trade is shown in Figure 6.2.

When you sell straddles, it is vital to calculate the profit range to determine the point at which potential losses begin (Table 6.7). The upside breakeven occurs when the underlying asset's price equals the strike price plus the net credit divided by 100. In this example, the upside breakeven is 150 [135 + (1500 ÷ 100) = 150]. The downside breakeven occurs when the underlying asset's price equals the strike price minus the net credit divided by 100. In this case, the downside breakeven equals 120 [135 – (1500 ÷ 100) = 120]. Microsoft must continue to stabilize and move in a straight line—trading between 120 and 150—for this trade to remain profitable. Although at expiration only one side can be wrong, the options also run the risk of being exercised if they move too far in-the-money. Since short straddles offer unlimited risk, it is vital to keep a close watch on the market and move quickly at the first sign of trouble.

By expiration on the third Friday of January, Microsoft is priced at $149^3/_4$. (Table 6.8.) This trade has managed to just barely stay between the breakevens. The short call is in-the-money and the short put is out-of-the-money. There's a good chance that the call would be exercised and we'd have to deliver 100 shares of Microsoft to the option holder at $135 per share. This means that you would have to buy

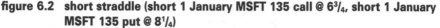

figure 6.2   **short straddle (short 1 January MSFT 135 call @ 6³/₄, short 1 January MSFT 135 put @ 8¹/₄)**

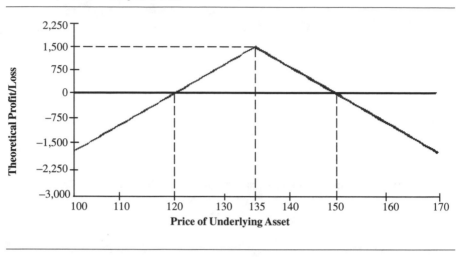

table 6.7   **short straddle trade calculations**

Short Straddle Using Microsoft Corp. @ 133⁹/₁₆

Maximum Risk = Unlimited above and below breakeven	Unlimited
Maximum Reward = Net credit	$1,500
Downside Breakeven = Strike price − (net debit ÷ 100)	120
Upside Breakeven = Strike price + (net debit ÷ 100)	150

100 shares of Microsoft at the current price. If the option were exercised on the last day before expiration when Microsoft is priced at 149³/₄, then you would lose $1,475 [(149³/₄ − 135) × 100 = $1,475]. Taken from the $1,500 net credit received, it would leave you with a big $25 to pay for part of your commissions ($1,500 − $1,475 = $25). This trade basically broke even—a bit disappointing perhaps but not the end of the world.

Obviously, the most advantageous price the market could have settled at would have been the strike price at 135. Both of the short options would expire worthless and you would get to keep the net credit. Before placing a trade, you have to assess just how likely it is for a market to close on the exact strike price of your short options. Review past price action by checking a stock's historical prices. Shorting straddles is a risky trade unless you find markets that are not likely to move away from a centerline.

table 6.8 short straddle results

Short 1 January MSFT 135 Call @ $6^3/_4$, Short 1 January MSFT 135 Put @ $8^1/_4$

Credit at Initiation	Stock Price at Initiation	Stock Price at Exit	Days in Trade	Profit/ Loss
$1,500	$133^9/_{16}$	$149^3/_4$	39	$25

---

rule of thumb
look for stable markets and use options with 45 days or less until expiration and enough premium to make the trade worthwhile.

long strangle

A strangle is similar to a straddle, except OTM options are used instead of ATM options. A long strangle is created by purchasing an OTM call and an OTM put with the same expiration month (Table 6.9). There are both drawbacks and advantages to this strategy over straddles. A long strangle costs less than a straddle because OTM options are less expensive than ATM options. Unfortunately, long strangles also require the underlying stock to make rather large unrealistic moves to make a profit.

---

long strangle strategy
a delta neutral options strategy best placed in a extremely volatile market that involves the simultaneous purchase of equal numbers of OTM puts and calls with the same expiration date.

Let's set up a long strangle using Amazon.com by going long 1 April AMZN 200 Call @ 36 and long 1 April AMZN 180 Put @ $39^1/_8$. (Table 6.10.) The maximum risk of a long strangle is equal to the cost of the double option premiums. In this example, the maximum risk is $7,512.50 [$(36 + 39^1/_8) \times 100 = \$7,512.50$]. The maximum profit is unlimited to the upside and downside beyond the breakevens. The upside breakeven occurs when the underlying asset equals the call strike price plus the net debit divided by 100, or $275^1/_8$ [200 + (7,512.50

table 6.9   amazon.com option premiums

Price of AMZN = $188^1/_2$ (12/4/98)

Expiration Date	Call Premium	Put Premium
January 180	32	22
January 200	$20^1/_4$	35
April 180	$56^7/_8$	$39^1/_8$
April 200	36	$50^1/_4$

table 6.10   long strangle trade calculations

Long Strangle Using Amazon.com @ $188^1/_2$

Maximum Risk = Net credit	$7,512.50
Maximum Reward = Unlimited above and below breakeven	Unlimited
Downside Breakeven = Put strike price – (net debit ÷ 100)	$104^7/_8$
Upside Breakeven = Call strike price + (net debit ÷ 100)	$275^1/_8$

÷ 100) = $275^1/_8$]. The downside breakeven occurs when the underlying asset equals the put strike price minus the net debit divided by 100, or $104^7/_8$ [180 – (7512.50 ÷ 100) = $104^7/_8$].

Figure 6.3 shows the risk profile for this trade. Once again, we see a U-shaped risk curve indicating a trade with unlimited profit potential and limited risk. Profit depends on a large move in the underlying stock. Luckily, Amazon.com at the time of this writing is an extremely volatile market with more than enough kick to place this trade in a winning position.

To exit a long strangle, you have to sell options with the identical strike prices and expiration date. After 24 days, Amazon.com peaks at $351^{15}/_{16}$, and the call can be sold at $156^1/_8$. The put can be sold at $9^1/_8$ for a net profit of $9,012.50 (Table 6.11). This kind of movement is quite unusual, but I use this scenario to illustrate the leverage that options can provide. Strangles will rarely work as a straightforward trade because they require the market to make a very large move in order to generate a profit. They are best used in combinations to create butterfly and condor spread strategies (see Chapter 8). However, they are an important piece of the options puzzle and can help traders to understand the difference between placing trades with ATM options versus placing trades with OTM options.

figure 6.3   long strangle (long 1 April AMZN 200 call @ 36, long 1 April AMZN 180 put @ 39^1/$_8$)

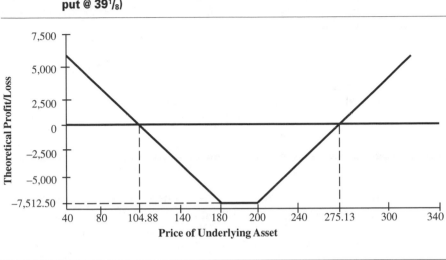

table 6.11   long strangle results

Long 1 April AMZN 200 Call @ 36, Long 1 April AMZN 180 Put @ 39^1/$_8$

Debit at Initiation	Call Price at Exit	Put Price at Exit	Days in Trade	Profit/ Loss	Return on Investment
$7,512.50	156^1/$_8$	9^1/$_8$	24	$9,012.50	120%

---

rule of thumb
look for high-volatility market with the capacity to make a very large move using options with at least 45 days until expiration.

---

short strangle

Shorting an OTM call and an OTM put with the same expiration date creates a short strangle. Short strangles are profitable only in stable markets that continue to trade between the breakevens of the trade. Just like the short straddle, the short strangle's maximum profit is limited to the net credit received from the double option premium. However, short strangles have even more limited profit potential because the OTM options are less expensive than the premium of ATM options. Risk is thereby reduced accordingly. However, the underlying stock has to make a major move to go beyond the breakevens. This strategy requires a large margin.

---

short strangle strategy
a delta neutral options strategy best placed in a stable market that involves the simultaneous sale of the same number of OTM puts and calls with the same expiration date.

Since the profit on a short strangle depends on the options expiring worthless, it is important to use options that do not have a lot of time until expiration. Let's use Microsoft (MSFT) to create a short strangle by going short 1 January MSFT 140 Call @ $4^1/_2$ and short 1 January MSFT 130 Put @ 5. (Tables 6.12 and 6.13.) The maximum reward is limited to the net credit of the option premiums, or \$950 $[(4^1/_2 + 5) \times 100 = \$950]$. The maximum risk is unlimited in both directions beyond the breakevens. The upside breakeven occurs when the underlying equals the call strike price plus the net credit divided by 100. In this example, the upside breakeven is equal to $149^1/_2$ $[140 + (950 \div 100) = 149^1/_2]$. To calculate the downside breakeven, subtract the net credit divided by 100 from the put strike price. In this trade, the downside breakeven is equal to $120^1/_2$ $[130 - (950 \div 100) = 120^1/_2]$. Microsoft has to stay between $149^1/_2$ and $120^1/_2$ for this trade to be profitable. Figure 6.4 shows the risk profile of this trade.

On January 15, Microsoft reaches $149^3/_4$. The short put is out-of-the-money, but the short call would expire in-the-money. There's a good chance that the short call would be exercised, triggering an obligation to deliver 100 shares of Microsoft to the option holder at \$140 per share. This means that you would have to buy 100 shares of

---

table 6.12   microsoft option premiums

Price of MSFT = $133^9/_{16}$ (12/7/98)

Expiration Date	Call Premium	Put Premium
December 130	$5^5/_8$	$2^1/_8$
December 140	4	$8^1/_4$
January 130	$9^3/_8$	5
January 140	$4^1/_2$	$11^1/_8$

---

table 6.13   **short strangle trade calculations**

Short Strangle Using Microsoft @ $133^9/_{16}$

Maximum Risk = Unlimited above and below breakeven	Unlimited
Maximum Reward = Net credit	$950
Downside Breakeven = Put strike price – (net debit ÷ 100)	$120^1/_2$
Upside Breakeven = Call strike price + (net debit ÷ 100)	$149^1/_2$

---

figure 6.4   short strangle (short 1 January MSFT 140 call @ $4^1/_2$, short 1 January MSFT 130 put @ 5)

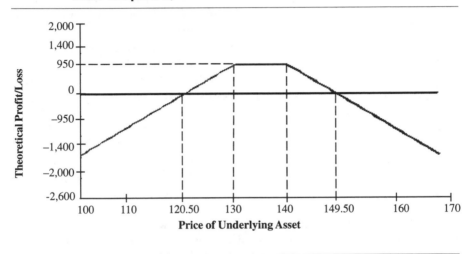

Microsoft at the current price of $149^3/_4$ for a loss of $975 [$(149^3/_4 – 140)$ × 100 = $975]. Taken from the $950 net credit received, it would leave you with a loss of $25 ($975 – $950 = $25). (Table 6.14.) This example illustrates how short strangles can be very dangerous to place in an unstable market. I prefer to trade short options in conjunction with long options to create complex strategies with limited risk.

---

rule of thumb
look for a wildly volatile market where you anticipate a drop-off into a very stable market with low volatility. Look for overpriced options with less than 45 days until expiration.

table 6.14 short strangle results

Short 1 January MSFT 140 Call @ $4^{1}/_{2}$, Short 1 January MSFT 130 Put @ 5

Credit at Initiation	Stock Price at Initiation	Stock Price at Exit	Days in Trade	Profit/ Loss
$950	$133^{9}/_{16}$	$149^{3}/_{4}$	39	–$25

conclusion

Delta neutral trades offer a divergence from traditional directional strategies. I usually allow the cost of the trades to inspire me to choose one position over another. Some brokerages simply do not allow their clients to short the market using uncovered options. Others require expensive margin deposits of more than $50,000. Either way, it is imperative to execute paper trades before using real money in order to recognize the subtle dynamics of each strategy.

Options at different strikes will have different deltas and will change as the underlying security changes. The object of the game is to keep your trade as close to zero deltas as possible. When the next uptick changes the market you are trading, you are no longer neutral. You may be able to make an additional profit by making an adjustment by purchasing or selling options to get the trade back to delta neutral again. This is especially true of trades that use multiple contracts.

When you are trading delta neutral, think of one side of your straddle as your hedge and the other side as your directional bet. If you are 100% wrong, you still can profit. It doesn't matter which way the trade goes because, theoretically, you are going to make a comparable amount on either side. When you start factoring in things like time decay and volatility, that figure may change. To find an appropriate market for a delta neutral trade, just surf the Net to a site that provides real-time or delayed quotes and see what you can find.

chapter 7

ratio spreads and backspreads

ratio call spread

Unlike straddles and strangles that use an equal proportion of options on either side of a trade, ratio spreads offset an uneven number of different types of options with the same expiration. A ratio call spread involves buying a lower strike call option and selling a greater number of OTM higher strike call options. This technique is also called a long ratio spread and can be thought of as a bull call spread with an extra short call (or two or three depending on the trade specifics). In general, it has an overall position delta of zero and is best placed in a bearish market. The maximum profit is realized when the market is at the higher strike price, but not above it, at expiration.

> **ratio spread**
> a strategy involving disproportionate numbers of puts and calls with the same expiration date to create a trade that offers limited risk and unlimited profit potential.

> **ratio call spread strategy**
> a bearish or stable strategy in which a trader buys 2 higher strike call and sells a greater number of lower strike calls. This strategy offers limited risk and unlimited profit potential.

There are a variety of ways to set up a ratio call spread. For example, you can buy one OTM call option and sell two call options that are even further out-of-the-money. You can also use a different ratio other than one to two. For instance, you might buy one ATM option and sell three OTM options. A ratio call spread is useful when a trader sees a slight rise in a market followed by a sell-off or a slight decline. If this trade is placed at a net credit, you have an increased chance of success. Unlimited risk exists to the upside due to the extra short calls, and therefore a large margin is required to place a trade using this strategy.

Referring to Excite Inc.'s fundamentals in Table 7.1 and using the values in Table 7.2, let's create a ratio call spread using Excite as our underlying stock by going long 1 February XCIT 45 Call @ $14^{1}/_{4}$ and short 3 February XCIT 60 Calls @ $7^{3}/_{4}$. The net credit of this trade is $900 {[(3 \times 7^{3}/_{4}) - (1 \times 14^{1}/_{4})] \times 100 = \$900}$. The maximum profit of a ratio call spread is calculated by multiplying the number of long contracts times the difference in strike prices by the value per point, plus the net credit received (or minus the net debit). (Table 7.3.) In this example, the maximum profit is equal to $2,400 {[1 \times (60 - 45) \times 100] + 900 = \$2,400}$. The maximum risk is unlimited to the upside above the breakeven. To calculate the upside breakeven of a ratio call spread, multiply the number of short calls times the sum of the short call premium plus the strike price of the short call, and then subtract the number of long calls times the sum of the premium plus the strike price of the long call. Finally, divide this number by the number of short calls minus the number of long calls. In this trade, the upside

---

table 7.1   excite inc. fundamentals

Excite Inc. (XCIT)

Last price	$56^{5}/_{8}$
Volume	7,888,500
52-week range	$13^{7}/_{8}$ to $58^{5}/_{8}$

source: www.bigcharts.com 12/8/98

table 7.2 excite inc. call premiums

Price of XCIT= $56^5/_8$ (12/8/98)

Call Strike Price	January	February
35	$17^3/_8$	$18^3/_4$
40	$14^1/_2$	16
45	$12^1/_4$	$14^1/_4$
50	9	12
55	$6^3/_{16}$	$9^1/_{16}$
60	$4^{15}/_{16}$	$7^3/_4$

table 7.3 ratio call spread trade calculations

Ratio Call Spread Using Excite Inc. @ $56^5/_8$

Net Credit = Net short call premium – net long call premium	$900
Maximum Risk = Unlimited above upside breakeven	Unlimited
Maximum Reward = [(# of long contacts × strike difference) × 100] + net credit (or – net debit)	$2,400
Upside Breakeven = {[# of short calls × (short call premium + short call strike price) – # of long calls × (long call premium + long call strike price)] / (# of short calls – # of long calls)}	72

breakeven is equal to 72 {[3 × ($7^3/_4$ + 60) – 1 × ($14^1/_4$ + 45)] / (3 – 1) = 72}. There is no risk to the downside because the trade was entered as a credit. The risk profile for this trade is found in Figure 7.1.

Closing this trade profitably has several possibilities depending on what happens in the underlying market. For this strategy to work well, the price of the underlying stock needs to fall sharply. Holding the position makes the most sense because you will make more money on the short options than on the loss of the long call. If the market gets bullish (price of the underlying stock rises), then you may have to liquidate two of the short options and retain the long call, offsetting it later to relieve some of the loss on the short options. You could also hold the position and wait (and pray) for a reversal. But the most prudent choice is to simply liquidate the entire trade when the prices seem optimal.

By tracking this trade, we find that after 28 days, Excite has fallen to 42 and appears to be heading for a reversal. To exit the trade, you need to buy back the short calls and sell the long call. Table 7.4

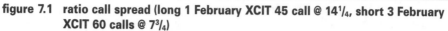

figure 7.1   ratio call spread (long 1 February XCIT 45 call @ 14¼, short 3 February XCIT 60 calls @ 7¾)

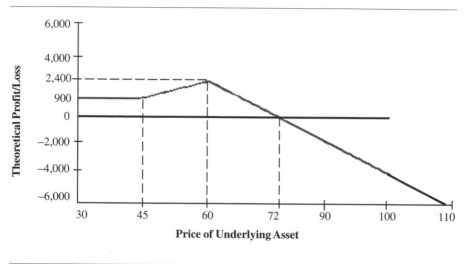

table 7.4   ratio call spread results

Long 1 February XCIT 45 Call @ 14¼, Short 3 February XCIT 60 Calls @ 7¾

Credit at Initiation	Price of 45 Call	Price of 60 Call	Days in Trade	Profit/ Loss
$900	6⁵⁄₈	1⁷⁄₁₆	28	$1,131.25

shows the results. If you sell the 45 call for 6⁵⁄₈, you will receive an additional $662.50. Buying the short calls back at 1⁷⁄₁₆ apiece will amount to $431.25. That leaves an additional profit of $231.25 to add to the initial credit received of $900. The total profit on this trade is $1,131.25.

rule of thumb
look for highly volatile markets with a bearish bias and options with a forward volatility skew

ratio put spread

A ratio put spread can be implemented when a slight fall in the market is anticipated followed by a sharp rise. Although it resembles a bear put spread with an extra short put (or two or three), a ratio put spread should be implemented in a bullish market, preferably one with a reverse volatility skew. This strategy works well in the stock market, as stocks generally want to move up in price. However, it is important to place this trade only on stocks that are high-quality stocks. If the company has reported lower than expected earnings or bad news is released, exit the position.

---

ratio put spread strategy
a bullish or stable strategy in which a trader buys a higher strike put and sells a greater number of lower strike puts. This strategy offers limited risk and unlimited profit potential.

---

reverse volatility skew
markets in which lower strike options have high implied volatility and are therefore overpriced, and higher strike options have low implied volatility and are often underpriced.

A ratio put spread consists of going long a higher strike put and going short a greater number of OTM lower strike puts. The maximum profit is realized when the market is at the lower strike, but not below that strike price at expiration. Note that the short options are not covered by long options, which is where the downside risk exists. For example, if you bought one and sold three, two of the short puts would be at risk. If you are doing an uneven number, you will have expensive margin requirements on the uncovered short options.

Some fundamentals of Sun Microsystems are shown in Table 7.5. Using the values in Table 7.6, let's create a ratio put spread by going long 1 January SUNW 100 Put @ 26 and short 4 January SUNW 75 Puts @ $7^{1}/_{4}$. The maximum profit of a ratio put spread is limited to the number of long puts times the difference in strike prices plus the net credit (or minus the net debit). This example has a net credit of $300 $\{[(4 \times 7^{1}/_{4}) - 26] \times 100 = \$300\}$ and a maximum profit of $2,800 $\{[(100 - 75) \times 100] + 300 = \$2,800\}$. (Table 7.7.) The maximum risk is unlimited to the downside beyond the breakeven. The downside breakeven is calculated by multiplying the number of short puts times the short put

---

table 7.5   sun microsystems fundamentals

Sun Microsystems (SUNW)

Last price	$74^1/_{16}$
Volume	20,245,600
52-week range	$34^5/_8$ to $82^1/_2$
P/E ratio	34.96

---

source: www.bigcharts.com 12/2/98

---

table 7.6   sun microsystems put premiums

Price of SUNW = $74^1/_{16}$ (12/2/98)

Put Strike Price	January	April
65	2	$4^1/_2$
70	4	$6^1/_8$
75	$7^1/_4$	$8^1/_2$
80	$9^1/_2$	$12^1/_8$
85	11	$14^1/_2$
90	$16^7/_8$	$18^1/_4$
95	$21^3/_8$	$24^1/_2$
100	27	$29^1/_2$

---

strike price minus the short put premium, and then subtracting the number of long puts times the long put strike price minus the long put premium. Then divide this number by the number of short puts minus the number of long puts. In this example, the downside beakeven is $65^2/_3$ {[$4 \times (75 - 7^1/_4) - 1 \times (100 - 26)$] / $(4 - 1) = 65^2/_3$}. The risk graph for this trade is shown in Figure 7.2.

Closing a ratio put spread profitably depends on the price movement of the underlying stock. In the best scenario, SUNW would have closed at the strike price of the short put. The short options would have expired worthless so that you get to keep the net credit and the long put could have been sold at a relatively high premium, thereby mitigating any loss. There is no risk to the upside because the trade is done at a net credit. If the market turns bearish, you should liquidate the position before the short puts are exercised to avoid heavy losses. In this example, SUNW closes at $97^1/_2$, an increase of $23^7/_{16}$ (Table 7.8). The short options expire worthless and you can sell the long option

table 7.7 ratio put spread trade calculations

Ratio Put Spread Using Sun Microsystems Corp. @ $74^1/_{16}$

Net Credit/Debit = Net short put premium − net long put premium	$300
Maximum Risk = Unlimited below downside breakeven	Unlimited
Maximum Reward = [(# of long contracts × strike difference) × 100] + net credit (or − net debit)	$2,800
Downside Breakeven = {[# of short puts × (short put strike price − short put premium) − # of long puts × (long put strike price − long put premium)] / (# of short puts − # of long puts)}	$65^2/_3$

figure 7.2 ratio put spread (long 1 January SUNW 100 put @ 26, short 4 January SUNW 75 puts @ 7¹/₄)

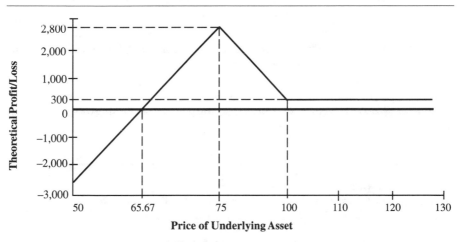

table 7.8 ratio put spread results

Long 1 January SUNW 100 Put @ 26, Short 4 January SUNW 75 Puts @ $7^1/_4$

Credit at Initiation	Stock Price at Initiation	Stock Price at Exit	Price of 75 Put at Expiration	Price of 100 Put at Expiration	Days in Trade	Profit/ Loss
$300	$74^1/_{16}$	$97^1/_2$	0	$16^3/_4$	44	$1,975

for $16^3/_4$. This corresponds to a total profit of $1,975 ($1,675 + $300 = $1,975) in 44 days.

---

rule of thumb
use highly volatile markets with a bullish bias and options with a reverse volatility skew.

---

ratio backspreads

Ratio backspreads are a very popular nondirectional trading strategy that offer unlimited profit potential and limited risk. This volatility-based strategy involves the buying of one leg and selling of another at a disproportionate ratio. This strategy in particular can be effectively used to minimize option time decay. If the markets move, you make money; and if they don't move, you still won't lose money. That's one of the reasons ratio backspreads are also called "vacation trades." They do not need to be monitored very closely as long as the options are at least 30 days out. In many cases, traders can place a ratio backspread and then turn their attention elsewhere as the trade continues to make money. This is partially due to the fact that correctly forecasting market direction is not essential to profit making. However, having a good feel for volatility is important to picking the right strategy.

---

ratio backspread
a delta neutral spread where an uneven number of contracts are bought and sold. Optimally no net credit or net debit occurs.

There are two kinds of ratio backspreads: call ratio and put ratio backspreads. Both of these strategies must be applied in a market with a specific volatility situation to be effective. Call ratio backspreads are best placed in markets where a rise in volatility is anticipated. Markets that are about to experience a lull in volatility are ripe for a put ratio backspread. In order to place either kind of ratio backspread, the following rules must be observed:

1. Choose markets with high volatility.
2. Avoid markets with consistent low volatility. If you really want to place a ratio backspread in a market that does not move, pay close attention to Rule #4.

3. Do not use ratios of options greater than .67—use ratios that are a multiple of 1 to 2 or 2 to 3.

4. If you choose to trade a slow market, a .75 ratio or higher is acceptable only by buying the lower strike and selling the higher. However, there is more risk.

5. To create a call ratio backspread, sell the lower strike call and buy a greater number of higher strike calls.

6. To create a put ratio backspread, sell the higher strike put and buy a greater number of lower strike puts.

7. Avoid debit trades. If you do place a ratio backspread with a debit, you must be willing to lose this amount.

One way to figure out the most effective ratio is to accurately calculate the net credit of a trade. This can be accomplished by calculating the full credit realized from the short options and dividing it by the debit of one long option. You then use up as much of the credit as you can to make the most profitable ratio.

Credit = # of short contracts × short option premium × $ value of each point

Debit = # of long contracts × long option premium × $ value of each point

It can be difficult to find ratio backspread opportunities in highly volatile markets with expensive stocks. Focus on medium-priced stocks and look for volatility skews by studying the implied volatility of the stock's options. Locating the right markets can be frustrating at first. Learn to be persistent. They're out there; you just have to keep looking.

call ratio backspread

Call ratio backspreads are created by simultaneously selling a lower strike call and purchasing a greater number of higher strike calls in a ratio less than two to three. Call ratio backspreads are best placed in bullish markets with a reverse volatility skew. In these markets, the lower strike options (the ones you want to sell) have higher implied volatility and may be overpriced. The lower strike options (the ones you have to buy) enjoy lower implied volatility and are often underpriced. By trading the reverse volatility skew, you can capture the implied volatility differential between the short and long options.

---

call ratio backspread strategy
option combination trades that involve the simultaneous sale of
lower strike calls and the purchase of a greater number of higher
strike calls with the same expiration date.

Let's introduce the delta to this situation. As previously discussed, the delta is the probability of an option closing in-the-money at expiration. Obviously an option that's already in-the-money has a higher probability of closing in-the-money than an option that's out-of-the-money. Therefore, the delta for an ITM option is higher than the delta for the ATM option or an OTM option. The higher the probability an option has of closing in-the-money, the higher its premium. Ratio backspreads take full advantage of this relationship by enabling a trader to create trades that are virtually free of charge.

Table 7.9 shows some fundamentals for Yahoo!, an Internet stock that has been absolutely raging in the past year, especially right before its quarterly earnings reports are released. Using the values in Table 7.10, and keeping in mind that ratio backspreads, unlike ratio spreads, offer unlimited profit, let's create a call ratio backspread by going short 2 April YHOO 160 Calls @ $16^7/_8$ and long 3 April YHOO 170 Calls @ $11^1/_2$. The net debit on this trade is –\$75 $\{[(3 \times 11^1/_2) - (2 \times 16^7/_8)] \times 100 = -\$75\}$. (Table 7.11.) The maximum risk is calculated by multiplying the number of short calls by the difference in strike prices by the value per point and then subtracting the net credit (or adding the net debit). The maximum risk on this trade is \$2,075 $\{[2 \times (170 - 160) \times 100] + 75 = \$2,075\}$. The upside breakeven is calculated by adding the strike price of the long calls to the following number: Take the difference in strike prices times the number of short calls minus the net credit divided by 100 (or plus the net debit divided by 100) and divide this number by the number of long calls minus the number

---

table 7.9 yahoo! fundamentals

	Yahoo! Inc. (YHOO)

Last price	$183^3/_{24}$
Volume	8,450,000
52-week range	$15^7/_{32}$ to $222^1/_2$
P/E ratio	371.11

source: www.bigcharts.com 12/3/98

table 7.10   yahoo! option premiums

Price of YHOO = $175^3/_8$ (12/3/98)

Expiration Date	Call Premium
April 160	$16^7/_8$
April 170	$11^1/_2$

table 7.11   call ratio backspread trade calculations

Call Ratio Backspread Using Yahoo! Inc. @ $183^3/_4$

Net Debit/Credit = Net short call premium – net long call premium	–$75
Maximum Risk = [(# of short calls × difference in strikes) × 100 – net credit (or + net debit)]	$2,075
Maximum Reward = Unlimited to the upside and limited to the net credit on the downside (if any)	Unlimited
Upside Breakeven = {[Long call strike price + [(difference in strikes × # of short calls) – (net credit / 100)} or + [(net debit / 100) / (# of long calls – # of short calls)]	$190^3/_4$
Downside Breakeven = If the trade has a net debit, the net debit is lost at the strike price of the short call or below. If the trade has a net credit, then breakeven = {short call strike price + [(net credit / 100) / # of short calls]}	160

of short calls. In this example, the upside breakeven is $190^3/_4$ (170 + {[(170 – 160) × 2 + 75 / 100] / (3 – 2)} = $190^3/_4$). This trade has an unlimited profit potential above $190^3/_4$. Although there is no breakeven for this trade to the downside since it was entered as a net debit, you can calculate the point at which you lose the net debit. That point is at the strike price of the short calls, or 160. For convenience, I will still refer to it as the downside breakeven. To derive the downside breakeven for a call ratio backspread with a net credit add the net credit (divided by 100) divided by the number of short calls to the strike price of the short calls. Figure 7.3 shows the limited risk and unlimited profit potential this strategy offers.

By tracking this trade, we find that after 25 days, Yahoo! has increased to $275^1/_2$ per share. The Yahoo! 170 calls are now priced at 105. (Table 7.12.) Selling the three long calls will bring in $31,500. But to avoid exercise, the short calls have to be bought back. Since a 160 call now goes for $115^7/_8$, two 160 calls will cost $23,175. The resulting profit of

figure 7.3 call ratio backspread (short 2 April YHOO 160 calls @ 16⁷/₈, long 3 April YHOO 170 calls @ 11¹/₂)

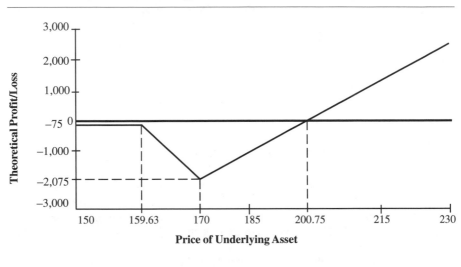

table 7.12 call ratio backspread results

Short 2 April YHOO 160 Calls @ 16⁷/₈, Long 3 April YHOO 170 Calls @ 11¹/₂

Debit at Initiation	Price of Long Call	Price of Short Call	Days in Trade	Profit/ Loss	Return on Investment
$75	105	115⁷/₈	25	$8,250 or $8,425	11,000%+

$8,325, minus the $75 debit, creates a final profit of $8,250—an amazing 11,000% return on the $75 investment. If the short 160 calls were assigned and exercised, you can exercise two of the long 170 calls and deliver 200 shares to the option buyer at a loss of $2,000. By selling the additional long call at 105, you can make a profit of $8,425 {[(105 × 100) − (2,000 + 75)] = $8,425}. Either exit scenario provides an excellent return on investment.

---

rule of thumb
use highly volatile markets with a bullish bias and options with a reverse volatility skew.

put ratio backspread

A put ratio backspread is basically the opposite of call ratio backspread. In a put ratio backspread, you sell the higher strike put and simultaneously buy a greater number of lower strike puts. In a call ratio backspread, you want the market to go up; however, you don't necessarily lose money if it goes down. With a put ratio backspread, you want the market to go down (bearish). In addition, put ratio backspreads are best placed in markets with a forward volatility skew. In these markets, the higher strike options (the ones you want to sell) have higher implied volatiliity and are therefore overpriced. The lower strike options (the ones you have to buy) enjoy lower implied volatility and are not quite so expensive.

---

put ratio backspread strategy
option combination trades that involve the simultaneous sale of higher strike puts and the purchase of a greater number of lower strike puts with the same expiration date.

---

forward volatility skew
markets in which higher strike options have high implied volatility and are therefore overpriced, and lower strike options have low implied volatility and are often underpriced.

The key to finding a profitable ratio backspread is arranging options premiums to create a downside breakeven that fits the stock's profile. Using the values for Excite in Table 7.13, let's create a put ratio backspread by going short 2 February XCIT 60 Puts @ 17 and long 3 February XCIT 55 Puts @ $11^1/_2$. The net debit is equal to –$50 [$(3 \times 11^1/_2) - (2 \times 17) \times 100 = -50]. (Table 7.14.) The maximum risk is equal to the number of short puts times the difference in strike prices multiplied by the value per point (100) minus the net credit or plus the net debit. In this trade, the maximum risk is $1,050 {$[2 \times (60 - 55) \times 100] + $50 = $1,050$}. The upside breakeven is the higher strike put option minus the net credit divided by 100 and then divided by the number of short puts. In this case, there is no upside breakeven because the trade was entered at a net debit. If the market closes above the strike price of the short puts—60 in this example—you'll lose the net debit of $50. The maximum profit is unlimited to the downside below the downside breakeven. The downside breakeven is calculated by multiplying the number of short

---

table 7.13   excite, inc. put option premiums

Price of XCIT = $53^1/_4$ (12/10/98)

Expiration Date	Put Premium
February 50	$8^5/_8$
February 55	$11^1/_2$
February 60	17

---

table 7.14   put ratio backspread trade calculations

Put Ratio Backspread Using Excite @ $56^5/_8$

Net Debit/Credit = Net short put premium − net long put premium	−$50
Maximum Risk = [(# of short calls × difference in strikes) × 100 − net credit (or + net debit)]	$1,050
Maximum Reward = Unlimited to the downside below the breakeven. Limited on the upside to the net credit (if any)	Unlimited
Upside Breakeven = If the trade has a net debit, the net debit is lost at the strike price of the short put or above. If the trade has a net credit, then breakeven = {short put strike price − [(net credit / 100) / # of short puts]}	60
Downside Breakeven = Long put strike price − {[(# of short puts × difference in strikes) − net credit / 100 *or* + (net debit / 100)] / (# of long puts − # of short puts)}	$44^1/_2$

---

contracts times the difference in strike prices, and subtracting the net credit divided by 100 or adding the net debit divided by 100. Then divide that amount by the number of long puts minus the number of short puts. Finally, subtract that amount from the lower strike price. In this trade, the downside breakeven is $44^1/_2$ {55 − [2 × (60 − 55) + 50/100] / (3 − 2) = $44^1/_2$}. This trade will make money as long as the price of excite closes below $44^1/_2$. The risk profile for this example is shown in Figure 7.4.

By tracking this trade, we find that after 26 days, Excite falls to 42 and looks poised for a rebound. To exit the trade, you have to buy back the short 60 puts at 19 and can sell the 55 puts for $16^7/_8$ each for a total net profit of $1,262.50. (Table 7.15.) Subtracting the net debit of $50, the total profit on this trade (not including commissions) is $1,212.50 {[(3 × $16^7/_8$) × 100] − [(2 × 19) × 100] − 50 = $1,212.50}. If the short 60 puts are assigned and exercised, you have to buy 200 shares of Excite at $60 per

figure 7.4   put ratio backspread (short 2 February XCIT 60 puts @ 17, long 3 February XCIT 50 puts @ 11½)

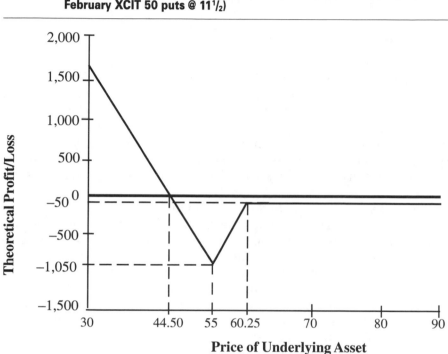

table 7.15   put ratio backspread results

Short 2 February XCIT 60 Puts @ 17, Long 3 February XCIT 55 Puts @ 11½

Debit at Initiation	Price of 60 Put	Price of 55 Put	Days in Trade	Profit/Loss
–$50	19	16⅞	26	$1,212.50 or $637.50

rule of thumb
use highly volatile markets with a bearish bias and options with a forward volatility skew.

share. However, by exercising 2 of the long 55 puts, you can still make a net profit of $637.50 {1687.50 − [2 × (60 − 55) × 100] − 50 = $637.50}.

conclusion

The best markets for ratio backspread trades have high volatility. Before placing a call or put ratio backspread, I spend a lot of time analyzing the overall risk of the trade. Once a trade is executed, patience is required to let the trade do what it was constructed to do. Sometimes it's the hardest thing in the world just leaving a ratio backspread alone. It's a good practice to monitor the trade once a day, but get in the habit of allowing it to mature to profitability. This is especially difficult for those traders who spend the entire day poring over real-time quotes.

For example, Yahoo! is a super high-flying market. What can you do to take advantage of Yahoo!'s sharp price movement? If it moves up quickly over a three-day period, you have two choices. You can certainly follow the upward trend and do a put ratio spread or a call ratio backspread; or you could bet on a correction and place a call ratio spread or a put ratio backspread. It's a tough choice. Sometimes, a contrarian trade is a good idea. Other times it's best to just go ahead and follow the trend. Only personal experience can guide you when it comes to making these kinds of critical choices.

To arrive at a decision, there are a host of economic variables that you may want to investigate. In the pre-Internet era, I could get the big picture and pay attention to details just by picking up the *Wall Street Journal* and *Investor's Business Daily*. Now I jump online and the information is right there. Anyone can buzz from site to site in seconds. If you learn that stocks are going up, interest rates are going down, the commodities markets are stable, and the dollar is going down, which is the only one that worries you? Everything is betting for an up move in stocks, except for the dollar going down. Why? Because the Federal Reserve at one point may say the dollar's too weak. Since the Fed is in the business of trying to support the dollar, I translate the Fed's comments as meaning that the dollar will be okay for a little while; but sooner or later, the dollar is going to be killed again. This may be a simple way of looking at the markets; but it's also a good example of intermarket analysis. You have to keep a close eye on the circle of money flow both within the United States and internationally.

When I investigate individual stocks, I focus in on volatility skews. As previously discussed, volatility measures the speed of change in the price of a market. High volatility leads to inflated stock prices. A volatility skew exists when different options with the same expiration and the same underlying instrument have substantially different implied volatilities. Higher implied volatility leads to inflated option premiums. Don't let the imposing nature of volatility intimidate you. Recognizing volatility skews is a viable method of finding markets with profitable option premium interrelationships. If a stock's options have lower strikes with high implied volatility, a reverse volatility skew exists. This is recognizable when lower strike options are priced higher in comparison to the premiums of higher strikes. In these kinds of markets you should aim to buy the higher strike options and sell the lower strikes. This works in your favor when looking for profit-making price quotes for call ratio backspreads or ratio put spreads. A forward volatility skew exists when higher strikes have high implied volatilities and lower strikes are less expensive in comparison. Markets with forward volatility skews are ripe for placing a put ratio backspread or a ratio call spread, since you want to sell the higher priced strikes and buy the lower priced strikes.

The method of locating volatility skews is easier than ever. Although there are several option analysis software programs that let traders calculate implied volatilities, you can just as easily access implied volatility data at various financial web sites. Monitor the implied volatility of options with the same expiration date but differing strikes with an eye for abnormalities.

chapter 8

sideways spread strategies

trading sideways markets

Many stocks do not trend up or down but move sideways between two prices for a few months or even years. The minimum time frame I prefer to use is two months, although a longer time frame can mean a more stable sideways market. Although sideways markets may not be the most appropriate markets for aggressive buy-and-hold investors, there are limited risk options strategies that take advantage of the price consistency rangebound markets offer.

---

sideways markets
stable markets that tend to trade in a range, fluctuating between specific support (low) and resistance (high) levels. Resistance is a historical price level of a market at which rising prices have a hard time breaking through to the upside. Support is a historical price level at which falling prices generally stop falling and either move sideways or reverse direction.

The two price caps of a sideways market are commonly referred to as support and resistance. For example, if every time IBM declines to $100 per share, the market rebounds, this would establish the support level. If IBM trades up in price to reach $130 and then sells off again, this would establish the resistance level. These two levels can then be used to create an effective options strategy that enables traders to collect time premium.

The primary determinants of an option's premium are intrinsic value, time value, and volatility. Time value is lost due to the theta decay of the option. Options lose the most time value in the last 30 days of the life of the option. The closer the expiration date comes, the faster the theta decay. Therefore, on the last day there will be the most loss of value due to time. Options lose value over time if markets do not move. This basic option characteristic can be used to create strategies that work in markets that are moving sideways.

Charts are very helpful when looking for nontrending markets. You can scan daily price and volume charts and basically just eyeball them for the support and resistance levels. If I spot a market that looks like it is going sideways, I take a ruler and see if I can draw support and resistance lines. Once this is accomplished, I look for the most effective option strategy to take advantage of the circumstances of the chosen market. Let's take a look at some of my favorite sideways strategies.

long butterfly

One of the most popular option strategies, the butterfly spread is actually a combination of a bull and a bear credit spread. There are two basic long butterfly scenarios: One uses calls and the other uses puts. Both consist of three different strikes—the body and the two wings. The body contains an option with the strike price between the support and resistance levels. The wings are composed of options with the strike prices at both ends of the trading range.

---

long butterfly strategy
a complex option strategy where two identical options are sold or bought together with the purchase (sale) of one option with an immediately higher strike, and one option with an immediately lower strike. All options must be the same type, have the same underlying asset, and have the same expiration date.

To create a long butterfly, you go long the wings and go short the body (the middle strike options) by purchasing as many option contracts as you sell. The trick is to sell more value in the body than in the wings. This trade offers a limited profit in a sideways-moving market when the underlying stock closes in between the upside and downside breakevens.

Table 8.1 shows some fundamental measurements for Hewlett-Packard Company (HWP). Looking at the prices in Table 8.2, let's create a long butterfly spread using options with 60 days or less so that the short options have a better chance of expiring worthless. However, the January prices may not create enough of a profit to make the trade worthwhile, so let's go long 1 February HWP 55 Call @ 11, short 2 February HWP 65 Calls @ $4^3/_8$, and long 1 February HWP 75 Call @ 1. The maximum risk of a long butterfly spread is the net debit paid for the trade. In this example, the net debit is $325 $\{[(11 + 1) - (2 \times 4^3/_8)] \times 100 = \$325\}$. (Table 8.3.) The maximum profit potential of the trade is calculated by taking the difference in the strike prices of the middle and lower strikes times the number of lower strike options times the value per point, minus the net debit paid. The maximum reward for this example is $675 $\{[(65 - 55) \times (1 \times 100)] - \$325 = \$675\}$. The downside breakeven for the trade is calculated by adding the lowest strike price to the net debit of the trade divided by the number of lowest strike options times 100, or $58^1/_4$ $\{55 + [325 / (1 \times 100)] = 58^1/_4\}$. The upside breakeven is calculated by taking the highest strike price minus the net debit divided by the number of highest strike contracts times 100, or $71^3/_4$ $\{75 - [325 / (1 \times 100)] = 71^3/_4\}$. Therefore, the breakeven range for this trade is between $58^1/_4$ and $71^3/_4$. The risk profile for this trade is shown in Figure 8.1.

Although you can leg out of the trade, it is important to monitor the market as a spread every day until the prices enable you to exit the trade with a good profit. Table 8.4 shows the results of the trade.

---

table 8.1   hewlett-packard company fundamentals

Hewlett-Packard Company (HPW)

Last price	$64^1/_8$
Volume	2,073,500
52-week range	$47^1/_{16}$ to $82^3/_8$
P/E ratio	22.37

source: www.bigcharts.com 12/10/98

---

table 8.2   HWP call option premiums

Price of HWP = $64^{1}/_{8}$ (12/10/98)

Call Strike Price	January	February
45	20	$22^{7}/_{8}$
50	$15^{1}/_{2}$	$16^{1}/_{8}$
55	$10^{1}/_{2}$	11
60	$5^{7}/_{8}$	$8^{1}/_{4}$
65	3	$4^{3}/_{8}$
70	$1^{1}/_{16}$	$2^{1}/_{4}$
75	$^{7}/_{16}$	1

---

table 8.3   long butterfly trade calculations

Long Butterfly Using Hewlett-Packard Company @ $64^{1}/_{8}$

Maximum Risk = Net debit	$325
Maximum Reward = (# of lower strike options) × (strike difference × 100) – net debit	$675
Downside Breakeven = Lowest strike price + [net debit / (# of lowest strike options × 100)]	$58^{1}/_{4}$
Upside Breakeven = Highest strike price – [net debit / (# of highest strike options × 100)]	$71^{3}/_{4}$
Risk to Reward Ratio = Reward / risk	208%

After fifteen days, Hewlett-Packard falls to $63^{1}/_{2}$. The 55 call is still priced at 11, the 65 call has dropped to $2^{1}/_{2}$ and the 75 call increased to $1^{1}/_{8}$. The trade has profited $387.50 {[(11 × 1) – (2 × 2^{1}/_{2}) + (1 × 1^{1}/_{8})] × 100 – 325 = $387.50}—a 119% return on investment. Although you may be tempted to stay in the trade longer to see if a bigger profit can be made, I recommend taking a profit once you've made 100% back on your investment. It's a judgment call at best, and these kinds of decisions get easier as you gather experience in the markets.

The long butterfly trade is a very popular strategy that captures time premium as the market trades back and forth between the wings. Since the premise for this trade is to capture time premium, it's best to use this strategy in the optimal time decay zone, which is the last 30 days of the life of the option. However, if you find a market that has been going sideways for a long time, the options premium you receive may be very low due to a decreased volatility premium

figure 8.1   long butterfly spread (long 1 February HWP 55 call @ 11, short 2 February HWP 65 calls @ 4³/₈, long 1 February HWP 75 call @ 1)

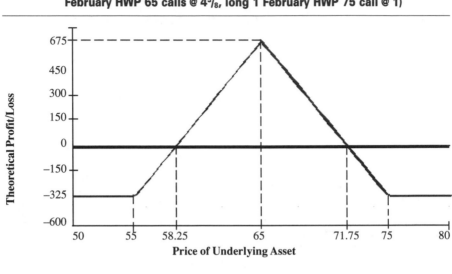

table 8.4   long butterfly results

Long Butterfly: Long 1 February HWP 55 Call @ 11,
Short 2 February HWP 65 Calls @ 4³/₈, Long 1 February HWP 75 Call @ 1

Closing Price of HWP Stock	Price of 55 Call	Price of 65 Call	Price of 75 Call	Days in Trade	Profit/ Loss	Return on Investment
63¹/₂	11	2¹/₂	1¹/₈	15	$387.50	119%

attached to the options. Therefore, when you sell short the body of the butterfly you will receive less of a premium for time than in a market that has higher volatility. You will likely have to go out at least another 30 days in the expiration cycle to make the trade reasonably profitable.

rule of thumb
look for sideways-moving markets with option prices that make the limited profit of this strategy worthwhile.

long condor

The long condor is one of my favorite nontrending market strategies. It can be thought of as a butterfly spread with an extra short strike price or a combination of a bull and bear (all call or all put) spread. In a long condor, you need to go short the two inner option strikes that make up the body of the condor and buy the wings. You are shorting the middle options to collect time premium as the underlying stock continues to trade in between the wings. This strategy usually creates a net debit, which is also the maximum risk.

---

long condor strategy
the sale or purchase of two options with consecutive exercise prices, together with the sale or purchase of one option with an immediately lower exercise price and one option with an immediately higher exercise price. All options must be the same type and have the same underlying asset and the same expiration date.

This strategy should make money with the passage of time as long as the price of the underlying stock stays between the wings. Using the prices in Table 8.2, let's create a long condor by going long 1 February HWP 55 Call @ 11, short 1 February HWP 60 Call @ $8^1/_4$, short 1 February HWP 65 Call @ $4^3/_8$, and long 1 February HWP 70 Call @ $2^1/_4$. The maximum risk for the trade is equal to the net debit, or \$62.50 $[(11 + 2^1/_4) − (8^1/_4 + 4^3/_8) \times 100 = \$62.50]$. (Table 8.5.) The maximum reward is equal to the number of lowest options times the difference in the strike price of the lower short option and the lower long option, multiplied by the value for each point less the net debit paid (or plus the net credit taken, if any). In this case, the maximum reward is \$437.50 $\{[1 \times (60 − 55) \times 100] − 62.50 = \$437.50\}$. The upside breakeven is equal to the highest strike price minus the net debit divided by the number of highest strike options multiplied by 100. In this example, the upside breakeven is $69^3/_8$ $[70 − (62.50 / 1 \times 100) = 69^3/_8]$. The downside breakeven is equal to the lowest strike price plus the net debit divided by the number of lowest strike options times 100. In this example, the downside breakeven is equal to $55^5/_8$ $[55 + (62.50 / 1 \times 100) = 55^5/_8]$. The profit range is therefore between $55^5/_8$ and $69^3/_8$. The risk profile of this example is shown in Figure 8.2.

To exit a condor, you have to sell the long options and buy back the short options. Since timing is critical, a condor must be monitored daily so that you can strike while the iron is hot. This can be accomplished by

table 8.5 **long condor trade calculations**

Long Condor Using Hewlett-Packard @ $64^1/_8$

Maximum Risk = Net debit	$62.50
Maximum Reward = [(# of lowest strike contracts × difference in strikes) × 100] – net debit	$437.50
Downside Breakeven = Lowest strike price + [net debit / (# of lowest strike options × 100)]	$55^5/_8$
Upside Breakeven = Highest strike price – [net debit / (# of highest strike options × 100)]	$69^3/_8$
Risk to Reward Ratio = Reward / risk	700%

figure 8.2 **long condor (long 1 February HWP 55 call @ 11, short 1 February HWP 60 call @ $8^1/_4$, short 1 February HWP 65 call @ $4^3/_8$, long 1 February HWP 70 call @ $2^1/_4$)**

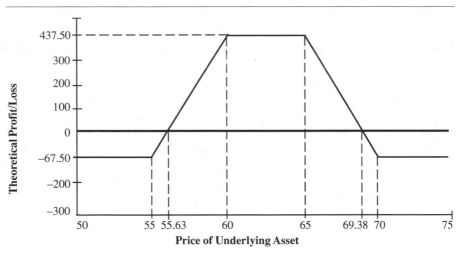

watching real-time prices throughout the day or with end-of-day prices for a morning placement. After 22 days, HWP bounces back to $68^5/_{16}$. The 55 call's premium is $16^3/_8$, the 60 call increases to $10^1/_8$, the 65 call is now $6^1/_8$, and the 70 call is $4^1/_2$. This creates a $400 profit $\{[(16^3/_8 + 4^1/_2) – (10^1/_8 + 6^1/_8) \times 100] – \$62.50 = \$400\}$—a 640% return on investment (Table 8.6). In addition, it can be interesting to leg out of this trade to cover the net debit and wait to see if the other half of the trade makes a free profit. This is easily accomplished because a condor is the combination of a bull call spread and a bear call spread. You can simply close one and wait to see what happens to the other.

table 8.6 long condor results

Long 1 February HWP 55 Call @ 11, Short 1 February HWP 60 Call @ $8^1/_4$,
Short 1 February HWP 65 Call @ $4^3/_8$, Long 1 February HWP 70 Call @ $2^1/_4$

Closing Price of HWP Stock	Price of 55 Call	Price of 60 Call	Price of 65 Call	Price of 70 Call	Days in Trade	Profit/ Loss	Return on Investment
$68^5/_{16}$	$16^3/_8$	$10^1/_8$	$6^1/_8$	$4^1/_2$	22	$400	640%

A long condor trade can use strikes that are further apart as long as you sell the body and buy the wings. You can also use puts instead of calls. In most cases, the option premiums will determine the optimal trade to place. Make sure you have enough time premium to make the trade worthwhile.

---

rule of thumb
look for a market that has been trading in a range for at least three months with option premiums that make the limited nature of the strategy worthwhile.

---

long iron butterfly

The long iron butterfly spread is the third strategy that can be used in a sideways market. It combines two more basic option strategies: the bear call spread (short lower call and long higher call) and the bull put spread (long lower put and short higher put). It is similar to a long condor, but has a particular twist. This shift is illustrated in Table 8.7. As you can see, the long iron butterfly is created by using a combination of calls and puts instead of all calls or all puts.

---

long Iron butterfly strategy
an options strategy that combines two more basic option strategies: the bear call spread (short lower call and long higher call) and the bull put spread (long lower put and short higher put). All options must have the same underlying asset and the same expiration.

---

table 8.7   long iron butterfly strategy shift

	Condor	Iron Butterfly	
Strike Price	Calls	Calls	Puts
135	Buy 1	Buy 1	
125	Short 1	Short 1	
115	Short 1		Short 1
105	Buy 1		Buy 1

table 8.8   HWP call and put option premiums

Price of HWP = $64^1/_8$ (12/10/98)

	Calls		Puts	
Strike Price	January	February	January	February
45	20	$22^7/_8$	$^1/_{16}$	$^1/_8$
50	$15^1/_2$	$16^1/_8$	$^1/_8$	$^7/_{16}$
55	$10^1/_2$	11	$^3/_8$	$^{15}/_{16}$
60	$5^7/_8$	$8^1/_4$	$1^5/_{16}$	$2^3/_{16}$
65	3	$4^3/_8$	$3^1/_4$	$3^3/_4$
70	$1^1/_{16}$	$2^1/_4$	7	6
75	$^7/_{16}$	1	$11^1/_8$	12

Let's create a long iron butterfly using the prices in Table 8.8 for Hewlett-Packard, by going long 1 February HWP 45 Put @ $^1/_8$, short 1 February HWP 55 Put @ $^{15}/_{16}$, short 1 February HWP 65 Call @ $4^3/_8$, and long 1 February HWP 75 Call @ 1. The maximum reward is equal to the net credit of the spread. In this example, the maximum reward is $418.75 {[($^{15}/_{16}$ + $4^3/_8$) − ($^1/_8$ + 1)] × 100 = $418.75}. (Table 8.9.) The maximum risk is equal to the number of lowest strike options times the difference between the long and short strike prices times the value per point, minus the net credit received. In this case, the maximum risk is $581.25 {[1 × (55 − 45) × 100] − 418.75 = $581.25}. The upside breakeven is equal to the highest short strike plus the net credit divided by the number of highest strike options times 100. In this example, the upside breakeven is $69^3/_{16}$ [65 + (418.75 / 1 × 100) = $69^3/_{16}$]. The downside breakeven is equal to the lowest short strike minus the net credit di-

table 8.9 long iron butterfly trade calculations

Long Iron Butterfly Using Hewlett-Packard Company @ 64$^1/_8$

Maximum Risk = [(# of lowest strike options × the difference in strikes) × 100] – net credit	$581.25
Maximum Reward = Net credit	$418.75
Downside Breakeven = Lowest short strike – (net credit / # of lowest strike options × 100)	50$^{13}/_{16}$
Upside Breakeven = Highest short strike + (net credit / # of highest strike options × 100)	69$^3/_{16}$
Risk to Reward Ratio = Reward / risk	72%

figure 8.3   long iron butterfly (long 1 February HWP 45 put @ $^1/_8$, short 1 February HWP 55 put @ $^{15}/_{16}$, short 1 February HWP 65 call @ 4$^3/_8$, long 1 February HWP 75 call @ 1)

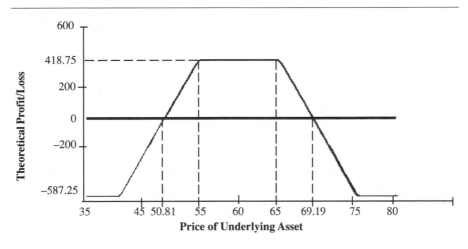

vided by the number of lowest strike options times 100. In this example, the downside breakeven is 50$^{13}/_{16}$ [55 – (418.75 / 1 × 100) = 50$^{13}/_{16}$]. Therefore, the profit range for this trade is between 50$^{13}/_{16}$ and 69$^3/_{16}$. The risk graph for this trade is shown in Figure 8.3.

To exit this trade, you need to monitor the underlying market daily. In the best of all possible scenarios, the underlying stock continues to move sideways between the strikes of the short options so that neither one is exercised. In this example, HWP generally moves sideways to 60$^1/_4$ at expiration, leaving the short options to expire worthless. This means that we get to keep the net credit of $418.75 (Table 8.10).

table 8.10   long iron butterfly results

Long 1 February HWP 45 Put @ $^1/_8$,
Short 1 February HWP 55 Put @ $^{15}/_{16}$, Short 1 February HWP 65 Call @ $4^3/_8$,
Long 1 February HWP 75 Call @ 1

Closing Price of HWP Stock at Expiration	Price of 45 Put	Price of 55 Put	Price of 65 Call	Price of 75 Call	Days in Trade	Profit/ Loss
$60^1/_4$	0	0	0	0	40	$418.75

It's truly amazing how each strategy's profit margin fluctuates slightly using primarily the same premiums. As a rule, I look for the trade with the best reward to risk ratio and the least risk. In general, if my calculations show an increased reward to risk ratio, I prefer to place an iron butterfly instead of a condor. This often happens when the puts and calls have different implied volatilities. But finding the right markets for these strategies is quite difficult if you are searching manually. This is where options trading software really comes in handy.

For example, in OptionStation you can customize the filter to search for only bullish, limited-risk butterfly trades. In seconds you'll have your choice of a variety of trades as well as each trade's maximum risk, maximum reward, and theoretical profit and loss. If you find one you like, you can then set up the trade's risk profile, calculate the breakevens, and even run a probability check to ascertain the trade's probability of ending up in-the-money. These kinds of tools are invaluable as you cascade from market to market looking for trading opportunities. Perhaps this is the real crux of the business; trading online increases your capacity to sift through all the numbers looking for that winning opportunity. When you unleash the power of your computer to hunt down optimal opportunities for making money, you have the competitive edge necessary to make money in the markets.

rule of thumb
look for a sideways market and then try out a variety of put and call premiums until an optimal trade is located

table 8.11 comparisons of sideways spread results

Comparison of Trade Results

Trade	Maximum Risk	Maximum Gain	Break-evens	Days in Trade	Profit Exit	Return on Investment
Long butterfly	−$325	$675	$58^1/_4$ and $78^3/_4$	15	$387.50	119%
Long condor	−$62.50	$437.50	$55^5/_8$ and $70^3/_8$	22	$400	640%
Long iron butterfly	−$581.25	$418.75	$50^{13}/_{16}$ and $69^3/_{16}$	40	$418.75	Depends on margin

conclusion

The examples in this chapter show three very similar strategies that make money by capturing time premium. Table 8.11 details the results of each trade so that you can easily compare them. If I stumble on a really stable market, the numbers will tell me which strategy to apply. But to keep it simple, I usually start by running the numbers on a butterfly strategy; if the numbers look good, I check out the difference when the spread is expanded into a condor. If this looks unusually promising, I'll do the calculations for an iron butterfly and see which has the optimal numbers.

Butterflies and backspreads are techniques that professional floor traders use all the time to hedge their risk. They are successful strategies to use because the risks are not as great as they might appear to be. These spreads are always hedging themselves one way or the other and do not require adjustments. Sometimes, the hardest part of trading is to believe that you have a good trade in your hands and simply leave those trades alone.

chapter 9

cybervesting from a to z

streamlining your approach

It's time to pull everything together. This chapter is designed to walk you step-by-step through a series of online sites in preparation for looking for a promising market. We will not be surfing from web site to web site. Instead, I intend to concentrate on a few select sites that have the most useful information available. If I am looking for information on the web, it had better be easy to obtain. So let's get started on our final cybertour into the online trading matrix.

First things first. . . . The following step-by-step process has been designed to help you to pick profitable trades, regardless of whether the markets are bullish, bearish, or sideways-moving. Each step will be followed by a breakdown of how it can best be used. These steps are as follows:

1. Charting—looking at chart patterns.
2. News—looking at the fundamental picture.
3. Strategies—developing an options strategy.
4. Tracking—tracking open positions.

charting

Many people who start trading options have a dart-throwing mentality for picking trades. I'm constantly amazed by the number of people who trade options without any knowledge of the underlying asset they are trading options against. In my system of finding profitable trades, I don't even look at the options until step 3. I prefer to start by looking at charts to determine whether a stock is in an uptrend, in a downtrend, or moving sideways.

As discussed in Chapter 1, there are a wide variety of charts that can be analyzed to assess a stock's movement. Before we start looking at trends, let's do a short review of charting basics. A chart is a series of data and numbers that consist of price (or volume) and time. Charts enable investors to visually survey a stock's price movement and volume activity in order to observe patterns and trends that aid in forecasting future price movement. There is an abundance of charting techniques, and even more technical analysis methods that can be used to analyze price fluctuations.

Charts for individual stocks are as unique as fingerprints. However, bar charts do have the following four things in common: opening price, high for the day (or hour, week, etc.), low for the day (hour, week, etc.), and closing price (Figure 9.1). The four parts of a simple bar chart show the price change of a stock over a specific time period. As time passes, other bars are created that start to form the

figure 9.1 bar chart basics

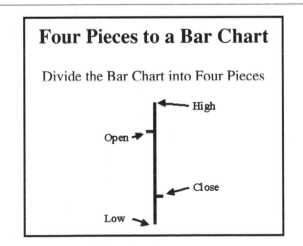

chart pattern. Patterns can be up, down, sideways, or a combination of one or more. Once you put enough of the bars together, you have the makings of a historical chart.

Bar series can range from minutes to months. It all depends on the time interval you choose. If you're a day trader, then looking at monthly bar charts is waste of time. Looking at five-minute bar charts will better suit you. As an options trader, I spend most of my time reviewing daily bar charts. There is an abundance of sites that offer charting services, but my two favorites are eSignal (www.esignal .com) and BigCharts.com (www.bigcharts.com). eSignal is one of the best subscription real-time quotes services available. The eSignal system offers nine kinds of charts and tables and two ways to create them. You can position the pointer on a stock symbol in a portfolio or quote window and then right click your way to "Chart Window" or go to "File," click "New," and then click "Chart Window." Entering a stock symbol causes the default to present an interval chart of that day's prices. If you want to see a different kind of chart, click the box next to the symbol box and a pull-down list of the following options is available:

---

day trader
an active trader who limits his or her trading to intraday positions by entering and holding positions from a few minutes to hours and exiting or offsetting these positions by the end of the day.

- *Interval charts* display the price range of a stock in a time frame of your choice as well as a selection of 20 technical analysis methods.

- *Tick charts* feature incremental price and volume movement over a time span of your choice that enables you to watch price changes as they happen.

- *Interval Tabular* is a table of the price range of a stock over the time span of your choice.

- *Time & Sales* is a table that shows the time, exchanges, price, and number of shares of each trade of stock. Pay attention to the volume that's coming in at specific prices. For example, if a stock is moving down very quickly and all of a sudden it starts to bounce back up and the price increase is accompanied by heavy volume, that price may indicate a strong support level. The next time it hits that price may indicate a very good buying opportunity.

- *Price/Volume* is a bar graph that shows the trade volume at different prices each day.
- *Time/Volume* is a bar graph that shows the trade volume at the time interval of your choice.
- *Daily Chart* is a visual graph of the historical price movement of a stock using a variety of analytical tools and the time frame of your choice.
- *Daily Tabular* is a table that displays the price movement over the time frame of your choice.
- *Point & Figure* is a graph that reveals a stock's significant upward and downward moves using closing prices through a pattern of *X*s and *O*s.

If you're not ready to take on a real-time subscription service, surf on over to BigCharts.com, an excellent fundamental and technical analysis site that's free. Let's explore this site by typing in "DELL" at the home page and then clicking on "Quick Chart." Within a few seconds, a new screen appears with an abundance of information (Figure 9.2). At the top of the screen, you'll find a variety of data, including access to news, analyst estimates, and broker research. Just below the price information, you'll find a snapshot view of Dell's current position, including the last price, change, P/E ratio, and 52-week range. Figure 9.2 shows a historical daily bar chart on Dell that consists of one year's opens, highs, lows, and closes. Below this chart lies a one-year daily volume chart for Dell Computer. Looking at Dell's price chart, can you tell whether Dell is in an uptrend, in a downtrend, or moving sideways? The following indicators can be used to interpret a stock's trend (if any) from looking at a chart.

52-week highs

The 52-week range can be found in the second line of information in the bar above the chart. Stocks that have recently experienced a 52-week high are considered momentum bull stocks. This means that there are very few sellers when compared to the buyers in the marketplace. Any stock that is at or near a 52-week high has a greater chance of continuing in an uptrend in the belief that strength leads to more strength. As Bill O'Neil, the editor of *Investor's Business Daily*, says, "I don't buy low and sell high. I buy high and sell higher."

52-week highs
this figure tells you the highest price a stock has reached over the past year.

figure 9.2   **interactive chart of dell computer with moving average**

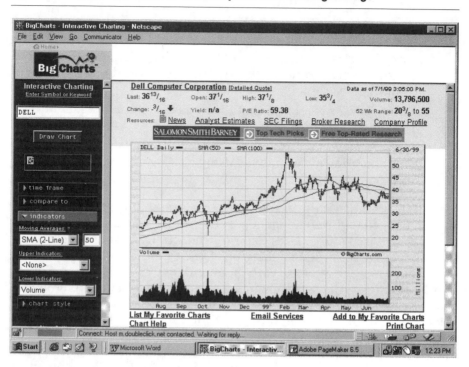

source: www.bigcharts.com. reprinted with permission.

simple moving average (SMA)

A moving average is one of the best technical analysis tools out there. Most institutional traders and newspapers use both a 50-day and a 200-day moving average and you should, too, since it will give you an idea as to what the people with the real money are going to do. A really strong stock will try to stay above its 50-day moving average. But if it breaks below its 50-day moving average, it had better bounce off its 200-day moving average. This is often accompanied by a large increase in volume (aka a volume spike) that drives the price back up to its 50-day moving average. If a stock closes below this number, it tells me that there is a possible trend change and to avoid this market due to uncertainty in the trend. Bearish stocks react in the opposite way. When a stock is breaking down it may fall to its 50-day average, encounter a volume spike, and then try to climb back up to its 200-day moving average. If it can't break through, it is probably headed back down to its 50-day moving average. To create a moving average, simply click on "Interactive Chart" to the right of the stock symbol box and then click on the "Indicators" button on the left-hand side of the screen. Beneath "Moving Averages," scroll down to "SMA (2-line)," type in "50 and 200" in the space next to it, and click "Draw Chart."

---

moving averages
a mathematical procedure employed by adding together a stock's closing prices (usually 50 and 200 days) and then dividing that number by the number of days. The result is noted on a chart. The next day the same calculations are performed with the new result being connected (using a solid or dotted line) to yesterday's, and so forth.

---

volume as an indicator

Volume can be used to determine setbacks and retracements before a trend continues to move. The volume part of the chart is located at the bottom of the screen beneath the price chart. Figure 9.2 shows some excellent volume indicators for Dell. Notice the volume spikes that occurred during the months of September and October 1998. On those days, volume increased to twice that of its average daily volume and the price of Dell had a big move down in price. However, by consulting the day's closing price on the day of extra volume, you'll find that buyers come rushing in before the close and pushed the price off the low. This is an excellent bullish sign, and when coupled with the 200-day moving average, can be a useful indicator when timing bullish trade entries. One more note on volume: Don't try to use volume spikes with short-term, intraday price bars. This can spell disaster because most of the volume in a stock usually comes in the first and last trading hours of the day.

---

volume spike
an extreme rise in a market's volume—the number of shares bought and sold—often resulting in a big price movement in either direction.

---

the KISS principle: keep it simple, stupid

Although a wide variety of additional indicators can be applied to any one chart, using too many crowds the chart with too much data and leads to trading indecision. There are probably more than 300 indicators available. If you applied all of them to one chart, half would be telling you that the chart is bullish, and the other half would be telling you that the chart is bearish. You can even create your own custom indicators. But the point I am trying to make here is that simple indicators are sometimes best.

So what am I looking for in an uptrend? I am looking for a strong stock, preferably one that has made a 52-week high recently. I am also looking for a pullback off the highs, but not below a 200-day moving average. To time my entry, I look for a volume spike which lets me know that the majority of the selling in that stock has been done, and it's time to move back up. I need at least two of these criteria to be met before continuing to the next step: news.

news

News plays a quintessential role in the business of trading. The effect of news is constantly reflected in the price of a stock. For instance, if you were online and saw that a stock you were tracking had a change of +10 points on the day, there is probably some news behind why that stock moved up so much. News is categorized into two different types: breaking news and scheduled news.

breaking news

Spontaneous news that comes with little or no warning to the public is breaking news. Examples of breaking news include tragedies, violent weather, pre-earnings announcements, the death of world leaders, and accounting irregularities. Most of these newsworthy events have very little correlation to one another, but they all contribute to market movement. Since breaking news comes as a surprise, we cannot use it to anticipate price movement. But once an event occurs, we can ride the trend that the news inspires.

---

breaking news
spontaneous news regarding sudden changes including management shake-ups, mergers and takeovers, or international crises.

If you're looking for the quintessential market news site, check out CBS MarketWatch (www.cbsmarketwatch.com). Designed to keep traders and investors in-the-know, this site features top-notch journalists, insightful commentary, and superior news reporting. From its home page—also referred to as the "Front Page"—click on "News Headlines" to get a list of breaking news articles, or "NewsWatch" for the latest buzz from the markets. In the left-hand column, click on "Columns" and you'll find a multitude of articles that will keep you abreast of market happenings. I'm especially fond of two regular features: Brenon Daly's "OptionWatch" and Thom Calandra's "StockWatch." There's even a column called "Breaking News" that highlights a controversial market news story and offers an online discussion group on the day's subject. As an online trader, I visit CBS MarketWatch every day—and so do millions of others. It gives me the straight scoop without any hype.

Another one of the best sites to monitor breaking news can be found at www.yahoo.com. Figure 9.3 shows Yahoo!'s home page, which features a variety of categories and special announcements. I usually click on "News & Media" to access the up-to-the-minute headlines and then move on to the day's business news by clicking on "Business & Economy." There are a multitude of online news sites— from CBS MarketWatch to Reuters. I just happen to enjoy Yahoo!'s

figure 9.3 yahoo! home page

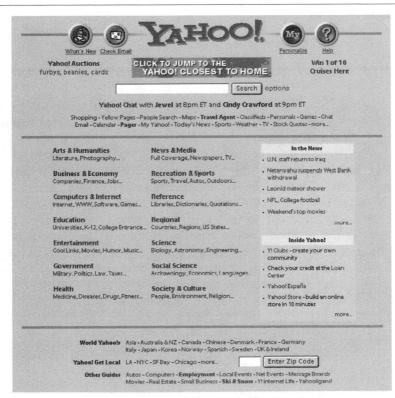

source: www.yahoo.com. reprinted with permission.

format, and judging from Yahoo!'s popularity, so do millions of other Internet users.

scheduled news

Scheduled news can be anticipated and is easily accessible. Examples include government reports, company reports, product announcements, and weather reports (for you cyclical traders). Let's return to Yahoo! and click on "Business & Economy" and then click on "Y! Finance" in the right-hand sidebar. A news screen appears with a variety of topics at the top. Scroll down the page and you'll find a list of articles in the "Latest Market News" section (Figure 9.4). To get information about a specific stock, click on "U.S. Markets" next to the "Financial News" category; then type in the stock's symbol and click "Search." A list of specific stories about that stock will appear. Not all stories will have your stock in the headline, but the company is mentioned somewhere in the article, which is why it is displayed.

---

scheduled news
news that can be anticipated for release including earnings reports, stock splits, and government reports.

Scheduled news is important because it can help you determine the right time to get into or out of a market. Learning to prioritize information is an important part of a trader's training since some facts are more useful than others are. Knowing how a company's last quarter's numbers look may be important, but not as crucial as knowing when an earnings report will be released. Many traders buy options just before earnings reports are released, hoping to get in prior to a big breakout.

Perhaps the biggest benefit you can derive from receiving scheduled news is the ability to enter, adjust, or exit a trade immediately before a big report is announced. Keeping track of stocks that are on your watch list or that you are trading is easier than ever before. Various financial web sites will e-mail you scheduled and breaking news on the stocks of your choice. Check out CBS MarketWatch (www.cbsmarket watch.com) or INO (www.ino.com) to avail yourself of this kind of free service. Once you have what you need, it's on to Step 3.

strategies

Finding the right strategy depends on how well you've done your homework using steps 1 and 2. The right options strategy is determined by

figure 9.4   latest news from yahoo!

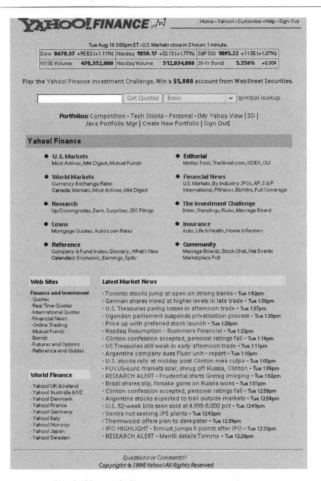

whether you're bullish, bearish, or neutral on a specific stock. Having a good base of options knowledge will help you here. If you're a novice to options trading, I suggest a visit to the Optionetics web site—www.optionetics.com—where you can find a wealth of information designed specifically to help options traders locate the tools needed to compete in the marketplace (Figure 9.5). If you are new to options trading, click on "Optionetics 101" and you'll find an abundance of educational information, as well as tests and answers, too. Just click on the topic you wish to see more information on and learn as you go.

To determine the right options strategy to use in a particular market, surf over to OptionsAnalysis.com (www.optionsanalysis.com), a

figure 9.5 optionetics home page

source: optionetics.com. reprinted with permission.

site I helped to develop (Figure 9.6). Just key in a stock symbol and click on "List." Once the description appears, you can click on it to review a stock's option premiums. This site lists all the options as well as the LEAPS (Long-term Equity AnticiPation Securities) that a stock has available. For traders with a traditional buy-and-hold orientation, options often carry with them the stigma of being short-term trading tools with tax consequences. LEAPS, by the very nature of their long-term expiration dates, help to overcome this stigma by giving traders significantly more time to be right about market movement.

LEAPS®
Long-term Equity AnticiPation Securities are long-term stock or index options with up to three years until expiration.

Continuing with our previous example, let's key in "DELL." The Options Value screen appears displaying a variety of at-the-money op-

figure 9.6   optionsanalysis.com home page

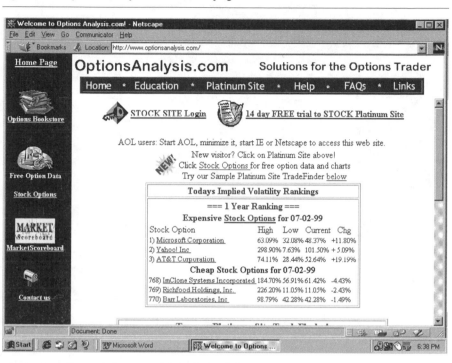

source: www.optionsanalysis.com. reprinted with permission.

tions (Figure 9.7). Beneath each option you'll find an assortment of option values. The first number is the price of the option. Note that the
January 2000 Dell 45 had a last price of $12^5/_8$ or $1,262.50. Mcall is the
price the option model thinks the option should be trading at (aka the
theoretical price). The Mcall value often differs from the actual price
for a variety of reasons—maybe the option hasn't traded for some
time or demand for a certain strike price is extremely high.

Mcall
an option value generated by a mathematical options pricing model
to determine what an option is really worth.

The next thing I look at is the option's historical premium levels,
otherwise called implied volatility. OptionsAnalysis.com has this taken
care of at the bottom of the quotes pages. I simply scroll down to the
bottom and locate the six-month and two-year implied volatility histo-

figure 9.7   options value screen

source: www.optionsanalysis.com. reprinted with permission.

ries chart (Figure 9.8). I am looking for an option's prices to be relatively cheap or expensive compared to its range. This is accomplished by looking at the last point of the graph (current implied volatility) and determining where it is versus the range (rest of the graph). The example in Figure 9.8 shows Dell with current implied volatility at just over 58. Its six-month range is between 50 and 90. This tells me that Dell options at this time are relatively cheap within a six-month time frame.

---

implied volatility
volatility computed using the actual market price of an option and a pricing model (Black-Scholes). For example, if the market price of an option rises without a change in the price of the underlying stock, implied volatility will have risen.

The information so far indicates that Dell is in an uptrend. Since the options appear to be relatively cheap, it's time to look for the right strategy. One of the great things about online research is that it appeals to the lazy and workaholic alike. Let's take a lazy approach to finding a good trade using Dell. Simply key in "DELL" in the stock symbol box,

figure 9.8   implied volatility chart

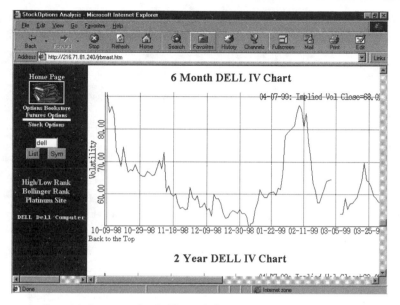

source: www.optionsanalysis.com. reprinted with permission.

and then move to the first row below it to initiate a quick search. Thinking Dell is going to move up big in the next 30 days, I program the stock screener to search for trades with a risk no higher than $1,000 and rank them in order by the highest probability of profit. Play around with this feature until you become familiar with the various screening criteria. After a while, you'll be able to tailor the screening parameters to fit anything you wish. When everything is set, click on the "Search" button to the left. The search immediately commences and Figure 9.9 shows the results, including the following columns of information:

- **Rk:** The rank of the given trade (a number from 1 to 50). A maximum of 50 trades can be displayed.
- **St:** The stock for this trade. The web site uses stock symbols here to save space.
- **OpMnth:** The expiration month of the options in the trade.
- **Strategy:** The kind of options strategy employed.
- **Composed of:** The web site is using a shorthand notation here to convey all the specific trade information.
- **Stkprc:** The underlying stock price. For calendar spreads, it's the near month.

figure 9.9 screening results

Rk	Stk	OpMnth	Strategy	Composed of	Stkprc	Prjct'd Price	Cost	Vega	Theta	Gamma	Delta	MaxProfit	MaxRisk	
1	DELL	MAY99	Call Vert (Debit) Spread	1xMAY45C@5 1/4 -1xMAY50C@2 15/16	46 7/16	63 1/2 in 30 days	$ 231.00	$ -0.14	$ 0.13	-0.0008	0.1792	$ 269.00	$ -231.00	9
2	DELL	MAY99	Put Vert (Credit) Spread	1xMAY45P@3 1/2 -1xMAY50P@5 7/8	46 7/16	63 1/2 in 30 days	$ -238.00	$ -0.13	$ 0.06	-0.0008	0.1821	$ 238.00	$ -262.00	9
3	DELL	MAY99	Call Vert (Debit) Spread	1xMAY45C@5 1/4 -1xMAY55C@1 1/2	46 7/16	63 1/2 in 30 days	$ 375.00	$ 0.78	$ -0.55	0.0045	0.3303	$ 625.00	$ -375.00	9
4	DELL	MAY99	Put Vert (Credit) Spread	1xMAY45P@3 1/2 -1xMAY55P@9 1/2	46 7/16	63 1/2 in 30 days	$ -600.00	$ 0.83	$ -0.70	0.0049	0.3351	$ 600.00	$ -400.00	9
5	DELL	MAY99	Buy Call	1xMAY45C@5 1/4	46 7/16	63 1/2 in 30	$ 525.00	$ 6.15	$ -4.58	0.0356	0.6057	Unlimited	$ -525.00	9

source: www.optionsanalysis.com. reprinted with permission.

- **Prjctd Price:** Where the underlying stock has to get to for the trade to start making a profit.
- **Cost:** The combined trade cost in dollars. A negative means a credit to your account.
- **Option Greeks:** Vega, theta, gamma, and delta are the "Greeks" of the trade.
- **Maximum Profit:** The greatest amount of money you can make from this trade. Some trades are unlimited. This number should be positive. If it is negative, this means you can't win!
- **Maximum Risk:** The probable greatest amount of money you can lose from this trade. Some trades can have unlimited risk.
- **Expiration:** The number of days remaining in the trade. For calendar spreads, the near month leg is used for days until expiration.
- **Vol:** The prior day's volume of shares traded.

The next step is to scan this screen for something that fits our risk and reward profile. Once you locate a position that appears worthwhile, click on it to see more details and a graph. Charts can be modified to show higher and lower price ranges, as well as different time frames. The possibilities are limitless.

From the table in Figure 9.9, I chose the following trade: long 1 May 99 Dell 45 call and short 1 May 99 Dell 50 call. Figure 9.10 shows the current volatility of Dell as well as a table detailing the probabilities of success in diferent time frames. Any of these fields can be changed to reflect a variation of this position. You can also check out the adjustment possibilities of the trade by using the bottom section to add more options or additional shares of the underlying stock.

After reviewing the trade, you may feel like looking at a different spread or strategy for Dell. Scroll down a little further and change your trade using the strategy matrix feature (Figure 9.11). This strategy matrix allows you to pick a bullish, bearish, or neutral

---

figure 9.10   probabilities and volatility for dell trade #1

source: www.optionsanalysis.com. reprinted with permission.

figure 9.11 strategy matrix

Implied Volatility	Price (Table shows Probability of Profit at Expiration)		
	Bullish	Neutral	Bearish
Low	○ Buy Call (32.0%) ○ Long Synthetic Call (32.0%) ○ Call Vert Spread (DB) (34.8%) ○ Put Vert Spread (CR) (34.8%) ○ Sell ITM Call Fly (59.4%) ○ Sell OTM Put Fly (59.4%) ○ Buy OTM Call TSpread (49.8%) ○ Buy ITM Put TSpread (49.8%)	○ Buy Straddle (40.5%) ○ Buy Strangle (26.1%) ○ Sell ATM Call Fly (53.1%) ○ Sell ATM Put Fly (53.1%) ○ Call Backspread (Bullish) (47.8%) ○ Put Backspread (Bearish) (45.3%) ○ Buy ATM Call TSpread (56.9%) ○ Buy ATM Put TSpread (56.9%)	○ Buy Put (36.0%) ○ Long Synthetic Put (36.0%) ○ Call Vert Spread (CR) (41.0%) ○ Put Vert Spread (DB) (41.0%) ○ Sell OTM Call Fly (68.0%) ○ Sell ITM Put Fly (68.0%) ○ Buy ITM Call TSpread (50.5%) ○ Buy OTM Put TSpread (50.5%)
Mixed	Buy the Stock! ○ Long Call, Short Put (50.7%)	◉ Do not use this table	Sell the Stock! ○ Long Put, Short Call (49.3%)
High	○ Sell Put (64.0%) ○ Covered Write (64.0%) ○ Call Vert Spread (DB) (59.0%) ○ Put Vert Spread (CR) (59.0%) ○ Buy OTM Call Fly (32.0%) ○ Buy ITM Put Fly (32.0%) ○ Sell ITM Call TSpread (49.5%) ○ Sell OTM Put TSpread (49.5%)	○ Sell Straddle (59.5%) ○ Sell Strangle (73.8%) ○ Buy ATM Call Fly (46.9%) ○ Buy ATM Put Fly (46.9%) ○ Call Ratio Spread (52.1%) ○ Put Ratio Spread (54.7%) ○ Sell ATM Call TSpread (43.1%) ○ Sell ATM Put TSpread (43.1%)	○ Sell Call (68.0%) ○ Covered Write (68.0%) ○ Call Vert Spread (CR) (65.1%) ○ Put Vert Spread (DB) (65.1%) ○ Buy ITM Call Fly (40.6%) ○ Buy OTM Put Fly (40.6%) ○ Sell OTM Call TSpread (50.2%) ○ Sell ITM Put TSpread (50.2%)

source: www.optionsanalysis.com. reprinted with permission.

strategy within a variety of volatility periods. Notice also that there is a percentage number just to the right of each strategy. That number is a probability that the specific strategy beside it will be profitable by expiration. Not all strategies have the same probability. Once you have finished your analysis and you like the strategy that you have reviewed, scroll to the very bottom of the screen and click on "Save." This strategy will be added to your portfolio of strategies and can be accessed at any time to review the risk graph, or to copy or delete the report. You can also set it up to automatically e-mail you the net profit/loss of each strategy using closing prices.

tracking

One of the best ways to learn how to trade is to use online portfolio trackers to monitor strategies that seem profitable. A tracking service will enable you to study what happens to these trades as the market prices fluctuate. This is an excellent way to learn and experience the effects various events and news can have on a market. Various web sites and online brokerages offer portfolio tracking without making you invest a penny. Each site has its own protocol when it comes to setting up a portfolio. Many will automatically e-mail you the profit and loss combo each evening, as well as news highlights on your chosen stocks. You can also watch the trade develop by creating a corresponding risk graph using options software.

To back-test a trading strategy or set of parameters using real market prices, check out Strikeprice.com (www.strikeprice.com) or Options Analysis.com (www.optionsanalysis.com). Both sites provide a full year of stock options' closing prices archived in the server. This means you can back-test any stock options strategy using the real options prices from the past. You simply enter a past date when creating a trade and the server accesses the past information. You can then track it forward to determine certain criteria and patterns in specific stock options. This is an excellent tool for garnering experience without risking any cash.

conclusion

In this chapter, I have tried to give you a sense of what it's like to go online and search for a moneymaking trade. As you become more comfortable, each of these steps will become second nature to you. But in the beginning, it can be of great help to keep an online journal so that you can remember where you've been and what you've learned. Let's review the steps for researching a trade:

1. *Charting*—Monitor chart patterns of specific stocks for signs of impending runs. Look for stocks that are approaching 52-week highs. If they have pullbacks, make sure they don't pull back below the 200-day or 50-day moving average. Keep an eye on volume and make sure that during pullbacks, volume has spiked to double its average daily volume before confirming a stock as bullish. A volume spike often washes out most of the sellers and is a clear sign that the stock is hitting the bottom.

2. *News*—Look at the fundamental picture. Watch scheduled news and be ready when surprises happen. Read company reports as well as outlooks of earnings reports to come. Be careful getting into a trade just before an earnings report is released because that's what the crowd does and the crowd isn't always right.

3. *Strategies*—Once you've located a promising market, find a strategy that fits the market's profile. Check out options premiums to find a position with the best probability of profit.

Use implied volatilities to locate abnormal patterns in option premiums.

4. *Tracking*—Track your open positions on a day-to-day basis, rather than minute-by-minute. Using a longer time frame gives you the opportunity to use a variety of research tools. Plenty of web sites and online brokerages will also send you nightly e-mails summarizing your open portfolio positions.

This four-point process for evaluating and tracking trades has been developed over my past few years as an online trader. The most important part of trading is to do your homework on a stock. It doesn't take long to develop a consistent procedure using a few web sites to research a stock's profit-making potential. Feel free to integrate my process into your own plan. Execute this plan just like a business. A lot of people think that I trade just for the fun of it or that I treat it like a game. I do like to say that trading is like grown-up Nintendo, but it's no laughing matter. Money is the bottom line for trading, and generating profits is the reward for all of your hard work, knowledge, and discipline.

chapter 10

the quest for the ultimate online brokerage

taking the plunge: paper trading whiz to armchair millionaire

The final link in a cyber-trader's world is the online brokerage. Back in 1995, there were only a handful of brokerages bold enough to take their business to the Net. But as more and more investors started using their computers to trade, the demand for lower commissions and online brokers grew exponentially. There are now more than 100 online brokers with approximately $420 billion in customer assets (as of May 1999). By the year 2002, it is estimated that the number of online investing accounts will increase to approximately 14.4 million with more than $688 billion in assets.

A huge difference exists between the kind of clients full-service and online brokerages attract. Full-service brokers tend to have older, more affluent clients with diverse portfolios while online brokerages' customers are younger with an account average of $25,000. Full-service clients enjoy being able to ask their brokers for advice while most online traders are self-directed and quick to scorn the stale advice of the traditional big brokerages. Then again, many online brokers have only experienced the bull market. We have yet to experience the full force of a bearish market. Although full-service brokers still handle the bulk of investment accounts, the online brokerage industry is definitely giving them a run for their money, and the consumer is reaping the benefits in the form of lower commissions.

Currently, Charles Schwab Online and E*Trade lead the pack as the most prominent online brokerages. Charles Schwab is a longtime discount broker and therefore had an infrastructure of accounts from which to draw when it opened up its online services in 1996. E*Trade, on the other hand, started from scratch and has become an online brokerage empire. Launching a massive advertising campaign, E*Trade has spent three times as much on advertising as on technology. However, this strategy may have backfired. In 1999, service went down several times and inspired an online cacophony of discontent as well as an abundance of complaints filed directly with the SEC. Despite these setbacks, the online giant is still growing by leaps and bounds and some online analysts continue to recommend it.

Growing pains aside, the online brokerage industry is just beginning to assess the needs of the option trader. Option trading is different from traditional stock trading because it requires customized services that online technology is just beginning to address. First of all, the complexity of putting on an options trade requires brokers to install a series of complicated mechanisms in order to meet an option trader's unique needs. Just the basic task of providing options quotes requires a complex infrastructure. There are more than 2,500 stocks that offer options. The options on each stock are called an option chain, and this chain may contain 100 individual options. Options are denoted using a base code combined with a code for the strike price and another code for the expiration month. Strike price codes use the 26 letters of our alphabet. Since there are sometimes more strike prices than there are letters, you sometimes have to switch base codes. For example, the letter "A" denotes the strike prices of 5, 105, 205, and 305 (see Appendix A). Usually, the strike price is the one closest to the current stock price. The problem in the Internet era is that when stocks can move over $100 in a matter of days, the options codes can change very quickly. This requires some very clever programming.

---

strike price codes
a system of alphabetical symbols that represent option strike prices used to describe an option when actually placing an order through an exchange.

Second, options traders represent a niche market. Many brokerages may not want to cater to this smaller group when they have the onslaught of the stock trading masses to deal with. The point that they may have missed, however, is that options trading volume is growing much faster than stock trading volume and options traders trade more frequently, generating greater commissions.

Although many of the larger online brokerages offer option services, many do not have the capacity to handle spreads directly online. Unlike stocks, options are often bought in combinations with specific pricing relationships between the different parts of the trade. That means that multiple trades have to be placed simultaneously, and only under certain conditions. Most brokers are set up to handle single transactions—simply buying or selling one trading instrument at a time. If you change the transaction to be "Buy this call and sell that call, but only do it if the difference between the two prices is $X," then most stock execution systems grind to a screeching halt. Buying and selling options online is a common occurrence, but employing spread and combination strategies online is still a work in progress. The infrastructure to handle direct online spread trading is currently available at five brokerages: WallStreet Electronica, Wall Street Access, Mr. Stock, Accutrade, and Ameritrade.

On the bright side, there is little to fear from "cybersnoopers," since major online brokerages have developed superb security systems. Due to an increase in the use of wireless modems and portable Web devices, a few firms are already beginning to offer traders the opportunity to trade from a pager or a personal digital assistant. That means you can get a price alert, check the activity of your favorite stocks and options, and place a trade all from a beach in Maui. But before you go online to check out the best prices on tickets to Hawaii, let's take an in-depth look at online brokerages and what makes one better than the other.

criteria for brokerage reviews

A conundrum is defined as a brain-teasing enigma. Finding the best broker has always been and continues to be a conundrum of the highest degree. Obviously "best" means the ultimate combination of brokerage attributes: low commissions, swift executions, and reliability. Since this book focuses on options trading, I have also looked for online brokerages to provide the customized features that option traders need to compete in the marketplace. Therefore, before launching into the reviews of the 10 best online brokerages, I will clarify the ground rules used to assess the 70 online brokerages included in Appendix E.

1. *Stock and options experience, screening, and portfolio tracking.* Not all brokerages handle options. So, it is important to make sure that the brokerage you choose to work

through not only handles options, but has an interest in catering to option traders' needs. Your broker must have an extensive background in options trading to be able to get your complex option orders filled and exited at a profitable price. In addition, brokerages that offer stock and options screening services are a real plus. You should also be able to easily track several portfolios in order to monitor your investments and observe the movement of stocks and options for potential future trades.

2. *Low commission rates.* From the start, online brokerages have been able to offer much lower commission rates than conventional full-service brokerages. Online rates for 100 shares of stock are as low as $5, whereas conventional discount brokers start at around $30 and go as high as $150. Option orders usually have a minimum commission per trade plus a per contract fee. Lower rates are especially important to option traders because combination spread orders consist of multiple contracts. Since the maximum reward on many spread trades is limited, profits can be severely reduced by high commission rates. However, low commissions also mean bare-bones services while traditional brokers offer a variety of money management services including investment advice. Look out for hidden costs.

3. *Margin rates.* You can trade stocks on margin, but not options. In the past, most brokerages required a 50% margin on stocks. But these days, due to the intense volume of certain Internet stocks, many brokerages have altered their margin policy and now require up to 100% of the price of the stock. When margin is offered, traders are charged interest on the loan. This amount of interest is referred to as the margin rate. Margin rates vary from brokerage to brokerage. In addition, many brokerages require high margin deposits (up to $100,000) to be held on account if you want to trade spreads and naked options. Straightforward debit spreads and straddles should not require more than the maximum risk for the trade.

4. *Trading account size.* Many brokerages require a minimum amount of money to establish an account. This number varies from nothing at all to $15,000. Low minimums have undoubtedly inspired more new traders than ever before to jump into the fray.

5. *Option spreads.* As this book goes to press, the standard procedure for placing combination option spread trades is to call the online broker's order desk and verbally make the

trade. Many online brokerages charge a higher commission fee for placing a trade using a broker. As the infrastructure of online trading progresses, placing spread orders online will hopefully become the norm. But until then, there are only a few brokerages pioneering the development of an option-friendly infrastructure that processes spread orders online. Some firms are accomplishing this feat by switching from a third-party clearing firm to a self-clearing organization.

6. *Order execution.* Order execution is based on a brokerage's ability to buy at the lowest price or sell at the highest price once your order has been placed. When you place an online order (or through a broker by phone), your order is either sent directly to an ECN (electronic communication network) or relayed to a floor broker who approaches a market maker or a specialist to get your order filled. If you place a market order, especially in a fast market, there is a good chance that you won't get the price on your screen. You can eliminate this problem by placing a limit order. Although limit orders are not always filled, at least if they are filled you get the price you want. Reliable order execution is by far the most important link in your chain to making money in the markets. Unfortunately, this area is very hard to rate until you actually have an account. Forays into countless chat rooms have made me realize that for every trader who relates a bad experience there are many more who never have a problem. Therefore (although I have made it a point to keep track of the complaints I've encountered), this part of my review has been restricted to the following areas:

A broker's ability to issue all types of orders online, including short sales, AON (all-or-nothing) orders, and stop orders.

Additional fees for processing orders other than market orders.

The time it takes to receive confirmation of executed orders or option assignments.

Customer comments as to the consistency of a firm's ability to get good fills.

7. *Quotes.* There are two basic kinds of quote services: real-time and delayed. A few firms offer unlimited streaming real-time quotes. Others offer a limited amount of free real-time access when someone opens up a new account plus so many real-time snapshot quotes per executed trade. More often, companies automatically supply delayed quotes and charge

a monthly fee for a link to a dynamic real-time quotes system. A handful of smaller firms offer only delayed quotes. Although I think that unlimited real-time quotes should be standard, don't dismiss a brokerage that doesn't offer real-time quotes until you have assessed your needs. Unless you are a serious day trader, real-time quotes may be overkill. Also, since many software programs require specific data servers to function properly, it might be provident to go that route.

8. *Account updates.* Instant account updating after the completion of each order is a big plus for options traders. Unfortunately, many firms provide account updates only by the beginning of each business day. Although this is satisfactory, instant account updating is much more useful to the active options trader because it's vital for traders with smaller accounts to know if a trade has been filled before placing another.

9. *Customer service.* There's nothing like really needing to talk with your broker and not being able to get through, especially when you have a problem getting online. It drives me crazy when I start getting the Touch-Tone runaround. ("Please press '1' if you'd like to talk a broker before you have a heart attack.") No matter how automated trading may become, nothing will ever take the place of having a knowledgeable and courteous person available to talk to when you have a question. Good customer service is in everyone's best interest. Although a few select firms offer customer service 24 hours a day, the customer service department in most firms is open only from one hour before the market opens until one hour after it closes. You can also contact brokerages by e-mail. In some cases, you will even receive a personal answer back from a knowledgeable brokerage employee who is intent on solving your issues. There are also those that have automated this system and all you get back is a form letter. These letters run the gamut from relatively helpful to completely inadequate and frustrating.

10. *Reliability.* As long as online trading continues to experience growing pains, reliability of service will be a key issue. System failure is simply unacceptable when it creates losses that could have been avoided if service was functioning properly. Online brokerages are steadily increasing capacity to meet demands, but we're not out of the woods yet. In judging a brokerage, it is important to note the alternative methods for reaching the brokerage in case there is a system failure.

11. *User-friendliness.* Web design is more than a matter of creativity. Although I like creative sites filled with exotic and colorful designs, I am mainly interested in efficiency. Time is the bottom line. If it takes five screens to get you to your account information, that's four too many. How long does it take to cough up a stock's various options premiums? Does your service offer 24-hour order entry? Do you have fast access to charts, news, and research information? Regardless of whether you are looking for a trade or placing one, an online brokerage needs to be easy-to-use and fast.

12. *Perks.* There are myriad perks offered by online brokerages to tempt the masses, including individual retirement accounts (IRAs), mutual funds, free checking, Visa cards, debit cards, WebTV compatibility, local offices, dividend reinvestment, no discrimination against odd-lot orders, foreign accounts available, and access to IPOs. The more a brokerage offers, the less surfing a trader has to do to find what he or she is looking for—one-stop shopping at its finest.

These criteria have been the basis for judging the following online brokerages to be the best of the bunch for options traders. What follows is an in-depth review of my favorite (top 10) picks. Additional online brokerage reviews can be found in Appendix E.

top 10 picks

Speculations aside, I have spent a considerable amount of time exhaustively investigating online options trading services. Since options traders have very different needs from stock traders, my final top 10 list is not the same as those of other rating services found on the Net. To create this list, I investigated the criteria detailed in the previous section and used the following four points to make my final decisions:

- The capacity to process option spread orders online.
- Commission and margin requirements.
- Service reliability and execution timeliness.
- How much money is required to get started.

The list in Table 10.1 represents my personal opinion, and my opinion can change quickly depending on how each company evolves. So please keep in mind that in the tremendously dynamic environment of the Internet, some of the information published in this book may have changed by the time you read it. To keep up with this evolutionary process, we will be continually updating this list at our web

table 10.1 online brokerage top 10 list

Online Brokerage	Commission					Complex Options Orders Online	Account Minimum
	Option	Bull Call Spread*	Stock Market Order	Stock Limit Order			
#1 WallStreet Electronica www.wallstreete.com	$25 + $2.50 per contract	$55	$14.95 up to 1,000 plus $.02 for each additional share	$19.95 per trade + $.02 per share		Yes	$2,500
#2 Wall Street Access www.wsaccess.com	$25 plus $1.50 to $2 per contract	$54	$25 (up to 5,000 shares)	$25 up to 5,000 shares		Yes	$10,000
#3 Mr. Stock www.mrstock.com	$19.95 + $1.75 per contract	$33	$14.95	$19.95		Yes	$2,000
#4 Accutrade www.accutrade.com	Minimum commission $35; $1.50 to $8 per contract	$70	$29.95 up to 1,000 shares, then add $.02 per share	$29.95 up to 1,000 shares, then add $.02 per share		Yes	$5,000
#5 Ameritrade www.ameritrade.com	$25 + $1.75 per contract; $35 minimum	$58	$8 flat rate	$13 flat rate		Yes	$2,000

#6 Preferred Trade www.preferredtrade.com	$19.95 minimum; plus $2 to $3	$45.90	$7.75 (routed to a third-party dealer) or $15 plus $.02 per share	$22.50 plus $.03 per share	No	$10,000
#7 Dreyfus Brokerage Services www.edreyfus.com	$15 plus $1.75 per contract	$30	$15	$15	No	$5,000
#8 CompuTEL Securities www.computel.com	$24 plus $1 per contract, fixed commission	$50	$14 for 999 shares or less, $9 for 1,000 shares or more	$19	No	$5,000
#9 Brown & Co. www.brownco.com	$19.95 plus $2.50 or $3 per contract	$50	$5 up to 5,000 shares, then add $.01 per share	$10 up to 5,000 shares, then add $.01 per share	No	$15,000
#10 Charles Schwab Online www.eschwab.com	$35 plus $1.75 per contract	$64	$29.95 plus $.03 per share for over 1,000 shares	$29.95 up to 1,000, then $.03 per share	No	$2,500

*The bull call spread used in this example: long 1 February DELL 60 Call @ $9^1/_4$ and short 1 February DELL 65 Call @ $7^1/_2$.

site, www.optionetics.com. Please feel free to e-mail me with information on your favorite firm on the list or let me know when a brokerage is failing to keep up its end of the bargain. After all, thanks to the Internet, freedom of speech has never been so free.

In the following pages, you'll find detailed information regarding the services and costs of each of the brokerages in our top 10 list. You need to be aware that the account minimum required to open an account and the minimum amount required for spread trading are not always the same. And sometimes the difference is staggering! Dreyfus Brokerage Services, for example, requires an initial deposit of only $2,000 to open an account, but that minimum jumps up to $20,000 if you want to do spread trading. Where the brokerages were willing to provide the information to us directly, we used their information. In other cases, I pulled the information off their web sites. Here, however, are the highlights of my list-making thought process.

The #1 and #2 spots were very difficult to decide. Both WallStreet Electronica (WSE) and Wall Street Access (WSA) have very professional staffs with extensive options experience. Both handle margin exactly the way they should, accounting for the actual risk of each trade. They both have the capacity to handle online order entry for complex options positions. In the end, the tiebreaker came down to which brokerage requires less money to start trading. WallStreet Electronica requires $2,500 to open an account in comparison to the $10,000 required by Wall Street Access. In addition, WallStreet Electronica—a bilingual brokerage offering Spanish and English translations—offers lower stock commission rates than Wall Street Access. However, WSA has a very strong dedication to customer satisfaction—a commission refund is offered on any trade if clients are not completely satisfied with the service.

I like Mr. Stock (www.mrstock.com) very much. Attention to details and commitment to the needs of option traders makes Mr. Stock an easy choice for #3. The principals at this firm are all ex–floor traders with extensive personal options trading experience. They have specifically targeted their site to cater to options traders and it shows—including an option volatility charting function that I find very useful. As this book goes to press, they are in the final phase of setting up their online spread capabilities to provide options traders with the ability to place all of the strategies detailed in this book without the use of a live broker. In anticipation, they are currently offering the use of a live broker for these types of trades, for the same commission as online trading. Once this process is in place, look for this site to give the first two firms on this list a run for their money. Mr. Stock requires only $2,000 to open an account and a minimum balance of $2,000 for spread trades.

At #4, Accutrade slimly beat out its rival Ameritrade at #5. Both brokerages have the same parent company and offer a variety of helpful option tools, including online spread order services. But in the final analysis, Accutrade scored higher than Ameritrade on reliability. Ameritrade is working to alleviate these growing pains by enlarging the capacity of its infrastructure.

You'll notice that the top five brokerages all offer—or intend to offer by the time this book is published—the ability to place complex options strategies online. Given that this is a book about online options trading, the capacity to trade spreads online is the number one qualifier in my rating scale. Beyond the top five, I found four smaller brokerages that focus on attracting options traders and one large brokerage that does it all.

Coming in at #6, Preferred Trade is option-friendly with brokers on the floors of the four main options exchanges helping to achieve the best execution possible in the equity and index options trading pits. They were friendly and easy to contact by phone, too, and that's a big plus as far as I'm concerned. Customer comments report this site as helpful and responsive. Extra charges are not required for phone orders and their RAES (Retail Automatic Execution System) interface speeds up the execution process considerably.

RAES
developed by the CBOE, the Retail Automatic Execution System (RAES) provides retail customers with the fastest order executions possible. Orders are guaranteed a fill at the current market bid and offer if they fall within designated parameters (i.e., 20 options contracts or less with a premium below $10; some exceptions apply). More than 26% of public customer orders are currently executed on RAES. For more information, check out the CBOE web site at www.cboe.com.

I was also quite impressed by the folks at Dreyfus Brokerage Services, and they capture the #7 spot. The friendly, solid staff provides a substantial amount of options services. Dreyfus has earned a reputation for being fast and reliable for option traders even though it requires a hefty account minimum for spread trades. It also offers the lowest options commissions of any brokerage I could find. Customer comments are mainly positive—good executions, customer service, and reliability.

CompuTEL gained the #8 spot. It has a straightforward attitude that I find appealing, with no hidden costs and an easy commission schedule. Although its capable team welcomes options combination trades, you still have to call a live broker to place an options spread order. However, look for CompuTEL to move up on the list as it adds online spread trade capabilities to its list of services in the near future.

At #9, Brown & Co. adds a touch of class to our top 10 list. Brown & Co. specifically focuses attention on active, experienced traders and has a very high requirement to open an account ($15,000). I include the firm because I am attracted by its no-frills online environment. I also like the fact that orders are sent directly to market makers and ECNs, bypassing third-party market centers that impose charges on each order. In addition, Brown & Co. has extremely low commissions—only $5 for up to 5,000 shares. Brown & Co. is not afraid of spread orders in the least and has developed a reputation for good fills, low commissions, and reliability.

Charles Schwab Online nabbed the #10 spot. While known in general for being the largest of the online brokerages, Schwab is very much up to speed on the needs of options traders. It offers exceptional services for options traders and has special brokers carefully screened for their options trading knowledge who handle active options trading accounts. On the downside, Schwab's commissions, while discounted, are not cheap and they are quite confusing. In addition, Schwab has not yet developed the infrastructure to handle online spread orders, but is working on developing this capacity. According to Schwab's management, complex option order screens will be online by the end of 1999.

That's it for the highlights. What follows is our list of the details of each of the top 10 brokerages so that you can do your own comparison. Remember, if you are paying a premium for live brokers, make sure that they are knowledgeable enough to earn that premium. And don't be afraid to interview a long list of brokers before making your final choice. Brokerages are the intermediaries of trading. To effectively compete in the new online trading arena, make sure you choose the firm that gives you what you need at a fair price.

#1 wallstreet electronica

www.wallstreete.com
5900 SW 41st St., Miami, FL 33155
phone: 305-669-3026
toll-free: 888-WALL-STE (925-5783)
fax: 305-661-7402
e-mail: info@wallstreete.com
category: Middle-cost discount brokerage
slogan: "*WallStreetE* . . . where *MONEY* meets *TECHNOLOGY*"

site design = 9
user-friendliness = 10
options usefulness = 9

general description: WallStreetE has been receiving some excellent press regarding its leadership in the online brokerage community and online accessibility. It easily placed high on our top 10 list because it offers online spread trading. Although its commissions are not as inexpensive as others on this list (you pay an additional 1.5 cents per share over the $14.95 base rate on all trades over 1,000 shares), it does offer commission breaks for frequent traders. WallStreetE is also highly respected for its research services, offering screening tools for mutual funds and stocks as well as analyst recommendations and charting. Additional bonus: The site is bilingual, with both Spanish and English translations.

features: WallStreetE offers three distinct service levels for trading stocks, bonds, mutual funds, and options: do-it-yourself Deep Discounted Brokerage, Full Brokerage On-line Advisors, and Valet Brokerage Service. The deep-discount service is geared for independent-thinking, self-directed investors who want to research and manage their own accounts using online interactive services. They have access to all the usual electronic bells and whistles from online research and analytical tools to real-time quotes and news alerts. The full advisory service provides traders with limited time availability with professional investment guidance and assistance in developing a wide range of investment strategies. The final "valet" service is in between the two previous alternatives and enables traders to personally trade and manage a variety of products and also seek help from an adviser.

additional services: Free money market sweep, free checkbook, cash and asset allocation account with a Visa card, checking account, money market account, trust services, investments in fixed income instruments including CDs, corporate bonds, emerging market sovereign debt, and Brady bonds; retirement accounts, IRAs, SEPs, and 401(k)s. Trading tools include real-time quotes, charts, and news. Trading in major markets outside the United States is available as well as U.S. tax–exempt accounts for non-U.S. citizens.

options: $25 plus $2.50 per contract plus frequent trader bonuses— 10 trades in one week entitle you to a complimentary ticket charge. WallStreetE offers option chains and 15-minute delayed quotes free of charge. An options calculator can be downloaded for use in determining complex options strategies. Stop orders on options are sometimes allowed depending on market conditions. Stop orders are not allowed on highly volatile Internet stock options. For a short option in a spread to be considered covered, the long part of the option contract has to expire on the same month or further out than the short contract and the strike price of the long option must be lower than the short option. The same applies to a short call, except the long call has to have a higher strike price. (Table 10.2.)

stocks: Nasdaq—OTC market orders are $14.95 per trade ($.02 per share above 1,000 shares). Frequent trader bonuses—If during the qualifying period your commissions exceed $1,000 but are less than $2,000, you'll get a 15% credit on the commissions in excess of $1,000. If they exceed $2,000, you'll earn a 20% credit. All other orders—NYSE listed, limit, stop, and GTC—are $19.95 per trade + $.02 per share plus frequent trader bonuses.

account minimum: $2,500 minimum to open an account; $10,000 minimum for spread trades; $50,000 minimum for index options; $2,000 minimum maintenance requirement for equity options plus 100% of the option proceeds plus 20% of the underlying stock value. These requirements may vary depending on the size of your account and your quantity of trading.

quotes: 100 free real-time quotes per day.

table 10.2   #1 wallstreet electronica

Trade	Margin	Commission
Long synthetic straddle: Short 100 shares of IBM @ 125 Long 2 February IBM 125 calls @ 8	$7,850	$51.95
Long straddle: AMZN @ 190 Long 1 February AMZN 190 Call @ $26^7/_8$ Long 1 February AMZN 190 Put @ 32	$5,888	$55
Short straddle: AMZN @ 190 Short 1 February AMZN 190 Call @ $26^7/_8$ Short 1 February AMZN 190 Put @ 32	$8,748	$55
Bull call spread: Long 1 February DELL 60 Call @ $9^1/_4$ Short 1 February DELL 65 Call @ $7^1/_2$	$175; $10,000 minimum account required	$55
Put ratio backspread: Short 3 February XCIT 60 Puts @ 17 Long 5 February XCIT 50 Puts @ $8^5/_8$	$3,787; $10,000 minimum account required	$70
Iron butterfly spread: Long 1 February HWP 45 Put @ $^1/_8$ Short 1 February HWP 55 Put @ $^{15}/_{16}$ Short 1 February HWP 65 Call @ $4^3/_8$ Long 1 February HWP 75 Call @ 1	$850; $10,000 minimum account required	$110

miscellaneous: Investment newsletters, portfolios, article archives, free unlimited access to real-time corporate data filed with the Securities and Exchange Commission (SEC Edgar Reports), portfolios, criteria searches, bond quotes. WSE also has a mirror site with dedicated lines through another service provider (PSI) on a separate network from its primary service provider in case a system failure occurs, as well as "cold" backup servers and routers ready to be used at any time in case of system difficulty.

#2 wall street access

www.wsaccess.com
17 Battery Place, New York, NY 10004
phone: 212-709-9400
toll-free: 800-925-5781
fax: 212-709-9522
e-mail: info@wsaccess.com
category: High-cost discount broker
slogan: "Where serious traders trade."
site design = 9
user-friendliness = 9
options usefulness = 9

general description: Wall Street Access is definitely one of the best online brokerages for option trading. Originally founded in 1981, Wall Street Access (WSA) debuted its premium online brokerage services in 1993, including a wide variety of useful amenities for option traders. Perhaps its biggest claim to fame is that it was the first online brokerage to allow complex option spreads to be electronically placed. WSA requires $10,000 to open an account, thereby catering to a more professional clientele. They do not sell proprietary products and are very proud of being independently owned and operated. WSA provides direct representation on every exchange floor and that enables them to find the best price for your trade. By working in client-assigned teams, WSA tries to offer clients maximum service with a personal touch. Trader commentary on the Net has been quite positive. WSA even offers a refund on your commission on any trade if you are not completely satisfied with the service. As a midsize brokerage (taking on around 300 new accounts a month), it has experienced a few "momentary" system failures, but guarantees direct access to a live broker by phone. It has one of the friendliest, most competent staffs around and that's a big plus!

features: Wall Street Access enables traders to trade stocks, options, mutual funds, index options, American depositary receipts (ADRs), and bonds. It offers four ways to place orders: using the Internet through Wall Street Access Online; online with Wall Street Access for Windows software; by phone with your personal trading team; or through Touch-Tone trading. Customer confirmation is sent via mail for every order placed as well as a monthly account statement detailing closing balances, dividends, interest payments, or receipts of interest in the account. All types of orders (from fill-or-kill to stop orders) can be processed.

additional services: Portfolio tracking, free real-time quotes during market hours (100 free quotes per trade), viewing account positions and trading activity 24 hours a day, and complimentary research (TheStreet.com, Zacks, and Briefing.com). In addition, when you call Wall Street Access, your call does not go to a voice-mail holding pattern. It reaches an experienced broker at the trading desk, not just an order taker.

options: $25 plus $1.50 to $2 per contract. Spread orders can be processed online. (Table 10.3.) Naked options require a $50,000 minimum account balance and 25% of underlying market value + premium received + any out-of-the-money amount. The short option in a

table 10.3 #2 wall street access

Trade	Margin	Commission
Long synthetic straddle: Short 100 shares of IBM @ 125 Long 2 February IBM 125 calls @ 8	$7,850	$54
Long straddle: AMZN @ 190 Long 1 February AMZN 190 Call @ $26^7/_8$ Long 1 February AMZN 190 Put @ 32	$5,887.50	$54
Short straddle: AMZN @ 190 Short 1 February AMZN 190 Call @ $26^7/_8$ Short 1 February AMZN 190 Put @ 32	$7,950; $50,000 minimum account required	$54
Bull call spread: Long 1 February DELL 60 Call @ $9^1/_4$ Short 1 February DELL 65 Call @ $7^1/_2$	$175	$54
Put ratio backspread: Short 3 February XCIT 60 Puts @ 17 Long 5 February XCIT 50 Puts @ $8^5/_8$	$2,213	$66
Iron butterfly spread: Long 1 February HWP 45 Put @ $^1/_8$ Short 1 February HWP 55 Put @ $^{15}/_{16}$ Short 1 February HWP 65 Call @ $4^3/_8$ Long 1 February HWP 75 Call @ 1	$1,581.25	$106

spread is considered covered as long as the short side expires before the long side. In addition to standard brokerage licenses, WSA specially trains its brokers to handle sophisticated option trades. Electronic placement of these spreads is offered. WSA calls all electronically placed spread orders directly to the floor so they will be placed as a spread—not legged into.

stocks: $25 (up to 5,000 shares) for market and limit orders.

account minimum: $10,000 to open an account and $50,000 for naked options.

quotes: 100 free real-time quotes for every executed trade.

miscellaneous: Browser and software services are available. Clients receive free subscriptions to CBS MarketWatch, Zacks, Wall Street Source, TheStreet.com, Briefing.com, BT Alex. Brown Morning Notes, Fundamental Data, Charts & Snapshots. If outages occur, direct access to a live trading team via the phone is guaranteed.

#3 mr. stock

www.mrstock.com
220 Bush St., Suite 360, San Francisco, CA 94104
phone: 415-249-4384
toll-free: 800-467-7865 or 800-470-1896
e-mail: info@mrstock.com
category: Middle-cost discount brokerage
slogan: "Reliable, accessible, fast & cheap."
site design = 9
user-friendliness = 8
options usefulness = 9

general description: In 1993, members of NASD had a monopoly over the Nasdaq markets. Using the old adage "If you can't beat 'em, join 'em," five Pacific Exchange options floor traders formed a brokerage firm called Mr. Stock, which subsequently became a NASD member. In the beginning, Mr. Stock primarily offered professional stock execution services to its owners and institutional clients. But in December of 1997, Mr. Stock became a full-service online brokerage specializing in options. Perhaps the reason that I rate Mr. Stock so highly is because they've really used their expertise as options floor traders to include all of the customized features necessary to trade options online. At Mr. Stock, real people answer the phone without a lot of bureaucracy.

features: This is an extremely comfortable brokerage. Everything is fully automated that could conceivably be automated, including:

- *Accounts.* Open any type of account (margin, cash, IRA, corporate, trust, etc.); transfer account; change account information.
- *Trading.* Mr. Stock provides a lengthy list of primary services including the following: orders entry 24 hours/day, 7 days/week; online stock orders; stock price charts and graphs; the ability to specify your preferred exchange route; access to LEAPS options; account execution confirmations via e-mail; hypothetical portfolio accounts and e-mailed updates; and an easy download of trades at year-end for tax calculations.

additional services: Mutual funds and IPOs (investors must be qualified), cash management services, cash sweep, and IRAs. Phone order service is available for an additional $10 per trade. Mutual funds, investment tools include Reuters, Zacks, 2nd Opinion, Edgar's, CBS MarketWatch Headline News, Proprietary Volatility and Stock Charts, Option Theoretical Calculator.

options: $19.95 + $1.75 per contract. All kinds of complex options combinations and spread orders (Table 10.4) can be processed online.

table 10.4   #3 mr. stock

Trade	Margin	Commission
Long synthetic straddle: Short 100 shares of IBM @ 125 Long 2 February IBM 125 calls @ 8	$7,850	$37
Long straddle: AMZN @ 190 Long 1 February AMZN 190 Call @ $26^7/_8$ Long 1 February AMZN 190 Put @ 32	$5,887.50	$18
Short straddle: AMZN @ 190 Short 1 February AMZN 190 Call @ $26^7/_8$ Short 1 February AMZN 190 Put @ 32	$11,587.50	$18
Bull call spread: Long 1 February DELL 60 Call @ $9^1/_4$ Short 1 February DELL 65 Call @ $7^1/_2$	$175 $2,000 minimum account balance	$33
Put ratio backspread: Short 3 February XCIT 60 Puts @ 17 Long 5 February XCIT 50 Puts @ $8^5/_8$	$4,737.50, to which the credit of $2,512.50 from the three-lot spread may be applied	$42
Iron butterfly spread: Long 1 February HWP 45 Put @ $^1/_8$ Short 1 February HWP 55 Put @ $^{15}/_{16}$ Short 1 February HWP 65 Call @ $4^3/_8$ Long 1 February HWP 75 Call @ 1	$2,000, to which the credit of $418.75 may be applied	$66

Mr. Stock then directly routes them to the exchange floor to be traded as spreads, not legged into. Stop orders on options are allowed. It also offers some very unique option services including a volatility charting service. To place orders with naked options, Mr. Stock requires 30% of the underlying stock, less any out-of-the-money amount (but not less than 10% of the stock). Stop orders on options are allowed.

stocks: Market orders—$14.95 for up to 5,000 shares; add $.015 per share for over 5,000. Limit orders—$19.95 for up to 5,000 shares; add $.015 per share for over 5,000.

account minimum: Mr. Stock requires a minimum of $2,000 to open a trading account and a minimum balance of $2,000 for spread trades.

quotes: 100 free real-time quotes are provided with every trade. Otherwise, real-time quotes are available for Mr. Stock customers through DBC and MyTrack for a monthly fee.

miscellaneous: Mr. Stock uses a browser. There is an additional $10 fee for telephone orders. IRA accounts do not require an annual fee. No system failures to date.

#4 accutrade

www.accutrade.com
4211 South 102d St., Omaha, NE 68127
toll-free: 800-882-4887 or 800-494-8949
e-mail: info@accutrade.com
category: Middle-cost discount brokerage
slogan: "Making Investors Smarter One by One"
site design = 9
user-friendliness = 8
options usefulness = 8

general description: Accutrade started offering online services back in July 1993. The Ameritrade Holding Corporation recently acquired Accutrade and added spread trading capabilities to its lineup of options services. It offers both browser and software-based accounts. Its Windows program has received enthusiastic reviews from customers and rave reviews from *Forbes* magazine. Since it is a smaller brokerage, it has not been plagued by system failures, and most comments praise its executions, customer service, and reliability. Although commissions run a little high, customer commentary reflects an excellent track record for customer service and reliability.

features: Accutrade offers stock, options, mutual funds, and bond services. Online option spread orders are available. Accutrade provides an extensive collection of online financial research tools including access to PR Newswire, BusinessWire, Dow Jones News, MarketEdge, First Call from Market Guide, and research reports from Market Guide on over 10,000 publicly traded companies.

additional services: Highly trained and available representatives, large mutual fund program, debit cards, checking accounts.

options: Minimum commission $35; $1.50 to $8 per contract. Accutrade offers an option order page for combined option order tickets for spreads, straddles, and strangles. Stop limits on options are available depending on the exchange. Access to option chains are available to check the entire option market on a stock. (Table 10.5.)

stocks: Market and limit orders—$29.95 up to 1,000 shares, and $.02 per share over 1,000.

account minimum: $5,000. A minimum of $10,000 for naked equity options and $50,000 for naked index options. Maintenance requirements are 30% of the underlying plus the premium minus any out-of-the-money, with a minimum of $500 per contract.

table 10.5   #4 accutrade

Trade	Margin	Commission
Long synthetic straddle: Short 100 shares of IBM @ 125 Long 2 February IBM 125 calls @ 8	$7,850	$65
Long straddle: AMZN @ 190 Long 1 February AMZN 190 Call @ $26^7/_8$ Long 1 February AMZN 190 Put @ 32	$5,887.50	$70
Short straddle: AMZN @ 190 Short 1 February AMZN 190 Call @ $26^7/_8$ Short 1 February AMZN 190 Put @ 32	$11,587.50	$70
Bull call spread: Long 1 February DELL 60 Call @ $9^1/_4$ Short 1 February DELL 65 Call @ $7^1/_2$	$175; $2,000 minimum account required	$70
Put ratio backspread: Short 3 February XCIT 60 Puts @ 17 Long 5 February XCIT 50 Puts @ $8^5/_8$	$2,212.50; $2,000 minimum account required	$75
Iron butterfly spread: Long 1 February HWP 45 Put @ $^1/_8$ Short 1 February HWP 55 Put @ $^{15}/_{16}$ Short 1 February HWP 65 Call @ $4^3/_8$ Long 1 February HWP 75 Call @ 1	$1,581.25; $2,000 minimum account required	$140

quotes: 100 free real-time quotes per trade.

miscellaneous: Quote lists offer up to 35 symbols at a time of stocks you want to track. One free S&P report per executed trade. Download your Accutrade account information into Quicken 98 software.

#5 ameritrade

www.ameritrade.com
1005 N. Ameritrade Place, Bellevue, NE 68005
toll-free: 800-400-3603 or 800-454-9272
e-mail: starting@ameritrade.com
category: Deep discount brokerage
slogan: "The way to trade. Period."
site design = 8
user-friendliness = 7
options usefulness = 8

general description: Ameritrade offers online spread trading capabilities, but differs greatly from the other leading online brokerages in other areas. Ameritrade is a large deep-discount brokerage that offers low commission rates for stocks (only $8 a pop), but higher rates for options ($29 minimum). As an added perk, it has developed and offers an excellent trading simulation game called "Darwin: Survival of the Fittest" that can be downloaded for free. Unfortunately, it has had a rash of system failures, which have immeasurably lowered its service ratings by several brokerage analyst sites.

features: Ameritrade provides extensive services for stock, options, mutual funds, and bond trading. It offers free Dow Jones news, S&P stock reports, and direct links to a variety of research services, including the Motley Fool, EDGAR Online, Morningstar.Net, and BigCharts. It also offers comprehensive stock screening programs, trade confirmations by e-mail or telephone, and free real-time snapshot quotes.

additional services: Checking accounts, mutual funds, free checking, Visa cards, WebTV compatible, dividend reinvestment, and no discrimination against odd-lot orders. Direct deposit and automatic monthly mutual fund investments are also available.

options: $25 + $1.75 per contract, $29 minimum. Ameritrade offers advanced option order tickets where you can place spreads, straddles, and strangles online (Table 10.6). Option chains are available in order to check all options on a stock. Stop orders on options are allowed.

stocks: $8 flat rate on market orders and $13 for limit orders.

table 10.6   #5 ameritrade

Trade	Margin	Commission
Long synthetic straddle: Short 100 shares of IBM @ 125 Long 2 February IBM 125 calls @ 8	$7,850	$42
Long straddle: AMZN @ 190 Long 1 February AMZN 190 Call @ 26$^7/_8$ Long 1 February AMZN 190 Put @ 32	$5,887.50	$58
Short straddle: AMZN @ 190 Short 1 February AMZN 190 Call @ 26$^7/_8$ Short 1 February AMZN 190 Put @ 32	$11,587.50	$58
Bull call spread: Long 1 February DELL 60 Call @ 9$^1/_4$ Short 1 February DELL 65 Call @ 7$^1/_2$	$175; $2,000 minimum account required	$58
Put ratio backspread: Short 3 February XCIT 60 Puts @ 17 Long 5 February XCIT 50 Puts @ 8$^5/_8$	$2,212.50	$64
Iron butterfly spread: Long 1 February HWP 45 Put @ $^1/_8$ Short 1 February HWP 55 Put @ $^{15}/_{16}$ Short 1 February HWP 65 Call @ 4$^3/_8$ Long 1 February HWP 75 Call @ 1	$2,000	$116

account minimum: $10,000 naked equity options and $50,000 naked index options. Maintenance requirements are 30% of the underlying plus the premium minus any out-of-the-money, with a minimum of $500 per contract.

quotes: 100 real-time quotes when you sign up, and 100 more real-time quotes for every Internet order filled. $20 per month for unlimited real-time quotes.

miscellaneous: Although it has a long list of excellent services, Ameritrade is definitely experiencing growing pains. Customer comments go from mediocre to poor. Reliability and availability need definite improvement.

#6 preferred trade

www.preferredtrade.com
220 Montgomery, Suite 777, San Francisco, CA 94104
phone: 415-781-0205
toll-free: 800-949-3504 or 888-781-0283

fax: 415-781-0292
e-mail: info@preftech.com
category: Middle-cost discount brokerage
slogan: "Anything else is too slow."
site design = 9
user-friendliness = 8
options usefulness = 7

general description: This online brokerage caters to option traders and active day traders and offers direct access to all four options exchanges. Preferred Trade sends stock and index option orders for 20 contracts or less to the electronic systems of the Chicago Board Options Exchange (the RAES system), the Pacific Exchange (POETS), the American Stock Exchange (AMOS), and the Philadelphia Stock Exchange (AUTOM). The management team has extensive experience trading on registered options exchanges as well as operating trading desks. Many of the firm's staff have worked on the trading floors of U.S. options exchanges or in the back offices of options clearing firms. Preferred Trade offers two distinct levels of service: browser and nonbrowser (for the more active investor). New visitors to the Preferred Trade site can access free stock and option quotes on a delayed basis, and review a detailed demonstration of the customer access and order entry system.

features: Services include stocks, stock options, bonds, and mutual funds. Follow your portfolio of stocks and options with free delayed quotes and intraday updated account positions. Quickly retrieve quotes, charts, news, and market recaps. Customer comments report this site as helpful and responsive. Extra charges are not required for phone orders. There is 24-hour order entry with orders executed during market hours (browser only). Real-time order status and portfolio information (nonbrowser only) are offered.

additional services: Access charts and news items on the stocks you are following. Online customer account access for viewing your positions. Trade listing of orders per security or by date. Equity review gives you daily statistics on your account balance. E-mail and toll-free telephone customer service with a licensed registered representative. Direct access for assistance with IRA and other retirement accounts. Preferred Trade offers a mutual fund network of hundreds of no-load funds through a live broker.

options: $19.95 minimum, plus $2.50 or $3 per contract. Options priced up to $10 are $2.50 per contract. Options priced $10 and above are $3 per contract. For options, users can enter online opening and closing buy orders, opening and closing sell orders for stock, and index option orders. Day and GTC orders for options can be entered online. Other option spread orders must be entered by phone. No specific criteria for option trading approval in customer accounts. Each application for option trading is treated individually based primarily on the customer's trading experience and financial condition. Only investors with significant option trading experience are approved to conduct naked option writing, which requires $100,000. Delayed option quotes can be easily accessed. Options analytics include volatility (historical and implied), profit and delta graphs, gamma graphs, and vega graphs. Stop orders on options are not offered. (Table 10.7.)

stocks: Market orders require a $15 minimum per trade for direct access to market maker ECNs. Based on $.02 (2 cents) per share for the first 2,000 shares and $.01 for each additional share. Or, if an OTC stock is eligible, $7.75 routed to a third-party dealer. Listed limit orders—$22.50 for the first 2,000 shares and then $.03 per share for additional shares.

account minimum: A minimum of $1,000 for a browser or cash account; $10,000 nonbrowser account; margin accounts require $5,000

table 10.7 #6 preferred trade

Trade	Margin	Commission
Long synthetic straddle: Short 100 shares of IBM @ 125 Long 2 February IBM 125 calls @ 8	$7,850	$34.95
Long straddle: AMZN @ 190 Long 1 February AMZN 190 Call @ $26^7/_8$ Long 1 February AMZN 190 Put @ 32	$5,887.50	$45.90
Short straddle: AMZN @ 190 Short 1 February AMZN 190 Call @ $26^7/_8$ Short 1 February AMZN 190 Put @ 32	$3,800; $100,000 minimum account required	$45.90
Bull call spread: Long 1 February DELL 60 Call @ $9^1/_4$ Short 1 February DELL 65 Call @ $7^1/_2$	$175; $10,000 minimum account required	$45.90
Put ratio backspread: Short 3 February XCIT 60 Puts @ 17 Long 5 February XCIT 50 Puts @ $8^5/_8$	$2,212.50; $10,000 minimum account required	$63.90
Iron butterfly spread: Long 1 February HWP 45 Put @ $^1/_8$ Short 1 February HWP 55 Put @ $^{15}/_{16}$ Short 1 February HWP 65 Call @ $4^3/_8$ Long 1 February HWP 75 Call @ 1	$1,581; $10,000 minimum account required	$91.80

cash; $10,000 minimum for covered spreads and $100,000 for uncovered positions; 20% of premium plus 20% of underlying stock value minus out-of-the-money amount plus 10% of underlying stock value. Minimum equity of $100,000 in the account plus cash available to put up for the requirement to sell calls or puts naked, as per the following formulas:

> *Equity requirement:* 20% of the stock + Premium – Amount out-of-the-money × # of contracts × 100

> *Index requirement:* 15% of the index + Premium – Amount out-of-the-money × # of contracts × 100

quotes: Real-time snapshot quotes are available at no additional charge to clients. Real-time dynamic quotes are not available for the browser, but they are available as part of the nonbrowser package.

miscellaneous: Mutual funds, rapid and/or automatic portfolio updating, no discrimination against odd-lot orders, 24-hour order entry (orders executed during market hours). Account holders can call toll-free (888-781-0283) in order to place trades over the telephone if they cannot access the Internet from their computer due to technical difficulties, computer failure, or system traffic on the Internet. These trades will be executed at the same online rates. The hours are 6:00 A.M. to 1:00 P.M. Pacific Time for telephone orders. Fax orders or voice mail orders are not accepted.

#7 dreyfus brokerage services, inc.

www.edreyfus.com
5757 Wilshire Boulevard, Suite 3, Los Angeles, CA 90036; 401 N. Maple Drive, Beverly Hills, CA 90210
toll-free: phone: 310-276-0200 or 800-416-7113
e-mail: support@edreyfus.com
category: Middle-cost discount brokerage
site design = 8
user-friendliness = 7
options usefulness = 7

general description: Established in 1976, Dreyfus Brokerage Services, Inc., formerly Pacific Brokerage Services, Inc., is a member firm of the New York Stock Exchange and other principal U.S. securities exchanges. In 1996, Dreyfus established its online services specializing in prompt executions in stocks and options at discount commission rates.

features: Dreyfus offers online stocks and options services entered and executed on all major exchanges via a direct computer to computer link with the New York Stock Exchange and the Nasdaq stock

table 10.8   #7 dreyfus brokerage services, inc.

Trade	Margin	Commission
Long synthetic straddle:	$7,850	$30
Short 100 shares of IBM @ 125		
Long 2 February IBM 125 calls @ 8		
Long straddle: AMZN @ 190	$5,887.50	$30
Long 1 February AMZN 190 Call @ $26^7/_8$		
Long 1 February AMZN 190 Put @ 32		
Short straddle: AMZN @ 190	$15,387.50;	$30
Short 1 February AMZN 190 Call @ $26^7/_8$	$20,000 minimum	
Short 1 February AMZN 190 Put @ 32	account required	
Bull call spread:	$175;	$30
Long 1 February DELL 60 Call @ $9^1/_4$	$10,000 minimum	
Short 1 February DELL 65 Call @ $7^1/_2$	account required	
Put ratio backspread:	$3,000;	$30
Short 3 February XCIT 60 Puts @ 17	$10,000 minimum	
Long 5 February XCIT 50 Puts @ $8^5/_8$	account required	
Iron butterfly spread:	$2,000;	$60
Long 1 February HWP 45 Put @ $^1/_8$	$10,000 minimum	
Short 1 February HWP 55 Put @ $^{15}/_{16}$	account required	
Short 1 February HWP 65 Call @ $4^3/_8$		
Long 1 February HWP 75 Call @ 1		

market, as well as various options exchanges. Trade history is available in either date or symbol order. Prices of security positions are updated constantly during market hours. Stock prices are delayed 20 minutes during market hours.

additional services: You can obtain important stock market information including the following: market indexes and statistics; market leaders; real-time quotations; order entry; account status reflecting security positions and money balances. There are links to Zacks, market indexes and statistics, market leaders, and StockEdge Online. Dreyfus does not do intraday update balances. Comprehensive services include retirement planning, estate planning, college planning, and tax planning are available.

options: $15 or $1.75 per contract (whichever comes first). Complex spread options trading is processed through a live broker at Web prices. Option quotes require only one base symbol for the underlying security. Extremely low options commissions (only $15). Stop orders on options are allowed depending on market conditions—but you have to call them in to a live broker. There is no process offering simultaneous trades of options and stocks; therefore, you have to leg into any spreads that involve stocks and options. Orders for the purchase or sale of options are entered and executed on all major exchanges via a direct computer-to-computer link with the New York Stock Exchange, the Nasdaq stock market, and selected dealers, as well as various options and other exchanges. (Table 10.8.)

stocks: $15 for limit and market orders. Above 5,000 shares, add $.01 per share.

account minimum: $1,000 to open an account; $20,000 for spreads and naked options.

quotes: Delayed quotes only. However, you may subscribe to eSignal for $130 to $155 per month or receive five free StockEdge quotes per month or pay a discounted rate of $59 to $79 per month for a StockEdge subscription.

miscellaneous: Download stock prices (symbol, last, volume, change, high & low) on 5,000+ securities, after market hours, for import to a database management or spreadsheet program on your personal computer.

#8 computel securities

www.computel.com
301 Mission St., 5th Floor, San Francisco, CA 94105
toll-free: To Open an Account: 800-432-0327
  Account Holder Support: 888-597-6840
  Trading Desk: 888-240-2835
fax: 415-543-3714
e-mail: support@computel.com
category: High-cost discount brokerage
site design = 7
user-friendliness = 8
options usefulness = 7

general description: CompuTEL Securities, a division of Thomas F. White (the firm that founded Lombard Securities and now Discover), has been in operation since June 1995, providing trading in equities and options, mutual funds, and fixed income products. One of the first brokerages to offer Internet trading, CompuTEL has an excellent record for executions and reliability.

features: Trading on stocks, options (Table 10.9), bonds, and over 1,000 mutual funds. Account information includes 24-hour access to positions, balances, order status, and execution reports.

additional services: CompuTEL offers news and research from Reuters Information Services, Inc., Link (detailed company profiles on more than 6,000 U.S. public companies); personalized market snapshot (up-to-the-minute late-breaking news and financial data from Reuters, intraday graphs, indexes, statistics, news headlines, commentaries, and financial reports); portfolio tracker (track up to 10 personalized portfolios with up to 30 securities each); personalized portfolio summary e-mailed twice daily; charting (price history charts and graphs—daily, weekly, and yearly—graphs on over 6,000 U.S. companies); 20-minute-delayed quotes; and option chain price information for most securities; also, eSignal or StockEdge Online (real-time quotes), BigCharts, Business Wire, and PR Newswire stories, free access to Briefing.com, Zacks Investment Research, and EDGAR Online SEC filings.

options: $24 plus $1 per contract, fixed commission. Comprehensive option services. Easy and cheap commission schedule with no hidden

---

table 10.9   #8 computel securities

Trade	Margin	Commission
Long synthetic straddle: Short 100 shares of IBM @ 125 Long 2 February IBM 125 calls @ 8	$7,850	$45
Long straddle: AMZN @ 190 Long 1 February AMZN 190 Call @ $26^7/_8$ Long 1 February AMZN 190 Put @ 32	$5,887.50	$50
Short straddle: AMZN @ 190 Short 1 February AMZN 190 Call @ $26^7/_8$ Short 1 February AMZN 190 Put @ 32	$9,500	$50
Bull call spread: Long 1 February DELL 60 Call @ $9^1/_4$ Short 1 February DELL 65 Call @ $7^1/_2$	$175; $2,300 minimum account required	$50
Put ratio backspread: Short 3 February XCIT 60 Puts @ 17 Long 5 February XCIT 50 Puts @ $8^5/_8$	$4,725; $2,000 minimum account required	$56
Iron butterfly spread: Long 1 February HWP 45 Put @ $^1/_8$ Short 1 February HWP 55 Put @ $^{15}/_{16}$ Short 1 February HWP 65 Call @ $4^3/_8$ Long 1 February HWP 75 Call @ 1	$1,500; $2,000 minimum account required	$100

costs. Spread orders welcomed although online spread services are not offered. CompuTEL is planning to expand its online capacity, including making the simultaneous placing of spread orders and other combination strategies available through online services.

stocks: $14 market orders of 999 shares or fewer; $9 for market orders of 1,000 shares or more. All limit orders are $19.

account minimum: $5,000. Equity options—$2,000 minimum balance. The margin required for naked short options is 25% of underlying stock value.

quotes: Each day 25 free real-time quotes are provided.

miscellaneous: Trade any domestic listed exchange or Nasdaq stock, including foreign company ADRs. Foreign securities are available through your personal representative. Foreign accounts are available.

#9 brown & co.

www.brownco.com
1 Beacon St., 18th Floor, Boston, MA 02108
phone: 617-624-6513
trading desk: 617-742-2600
toll-free: 800-357-4410
category: Deep discount brokerage
slogan: "Where your experience pays off."
site design = 8
user-friendliness = 7
options usefulness = 6

general description: Brown & Co. is a deep discount broker for active, experienced clients that do not need investment advice or handholding. The unusually high account minimum helps to streamline clients to those with a high level of trading experience. Brown & Co. directs orders to market makers and ECNs, thereby bypassing market centers that impose charges on each order that in turn reduce a brokerage's profit. In this way, Brown & Co. has developed a reputation for excellent fills, low commissions, and reliability.

features: Brown & Co. allows investors to trade stocks and stock options, as well as bonds and Treasuries. All accounts are considered margin accounts.

additional services: Check writing is one of the few additional features. Brown & Co. does not offer free research because their clients are experienced investors with their own techniques of researching companies. It offers a multitude of links, but no free services. A rebate of 10% of the total commission amount is given any month when commissions exceed $350.

options: Market orders—$15 + $1.50 per contract ($25 minimum) for up to 30 contracts, then $1.75 per contract; limit orders—$15 + $1.75 per contract ($25 minimum). Spread orders and complex options combinations are allowed to be placed via a live broker if you receive approval to do so. (Table 10.10.) Stop orders on equity options are available. A special team comes in on expiration weekends and processes all assignments in order to alert clients of nonautomatic assignments.

stocks: Market orders (online and Touch-Tone)—$5 up to 5,000 shares, then add $.01 per share. Limit orders—$10 up to 5,000 shares, then add $.01 per share.

account minimum: $15,000. Naked option account requirements depend on the exchange used.

table 10.10   #9 brown & co.

Trade	Margin	Commission
Long synthetic straddle: Short 100 shares of IBM @ 125 Long 2 February IBM 125 calls @ 8	$7,850	$35
Long straddle: AMZN @ 190 Long 1 February AMZN 190 Call @ $26^7/_8$ Long 1 February AMZN 190 Put @ 32	$5,887	$50
Short straddle: AMZN @ 190 Short 1 February AMZN 190 Call @ $26^7/_8$ Short 1 February AMZN 190 Put @ 32	$9,687.50	$50
Bull call spread: Long 1 February DELL 60 Call @ $9^1/_4$ Short 1 February DELL 65 Call @ $7^1/_2$	$175	$50
Put ratio backspread: Short 3 February XCIT 60 Puts @ 17 Long 5 February XCIT 50 Puts @ $8^5/_8$	$2,212	$54
Iron butterfly spread: Long 1 February HWP 45 Put @ $^1/_8$ Short 1 February HWP 55 Put @ $^{15}/_{16}$ Short 1 February HWP 65 Call @ $4^3/_8$ Long 1 February HWP 75 Call @ 1	$1,582	$100

quotes: 100 free real-time quotes per executed trade.

miscellaneous: Automatic execution confirmation includes a special place on the site that shows "today's executions." If the server goes down, Brown & Co. will waive the commission fees. The firm has 150 live brokers, 13 branch offices, and Touch-Tone service to pick up the slack.

#10 charles schwab online

www.eschwab.com
101 Montgomery, MS120-12, San Francisco, CA 94104
toll-free: 800-435-4000
e-mail: Located at the web site
category: High-cost discount brokerage
slogan: "The online leader. The service you expect, the value you want."
site design = 8
user-friendliness = 6
options usefulness = 7

general description: Schwab is the largest brokerage of them all and therefore has the resources to offer one of the most advanced information retrieval systems available complete with the very latest news, research, and investment information concisely analyzed and tailored to fit your trading needs. With 450 branches all over the country, Schwab is everywhere. Commissions tend to run a little high but that hasn't stopped Schwab from leading the online trading market with a 33% share (according to a report from Piper Jaffray Companies, Inc.). Unfortunately, it can be very hard to get through to a live service representative in such a big brokerage at their main trading headquarters.

features: Schwab has it all: stock, stock options, mutual funds, bonds, Treasuries, stock screening, portfolio management, and everything from tax planning to college funds. There are two kinds of available service: Schwab Signature Services (priority service and enhanced research for active traders and investors with substantial portfolios) and Schwab AdvisorSource (easy-to-find, prescreened, independent investment advisers).

additional services: Certificates of deposit (CDs), life insurance, retirement services, special live interactive events with investment experts providing insightful answers to financial questions. Links to Market Buzz™ include Briefing.com, OneSource Online, Quote.com, BigCharts.com, CBOE, Market Guide, StockSmart, DBC Online.

table 10.11   #10 charles schwab online

Trade	Margin	Commission
Long synthetic straddle: Short 100 shares of IBM @ 125 Long 2 February IBM 125 calls @ 8	$4,375	$73.63
Long straddle: AMZN @ 190 Long 1 February AMZN 190 Call @ $26^7/_8$ Long 1 February AMZN 190 Put @ 32	$5,887.50	$64
Short straddle: AMZN @ 190 Short 1 February AMZN 190 Call @ $26^7/_8$ Short 1 February AMZN 190 Put @ 32	$10,637; naked equity $25,000	$64
Bull call spread: Long 1 February DELL 60 Call @ $9^1/_4$ Short 1 February DELL 65 Call @ $7^1/_2$	$2,000; $5,000 minimum account required	$64
Put ratio backspread: Short 3 February XCIT 60 Puts @ 17 Long 5 February XCIT 50 Puts @ $8^5/_8$	$3,000; $5,000 minimum account required	$134
Iron butterfly spread: Long 1 February HWP 45 Put @ $^1/_8$ Short 1 February HWP 55 Put @ $^{15}/_{16}$ Short 1 February HWP 65 Call @ $4^3/_8$ Long 1 February HWP 75 Call @ 1	$2,000; $5,000 minimum account required	$140

options: $35 plus $1.75 per contract (this varies due to the quantity of the order and the option premium). Schwab knows that option traders need seasoned expertise and fast order execution. Schwab Options Service offers fast access to a dedicated team of expert option specialists who provide prompt, efficient order execution on even the most complex orders through Schwab's advanced order execution technology. They can also help structure option trading strategies based on a trader's investment objectives. (Table 10.11.)

stocks: Market and limit orders are $29.95 up to 1,000 shares, then add $.03 per share.

account minimum: $2,500; minimum requirement on equity option spread orders is $5,000 and $25,000 on index options.

quotes: 100 free for opening an account and 100 free for each executed trade.

miscellaneous: Multilingual services: Schwab has several service centers for the non-English-speaking investor—life insurance, CDs, and money markets. Schwab has experienced several system failures—alternate contacts through channels: voice broker, tele-broker, live broker, and local branch broker.

conclusion

To decipher the needs of an online trader, I took a close look at the current advantages of a live broker. To become a broker, candidates must pass a test called a Series 7 to receive a license. Series 7 is designed to test a candidate's knowledge of the rules and regulations of stock trading, the formal definitions of various securities, the risks involved in trading, and some fairly basic macroeconomic variables that affect securities. The test does not assess a candidate's ability to make money in the markets. Many brokers are fairly young and get into this business with hopes of making lots of money in commissions—not necessarily making money in the markets.

I raise this issue because the most widely touted reason for having a live broker is to get his or her advice. The quality of the advice is directly proportional to your broker's ability to make money in the marketplace (commissions not included). There are lots of brokers out there who are very talented and could be a tremendous asset in your financial management. Then there are the others—the ones who may know less than you do about how to make money using stocks and options. That's why it is so important to interview prospective brokers carefully before you throw high commission dollars at them. All brokers are not created equal.

Brokers make money regardless of whether you do. That's a very important thing to keep in mind. Have you ever gotten a call from a broker who just had to tell you about the latest hot stock that you just had to buy? If you decide to take that timely advice and buy the stock, and the stock price subsequently plummets, your broker still makes a commission getting you into and then out of that very same stock. Getting advice from a broker is a double-edged sword. With the advent of online financial commentaries, advisories, and chat rooms, much of the information that was previously limited to the broker's world is now readily available on the Internet. Once you learn how to interpret market signals for yourself, you probably won't need a broker to advise you at all.

The next advantage that today's brokers have over computers is ease and speed. Calling your broker to place an order is just a matter of picking up the phone, dialing a few numbers, and reading off your order. In the computerized world, you have to turn on your computer, open your browser, go to your brokerage site, log on with a user name and password, go to the trading section of the site, type in the trade that you want, confirm the trade that you want, and then hit "Submit." You've missed 10 points in stock price move going through this process! Some of that time is shaved off if we assume that you are already on the computer, but the rest still takes time and energy.

To become more time efficient, many brokerages are working hard at becoming portals where you would spend most of your time online. In that case, you are probably already at the site and already logged on. Before long, as voice recognition applications become more proficient, you will no doubt be able to speak your order directly into the computer.

On the flip side, let's look at the advantages that computers already bring to the table today. Most traders are starting to use the Internet to get charts, news, and analysis information. Unless you have two lines, you have to log off to pick up the phone to place an order. Then there's the process of picking stocks. If you know that you are interested in buying mid-cap stocks, with a certain price earnings ratio and a certain volume, that have recently shown a certain pattern, there's no broker in the world that can find them all with the speed and accuracy of your computer.

As the marketplace evolves, brokerages are going to have to put more services and tools online to attract additional clients. Even commissions may become a thing of the past as more companies compete for clients. In the final analysis, the brokerage that ends up with your business will be the one that offers the highest level of reliability, ease of use, and execution expertise.

chapter 11

order processing

placing an online order

Technology has made the execution of an order almost unnoticeable to the average trader. You just key in the trade, dial in your password, and hit "Send." In many cases, the entire ordering process is completed in 10 seconds or less. Simple buy and sell orders are so effortless that many traditional investors do not concern themselves with this end of the investment process at all. But this does not hold true for complex option orders. Option traders have distinct needs that require special attention. If you are dealing with a brokerage firm that doesn't specialize in options, you may have a hard time getting a complex option order executed. As an option trader, you need a brokerage that understands the tricks of the trade so that your order will be filled at the best possible price.

Trade execution depends on the type of trade you want to execute, the exchange, and the mood of the market. There are an assortment of order instructions (see Appendix A for a list of "Types of Orders") and a variety of exchanges to choose from. In addition, the advent of the Internet has changed the ordering process dramatically. Let's take a closer look at what happens when you place an order.

To make a trade, you begin by placing an order with your broker, who in turn passes it along to a floor broker. The floor broker takes it to the appropriate pit and uses the open outcry system to try to find another floor broker who wants to buy or sell your order. If your floor broker cannot fill your order, it is left with a specialist who keeps a list of all the unfilled orders, matching them up as prices fluctuate. In this way, specialists are brokers to the floor brokers and receive a commission for every transaction they carry out. Groups of specialists trading similar markets are located near one another in trading pits. Once your order has been filled, the floor trader contacts your broker, who in turn sends confirmation of the execution of your trade. The amazing part of this process is that a market order—one that is to be executed immediately—may take only seconds to complete.

Computerized trading is used for smaller orders of less than 1,200 shares. Frequently, more than 50% of a day's trades use the Designated Order Turnaround (DOT) system to process small trades. No matter what, your broker gets paid a fee or commission for his or her efforts. Although some online brokerages have slashed commissions to less than $10 a trade, your chief concern as a trader should be to get the transaction executed as you desire and at the best possible price. That's why choosing the right broker is essential to your success. Brokers should be in the business of looking after your interests, not just generating commissions for their pockets.

Designated Order Turnaround (DOT)
the computerized order entry system maintained by the New York Stock Exchange.

In addition to the specialists, there are also market makers that create liquidity by narrowing the spread. Market makers trade for themselves or for a firm. Once an order hits the floor, the market makers can participate with the other players on a competitive basis. However, if there is no action in the pit, they are obligated to "make a market" happen. Market makers are truly pros. They play the bid-ask spread like no one else on the planet, making their money on the spread—the difference between the bid and the ask price. This difference may be only $.25 or less. However, they process a very large number of shares and this tiny difference adds up quickly. Market makers are also experts at hedging their trades for protection.

---

market maker
an independent trader or trading firm that is prepared to buy and sell shares or contracts in a designated market in order to facilitate trading by making a two-sided market (bid and ask).

Nasdaq offers brokers the ability to trade directly from their offices using telephones and continuously revised computerized prices. In this way, brokers bypass floor traders and the need to pass along a commission to them. This means that they get to keep more of the commission for themselves. There are no specialists, either; but there are market makers.

Options exchanges, although much newer, are very similar to stock exchanges. They provide a safe place for buyers and sellers to trade options. The Chicago Board Options Exchange (CBOE) handles the majority of the volume on stock options. However, the Philadelphia Stock Exchange, the American Stock Exchange, and the Pacific Stock Exchange also house options trading pits.

The process for placing option orders is very similar to that of placing a stock order. In many cases, if you are trading both the stock and the options, your order will be guided to an exchange that can process both. However, since they are individual orders, you will be charged a commission on both orders. Commissions are charged to place a trade and to exit one.

Unlike simple stock and option orders, option spread orders require special handling. Even though some online brokerage firms allow customers to place complex options strategies online, it still takes a floor broker to represent the order to the market-making crowd. None of the option exchanges (CBOE, AMEX, PHLX, and PCX) are equipped electronically to route the complex option spread order to the appropriate market-making crowd.

Behind each successful option spread trade stands a broker who understands the best method for executing a complex option order. Indeed, there are numerous decisions that contribute to an option spread order's success. The real trick of the trade comes into play when an option is dual or triple listed on various exchanges. Take AOL, for instance; currently AOL options trade on three different exchanges—CBOE, AMEX, and PCX. Each exchange has its own bid-ask spread, which may not be the same as other exchanges' bid-ask spreads. This can make things extremely confusing, especially since most quotes show the best inside market (best bid and best offer from an individual exchange). That's why choosing the right brokerage is essential to your trading success. Brokers with extensive options experience will know which exchange provides the better fill or if the order should be split (one leg to be executed on one exchange and the other leg to be executed on a different exchange).

Once an order has been filled, executions are verbally given to the brokerage firm from the floor broker with individual strike price fills, which then need to be communicated to the customer. This execution should be confirmed with the customer or appear immediately within the customer's online order execution screen. Simple stock orders and buy/sell option orders can be processed electronically. But complex option spreads require manual labor. This leaves a wide margin for human error. Firms without the expertise to process specific strategies are just more likely to make mistakes and possibly cause forfeiture of profits or even major losses. This leads to client frustration as an enormous amount of time and energy goes into complaining and trying to find a solution. Look for a brokerage that employs brokers with experience on the floor of an options exchange. There is no substitute for options experience.

inner workings of assignments and option exercising

The manner in which a trade is closed manifests the trade's profit or loss. There are three ways to exit a trade in which options are present. An option can be offset, exercised, or allowed to expire. Experience is the best teacher when it comes to choosing the best alternative. Since each alternative has an immediate result, learning how to profitably close out a trade is essential to becoming a successful trader.

If you want to exercise a long stock option, you simply notify your broker, who will then notify the Options Clearing Corporation (OCC). By the next day, you will own (call) or have sold (put) the corresponding underlying asset. You can exercise an option at any time; but primarily you will do it—if you do it at all—just prior to expiration. If the market rises, you may choose to exercise a call option. Your trading account will then be debited for 100 shares of the underlying stock (per option) at the call's strike price. If the market declines, you may choose to exercise a put option. You will then short the stock and receive a credit to your account for 100 shares at the put's strike price.

An option seller cannot exercise an option. By selling an option, you are taking on the risk of having a buyer assigned and exercise the option against you when market price movement makes it an ITM option. If you have an open position short call that is assigned and exercised, you are obligated to deliver 100 shares of the underlying stock to the option buyer at the strike price of your short call. If you have an open position short put that is assigned and exercised, you are obligated to buy 100 shares of the underlying stock from the option buyer at the strike price of your short put. The OCC randomly matches or "assigns" buyers and sellers to one another. If there is an excess of sellers by expiration, all open position ITM short options are automatically exercised by the OCC. In order to avoid being automatically exercised, short option holders can choose to offset their options instead.

Offsetting is a closing transaction that cancels an open position. It is accomplished by doing the opposite of the opening transaction. Obviously, the best time to offset an option is when it is in-the-money and therefore will realize a profit. Offsetting is also used to avoid incurring further losses. An option can be offset at any time—one second after it has been entered or one minute before expiration. It is very important to know the expiration dates of your open position options so that you avoid leaving a nice profit on the table. In contrast, the best way to realize a profit from a short option is to let it expire and keep the credit received from the premium. That's why time is a short option's enemy. The longer a short option has till expiration, the more chances it has of being exercised.

Although most option holders and writers close out their option positions with an offsetting closing transaction, investors should be familiar with assignment and exercise. Understanding assignments and exercises can help an option holder determine whether exercise might be more advantageous than an offsetting sale of the option. Offsetting an option is the most popular technique of closing an option. In fact, 95% of all the options with value are offset. However, there are various reasons why a trader might choose to exercise an option versus offset it. Of the 5% that are exercised, 95% are exercised at expiration.

In addition, option writers (short option sellers) need to understand exercise procedures because of the possibility of being assigned. Once a customer is assigned, he or she can no longer effect a closing transaction in that option, but must instead purchase (put) or deliver the underlying stock (call) for the exercise price (or, in the case of a cash-settled option, pay the cash settlement amount). Depending on the situation, it may be better for the customer to cover the assignment and deliver the underlying stock by hedging and selling a long option position or simply by exercising a long option position.

In the case of assignments, the OCC assigns exercises in standardized lots to clearing member accounts that reflect the writing of options identical to the exercised options. Once the exercises are assigned by the OCC to a clearing member firm, the clearing firm must then assign them to customers maintaining positions as writers of the exercised options series. These assignments are allocated either on a random selection basis or on a first in, first out basis.

To exercise an option, the holder must direct his or her brokerage firm to give exercise instructions to the OCC. In order to ensure that an option is exercised on a particular day, the holder must direct the brokerage firm to exercise before the firm's cutoff time for accepting instructions for that day—normally a half hour before the market closes. Once an exercise instruction has been given to a member clearing firm, it cannot ordinarily be revoked except to correct a bona fide error designated in a request filed by the clearing member prior to a deadline specified in OCC's rules.

Exercises and assignments may become somewhat tricky during expiration. Most online trading brokerages automatically offset long option positions that are $3/4$ point or greater in-the-money. If a short option position is greater than $1/4$ point in-the-money, it runs the risk of being assigned. Assignment places the short seller in a position of unlimited risk, which is why hedge strategies are so vital to an option trader's ability to succeed.

online order entry formats

Although each online brokerage site has its own unique design format, many of the available order screens are similar in scope. Let's take a walk through a few of these screens using Mr. Stock as our prototype brokerage. Mr. Stock has created the following order entry screens for six different types of options orders:

- Simple stock order
- Simple option order
- Spread
- Straddle
- Butterfly
- Condor

A custom option screen enables customers to revise a price or quantity prior to sending the order to the brokerage. Most brokerages also offer a symbol lookup feature that can be used to derive the symbol for the stock or option you want to trade.

stock order screen

There are several different variables that clients must enter to submit a stock order online (Figure 11.1). You can choose to buy, sell, sell short, or buy to cover the stock of your choice. You also need to choose the symbol; specify the quantity of shares; choose whether it's a market or limit order (and a price if you want a limit order); specify

figure 11.1   stock order entry screen

source: courtesy of mr. stock. reprinted with permission.

figure 11.2   option order entry screen

source: courtesy of mr. stock. reprinted with permission.

figure 11.3   vertical spread order entry screen

source: courtesy of mr. stock. reprinted with permission.

day or good till canceled (GTC); and add any special instructions you may have (stop order, stop limit, fill-or-kill, etc.). Additional fees may apply depending on your special instructions.

option order screen
There are nine different variables that the customer must enter to submit an option order (Figure 11.2): open buy/open sell, close buy/close sell; quantity; class; month; strike price; call or put; limit price; day or good till canceled; and any special instructions you may have. Once again, you may modify your order as to price and quantity or look up the option's symbol if needed.

spread order screen
There are two kinds of vertical spreads: credit and debit (Figure 11.3). Since a vertical spread consists of two options, the order screen has two rows of information that must be filled out to complete the order. Qualifiers such as day or GTC, limit price, and special instructions are entered only once.

straddle order entry

A straddle consists of two option transactions—a put and a call with the same strike price and expiration date—executed at one price. The straddle order screen (Figure 11.4) consists of the same selections as a basic option screen, except the option order selection has a pull-down menu with two-part buy or sell instructions.

butterfly order entry

Butterfly orders are simply three option transactions at one price. A butterfly must be in a 1:2:1 ratio with regular strike increments. This screen (Figure 11.5) is used to trade butterflies in which the customer only needs to specify one price, day or GTC, and any other qualifiers.

condor order entry

Condor orders consist of four option transactions at a time. This screen (Figure 11.6) can be used to place a condor or an iron butterfly order. There are four rows of option information that must be completed and one row of qualifiers.

These screens represent the kind of process that you will be required to go through to place a complex option order directly online. The graphics may change, but the content will remain the same. For the most part, you should include a limit price for spreads, straddles, butterflies, and condors. In today's highly volatile market, placing limits on the amount of money you are willing to spend is the key to managing your risk.

figure 11.4   straddle order entry screen

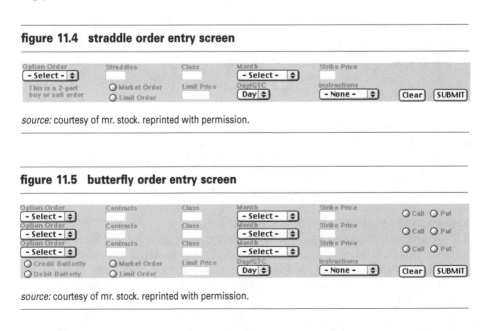

source: courtesy of mr. stock. reprinted with permission.

figure 11.5   butterfly order entry screen

source: courtesy of mr. stock. reprinted with permission.

figure 11.6   condor order entry screen

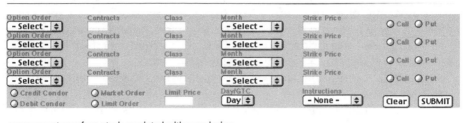

system failures

On Tuesday, October 28, 1997, the New York Stock Exchange at 1.2 billion shares' worth and Nasdaq at 1.36 billion shares' worth broke the record for trading volume. Markets plummeted that day, and bargain-hunting traders clamored to take advantage of extremely low prices. A feeding frenzy ensued, but many small investors couldn't reach their brokerage firms to get their hands in the pie. Unfortunately, many online brokerages simply did not have the capacity to handle the increased flow of orders. Investors found it impossible to log on and even brokerage phone lines were busy. As losses accumulated and profits were missed, investor frustration soared.

After the exchanges closed, online financial chat rooms were filled with negative tirades from impassioned investors. Each brokerage cited a variety of excuses for system failures. Many big online brokerages had misjudged the intense volume a major move in the marketplace could create and did not have the capacity to handle it. In contrast, many of the smaller brokerages had an easier time processing the increased flow of orders because they service fewer clients to begin with.

This initial incident of system failure gave the online brokerage industry a new demon to deal with. But solving these difficulties is not easy. System failures continue to plague electronic brokerages as online brokerages pursue various solutions to the high volume problem. Recent increases in stock trading volumes as well as wild price swings have produced a tidal wave of online brokerage failures. For example, E*Trade, the self-proclaimed leader of online brokerages, suffered critical outages on three consecutive days during the first week in February 1999. Thousands of E*Trade customers were unable to place orders. In addition, massive trading bottlenecks on a number of high-volume Internet stocks as well as periodic access problems in quieter markets have triggered a variety of problems for traders across the board.

Unfortunately, everyone wants to place the blame somewhere other than their own backyard and very few are bellying up to the bar with any concrete solutions. After the Securities and Exchange Commission (SEC) received 330% more investor complaints on online problems than the prior year, the SEC's chairman, Arthur Levitt, responded by warning investors to exercise caution when trading online. Not to be outdone, the NASD Regulation, the self-policing arm of the National Association of Securities Dealers, suggested that brokerage firms should warn investors of possible losses due to online capacity flaws. Meanwhile, brokerages have countered by increasing margins—sometimes to as much as 100%—on various high-tech stocks, thereby reducing the number of traders who can afford to trade these high-flying stocks. Others have countered by removing certain Internet stocks from online trading.

If you do get burned by a system failure, you can attempt to find consolation by lodging a complaint in writing to the compliance officer at your brokerage firm and sending copies to the Securities and Exchange Commission (SEC), National Association of Securities Dealers (NASD), and possibly your state regulator. Investors who want to take legal action do not have much of a case unless they can prove "a clear departure from established norms." Since antifraud provisions do not permit suits based on claims of lost profits, there is no recourse under federal antifraud provisions set up by national securities laws. If you still want to file a complaint, make sure to send a copy to the SEC at the Office of Investor Education and Assistance, Securities and Exchange Commission, Washington, DC 20549, or call your local NASD office (call 800-289-9999 to find it). You can also visit the NASD web site at www.nasd.com.

National Association of Securities Dealers (NASD)
the self-regulatory organization of the securities industry responsible for the regulation of Nasdaq and the over-the-counter markets (www.nasd.com).

---

conclusion

Order processing has come a long way since the late 1700s when traders met under a buttonwood tree on Wall Street. Today's floor traders can run up to 12 miles or more each trading day just to get the job done. As we cross into the twenty-first century, this process will probably become more electronically synchronized. It will be very interesting to see how it changes the nature of the trading game.

To make the most of any option, traders with open positions need to keep track of the price of the underlying asset very carefully each day. A momentary fluctuation in price can mean the difference between opportunity and crisis. Luckily, computers make this process easier than ever before. Most brokerages provide detailed listings of any orders that you may have open. You can also receive closing prices on the stocks and options of your choice directly to your e-mail address either from your brokerage or from a lengthy list of financial web site services. This is a far cry from checking prices in the *Wall Street Journal* every day.

Since the price execution of an option spread is critical to its success, I highly recommend working with smaller online brokerage firms that specialize in options. As online trading continues to evolve, we will most likely witness an all-around upgrade in online option spread order placing. Although only a handful of online brokerages offer this kind of service, more brokerages will undoubtedly follow suit in order to compete for the option trader's business. Since easy ordering formats are very important to the avid option trader, hopefully we will see a lot of advancement in this area over the next few years. What can the active online option trader do right now to minimize losses? Here's my list of 10 dos and don'ts to help you through the online trading growing pains.

1. First and foremost, you have to assume that glitches and delays are part of the online trading process.
2. Develop a backup plan for each trade beyond just calling your broker on the phone when your system is down.
3. Keep a hard copy of your trading account available for when your broker's server shuts down.
4. Place limited-risk trades; avoid naked positions.
5. Always calculate a trade's maximum risk before entering it and make sure you can afford to lose that amount.
6. Try using LEAPS options in the more volatile markets.
7. Don't expect instantaneous executions or confirmations, for sooner or later you will be disappointed.
8. If you believe the "fast" and "easy" claims advertised by online brokerages, get ready for disillusionment.
9. Always use limit orders. Market orders can be extremely dangerous in heavily volatile markets.
10. There are specific risks associated with buying on margin. Be aware of what is expected of you before entering a trade.

chapter 12

living online

reality check for online traders

Online trading is changing the nature of investing more than we can even begin to understand. Perhaps change is the only constant we can count on. In the past, the majority of the public's view of the stock market stemmed from television and movies. In fact, just last night I caught part of a movie where corporate raiders attempted a hostile takeover and the company's owner countered by buying back as much stock as he possibly could in his own company, which drove up the stock price. The raiders then started to sell, igniting a flurry of selling activity, which dropped the price to almost nothing. This left the company's owner with a bunch of worthless stock. The banks moved in on the company's owner and before long the whole family (rich, spoiled, and pathetic) was homeless.

I didn't say the movie was inspiring; but it was humorous in a Hollywood sort of way. It showed the insanity of it all—which is what we like to see as a moviegoing public—people screaming into their phones as floor brokers and market makers thrash it out in the trading pits. Movies have traditionally glorified trading by focusing on market extremes, and this misrepresentation has contributed to the public's fear of the stock market. But the Internet is changing this perspective once and for all by making trading easier than it's ever been before. It remains to be seen what changes will occur as online trading penetrates the mainstream's awareness.

But is the proliferation of online trading, especially in options, a dramatic shift in the way investors trade or just a hyped-up way for investors and traders to lose money faster in the markets? I hope it is not the latter; but we must be realistic. After all, the faster someone can trade, the more likely that person is to trade more often. Unfortunately, the ease with which investors or traders may be able to move in and out of the market may very well be inversely correlated to the amount of research they actually do to find and manage investment opportunities. It is paramount to your success as a trader to fight against this kind of gambler mentality when it comes to online trading disciplines. Let the power of the Internet work for you. Online trading services have not only increased the speed of the transaction and lowered the cost, but also given traders unimaginable access to information from which knowledgeable investment decisions can be made.

In reality, just like any job, there are fast days and there are slow days. You never know what might happen next. Perhaps it's the uncertainty that's so exhilarating. For me, trading is exciting. It's the most exciting game I know. Every morning I wake up early and have no idea what might happen next and I love it. But I do know that my ability to make good decisions quickly is the backbone of my ability to make a profit. Time waits for no one, especially the trader. However, the one attribute all traders must learn is patience. Many of the best trades take time to mature. So be patient, especially if you have placed a delta neutral options trade. Sometimes it is better to wait than to keep reacting to the market's every whim. Learn to utilize the Internet to provide you with the resources you need to trade well.

Entering the stock market for the first time is like walking in Daniel's shoes as he cha-chas into the lion's den. You have to have faith in your abilities to overcome every obstacle. On the outside, trading consists of buying and selling stocks and stock options. But on the inside, market sentiment and trader psychology can rip you apart. You have to be able to keep your wits about you to withstand everything the marketplace has to throw at you—from bidding wars to international market collapses. The first rule: Don't panic. By remaining calm, you harness the clarity to make decisions quickly in order to protect your investments against losses. Always look to protect your capital by using strong risk management techniques. Try to place yourself in a position to profit by choosing trades with limited risk and plenty of time to mature to profitability. And finally, have an exit plan already in place before placing a trade. The lack of a profit and loss plan is akin to not having a fire escape route—don't get burned.

electronic communication networks (ECNs)

As the speed by which information travels increases, the foundation on which the investing infrastructure is based is making a dynamic shift so fundamental that it challenges the imagination. Indications of this shift are clearly evident in the rise of electronic communication networks (ECNs). In 1997, ECNs began enabling brokerages to place stock trades via an electronic network so that the highest bid and lowest offer could be matched up between independent traders. Without the interference of market makers and other intermediaries that traditionally skim the cream off the top, a very efficient system has been developed that could lead to a fundamental change in the marketplace infrastructure. A handful of online brokerages—A. B. Watley, MB Trader, Datek Online, and Muriel Siebert, to name a few—are already using ECNs to match orders 24 hours a day. In fact, the SEC is currently seeking to implement new regulations for the development and operation of off-exchange trading systems. In the meantime, ECNs are growing at a phenomenal rate; and the more they grow, the higher liquidity they create for the trades pending execution. This should reduce the cost to the trader, increase the efficiency in which an order is placed, and create new markets in which an order can be placed. These factors which may result in making the markets much more competitive—all very good outcomes of the growth of ECNs.

---

electronic communication network (ECN)
a system that enables brokerages to place trades via an electronic network so that the highest bid and lowest offer can be matched up between independent traders.

However, there are still some major hurdles to be overcome before ECNs can become a major contender. First of all, brokerages develop strong relationships with market makers, and these heavyweight traders make their money on the bid-ask spread. If brokerages start to divert orders to ECNs they risk angering their market makers, and that is a potentially costly thing for a brokerage to do. Specialists on the New York Stock Exchange are not about to give up their lucrative positions without a fight. They may fight back by punishing offending brokerages by giving them lousy fills for their customers' orders.

But the advantages of ECNs—inexpensive trades and fast executions 24 hours a day—are not going to go away. According to a new Meridien Research report, "Exchanges that continue to resist these technological developments in favor of traditional trading practices risk erosion in market share and eventual extinction." (PR Newswire, January 20, 1999, 08:16; source: Meridien Research, Inc.) This kind of projection, as far as I'm concerned, is not too far off the mark.

Although an options ECN is currently slated for deployment in the not too distant future, there are still more than a few infrastructure obstacles to overcome. Current plans call for the inclusion of approximately 600 of the most popular options. Since it seems to be the nature of this generation to advance down the mind-boggling path of technological breakthroughs, I have no doubt that a vast network of electronic options exchanges will be up and running before too long.

The advent of an options ECN has both pros and cons. An electronic network in which we as traders could post our bids and offers to an electronic exchange seems wonderful. However, the question of liquidity will always be an issue. Even at exchanges, it is sometimes difficult to trade larger orders without giving up the trade for a wide bid-ask spread. In some markets trading 10 contracts may seem difficult while in others a large trader can trade thousands of options at a time, even as spread orders. For an options ECN to survive, there must be participation of all players: individual traders, market makers, and larger institutional traders. However, although there is a lot of talk in the market about an options ECN, it will take time for such a market to gain acceptance, and this will limit its growth in the early years. As options markets proliferate thanks to the advance of online trading, there may be enough liquidity for a comprehensive options ECN to create a new market for the trading of options that is competitive to the options specialist and market making system available at present. As an options trader who trades a large number of contracts, I dream of such a market where I do not have to worry about liquidity in the options market. But this new development will take time.

the effects of regulatory controls on online trading

As we move into the information age, the federal government is struggling to establish regulatory control over the content of the Internet. Information providers and software developers rally behind the First Amendment's freedom of speech clause while the federal government wages its battle in the name of protecting the public. Due to the Internet's interactive and seemingly uncontrollable nature, establishing some kind of regulatory control may prove to be an uphill battle.

The government's first tack was to try to get control over the content of the Internet through the Communications Decency Act. The judges from the U.S. Court of Appeals for the Third Circuit countered by recognizing that the Internet "has achieved, and continues to achieve, the most participatory marketplace of mass speech that this country—and indeed this world—has yet seen." [*American Civil Liberties Union (ACLU) v. Reno*, 929 F. Supp. 825 (E.D.Pa. 1996).] In June of 1997, the U.S. Supreme Court agreed, and the Communications Decency Act was successfully struck down [*Reno v. ACLU*, 65 U.S.L.W. 4715 (June 25, 1997)]. Proponents of a free Internet see this verdict as the Supreme Court's way of confirming First Amendment protection for freedom of speech on the Internet.

Communications Decency Act
an Act proposed by the U.S. federal government that sought to control the content of the Internet by confronting and defining online indecency.

But federal agencies and state governments have their own interpretations. Laws that uphold the government's claim for regulatory control of online information and software content are still being put forth in order to protect the public. For example, a Texas federal district court recently banned the sale of the Quicken Family Lawyer software package in order to protect "the uninformed and unwary from overly simplistic legal advice." [Institute for Justice (www.ij.org) web site, "Free Speech Case."] It was the court's stance that Quicken's software constituted the "unlicensed practice of law." (Ibid.) Although the decision is currently under appeal, federal agencies and other states are now free to use this precedent in their attempts to regulate software programs and web sites. For more information on regulation of the Internet, check out the Institute for Justice (www.ij.org) and click on their "First Amendment" Cases.

the big picture

When I first sat down to write this book, I was almost overwhelmed by the immensity of the project. How could I try to make heads or tails of the limitless nature of trading options online? As I headed into the homestretch, I realized that I needed to confirm some of my suspicions regarding online trading's prospects. In order to get the big picture, I interviewed two of the best online financial journalists in the business: Brenon Daly from CBS MarketWatch and Peter Henig of the Red Herring.

brenon daly

As a senior writer at CBS MarketWatch, Brenon Daly writes the daily "Software Report" and the twice-weekly "OptionsWatch" column, and covers large technology deals and investment conferences. Daly's extensive background in financial journalism includes bylines in the *East Bay Business Journal*, the *Economist*, and *Business Central Europe*. He also headed up the Vienna bureau of United Press International (UPI). He has more than paid his dues as a financial reporter and I sincerely value his insights on online trading.

When asked how the dramatic rise of online trading has affected investing in general, Daly acknowledged that "online trading has broadened the trading base. It's just easier than ever before. In fact, 50% of the American public own stocks in comparison to only 5% in Europe. I know that for myself, I trade more than I should since it's so easy—just point and click. Session-to-session trading has shifted away from the long-term view of investment." This shift has led to an exponential increase in trading volume. In fact, according to Schwab, the current leading online brokerage, 7 out of every 10 trades are done online. This shift means that more people than ever before are more than likely applying their savings in the markets, resulting in the astounding volatility of the past few years. But Daly still believes that there is "plenty of room for experienced brokers because inexperienced traders still need a helping hand."

When asked whether online trading will contribute to an increase in options trading, Daly stated, "Although options trading has grown over 35% over the last five years, the options market is limited because they are still not widely understood. Options are still a derivative industry. They are just too complicated and this caps the growth. Evidence of the limited nature of the options markets abounds." Although there may be a commentary or two from well-known options experts, "they never talk about the option pits on CNBC." Until the trading public becomes more educated about options, options will have limited use by the investing public regardless of how easy online brokerages make options trading.

When it comes to the rise of ECNs, Daly talked about how "market makers are getting fat, but lean days are coming for them because they are not passing along any cuts. ECNs are a tremendous threat to exchanges. They allow traders to get a better fill and reduce commissions. This will finally get exchanges to compete on price." But Daly was also ready to defend live brokers. "People are accountable; machines are not. No valuable information will come from ECNs, and personalization of information is so important. Besides, brokerages that opt to send orders to ECNs run the risk of pissing off their market makers, and connections are the key to good service."

Daly continued, "It's hard to imagine options ECNs. It's a very ambitious program. In the beginning, they plan on listing 600 options, which is a lot like skimming off the cream. ECNs may work to fill the big guys but not the less impressive ones. I'm not sure the ECNs will be able to compete. Options trading is a very insular world and the lines are pretty well drawn. Brokerages are unlikely to switch over to ECNs because if you've been sending your business to an ECN and then need a market maker, you'll likely get lousy fills. ECNs are still an untested, unproven system."

When the conversation returned to online brokerages, Daly had an interesting view on system failures and E*Trade in particular. "E*Trade is not worried about outages. They practically celebrate the free advertising. It's amazing, really. Not being able to process trades can be very frustrating. But despite all of that, people won't switch their accounts because it's too much of a hassle. It's just like AOL. Thousands of people may have complained about not being able to log on, but it didn't slow AOL's growth. As far as I'm concerned, people are way too tolerant of outages. Of course, settlements do occur, but account growth is everything while customer service sucks. The competitive bite is taking its toll on commissions already, and someday in the not too distant future we may be trading for free. Right now we're sitting at around $10 a trade. Someday the system will buckle completely. After all, Internet access is a service and an online stock trade is little more than a data transaction. Online brokerages like E*Trade are already branching out into other areas of the Internet. Being a brokerage is just not enough—they have to be able to diversify their assets."

My final questions focused on the radical change the Internet has had on the financial journalism profession. Daly believes that "the Web opens up new avenues for journalists. Opportunity is no longer limited to the newspaper, and journalists have made the transition to the Net just like any other business." But like many of his peers, Daly learned the ropes as a newspaperman. "It'll be interesting to see the next generation that never had to make that transition." This is as true of journalists as it is of online traders. The next generation will never know what it was like to be without the World Wide Web at their fingertips.

pete henig

After starting out on Wall Street as an analyst working on the floor of the commodities exchange, Pete Henig is now the highly respected investment editor for the Red Herring, one of the first financial web sites to hit the Net. In the following interview, Henig described how "TheStreet.com was still in its infancy, as was CBS MarketWatch. Bloomberg was resisting, and we [Red Herring] were just hanging on by the seat of our pants. In just a year and a half the competition has heated up and we have boomed." But as a writer, Henig was immediately smitten with his online prospects because "Internet journalism gives you ultimate freedom to write in your own personal voice, and be creative with ideas. It's a great gig for true writers but the deadline pressures are killer because investors want information *now*."

When asked how the dramatic rise of online trading has affected investing in general, Henig stated, "Overall, I think it's good for investing because it allows a more level playing field for all to trade the markets, and retail to have as much influence on the markets as institutions. However, the downside is it has lulled investors into a false sense of security that markets only go up. They don't, of course, and people get shell-shocked when they come crashing down. Also, there has not nearly been enough efforts out there to convince online traders to get educated as to what they are doing or should do, or even as to why they should be educated in the markets. There's way too much information and it's way too easy to trade. But people really need to read a good Peter Lynch book, because ultimately stocks are companies and companies make mistakes."

> **Peter Lynch**
> legendary founder of Fidelity Magellan—a major mutual fund—who consistently averaged an annual return of 23.83% throughout his tenure as manager of the fund. Lynch is now a best-selling author of books on financial analysis.

I went on to ask Henig about the positive or negative differences in the way people trade online in comparison to traditional methods. Henig replied, "I think there's a bit more of a haphazard attitude toward trading online, even though people have taken investing into their own hands rather than giving it over to some broker who may or may not care about their money. With that said, you'd be surprised at the level of sophistication of some of these online traders and the amount of information they are able to dig up about companies either through filings or chat boards or wherever. I'm often impressed. Yet, still many active online traders trade with momentum and that scares me because they have no idea that the market makers have already figured out the momentum game and how to lull online traders into the market only to whip it back against them in the other direction. The other negative is that the Internet has shortened our already short attention spans. Online investing for the long term might mean three to six months, whereas years ago, long-term investing meant holding it for your grandkids. The low opportunity costs for making trades mean that people can trade in and out of stocks all of the time. That ability inclines them against buying and holding, unfortunately, which, as we all know, is where the real money is made."

When asked how much online trading contributed to the frenzy of Internet stock trading, Henig responded with great excitement. "Online trading is *the* reason behind the frenzy in Internet stock trading. People trade what they know and online traders tend to know the Web. They believed in it even before the large institutions would touch it. The combination of low floats, high demand for individual investors, and mass hysteria over a fundamentally new economy makes this a ripe environment for nutty gains beyond all possible traditional valuations. Ultimately, I think some of these companies will grow into their valuations, others will get bought, and a lot will die on the vine."

Since this kind of mass trading hysteria borders on obsession, I asked Henig why online trading has become so popular. According to Henig, "It's about power and freedom and a game. It's fun, bottom line, especially when you can feel richer overnight. Why slave away at your desk when AOL goes up 20 points away and the guy sitting next to you has become a Dell-ionaire. People also love the feeling of getting a bargain, and trading is cheap. But it's the game. People just get hooked."

I then asked Henig if he thought that the addition of thousands of new online traders would boost options trading. Henig said, "Like everything else, if you give the investing public something to eat, a lot of them will start to chew on it just for the heck of it. So yes, I think just the availability of trading options will create its own demand. But the odd part about options is that if they are treated in the right way, they are all about managing risk, rather than incurring more risk. This is the fundamental paradox faced by those who know how to trade options and want to encourage others to do it. People hear the word options and they run—or they think they barely have enough money to trade stocks, how are they going to afford to trade options as well? If there is a learning curve with the investing public on equities alone, the learning curve on options has got to be 10 times steeper."

When asked about online brokerage system failures, Henig responded by saying that online brokerages "need to be honest about their capacity to handle not only the number of customers they have, but the number of trades that can occur at any one time. Brokerages should not try to market themselves as more they can deliver. E*Trade is a great marketing machine—the AOL of investing. But like AOL, the infrastructure and customer service couldn't live up to their great marketing and brand building. People were drawn in, then let down, and demanded their money and hit the road. I'd be curious to see how many customers E*Trade is losing per day, rather than how many it's signing up. The name of the game among online traders is the value per account, not the size of how much those accounts are worth. So there's every incentive for these online trading companies to sign up as many people as possible because that's how Wall Street is valuing them, either in the public markets or if they're going to be bought out." If investors want to protect themselves from online brokerage growing pains, Henig suggests taking the time to ask some serious questions before signing up with an online brokerage. "If I have a problem or question, and I'm new to this game, who's going to answer the phone or return an e-mail in the fastest amount of time? I can tell you from firsthand experience, it tends not to be the biggest names in the online trading business. They are only now catching on that customer service is the real driver of online trading, not commissions."

When asked about the future of online trading, Henig prolifically mused, "Let's be honest, it's all going online. I did an interview with the CEO of DLJ direct, Blake Darcy, and he says he's seeing million-dollar personal accounts leaving the moneyed halls of Goldman and Morgan and signing up online. We called it 'Brother, can you spare a million?' That's not to say everything will ultimately be online, but yes, I believe the stockbroker of the future is dead. The value add will be in educated customer service centers, although we'll still have professional money managers and portfolio managers for people who are socking away money in their 401(k)s. Online trading has obviously created a tremendous amount of extra liquidity in the markets, and that liquidity won't dry up anytime soon. There are even theories that a Dow at 20,000 is not inconceivable given the amount of cash and a world economy that's going borderless. With all of that said, I worry about the day when things might turn bad. Would the average online investor know what to do if his portfolio of stocks heads south? Does he or she understand bonds? Options? Commodities? And because the online trading firms can move money so fast, the velocity of downside moves can become ferocious. Who knows where things will stabilize before investors get hurt? But everyone's surely having a blast right now, right?"

As the interview drew to a close, Henig returned to our earlier conversation on how the rise of online trading has changed the fundamental nature of journalism. Henig stated, "It's stressed us out. The demand for investing information is insatiable, absolutely insatiable. So while that's great for business and for job opportunities and for building your brand name as a writer, it's downright miserable to try to fill every gap in that demand, on deadline. Red Herring's chosen to take the high road and provide an intelligent level of news and analysis on the Web as well as unique story ideas based on nuggets of news or information or emerging trends. In that sense, it's been great because it gives journalists the freedom to explore and dream and wonder, even within the investing landscape of news. That's a great feeling, and beats writing for a *Beverage and Soda* newsletter any day."

conclusion

The world of online trading is changing at an exponential pace. The introduction of online traders has created an explosion of players fashioning a whole new market dynamic. Technological innovations have changed the way we all trade. Megacomputers with faster modems have led us to the cutting edge of profit making in the markets. From the vast number of financial information resources the trading public can access to the lightning speed of the online transaction process, there has never before been a trading environment like there is today. Traders can either use this information intelligently or become so overwhelmed by the magnitude of the information overload that they develop analysis paralysis.

Online trading is an exhilarating activity. As the online trading phenomenon grows and millions of new traders develop chronic online trading addictions, options markets are bound to expand. Although many traders may learn how to use options effectively to manage trading risk, my fear is that too many individuals will get overconfident. It takes time and discipline to develop a sufficient trading knowledge base with which to make money in the markets—especially the options markets. After all, the marketplace is the greatest equalizer of education. Whether you are a Harvard MBA, a rocket scientist, or a high school dropout, the markets prove on a daily basis who wins and who loses. One way or another, you will get your education in the markets, so be well prepared.

Options trading is a specialized business. Informed traders have the opportunity for high rewards while uninformed traders may end up experiencing just how devastating sporadic market movement can be. Just as an Internet stock can go up 10 times in value in a year, it can also lose popularity and sink like a stone. Beware of naked options unless they are hedged as part of a spread!

Regardless of technology's effects on the markets, the characteristics of basic trading instruments remain the same. An option by any other name is still an option. Never underestimate the importance of a comprehensive working knowledge of options and just how critical the nuts and bolts of options trading is to your success. There is absolutely no substitute for a healthy understanding of options' risks and rewards. Success should be measured in terms of long-term gain, not yesterday's gain.

If you want to become a successful online trader, take the time to gain market experience. Don't worry about missing out on a market's wild bull ride. Trending markets happen every day. Start by setting up online portfolios to monitor market movement to get a sense of how things work. Remember—for every Dell Computer success story, there are a million sad stories from traders who lost their whole account on a bad tip.

When it comes to online trading, let caution be your guide until knowledge and experience coalesce to foster tangible trading intuition. To acquire experience, you need to be able to play the game long enough to get the big picture. Trading knowledge is acquired by knowing which details to pay attention to. Before placing a trade, calculate the maximum risk and reward as well as the breakeven points to clearly establish a trade's profit range. A successful trader must know whether a trade is worth the risk. The practical application of limited risk strategies can increase your chances of making consistent stock market profits and reducing trading-related stress.

The key to successful trading is the effective integration of the big picture coupled with a perceptive ability to prioritize small details. To become a confident trader, you need to be able to break down the complexities of trading strategies into simple, straightforward tasks that lead to moneymaking trades. Each time you study a new market, there are certain characteristics to be investigated. Likewise, every strategy has its own niche of applicability. By specializing in one or two markets at a time, you can learn which strategies work in which recognizable market conditions. As these conditions repeat themselves in other markets, the same strategy can be employed to reap rewards.

As we continue to experience the effects of technology on the investment community's evolution, it's up to you to find a balance—neither getting left behind nor moving too fast. I hope this book has helped to give you a foundation for competing in the online trading revolution. Learning to trade options takes true grit determination as well as passion, patience, and perseverance. The pursuit of this journey affirms your personal decision to strive for increased financial success through managed risk strategies. The Internet offers traders financial empowerment. With this in mind, you're ready to boldly go forth into cyberspace—mouse in hand—to seek out new web sites and explore trading opportunities the likes of which have never before been seen by civilization.

appendix a

informational charts, data, and strategy reviews

option expiration month codes

	Jan	Feb	Mar	Apr	May	Jun
Calls	A	B	C	D	E	F
Puts	M	N	O	P	Q	R

	Jul	Aug	Sep	Oct	Nov	Dec
Calls	G	H	I	J	K	L
Puts	S	T	U	V	W	X

strike price codes

A	B	C	D	E	F	G	H	I
5	10	15	20	25	30	35	40	45
105	110	115	120	125	130	135	140	145
205	210	215	220	225	230	235	240	245
305	310	315	320	325	330	335	340	345
405	410	415	420	425	430	435	440	445
505	510	515	520	525	530	535	540	545
605	610	615	620	625	630	635	640	645
705	710	715	720	725	730	735	740	745

J	K	L	M	N	O	P	Q	R
50	55	60	65	70	75	80	85	90
150	155	160	165	170	175	180	185	190
250	255	260	265	270	275	280	285	290
350	355	360	365	370	375	380	385	390
450	455	460	465	470	475	480	485	490
550	555	560	565	570	575	580	585	590
650	655	660	665	670	675	680	685	690
750	755	760	765	770	775	780	785	790

S	T	U	V	W	X	Y	Z
95	100	$7\frac{1}{2}$	$12\frac{1}{2}$	$17\frac{1}{2}$	$22\frac{1}{2}$	$27\frac{1}{2}$	$32\frac{1}{2}$
195	200	$37\frac{1}{2}$	$42\frac{1}{2}$	$47\frac{1}{2}$	$52\frac{1}{2}$	$57\frac{1}{2}$	$62\frac{1}{2}$
295	300	$67\frac{1}{2}$	$72\frac{1}{2}$	$77\frac{1}{2}$	$82\frac{1}{2}$	$87\frac{1}{2}$	$92\frac{1}{2}$
395	400	$97\frac{1}{2}$	$102\frac{1}{2}$	$107\frac{1}{2}$	$112\frac{1}{2}$	$117\frac{1}{2}$	$122\frac{1}{2}$
495	500	$127\frac{1}{2}$	$132\frac{1}{2}$	$137\frac{1}{2}$	$142\frac{1}{2}$	$147\frac{1}{2}$	$152\frac{1}{2}$
595	600	$157\frac{1}{2}$	$162\frac{1}{2}$	$167\frac{1}{2}$	$172\frac{1}{2}$	$177\frac{1}{2}$	$182\frac{1}{2}$
695	700	$187\frac{1}{2}$	$192\frac{1}{2}$	$197\frac{1}{2}$	$202\frac{1}{2}$	$207\frac{1}{2}$	$212\frac{1}{2}$
795	800	$217\frac{1}{2}$	$222\frac{1}{2}$	$227\frac{1}{2}$	$232\frac{1}{2}$	$237\frac{1}{2}$	$242\frac{1}{2}$

variable option deltas

All options are provided a delta relative to the 100 deltas of the underlying security. If 100 shares of stock are equal to 100 deltas, then the corresponding options must have delta values of less than 100. You can estimate an options delta as follows depending on the movement of the underlying stock.

Option	Calls		Puts	
Deltas	Long	Short	Long	Short
ATM	+50	−50	−50	+50
	ITM			
1 Strike	+ 60 to + 65	− 60 to − 65	− 60 to − 65	+ 60 to + 65
2 Strikes	+ 70 to + 75	− 70 to − 75	− 70 to − 75	+ 70 to + 75
3 Strikes	+ 80 to + 85	− 80 to − 85	− 80 to − 85	+ 80 to + 85
	OTM			
1 Strike	+ 35 to + 40	− 35 to − 40	− 35 to − 40	+ 35 to + 40
2 Strikes	+ 25 to + 30	− 25 to − 30	− 25 to − 30	+ 25 to + 30
3 Strikes	+ 15 to + 20	− 15 to − 20	− 15 to − 20	+ 15 to + 20

option symbols

To understand quotes, you must be able to decipher option symbols. Option symbols vary depending on their source. However, all option symbols are composed of the following components:

1. **Root symbol**—The symbol used to identify the underlying financial instrument on which an option is based.

2. **Expiration month**—The month in which the option contract expires is represented by a letter of the alphabet that also designates the option as a call or a put. (An "Option Expiration Month Codes" chart can be found on the first page of this Appendix.)

3. **Strike price**—The specific price at which the option gives the holder the right to buy or sell the underlying financial instrument. For stocks, strike prices are represented by a letter of the alphabet.

4. **Option type**—In stock options, calls and puts have a letter designating their expiration.

Stock Example: INTC-Intel   A   A
Intel January 105 Call

INTC = Intel stock
A = January call expiration
A = Strike price of 5, 105, 205, 305, 405, 505

intermarket relationships

Interest Rates	Bonds	Stocks	Dollar
Rising	Falling	Falling	Rising
Falling	Rising	Rising	Falling
Stable	Stable	Up/stable	Stable

Note: If these relationships do not hold then there is said to be a divergence. A good trader will look for reasons for a divergence and for opportunities to make money under the circumstances.

market opportunities

Bullish Limited Risk Strategies	Bullish Unlimited Risk Strategies	Bearish Limited Risk Strategies
Buy call	Buy underlying stock	Buy put
Bull call spread	Sell put	Bear put spread
Bull put spread	Covered call	Bear call spread
Call ratio backspread	Call ratio spread	Put ratio backspread

Bearish Unlimited Risk Strategies	Neutral Limited Risk Strategies	Neutral Unlimited Risk Strategies
Sell underlying	Long straddle	Short straddle
Sell call	Long strangle	Short strangle
Covered put	Long synthetic straddle	Call ratio spread
Put ratio spread	Long butterfly	Put ratio spread
	Long condor	
	Long iron butterfly	

risk profile basics

Use Figure A.1 to help you get the full benefits of the risk graphs scattered throughout this book. Risk graphs like this one enable traders to visually assess a trade's profitability in one glance. By analyzing the risk graph of a trade at expiration, you can assess the following important values:

- The dark line represents the actual profit or loss of the trade depending on the price of the underlying asset. By looking at any price on the bottom axis, you can figure out the corresponding profit or loss the trade makes when the underlying asset expires at a certain price.
- Line A tracks the downside breakeven ($32) of the trade to the corresponding price of the underlying asset. If the price of the underlying asset falls below this point, the trade starts to make a profit that is unlimited in nature (the line continues to move upward and to the left as the price of the underlying asset falls).
- Line B tracks the upside breakeven ($38) of the trade to the corresponding price of the underlying asset. When the price of

figure a.1 put ratio backspread (short 1 July MO 40 put @ 5½, long 2 July MO 35 puts @ 1¾ MO @ 35⅞)

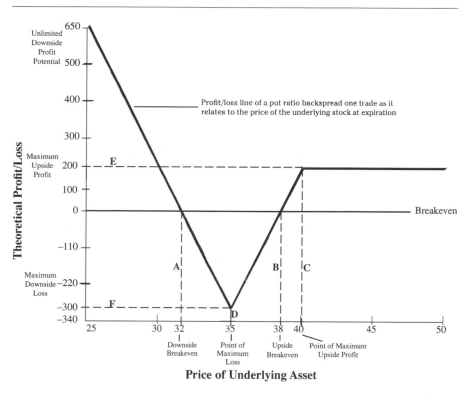

Profit/loss line of a put ratio backspread one trade as it relates to the price of the underlying stock at expiration

Price of Underlying Asset

the underlying asset rises above this point it starts to make a profit that is limited in nature.

- Line C tracks the point at which the trade hits a maximum limited profit ($40—the strike price of the short call). The underlying asset must move significantly in either direction for this trade to make a profit.
- Line D shows the price of the underlying asset at the point of maximum loss ($35—the strike price of the long option).
- Line E shows the maximum limited profit ($200).
- Line F shows the maximum loss amount (–$300).

options strategy quick reference guide

Strategy	Risk Profile	Strategy	Market Outlook	Profit Potential	Risk Potential	Time Decay Effect
Long Call		B1-C	Bullish	Unlimited	Limited	Detrimental
Short Call		S1-C	Bearish	Limited	Unlimited	Helpful
Long Put		B1-P	Bearish	Unlimited	Limited	Detrimental
Short Put		S1-P	Bullish	Limited	Unlimited	Helpful
Bull Call Spread		B1-LC S1-HC	Bullish	Limited	Limited	Mixed
Bull Put Spread		B1-LP S1-HP	Moderately Bullish	Limited	Limited	Mixed
Bear Call Spread		S1-LC B1-HC	Moderately Bearish	Limited	Limited	Mixed
Bear Put Spread		B1-HP S1-LP	Bearish	Limited	Limited	Mixed
Long Straddle		B1-ATM-C B1-ATM-P	Volatile	Unlimited	Limited	Detrimental
Short Straddle		S1-ATM-C S1-ATM-P	Stable	Limited	Unlimited	Helpful
Long Strangle		B1-OTM-C B1-OTM-P	Volatile	Unlimited	Limited	Detrimental
Short Strangle		S1-OTM-C S1-OTM-P	Stable	Limited	Unlimited	Helpful
Call Ratio Spread*		B1-LC S2-HC	Bearish / Stable	Limited	Unlimited	Mixed
Put Ratio Spread*		B1-HP S2-LP	Bullish / Stable	Limited	Unlimited	Mixed
Call Ratio Backspread*		S1-LC B2-HC	Very Bullish	Unlimited	Limited	Mixed
Put Ratio Backspread*		S1-HP B2-LP	Very Bearish	Unlimited	Limited	Mixed
Long Butterfly		B1-LC S2-HC B1-HC OR B1-LP S2-HP B1-HP	Stable	Limited	Limited	Helpful
Long Condor		B1-LC S1-HC S1-HC B1-HC OR B1-LP S1-HP S1-HP B1-HP	Stable	Limited	Limited	Helpful
Long Iron Butterfly		S1-ATM-C B1-OTM-C S1-ATM-P B1-OTM-P	Stable	Limited	Limited	Helpful

Quick Reference Guide Codes

B	Buy	HC	Higher Strike Call
S	Sell	LC	Lower Strike Call
1	1 Contract	HP	Higher Strike Put
2	2 Contracts	LP	Lower Strike Put
C	Call	U	Underlying Instrument
P	Put	ATM	At-the-money
		OTM	Out-of-the-money
		ITM	In-the-money
		*	Follow Ratio Rule

options strategy reviews

LONG STOCK

Strategy = Buy shares of stock.
Market Opportunity = Look for a bullish market where a rise in the price of the stock is anticipated.
Maximum Risk = Limited to the price of the stock as it approaches zero.
Maximum Profit = Unlimited as the stock price rises above the initial entry price.
Breakeven = Price of the stock at initiation.
Margin = Required; usually 50% of the total cost of the shares.

SHORT STOCK

Strategy = Sell shares of stock.
Market Opportunity = Look for a bearish market where a fall in the price of the stock is anticipated.
Maximum Risk = Unlimited as the stock price rises.
Maximum Profit = Limited to the full price of the stock shares as they fall to zero.
Breakeven = Price of the stock at initiation.
Margin = Required; usually 150% of the total cost of the shares.

LONG CALL

Strategy = Buy a call option.
Market Opportunity = Look for a bullish market where a rise above the breakeven is anticipated.
Maximum Risk = Limited to the amount paid for the call.
Maximum Profit = Unlimited as the price of the underlying instrument rises above the breakeven.
Breakeven = Call strike price + call option premium.
Margin = None.

SHORT CALL

Strategy = Sell a call option.
Market Opportunity = Look for a bearish or stable market where you anticipate a fall in the price of the underlying asset below the breakeven.
Maximum Risk = Unlimited as the stock price rises above the breakeven.
Maximum Profit = Limited to the credit received from the call option premium.
Breakeven = Call strike price + call option premium.
Margin = Required. Amount subject to broker's discretion.

LONG PUT
Strategy = Buy a put option.
Market Opportunity = Look for a bearish market where you anticipate a fall in the price of the underlying asset below the breakeven.
Maximum Risk = Limited to the price paid for the put option premium.
Maximum Profit = Limited as the stock price falls below the breakeven to zero.
Breakeven = Put strike price – put option premium.
Margin = None.

SHORT PUT
Strategy = Sell a put option.
Market Opportunity = Look for a bullish or stable market where a rise above the breakeven is anticipated.
Maximum Risk = Limited as the stock price falls below the breakeven until reaching a price of zero.
Maximum Profit = Limited to the credit received from the put option premium.
Breakeven = Put strike price – put option premium.
Margin = Required. Amount subject to broker's discretion.

BULL CALL SPREAD
Strategy = Buy a lower strike call and sell a higher strike call with the same expiration date.
Market Opportunity = Look for a bullish market where you anticipate a modest increase in the price of the underlying asset above the price of the short call option.
Maximum Risk = Limited to the net debit paid for the spread.
Maximum Profit = Limited [(difference in strike prices × value per point) – net debit paid].
Breakeven = Long strike price + (net debit ÷ 100)
Margin = Required. Amount subject to broker's discretion—should be limited to the net debit on the trade.

BEAR PUT SPREAD
Strategy = Buy a higher strike put and sell a lower strike put with the same expiration date.
Market Opportunity = Look for a bearish market where you anticipate a modest decrease in the price of the underlying asset below the strike price of the short put option.
Maximum Risk = Limited to the net debit paid.
Maximum Profit = Limited [(difference in strike prices × value per point) – net debit paid].
Breakeven = Long strike price – (net debit ÷ 100)
Margin = Required. Amount subject to broker's discretion.

BULL PUT SPREAD

Strategy = Buy a lower strike put and sell a higher strike put with the same expiration date.

Market Opportunity = Look for a bullish market where you anticipate an increase in the price of the underlying asset above the strike price of the short put option.

Maximum Risk = Limited [(difference in strike prices × value per point) – net credit].

Maximum Profit = Limited to the net credit received.

Breakeven = Short put strike price – (net credit ÷ 100)

Margin = Required. Amount subject to broker's discretion.

BEAR CALL SPREAD

Strategy = Buy a higher strike call and sell a lower strike call with the same expiration date.

Market Opportunity = Look for a bearish market where you anticipate a decrease in the price of the underlying asset below the strike price of the short call option.

Maximum Risk = Limited [(difference in strike prices × value per point) – net credit].

Maximum Profit = Limited to the net credit received.

Breakeven = Short call strike price + (net credit ÷ 100)

Margin = Required. Amount subject to broker's discretion.

LONG STRADDLE

Strategy = Purchase an ATM call and an ATM put with the same strike price and the same expiration date.

Market Opportunity = Look for a market with low volatility where you anticipate a sharp volatility increase.

Maximum Risk = Limited to the net debit paid.

Maximum Profit = Unlimited to the upside beyond the breakeven. Limited on the downside as the underlying asset falls to zero. Profit requires sufficient market movement but does not depend on market direction.

Upside Breakeven = ATM strike price + (net debit ÷ 100)

Downside Breakeven = ATM strike price – (net debit ÷ 100)

Margin = None.

SHORT STRADDLE

Strategy = Sell an ATM call and an ATM put with the same strike price and the same expiration date.

Market Opportunity = Look for a wildly volatile market where you anticipate a period of low volatility.

Maximum Risk = Unlimited to the upside; the downside is limited as the underlying asset falls to zero.

Maximum Profit = Limited to the net credit received. Profit is possible if the market stays between the breakevens.

Upside Breakeven = ATM strike price + (net credit ÷ 100).

Downside Breakeven = ATM strike price – (net credit ÷ 100)

Margin = Required. Amount subject to broker's discretion.

LONG STRANGLE

Strategy = Buy an OTM call and an OTM put with the same expiration date.

Market Opportunity = Look for a stable market where you anticipate a large volatility spike.

Maximum Risk = Limited to the net debit paid.

Maximum Profit = Unlimited to the upside beyond the breakeven. Limited on the downside as the underlying asset falls to zero.

Upside Breakeven = Call strike price + (net debit ÷ 100)

Downside Breakeven = Put strike price – (net debit ÷ 100)

Margin = None.

SHORT STRANGLE

Strategy = Sell an OTM call and an OTM put with the same expiration date.

Market Opportunity = Look for a wildly volatile market where you anticipate a drop-off into a very stable market with low volatility.

Maximum Risk = Unlimited to the upside. Limited on the downside as the underlying asset falls to zero.

Maximum Profit = Limited to the net credit received.

Upside Breakeven = Call strike price + (net credit ÷ 100)

Downside Breakeven = Put strike price – (net credit ÷ 100)

Margin = Required. Amount subject to broker's discretion.

RATIO CALL SPREAD

Strategy = Buy a lower strike call and sell a greater number of higher strike calls.

Market Opportunity = Look for a volatile market where you expect a decline or a small rise not to exceed the strike price of the short options.

Maximum Risk = Unlimited to the upside above the breakeven.

Maximum Profit = Limited [# of long contracts × (difference in strike prices × value per point) + net credit or – net debit].

Upside Breakeven = {[# of short calls × (short call premium + short call strike price) – # of long calls × (long call premium + long call strike price)] / (# of short calls – # of long calls)}.

Margin = Required. Amount subject to broker's discretion.

RATIO PUT SPREAD

Strategy = Buy a higher strike put and sell a greater number of lower strike puts.

Market Opportunity = Look for a volatile market where you expect a rise or slight fall not to exceed the strike price of the short options.

Maximum Risk = Limited to the downside below the breakeven as the underlying asset falls to zero.

Maximum Profit = Limited [# of long contracts × (difference in strike prices × value per point) + net credit or – net debit].

Downside Breakeven = {[# of short puts × (short put strike price – short put premium) – # of long puts × (long put strike price – long put premium)] / (# of short puts – # of long puts)}.

Margin = Required. Amount subject to broker's discretion.

CALL RATIO BACKSPREAD

Strategy = Sell lower strike calls and buy a greater number of higher strike calls (the ratio must be less than .67).

Market Opportunity = Look for a market where you anticipate a sharp rise with increasing volatility. Should be placed as a credit trade or at even.

Maximum Risk = Limited [(# of short calls × difference in strike prices) × value per point – net credit or + net debit].

Maximum Profit = Unlimited to the upside beyond the breakeven. Limited on the downside to the net credit (if any).

Upside Breakeven = Long call strike price + {[(difference in strike prices × # of short calls) – (net debit / 100) or + (net credit / 100)] / (# of long calls – # of short calls)}.

Downside Breakeven = If net debit, the net debit is lost at the strike price of the short call or below. If net credit, then downside breakeven = {short call strike price + [(net credit / 100) / # of short calls]}.

Margin = Required. Amount subject to broker's discretion.

PUT RATIO BACKSPREAD

Strategy = Sell higher strike puts and buy a greater number of lower strike puts with a ratio less than .67.

Market Opportunity = Look for a market where you anticipate a sharp decline with increased volatility. Place as a credit or at even if possible.

Maximum Risk = Limited [(# of short puts × difference in strike prices × value per point) – net credit or + net debit].

Maximum Profit = Unlimited to the downside below the breakeven. Limited on the upside to the net credit, if any.

Upside Breakeven = If net debit, the net debit is lost at the strike price of the short put or above. If net credit, then upside breakeven = {short put strike price – [(net credit / 100) / # of short puts]}.

Downside Breakeven = Long put strike price – {[(# of short puts × difference in strikes) – (net credit / 100) *or* + (net debit / 100)] / (# of long puts – # of short puts)}.

Margin = Required. Amount subject to broker's discretion.

LONG BUTTERFLY

Strategy = Buy lower strike option, sell two higher strike options, and buy an even higher strike option (all calls or all puts).

Market Opportunity = Look for a rangebound market that is expected to stay between the breakevens.

Maximum Risk = Limited to the net debit paid.

Maximum Profit = Limited [(# of lowest strike options × difference in strikes) × value per point] – net debit paid.

Upside Breakeven = Highest strike price – [net debit paid / (# of highest strike options × 100)].

Downside Breakeven = Lowest strike price + [net debit paid / (# of lowest strike options × 100)].

Margin = Required. Amount subject to broker's discretion.

LONG CONDOR

Strategy = Buy lower strike option, sell higher strike option, sell an even higher strike option, and buy an even higher strike option (all calls or all puts).

Market Opportunity = Look for a rangebound market that is expected to stay between the breakeven points.

Maximum Risk = Limited to the net debit paid.

Maximum Profit = Limited [# of lowest strike options × difference in strikes) × value per point) – net debit.

Upside Breakeven = Highest strike price – [net debit / (# of highest strike options × 100)].

Downside Breakeven = Lowest strike price + [net debit / (# of lowest strike options x 100)].

Margin = Required. Amount subject to broker's discretion.

LONG IRON BUTTERFLY

Strategy = Buy a higher strike call, sell a lower strike call, sell a never lower strike put, and buy an even lower strike put.

Market Opportunity = Look for a rangebound market that you anticipate to stay between the breakeven points.

Maximum Risk = Limited {[(# of lowest strike options × difference between long and short strikes) × value per point] − net credit received}.

Maximum Profit = Limited to the net credit received.

Upside Breakeven = Highest short strike price + (net credit / # of highest strike options × 100).

Downside Breakeven = Lowest short strike price − (net credit / # of lowest strike options × 100).

Margin = Required. Amount subject to broker's discretion.

---

types of orders

As you get ready to trade, you will have to decide what kind of order you wish to place. There are a wide variety of orders that you will need to become acquainted with. Let's take a look at the most prevalent order types.

1. **At-even orders** should be placed without a debit or a credit to the account. That means that you may have to wait until the market gets to the right prices for your trade to be placed.

2. **At-the-opening orders** should be executed at the opening of the market or should be canceled.

3. **Day orders** remain good only for the duration of the trading day that it is entered. It is canceled at the end of the trading day, if not executed.

4. **Fill-or-kill orders** must be executed immediately as a whole order. If not, the order is canceled.

5. **Good till canceled orders** remain in effect until executed or explicitly canceled, or the contract expires.

6. **Immediate or cancel orders** must be executed immediately in whole or part as soon as it is entered. Any part not executed is automatically canceled.

7. **Limit orders** specify a maximum buying price or a minimum selling price.

8. **Limit buy orders** must be executed below the current market price.

9. **Limit sell orders** must be executed above the current market price.

10. **Market orders** are the most common type of order. They are guaranteed execution at the best price prevailing in the market.

11. **Market-on-open orders** must be executed during the opening of trading.

12. **Market-on-close orders** must be executed during the closing of trading.

13. **Market-if-touched orders** combine market and limit orders, whereby the order becomes a market order when the options or stock reach a specified price.

14. **Market-if-touched buy orders** become a market order when the options or underlying asset fall below the current market price.

15. **Market-if-touched sell orders** become a market order when the options or underlying asset rise above the current market price.

16. **Stop orders** are used to limit risk. They become market orders when the options or stock reaches a certain price. However, **buy stop orders** must be executed when the specified price is above the current market price; and **sell stop orders** must be executed when the specified price falls below the current market price.

17. **Stop limit orders** are an extension of stop orders where the activated order becomes a limit order instead of a market order.

appendix b

market analysis terminology

fundamental analysis methodologies and indicators

Accumulation-Distribution: This indicator reflects a stock's daily long shares compared to short stock shares. This is important in that it attempts to evaluate two of the most important indicators of strength or weakness in a stock—the percentage change of a stock's price and volume. The accumulation-distribution rating is calculated by multiplying a stock's daily price change percentage by its volume. This number is then added to or subtracted from the cumulative total for the stock depending on whether the price increased or decreased. *IBD* uses the following rating: A (strongest accumulation), C (neutral), and E (weakest—distribution). In general, a stock with an A rating means there is plenty of demand for the stock (high volume) and the price will probably continue to rise. An E rating means that the supply for a stock is greater than the demand and could trigger a drop in price. I like to focus on A's only for buying and E's for a bearish perspective.

Annual Earnings Change (%): The historical earnings change between the most recently reported fiscal year earnings and the preceding.

Beta Coefficient: A means of measuring the volatility of a security or portfolio of securities in comparison with the market as a whole. A beta of 1 indicates that the security's price will move with the market. A beta greater than 1 indicates that the security's price will be more volatile than the market. A beta less than 1 means it will be less volatile than the market.

Closing Price, Net Change: These two points are important as they represent the dollar value by which a stock has changed. The net change value tells how much the price of the stock changed during yesterday's trading. If the fictitious stock Reality Check, Inc. (RCI) is trading at $10 today and closed yesterday at $8, then the stock has risen $2. This 20% increase is significant. If RCI is trading today at $10 and closed yesterday at $20, this $10 drop in value (50%) is very significant.

Dividend Yield: Dividend yield is calculated by dividing a stock's dividend rate expected for the next 12 months by the current price of the stock. Unless you are buying stocks based on dividend yield (the return you receive on a dividend payout) and earnings, this is not a critical number. If you are building a long-term portfolio based on yields, then you will want to compare one stock versus another using this information. Many stocks—especially high-technology stocks—have a low dividend yield, yet still are good investments.

Earnings Growth: This indicator is measured annually and quarterly. It divides a company's revenue by the outstanding shares. If a company starts to slump, you'll definitely see it on the quarterly earnings growth reports. If revenues decline, companies have to tighten their belts, and this can send out the bears.

Earnings per Share (EPS): EPS is a widely used measurement of a company's financial strength. EPS is calculated by dividing a company's net earnings for common stock by the number of outstanding common shares. The resulting number can then be compared to the EPS of the same quarter in the prior year to determine a company's earnings growth. The result of this comparison is used to forecast an increase or decrease in the future price of the stock. Also, pay attention to a stock's ability to consistently grow by researching the EPS at least five years back. If you find a consistent growth pattern, you can bet that investors are willing to pay more for that stock.

Earnings per Share Rank: This number is a measure of a company's growth over the past two quarters in comparison to the same quarters in the prior year. The past three- to five-year annual growth rate is factored in and the resulting number is compared to other companies and given a rank of 1 (lowest) to 99 (highest). The EPS rank basically tells a trader how profitable a stock is in comparison to the more than 10,000 stocks available to be traded. I like to focus on companies with stocks with the greatest strength when buying (an EPS ranking of 95 or better) and the weakest when selling (an EPS of 20 or less). It is a good idea to track the EPS rank of your stocks on at least a weekly basis. This will give you a chance to make changes to your portfolio if there is a dramatic change in the character of your investments.

52-Week High and Low: This figure tells you the price change of a stock over the past year. The difference between the high and the low is called the range. If a stock has moved only $1 in the past year, it is likely to stay in this range again in the coming year. Also, if a stock is at its 52-week high, it may be ready to make new highs. This is one you want to look at as a potential buy. If a stock is at a 52-week low, it could break down and go lower, which may be a selling opportunity (going short). It is generally stated on Wall Street that strength leads to strength and weakness leads to weakness. Since many investors use this information to make investment decisions, it can have great influence on the directions of many stocks.

Float (Mil): The float represents the number of securities that are in the public's possession. You can deduct shares that are held by pensions, mutual funds, and other large investors to arrive at a float. This daily column indicates how many shares are available for trading. This number is important if you want to keep track of how supply and demand affect price. For example, if Reality Check, Inc. (RCI) shares are in high demand, buyers will have to bid the price up to make it attractive to sellers to sell their shares to increase supply. When a company splits, it reduces demand by increasing supply. Therefore, a company with a smaller float will likely outperform one with a higher float.

Greatest % Rise in Volume: This is often more perceptive than a most active list because it highlights stocks with exceptional activity—not just those with the highest volume of shares being traded. Noting this figure may enable you to discover those small and mid-cap stocks with increasing volume above and beyond the norm.

Hi/Lo—High Price Yesterday/Low Price Yesterday: Unless you are day trading (going in and out during one trading session), this information is not critical. Investors and traders look at this information to signal if stock traders will be running stops. This technique can also be used to look for orders from public traders. For example, if a trader sold a stock yesterday, he or she may place a buy stop (to cover losses) above yesterday's high. This is referred to as a resistance point. If the trader bought a stock, he or she may place a sell stop (to sell the stock they purchased) below yesterday's low. This is referred to as a support point. The technique of using stops is used by many investors and traders for protection if the market moves against their original position; however, it is not what we recommend. I prefer to use options because I find them to be much more profitable and safer in the long run.

High-Low Index: The high-low index (H/L index) is constructed by taking the net 52-week yearly highs and lows over a six-day period (for displays of one year or less) or a six-week period (for displays greater than one year). The number of new 52-week highs and lows is calculated as a percent of total issues traded, to compensate for the addition and subtraction of stocks to an industry group average.

Management: Changes in a company's management can mean big news, which often triggers public reaction to be bearish or bullish.

Money Flow: A volume-weighted version of the relative strength index, but instead of using up closes versus down closes, money flow compares the current interval's average price to the previous interval's average price and then weighs the average price by volume to calculate money flow. The ratio of the summed positive and negative money flows are then normalized to be on a scale of 0 to 100.

Most Active Issue: The *IBD* and the *Wall Street Journal* list those stocks that are most active by volume—primarily blue-chip stocks with millions of shares available to be traded.

Most % Down in Price: This listing is interesting to watch, but the information only describes what is happening, not what will happen.

Most % Up in Price: These are stocks with the biggest increases in price. Although this information is interesting to scan, it can be dangerous to choose a stock solely depending on the change in its price.

Net Change: The daily change from time frame to time frame. An example would be the change from the close of yesterday to the close of today. It is the difference between the closing price of a security on the trading day reported and the previous day's closing price. In over-the-counter transactions, the term refers to the difference between the closing bids.

Net Earnings: That part of a company's profits remaining after all expenses and taxes have been paid and out of which dividends may be paid.

Odd Lot: An amount of a security that is less than the normal unit of trading for that security. Generally, an odd lot is fewer than 100 shares of stock or five bonds. An investor may pay a premium when trying to purchase with odd lots. Historical theory says that the odd-lot investor is traditionally a small personal investor trading in less than 100 shares at a time. Odd-lot traders are usually guilty of bad timing, and profits may be made by acting contrary to odd-lot trading patterns. Those who believe this theory interpret heavy odd lot buying in a rising market as an indication of technical weakness and the signal of a market reversal. Heavy odd lot buying in a declining market is seen as an indication of technical strength and is thus a signal to buy. Analysis of odd lot trading patterns over the years has failed to support this theory with any real consistency. Odd-lot investors tend to buy market leaders and have generally done well in the upward market of the past 50 years.

On Balance Volume: On balance volume is an accumulation of volume where the current interval's volume is added to the total if the stock closes up, and today's volume is subtracted from the total if the stock closes down.

Price/Book Ratio: Compares a stock's market value to the value of total assets less total liabilities (book). Determined by dividing current price by common stockholders' equity per share (book value), adjusted for stock splits. Also called market-to-book.

Price-Earnings Ratio (P/E): The price-earnings ratio—otherwise known as the P/E—is very important because it compares a company's stock price to the amount of earnings per share. This comparison attempts to assign a rating to the difference between a company's profits per share and the actual price of each stock share. The P/E ratio tells you how many times the earnings a stock is trading at. To calculate the P/E of a stock, simply divide the current stock price by the latest 12-month earnings per share. Let's use our fictitious high-technology stock, Reality Check, Inc. (RCI) to generate an example of how P/E can be calculated. If RCI is trading at $20 per share and the earnings per share are $1, it has a P/E of 20. If the average for the high-tech industry is a P/E of 40, then this stock may be undervalued. If RCI is trading at a P/E of 100 ($100 per share) with an industry average of 40, then the stock is overvalued; on any sign of weakness, the stock will likely come tumbling down. How are industry averages established? Brokerage firm analysts establish guidelines for each industry. For example, a slow-growth industry, such as the steel industry, may have a P/E of only 10, while a high-growth industry, such as the Internet businesses, may have a P/E of 40 or higher. The P/E ratio is used to describe the current state of a stock's price. It is not generally used to forecast future prices. It simply lets traders know how well the stock is doing right now. A general rule of thumb states that faster growing companies have higher P/Es. Since faster growth is linked to higher future earnings, a company with a high P/E may have high future earnings. The trick is never to assume anything that isn't carved in stone. Valuing a company by its future earnings is a dangerous game since these earnings may range significantly.

Price Percentage Gainers and Losers: This is one of my favorite *Wall Street Journal* columns. If there were only two pieces of information I could look at to make a smart investment, I would pick these two because they reveal the stocks with the greatest momentum (up or down). I have to admit that I believe that the best investments are based on momentum, at least in the short term. I like to watch these stocks like a hawk to see if they have momentum that is continuing (good or bad) or momentum that is slowing and reversing. I like to look for a chance to do the opposite on fast movers down (price percentage losers) by looking for buying opportunities. I also like to buy on a fast mover up (price percentage gainers). If I miss a move up, I look to sell as soon as I see the momentum slowing or reversing.

Price to Sales Ratio (PSR): Tracking this indicator can help you to understand when a stock is overpriced or undervalued. To calculate a stock's PSR, divide the price of a stock by the company's sales per share.

Quarterly EPS % Change: Quarterly Earnings Change (%): Historical earnings change between the earnings most recently reported and the quarter preceding.

Quick Ratio: Indicator of a company's financial strength (or weakness). Calculated by taking current assets less inventories, divided by current liabilities.

Relative Strength (RS): Relative strength weighting is used by *Investor's Business Daily* to compare one company to another, or one industry to another. Relative strength compares a stock's price change over the past year to all the other stocks traded on the NYSE, AMEX, and Nasdaq. A relative strength of 99 puts that stock at the top of the list; a relative strength of 1, at the bottom. I prefer to buy call options on stocks with a relative strength weighting of 80 or better, and 40 or lower when buying put options. A relative strength line can also be found on *IBD*'s price charts. It is usually the unbroken line below the price bars and the stock's 50-day moving average. The relative strength value can be found at the end of the RS line. It charts the ratio created when a stock's closing price is divided by the closing price of the S&P 500 index. The relative strength line can be used to provide clues to the future price movement of a stock. If the relative strength line continues to move up, the price will most likely rise (and vice versa).

Return on Equity (ROE): This indicator rates a stock's profitability. It is derived by dividing the net income of the past 12 months by the common stockholders' equity (adjusted for stock splits). The result is shown as a percentage. If you can find a stock with an ROE higher than 20 over the past five years, put it on your watch list.

Short Interest Ratio: A ratio that indicates the number of trading days required to repurchase all of the shares that have been sold short. A short interest ratio of 2.5 would tell us that based on the current volume of trading, it will take two and a half days' volume to cover all shorts.

Standard Deviation: A measure of the fluctuation in a stock's monthly return over the preceding year.

Stocks in the News: A section of the *Wall Street Journal* that graphs 24 NYSE, 24 Nasdaq, and 4 AMEX stocks trading at their 52-week high. Each graph features a stock's price and volume activity over the past year, annual and quarterly earnings per share growth rates, shares outstanding, earnings per share and relative strength rankings, industry group strength, volume percent change, price-earnings ratio, percentage debt, management ownership of company stock, and relative strength line, as well as other pertinent indicators. These important charts give you the opportunity to scan for potential investment opportunities.

Supply and Demand: The supply and demand for a company's shares is referred to as momentum. Companies typically issue earnings estimates and reports. In the meantime, street expectation drives the price of the stocks prior to the release of a report. If investors feel the report will beat the street expectation, then the price of the shares will be bid up, as there will be more buyers than sellers. If the majority of the investors feel that the company's earnings will disappoint the street, then the prices will be offer down. In many ways, a stock exchange is like an auction. If there are more buyers than sellers, prices will rise. If there are more sellers than buyers, prices will fall.

Volume (Vol): The number of shares of stock traded per day is important when the volume is increasing significantly. For example, when a stock has had an average share volume of 100,000 shares and one day the stock trades five times that (500,000), this information is useful. If the stock has a high trading volume and is found on the price percentage gainers and losers list, then you have a confirmation signal that the stock is making a move. When volume is decreasing or stable, the stock will likely go nowhere, as interest in the stock is dwindling. It is important to watch the volume of the stocks you own or are trading to see whether there is a momentum increase or decrease.

Volume Percent Change: This interesting addition to *IBD*'s table of information shows how a stock's volume compares to the previous 50 trading days. *IBD* will highlight stocks with prices greater than $10 when the volume increases by 50% or greater than the average volume over the past 50 trading days. Why is this so important? Volatility. Large increases in volume signal high volatility. Personally, I look for increases that at least double (200%) in average volume, because the larger the increase in volume, the more likely something important may be happening. This is a typical signal of momentum change that indicates either strong impending moves up or strong impending moves down in the price of a stock. Look for stocks that are lower than $10 in price that have volume percentage changes of 200% or greater. This could signal the beginning of explosive growth in the price of a stock.

technical analysis methodologies and indicators

Advance-Decline Line (A/D Line): A technical analysis tool representing the total differences between advances and declines of security prices. The advance-decline line is considered one of the best indicators of market movement as a whole. The A/D line is calculated by taking the percent of stocks advancing minus the percent of stocks declining (either daily or weekly) and adding this amount to a running total. This total is then plotted on top of the industry index so that when more stocks in the group are advancing than declining, the A/D line moves upward. A majority of stocks dropping in price causes the A/D line to move downward. Divergences are the most important feature of the A/D line. When a divergence occurs, the A/D line is believed to more accurately forecast the future because it reflects the action of the broad index rather than a small sample of the most highly market-capitalized issues. When a weighted industry index moves to new highs and the A/D line is in a decline, then an index top is indicated. The A/D line is usually much better at forecasting tops than bottoms. In general, it often turns at the same time or later than when an index bottoms.

Alpha-Beta Trend Channel: The alpha-beta trend channel uses the standard deviation of price variation to establish two trend lines, one above and one below the moving average of a price field. This creates a channel (band) where the great majority of price field values will occur.

Alpha Coefficient: This is a mathematical estimate of the amount of return expected from an investment's inherent values—such as the rate of growth in earnings per share—distinct from the amount of return caused by volatility, which is measured by the beta coefficient. An alpha coefficient of 1.3 indicates a stock is projected to rise 30% in price in a year when the return on the market and the stock's beta coefficient are both zero. When an investment price is low relative to its alpha, it is undervalued and considered a good selection.

Andrews Method: A technique whereby a technician will pick an extreme low or high to use as a pivot point and draw a line (called the median line) from this point that bisects a line drawn through the next corrective phase that occurs after the pivot point. Lines parallel to the median line are drawn through the high and low points of the corrective phase. The parallel lines define the resistance and support levels for the price channel.

Arms Ease of Movement: This technique quantifies the shape aspects of equivolume charting tool plotted boxes to determine the degree of ease or difficulty with which a particular issue is able to move in one direction or another. The ease with which an issue moves is a product of a ratio between the height (trading range) and width (volume) of the plotted box. In general, a higher ratio results from a wider box and indicates difficulty of movement. A lower ratio results from a narrower box and indicates easier movement.

Beta (Coefficient): A ratio of an individual stock's historical returns to the historical returns of the stock market. If a stock increased in value by 12% while the market increased by 10%, the stock's beta would be 1.2.

Bollinger Bands: Bollinger bands can be used to determine overbought and oversold levels, locate reversal areas, project targets for market moves, and determine appropriate stop levels by plotting trading levels above and below a simple moving average. The standard deviation of closing prices for a period equal to the moving average employed is used to determine the bandwidth with bands tightening in quiet markets and loosening in volatile markets. Often used in conjunction with indicators such as RSI, MACD histogram, CCI, and rate of change. Divergences between Bollinger bands and other indicators show potential action points. As a general guideline, look for buying opportunities when prices are in the lower band, and for selling opportunities when the price activity is in the upper band.

Box-Jenkins Linear Least Squares: The additive structure of Box-Jenkins models with a polynomial structure. The Box-Jenkins method is from G. E. P. Box and G. M. Jenkins, who authored *Time Series Analysis: Forecasting and Control*. The method refers to the use of autoregressive integrated moving averages (ARIMA), which fit seasonal models and nonseasonal models to a time series.

Breadth-of-Market Theory: A technical analysis theory that predicts the strength of the market according to the number of issues that advance or decline in a particular trading day.

Candlestick Charts: A candlestick chart provides a visual representation of price movement during a specified period of fixed intervals. The price range between the open and close of each interval is symbolized as a rectangle. If the close is above the open, the rectangle is white, and if the close is below the open, the rectangle is black. In addition, vertical lines extend from the rectangles indicating the high and low prices of that interval.

Chi-Square: A statistical test to determine if the patterns exhibited by data could have been produced by chance.

Cup and Handle: A price accumulation pattern that is often observed on bar charts. Patterns last from 7 to 65 weeks; the cup is U-shaped, and the handle, which is usually more than one or two weeks in duration, is a slight downward drift with low trading volume from the right-hand side of the formation.

Elliott Wave Theory: This method enables traders to determine where the market is currently in comparison to the overall market movement. There are three major aspects of wave analysis: pattern, time, and ratio. The basic Elliott pattern consists of a five-wave uptrend followed by a three-wave correction.

Exponential Smoothing: A mathematical-statistical method in which greater weight is given to more recent price action.

Fibonacci Ratios and Retracements: Originally used by Greek and Egyptian mathematicians as the golden mean and applied in music and architecture, a Fibonacci spiral is a logarithmic spiral that tracks natural growth patterns. In technical analysis, these can be applied to either price or time, although it is more common to use them on prices. The most common levels used in retracement analysis are 61.8%, 38%, and 50%. When a move starts to reverse, the three price levels are calculated (and drawn using horizontal lines) using movements low to high. These retracement levels are then interpreted as likely levels where countermoves will stop.

Gann Square: A mathematical system for finding support and resistance based on a market's extreme low or high price in a given period. Attainment of a particular price level in a square tells you the next probable price peak or decline of future movement.

Head and Shoulders: A bearish price pattern that has three peaks resembling a head and two shoulders. The stock price moves up to its first peak (the left shoulder), drops back, then moves to a higher peak (the top of the head), drops again but recovers to another, lower peak (the right shoulder). A head and shoulders top typically forms after a substantial rise and indicates a market reversal. A head and shoulders bottom (an inverted head and shoulders) indicates a market advance.

Kagi Chart: Originating in Japan, Kagi line charts display a series of connecting vertical lines where the thickness and direction are dependent on price action. If closing prices continue to move in the direction of the prior vertical Kagi line, then that line is extended. However, if the closing price reverses, a new Kagi line is drawn in the next column in the opposite direction. When closing prices penetrate the prior column's high or low, the thickness of the Kagi line changes.

Linear Regression: Used to forecast future price action, a linear regression consists of a center line and a set of channel lines. The center line, the linear regression, is generated by a least squares calculation. The channel lines are placed on both sides of the center line at a percentage distance away. A positive line signals bullish opportunities and a negative line signals bearish ones.

Maximum Entropy Method (MEM): MEM can be used in two ways: a tool for spectrum analysis and a method of adaptive filtering and trend forecasting. As a tool for spectrum analysis, the MEM system provides high resolution spectra for identifying the dominant data cycles within relatively short time series. As a forecasting tool, MEM can be used in conjunction with moving averages to forecast lower and upper trend channels in the data.

Momentum Indicator: A market indicator utilizing price and volume statistics for predicting the strength or weakness of a current market and any overbought or oversold conditions, and to note turning points within the market.

Moving Average: The moving average is probably the best known, and most versatile, indicator in the analyst's tool chest. It can be used with the price of your choice (highs, closes, or whatever) and can also be applied to other indicators, helping to smooth out volatility. It is a mathematical procedure to smooth or eliminate the fluctuations in data and to assist in determining when to buy and sell. A moving average emphasizes the direction of a trend, confirms trend reversals, and smooths out price and volume fluctuations or noise that can confuse interpretation of the market. It is the sum of a value plus a selected number of previous values divided by the total number of values. As the name implies, the moving average is the average of a given amount of data. For example, a 14-day average of closing prices is calculated by adding the last 14 closes and dividing by 14. The result is noted on a chart. The next day the same calculations are performed with the new result being connected (using a solid or dotted line) to yesterday's, and so forth.

Moving Average Convergence/Divergence (MACD): The MACD is used to determine overbought or oversold conditions in the market. A MACD is composed of two lines—two exponentially smoothed moving averages—plotted above and below a zero line. The first line is the difference between the long-term moving average and the short-term moving average. The second line is a short-term moving average of the MACD line. Buy and sell signals come from any crossovers—movements across the zero line—and any divergences.

Norton High/Low Indicator: An indicator that uses results from the demand index and the stochastic study in order to pick tops and bottoms on long-term price charts. Two lines are generated: the NLP line and the NHP line. The system also uses level lines at –2 and –3. The NLP line crossing –3 to the downside is the signal that a new bottom will occur in four to six periods, using daily, weekly, or monthly data. Similarly, the NHP line crossing –3 to the downside indicates a new top in the same time frame. The indicator tends to be more reliable using longer-term data (weekly or monthly). When either indicator drops below the –3 level, a reversal may be imminent. The reversal (or hook) is the signal to enter the market.

Notis %V: A way to measure volatility by measuring the daily price range. Volatility is high when the daily range is large and low when the daily range is small. The Notis %V study contains two separate indicators. It divides market volatility into upward and downward components (UVLT and DVLT). Both are plotted separately in the same window, and can be plotted as an oscillator. The upward component is also compared to the total volatility (UVLT + DVLT) and expressed as a percentage; thus the name %V.

On Balance Volume (OBV): A technical indicator that signals the buying and selling momentum of a stock by comparing price to volume. OBV works on the theory that when a stock closes up for the day, the volume of shares traded represents buying power; and when a stock closes down for the day, the volume of shares denotes selling power. Since trend changes in OBV often precede trend changes in price, OBV can be used to forecast market reversals.

Point and Figure Charts (PF): There are several types of PF charting methods that analyze price variations in stocks and commodities using trend lines, resistance levels, and various other criteria. PF charts are usually easy to read and interpret because they filter out the small, and often confusing, price movements leaving only the most important price action movements.

Price Oscillator: An indicator that displays the difference between a slow and fast time period, subtracting it from the current interval's price.

Price Patterns: Formations that appear on stock price charts that have been shown to have a certain degree of predictive value including: double bottom (bullish); double top (bearish); head and shoulders (bearish); inverse head and shoulders (bullish); triangles, flags, and pennants (can be bullish or bearish depending on the prevailing trend).

Rate of Change: A percentage indicator that calculates the market's change from the current interval's price versus the price _n_ intervals ago.

Stochastic Indicator: The stochastic indicator is based on the observation that as prices increase, closing prices tend to accumulate ever closer to the highs for the period. Conversely, as prices decrease, closing prices tend to accumulate ever closer to the lows for the period. Trading decisions are made with respect to divergence between % D (one of the two lines generated by the study) and the item's price, or when % K rises above % D (bullish) or below it (bearish).

Swing Chart: A chart that has a straight line drawn from each price extreme to the next price extreme based on a set of criteria such as percentages or number of days.

Trading Bands: A method of plotting lines in and around the price of a market to form an envelope and using this information to recognize when prices are high or low on a relative basis and predict when to buy or sell by using indicators that confirm price action.

True Strength Index: A momentum indicator that double-smooths the ratio of the market momentum to the absolute value of the market momentum.

Variable-Length Moving Average: A moving average where the number of periods selected for smoothing is based on the standard deviation of price—the more volatile the price is, the shorter the number of periods used for smoothing.

Weighted Moving Average: Similar to a simple moving average, but gives more weight to current data in the _n_-interval average calculation.

Williams' %R: An index that determines where the most recent closing price is in relation to the price range for an _n_-interval period. If Williams' %R rises above 80, it signals an overbought market. Conversely, if it falls below 20, it signals an oversold market.

appendix c

online software guide

There are more than 500 financial software programs currently available. I have used my fair share of trading programs and even designed a few of my own. Computers are well-suited to financial planning and trading because of their inherent ability to crunch numbers and perform complex calculations at the push of a button. Now that real-time data is readily available directly over the Internet, option software programs are easier and cheaper to use than ever before. However, assessing a specific program is a difficult task because they are in a constant state of revision. That's why this section is not intended as an in-depth review of these programs. Instead this is a list of trading software and the web sites where they can be found. Most programs offer a 30-day free trial and many can be directly downloaded from the Net. Always demo a program before buying it!

Alef Corporation	www.alef.com
Blue Note Analytics, Inc.	www.bluenoteinc.com
Consulting MicroHedge	www.may.com
The Edge	www.pnc.com.au/~mako
Investment Enhancing Systems, Inc.	www.ies-invest.com
Option-All Trading	www.option-all.com
OptionMax from DiamondBack Software, Inc.	www.optionmax.com
OptionPeer with Option Tutor	www.beyond.com/PKSN100681/prod.htm
OptionsCOURSE.com	www.optioncourse.com
OptionStation, SuperCharts, and TradeStation	www.omegaresearch.com
Option Trader	www.austin-soft.com
OptionVue Systems International, Inc.	www.optionvue.com
Option Wizard	www.optionwizard.com
PMpublishing's Daily Option Analysis	www.pmpublishing.com/volatility
Super Trade Software	www2.epix.net/~sts/
Zero Delta Analytics	www.ZeroDelta.com

appendix d

financial web guide

Appendix D contains 229 reviews of financial investment web sites broken down into the following 13 categories: Supersites, News, Research, Education, Technical Analysis, Options, Webzines, High Technology, Exchanges, Advisory Sites, Specialty Sites, Fun & Games, and Search Engines. Each review is designed to help you determine the site's content and scope and is rated for site design, user-friendliness, and real use, with 1 being the lowest and 10 the highest. Since the Internet is an evolving medium, updates, additions, and changes to this list can be found at www.optionetics.com.

Name	Web Address	Type of Site
ABC News.com	www.abcnews.com	News
Absolute Investments Webzine	www.absolute-investments.com	Webzine
Active Investment Research	www.stockresearch.com	Research
Active Traders Network	www.activetraders.net	Supersite
AltaVista Connections	www.altavista.com	Search Engine
AltaVista Finance	altavista.wallst.com	Supersite
American Association of Individual Investors	www.aaii.com	Education
Armchair Millionaire	www.armchairmillionaire.com	Education
Ask Research	www.askresearch.com	Tech Analysis
Atlantic Broadcasting System	www.abslive.com	News
Avid Trading Company	www.avidtrader.com	Advisory
Barchart.com	www.barchart.com	Tech Analysis
Barron's Online	www.barrons.com	Webzine
BBC News/ Business	news.bbc.co.uk/hi/english/ business	News
BigCharts	www.bigcharts.com	Tech Analysis
Biofind	www.biofind.com	Specialty
Bloomberg	www.bloomberg.com	News
Bonneville Market Information	www.bmiquotes.com	Supersite
Briefing.com	www.briefing.com	Research
Business Week	www.businessweek.com	Webzine

Name	Web Address	Type of Site
Buttonwood Financial Resources	www.buttonwood.net	Advisory
Buy Sell or Hold	www.buysellorhold.com	Research
Cassandra's Revenge	www.stockscape.com/ newsletters/cassandra	Education
CBS MarketWatch	www.cbsmarketwatch.com	News
Chicago Board of Trade	www.cbot.com	Exchanges
Chicago Board Options Exchange	www.cboe.com	Exchanges
ClearStation	www.clearstation.com	Tech Analysis
CMPnet	www.cmpnet.com	High Tech
CNBC	www.cnbc.com	News
CNNfn	www.cnnfn.com	News
Coalition of Black Investors	www.cobinvest.com	Specialty
Committee on Options Proposals	www.coop-options.com	Options
Companies Online	www.companiesonline.com	Research
CoveredCall.com	www.coveredcall.com	Options
CoveredCall Hotline	www.coveredcallhotline.com	Options
Crash Proof Advisors Services	www.crashproofadvisors.com	Advisory
CyberInvest	www.cyberinvest.com	Supersite
Cyberstocks	www.cyberstocks.com	High Tech
Daily Graphs Online	www.dailygraphs.com	Tech Analysis
Daily Picks	www.dailypicks.com	Advisory
Daily Rocket	www.dailyrocket.com	Webzine
Daily Stocks.com	www.dailystocks.com	Supersite
DartZ.com	www.dartz.com	News
Dataquest	www.dataquest.com	High Tech
DBC Online	www.dbc.com	Supersite
Direct Stock Market	www.dsm.com	Specialty
Disclosure	www.disclosure-investor.com	Research
Doh! Stock Picks	www.doh.com	Research
Dow Jones	www.dowjones.com	Research
Dr. Ed Yardeni's Economics Network	www.yardeni.com/ econews.html	Education
Dun & Bradstreet	www.dnb.com	Research
E*Trade	www.etrade.com	Supersite
Economist	www.economist.com	Webzine
EDGAR Online	www.edgar-online.com	Supersite
Einvestor	www.einvestor.com	Supersite
E-Line Financials	www.financials.com	Education
Elliott Wave International	www.elliottwave.com	Advisory
Equis International	www.equis.com	Tech Analysis
Equity Analytics	www.e-analytics.com/	Education
Equity Web	www.equityweb.com	Specialty
eSignal	www.dbc.com/seo/com	Supersite
Excite	www.excite.com	Search Engines
Final Bell	www.sandbox.net/finalbell/ pub-doc/home.html	Education
FinanceWise	www.financewise.com	Research
Financial Center	www.tfc.com	Education
Financial Newsletter Network	www.financialnewsletters.net	News
Financial Times	www.ft.com	News
Financial Web	www.financialweb.com	Supersite

Name	Web Address	Type of Site
FINweb	www.finweb.com	Research
First Call	www.firstcall.com	Research
Forbes Digital Toolbox	www.forbes.com	Webzine
Fortune	www.fortune.com	Webzine
Fox Market Wire	www.foxmarketwire.com	News
FreeRealTime.com	www.freerealtime.com	Specialty
FundTrader.com	www.fundtrader.com	Advisory
Galateia Corp.	www.voicenet.com/	
	~mitochon	Advisory
Gomez Advisors	www.gomez.com	Specialty
Good Money	www.goodmoney.com	Specialty
Good Morning Silicon Valley	www.gmsv.com	High Tech
Green Money Online Guide	www.greenmoney.com	Specialty
GreenJungle	www.greenjungle.com	Education
Hedgehog	www.hedge-hog.com	Advisory
Hey Idiot.Com	www.heyidiot.com	Fun & Games
Holt Stock Report	www.holtreport.com	News
Hoover's Online	www.hoovers.com	Research
Hotbot	www.hotbot.com	Search Engines
IBES	www.ibes.com	Research
Inc.Online	www.inc.com	Webzine
Individual Investor Online	www.individualinvestor.com	Supersite
InfoBeat	www.infobeat.com	Research
Infoseek	www.infoseek.com.	Search Engines
InfoSpace	quotes.infospace.com	Tech Analysis
INO	www.ino.com	Options
InSite	www.dbcms.com	Tech Analysis
Inter@ctive Investor	www.zdii.com	Research
Internet.com	www.internetnews.com/stocks	News
InterQuote	www.interquote.com	Specialty
Investment FAQ	www.invest-faq.com	Education
INVESTools	www.investools.com	Supersite
Investor Guide	www.investorguide.com	Supersite
Investor Home	www.investorhome.com	Specialty
Investor Words	www.investorwords.com	Specialty
Invest-O-Rama	www.investorama.com	Supersite
Investorlinks	www.investorlinks.com	Supersite
Investors Alley	www.investorsalley.com	News
Investor's Business Daily	www.investors.com	News
Investor's Forecast.com	www.investorsforecast.com	Advisory
Investors Free Forum	www.gate.net/	
	~matt5150/chat.html	Specialty
Investor's Galleria	www.centrex.com	Specialty
InvestorSoftware.com	www.invest-soft.com	Specialty
InvestViews	www.investviews.com	Tech Analysis
IQC.com	www.iqc.com	Tech Analysis
JagNotes	jagnotes.com	News
Kids' Money	pages.prodigy.com/kidsmoney	Fun & Games
Kiplinger Online	www.kiplinger.com	Webzine
Lycos	www.lycos.com/business	Search Engines
Lycos Investing	investing.lycos.com	Supersite

Name	Web Address	Type of Site
Market Guide Investor	www.marketguide.com	Research
MarketEdge	www.stkwtch.com	Tech Analysis
MarketScoreboard	www.marketscoreboard.com	George Fontanills
Max's Investment World	www.maxinvest.com	Education
Microsoft Investor	www.investor.msn.com	Supersite
Moby Data	www.mobydata.com	Specialty
Money.com	www.pathfinder.com/money	News
MoneyClub	www.moneyclub.com	Research
MoneyMinded	www.moneyminded.com	Specialty
Moody's Investors Service	www.moodys.com	Specialty
Morningstar	www.morningstar.net	Specialty
Motley Fool	www.fool.com	Supersite
MSN MoneyCentral	investor.msn.com	Research
MSNBC	www.msnbc.com	Webzine
Multex	www.multex.com	Research
Nasdaq-AMEX	www.nasdaq-amex.com	Exchanges
Netpicks	www.netpicks.com	Options
Netquote	www.netquote.com.au	Specialty
New York Stock Exchange	www.nyse.com	Exchanges
News Alert	www.newsalert.com	News
Nordby.com	www.nordby.com	Tech Analysis
North American Quotation	www.naq.com	Specialty
Online Investment Services	www.sonic.net/donaldj	Specialty
OnlineInvestor	www.onlineinvestor.com	Webzine
Optionetics	www.optionetics.com	George Fontanills
OptionInvestor.com	www.optioninvestor.com	Options
Options Industry Association	www.optionscentral.com	Options
OptionsAnalysis.com	www.optionsanalysis.com	George Fontanills
OptionSource.com	www.optionsource.com	Options
Option Strategist	www.optionstrategist.com	Options
Pacific Stock Exchange	www.pacificex.com	Exchanges
Pathfinder	www.pathfinder.com/welcome	News
PC Quote	www.pcquote.com	Specialty
Philadelphia Stock Exchange	www.phlx.com	Exchanges
Pristine	www.pristine.com	Tech Analysis
Quicken.com	www.quicken.com	Supersite
Quote.com	www.quote.com	Supersite
Red Chip Review	www.redchip.com	Webzine
Red Herring Online	www.herring.com	Webzine
Register	www.hubcom.com/register	High Tech
Reuters	www.reuters.com	News
Reuters MoneyNet	www.moneynet.com	Research
Securities and Exchange Commission	www.sec.gov	Exchanges
Securities and Industry Association	www.sia.com	Specialty
Silicon Investor	www.siliconinvestor.com	High Tech
Small Cap Investor	www.smallcapinvestor.com	Specialty
Small Stock News Network	www.ssnn.com	Research
Smart Portfolio.com	www.smartportfolio.com	Advisory
SmartMoney Interactive	www.smartmoney.com	Webzine

Name	Web Address	Type of Site
Social Investment Forum	www.socialinvest.org	Specialty
Standard & Poor's Equity Investment Service	www.stockinfo.standardpoor.com	Supersite
Stock City	www.stockcity.com	Specialty
Stock Club	www.stockclub.com	Specialty
Stock Detective	www.stockdetective.com	Specialty
Stock Research Group	www.stockgroup.com	Research
Stock Smart	www.stocksmart.com	Supersite
Stock Track	www.stocktrak.com	Fun & Games
Stock Valuation with Sense	www.stocksense.com	Education
StockMaster	www.stockmaster.com	Tech Analysis
Stockpage	www.thestockpage.com	Specialty
StockPicks	www.stockpicks.com	Advisory
Stockpoint	www.stockpoint.com	Supersite
StockRumors	www.stockrumors.com	Advisory
Stocks.com	www.stocks.com	Research
StockScreener	www.stockscreener.com	Research
StockSecrets	www.stocksecrets.com	Research
StockSite.com	www.stocksite.com	News
StockSmart Pro	www.stocksmartpro.com	Research
StockTalk	www.stock-talk.com	Specialty
StockTools	www.stocktools.com	Tech Analysis
StockZ.com	www.stockz.com	News
StreetForce.com	www.streetforce.com	Specialty
StreetNet	www.streetnet.com	News
Stricknet.com	www.stricknet.com	Options
Strikeprice.com	www.strikeprice.com	Options
SuperStockPicks.com	www.superstockpick.com	Advisory
Teachdaq	www.teachdaq.com	Education
Technical Analysis of Stocks & Commodities	www.traders.com	Webzine
Telescan Direct	www.telescandirect.com	Research
TheStreet.com	www.thestreet.com	News
Thomson Investors Network	www.thomsoninvest.net	News
Timely.com	www.timely.com	Tech Analysis
TradeLogic Financial Suite	www.tradelogic.com	High Tech
Trader's Bookstore.com	www.booksfortraders.com	Specialty
Traders Digest	www.tradersdigest.com	Webzine
Trading Tactics	www.tradingtactics.com	Specialty
TradInvestors.com	www.pages.prodigy.net/xliu	Advisory
Undergrad Investment News	www.uinews.com	Education
USA Today Money	www.usatoday.com/money/mfront.htm	News
Value Line	www.valueline.com	Tech Analysis
Value Point Analysis Financial Forum	www.eduvest.com	Specialty
VectorVest	www.vectorvest.com	Research
Virtual Stock Exchange	www.virtualstockexchange.com	Education
Wall Street City	www.wallstreetcity.com	Supersite
Wall Street Journal Interactive	interactive.wsj.com	News
Wall Street Research Net	www.wsrn.com	Research

Name	Web Address	Type of Site
Wall Street SOS Forum	www.sosadvisors.com	Advisory
Wall Street Sports	www.wallstreetsports.com	Fun & Games
WallStreetView.com	www.wallstreetview.com	Research
Web Investor	www.thewebinvestor.com	Supersite
Wired Magazine	www.wired.com	Webzine
Wolf	www.netword2000.com/wolf	Advisory
Women's Wire	womenswire.com/money	Specialty
World Mergers and Acquisitions Network	www.worldm-anetwork.com	Advisory
World Wide Financial Network	www.wwfn.com	Research
Worth Online	www.worth.com	Webzine
XOLIA Expert Online Investment Advocates	www.xolia.com/public	Specialty
Yahoo!	www.yahoo.com	Search Engine
Yahoo! Finance	quote.yahoo.com	Supersite
Young Investor Website	www.younginvestor.com	Education
Zacks Investment Research	www.zacks.com	Research
ZDNet	www.zdnet.com	Research

supersites

Active Traders Network
www.activetraders.net
This comprehensive site offers message boards, traders' chat rooms, stock charts, quotes, news, a daily e-mailed newsletter, major index charts, resource links, investment ideas, and technical analysis with global, domestic, and industrial views. It also presents a valuable mock trading portfolio analysis tutorial.
Site Design: 9
User-Friendliness: 8
Real Use: 8
Subscription: $30/month or $75/quarter

AltaVista Finance
altavista.wallst.com
Designed for the active online trader, this well-organized web site features earnings revisions, gainers, losers, annual reports, quotes, charts, graphs, a "Stock of the Day" feature, and industry analysis. There's not a lot of proprietary information, but they supply links to CBS MarketWatch, Hoover's Online, and Individual Investor magazine.
Site Design: 7
User-Friendliness: 8
Real Use: 7
Subscription: Free

Bonneville Market Information (BMI)
www.bmiquotes.com
BMI is a major dynamic quote service and supersite. It offers real-time, delayed, or end-of-day prices on stocks, futures, and options as well as up-to-the-minute news and market analysis for a fee. This information can be accessed in a variety of ways including cable, FM, wireless networks, and directly from the Internet, and is compatible with various trading software. The main site provides free 20-minute-delayed quotes, a link to CBS MarketWatch, and end-of-day global market information, including exchange rates and American depositary receipts (ADR) prices.

Site Design:	9
User-Friendliness:	9
Real Use:	10
Subscription:	Varies depending on service

CyberInvest
www.cyberinvest.com
CyberInvest hosts a free online Web directory to a multitude of investing sites. It also focuses on investor education by providing portfolio tracking, market monitors, and tips for global investing. Lots of advertising and ornate graphics tend to slow this site down, but it's still well worth visiting.

Site Design:	9
User-Friendliness:	9
Real Use:	9
Subscription:	Free

Daily Stocks.com
www.dailystocks.com
This mega-link site features a tremendous list of financial sites arranged by trading tool categories—from stock screening sites to market commentary sites. It also offers an excellent search tool that finds sites on the individual stocks of your choice. You can even opt to be notified of future postings by e-mail.

Site Design:	6
User-Friendliness:	8
Real Use:	9
Subscription:	Free

Data Broadcasting Corp. (DBC) Online
www.dbc.com
DBC is a major dynamic quote provider and an excellent research and analysis site. In addition to real-time, delayed, and end-of-day prices, you get a multitude of additional services including news, movers and shakers, charts, customized portfolios, and alerts for a fee. The comprehensive site also offers delayed snapshot quotes and lots of valuable information, news, and commentary. Many trading software programs are compatible with DBC (also known as Signal) to run their analysis systems.

Site Design:	9
User-Friendliness:	9
Real Use:	10
Subscription:	eSignal: real-time—$150/month; delayed—$79/month. Cable, FM, and wireless networks are also available at varying rates.

eSignal
www.dbc.com/seo/cam
This site is actually hosted by DBC Online and is *the* dynamic state-of-the-art, real-time quoting service. Broadcasting directly from the floors of the exchange, DBC operates a multimillion-dollar, proprietary network that provides real-time stock, futures, bonds, and options prices via the Internet, cable, and wireless networks. Access the "Trader's Toolbox" and you'll find an abundance of market commentary, calendars, market index charts—intraday, interval, and tick by tick—symbol lookup and market snapshots, *The Exchange Newsletter*, earnings reports, movers and shakers, IPO info, industry earnings, and more. Signal Online also offers e-mail, pager, and cell phone alerts and is compatible with a variety of investment and options trading programs.

Site Design:	10
User-Friendliness:	9
Real Use:	10
Subscription:	$79/month plus depending on service needs

E*Trade

www.etrade.com

One of the most popular online brokerages also provides the general public with an immense amount of financial trading tools. You have the market at your fingertips: Get quotes, charts, earnings estimates, and company profiles. Set up a portfolio of your favorite stocks and they'll even e-mail you with the latest breaking news and quotes.

Site Design:	8
User-Friendliness:	7
Real Use:	8
Subscription:	Free

EDGAR Online

www.edgar-online.com

This first-rate site is a classic financial resource. It allows you to access EDGAR filings using an electronic data-gathering analysis retrieval tool (now that's impressive) to locate the SEC filings that interest you. Check out the exclusive drill-down tools, the "IPO Express" feature, insider trading updates, or program an alert to let you know when a company you are watching files a new document. Although this is a subscription-based site, it does offer a few free services including custom portfolios.

Site Design:	9
User-Friendliness:	9
Real Use:	9
Subscription:	$9.95 to $99.95/month

Einvestor

www.einvestor.com

This site has a financial resource directory with more than 2,000 web sites in 59 categories. You can also find a generous sprinkling of financial news, securities research, chat rooms, free quotes, investors forums, and bulletin boards of today's postings, plus tips from experienced traders. In 1998, this comprehensive site received a Major Web Select Award from *Investor Day*'s Gold Site.

Site Design:	9
User-Friendliness:	8
Real Use:	8
Subscription:	Free

Financial Web

www.financialweb.com

The Financial Web lives up to its name by interweaving 18 smaller sites to create the total personal finance online solution. A well-organized site map gets you on track to help you navigate your way around the site with ease. Areas of focus include bearish and bullish stock watchers, e-mail price alerts on selected stocks, small-cap stock research, mutual funds, EDGAR documents, screening guides, a convenient quote search engine, and even a section on options. Make sure to check out the "Stock Detective" for the latest online fraud caper.

Site Design:	8
User-Friendliness:	9
Real Use:	10
Subscription:	Free

Individual Investor Online

www.individualinvestor.com

This site has top market stories and access to quotes, charts, strategies, the Magic 25, hot stocks, analysis, portfolio and mutual fund information. The message boards and forums are well used and filled with interesting trader insights on a huge variety of topics.

Site Design:	7
User-Friendliness:	8
Real Use:	7
Subscription:	Site tools—free; newsletter—$19.95/year

INVESTools

www.investools.com

This is a fully loaded, well-designed site dedicated to providing everything the savvy investor uses to make successful trading decisions. INVESTools features first-rate research tools and links, advisory groups, featured adviser articles, a free advisory newsletter, stock screening, stock and fund recommendations, and model portfolios, plus ticker search tools, custom portfolios, quotes, and charts.

Site Design:	9
User-Friendliness:	9
Real Use:	9
Subscription:	Free

Investor Guide

www.investorguide.com

This excellent, comprehensive site focuses on investing, personal finance, and education. In addition to quotes and news, it has a great FAQ section with more than 1,000 responses to investment questions. Subscribe to the weekly newsletter or try your luck at the Hedgehog Investment Competition. If you've ever wanted to create and manage your own $1,000,000 hedge fund, here's your chance.

Site Design:	9
User-Friendliness:	9
Real Use:	9
Subscription:	Consulting services from $75 to $95 an hour

Invest-O-Rama

www.investorama.com

Doug Gerlach's Invest-O-Rama hosts a wonderfully comprehensive directory link to more than 9,350 financial web sites. You can also research specific companies using an army of fundamental and technical analysis tools. All this as well as insightful articles by Gerlach and a handful of other financial journalistic experts. An all-around great site for savvy investors and novices alike.

Site Design:	9
User-Friendliness:	9
Real Use:	9
Subscription:	Free

Investorlinks

www.investorlinks.com

Investorlinks is an extensive financial web directory with daily and weekly reports, as well as articles and commentary. It offers links to advisories, mutual funds, options services, quotes, charts, stocks, financial news, investor services, brokerages, stocks and bonds, and research, and a free portfolio feature.

Site Design:	9
User Friendliness:	9
Real Use:	9
Subscription:	Free

Lycos Investing

investing.lycos.com

Lycos, a leading search engine, brings its resources to the complex world of investing, offering quick snapshot quotes and company profiles, customized charts and graphs, intraday charts, and recent news clips. You can also check out market commentary, mutual fund analysis, personal finance information, extensive Web directories, the usual chat rooms and message boards, and links to various news services.

Site Design:	8
User-Friendliness:	8
Real Use:	8
Subscription:	Free

Microsoft Investor

www.investor.msn.com

What don't they have at Microsoft's financial supersite? There are quotes, charts, graphs, market reports, finders, screeners, research, online workshops, custom portfolios, feature news and investment articles from MSNBC, as well as impressive commentary from prime financial journalists. For a small fee, you can receive e-mailed market reports or link up using with Microsoft Money software. Gates proves once again that he always goes the whole hog!

Site Design:	9
User-Friendliness:	9
Real Use:	9
Subscription:	$9.95/month

Motley Fool
www.fool.com
One of the most popular sites on the Internet! The Motley Fool site seeks to educate, amuse, and continually enrich the investment process for the hundreds of thousands of eager investors who use their books and this site to maximize their trading profits. This extremely entertaining site has a vast amount of current and educational investment information including quotes, charts, financials, portfolios, news and ideas, and some of the most heavily-trafficked bulletin boards of the Net. It also offers an e-mailed newsletter service, "Industry Focus," with refreshing articles and commentary on everything from market movement to specific companies for a small subscription fee and a free once-a-week wrap-up, "Notes from a Fool." For brokerage reviews, check out the Motley Fool Brokerage Center. Don't be fooled by their foolish bravado—this site has plenty of investor clout. In 1999, it received both the People's Choice and the Webby award for Best Finance Site. Truly a quintessential supersite!

Site Design:	10+
User-Friendliness:	10+
Real Use:	10+
Subscription:	Free, or $25/year for "Industry Focus" e-mailed newsletter

Quicken.com
www.quicken.com
The Quicken site is geared for novice investors, would-be homeowners, and small business entrepreneurs. It offers an extensive array of quotes, advanced charting, custom portfolios, home and mortgage information (including a convenient calculator), news and analysis, company profiles, SEC filings, and reports. You can also find small business help and Quicken's turbo tax software products.

Site Design:	7
User-Friendliness:	8
Real Use:	8
Subscription:	Free

Quote.com
www.quote.com
The Quote.com site offers a ton of useful information, including delayed and real-time quotes, charts, earnings estimates and reports, top business stories, NYSE most active gainers and losers, and a market guide with in-depth information on individual companies. You can also register for hourly updates, dynamic quote service, and timely news feeds. Check out their options education area—comprehensive and well-organized.

Site Design:	10
User-Friendliness:	10
Real Use:	10
Subscription:	$9.95 to $59.95 depending on the scope of service

Standard & Poor's Equity Investor Service
www.stockinfo.standardpoor.com
The S&P is not just a renowned index anymore. Thanks to the Internet, the S&P's web site offers top-notch "Personal Wealth" services including custom portfolios, news and commentary, real-time symbol searches and auto alerts. The real meat of the site comes from the company research services as well as S&P's "Advisor Insight" with stock reports and professional analysis.

Site Design:	10
User-Friendliness:	9
Real Use:	9
Subscription:	Basic subscription service $9.95/month. Reports are extra.

Stockpoint
www.stockpoint.com
This site is filled to the brim with investment information. Enjoy custom portfolios, charts, graphs, news commentary, featured articles, and links to more than 80 newsletters. The "StockFinder" feature will search the major exchanges (NYSE, AMEX, Nasdaq) to find the stocks that match your criteria. For companies or individuals looking to set up online, Stockpoint is also one of the Web's foremost web site builders with a proven record of successful sites. It made *Barron's* "Top Ten Investment Web Sites" in 1998.

Site Design:	8
User-Friendliness:	9
Real Use:	8
Subscription:	Free

Stock Smart
www.stocksmart.com
A well-designed, clean site that specializes in providing you with in-depth information on your chosen stocks and industry sectors. It offers excellent custom portfolios with automatic updates, earnings calendars, graphs and charts, research, stock screening, plus a look at the global markets. "Smart E-lerts" can give you timely stock prices plus the latest news.

Site Design:	10
User-Friendliness:	9
Real Use:	8
Subscription:	$12.95/month

Wall Street City
www.wallstreetcity.com
The Wall Street City site has it all, from market analysis, shrewd commentary, and consensus reports to breaking news, snapshot quotes, technical charts, customizable portfolios, company reports and powerful search engines. For beginner investors, the education center is one of the most comprehensive available on the Net and definitely worth a look. It made *Barron's* "Top Ten Investment Web Sites" in 1998.

Site Design:	9
User-Friendliness:	10
Real Use:	9
Subscription:	$9.95 to $34.95/month
	depending on level of service

Web Investor
www.thewebinvestor.com
This free site features an excellent guide to online investing sites as well as technical analysis, day trading alerts, stock analysis, portfolio management, daily stock reports, links to free quotes, charts and data providers, market research, and references. Access snapshot quotes, charts, company news, global and financial news, a newsletter, and features like the "Today's Chart of Interest" and the "Daytrader's Workshop."

Site Design:	8
User-Friendliness:	8
Real Use:	7
Subscription:	Free

Yahoo! Finance
quote.yahoo.com or www.yahoo.com/business
Yahoo! Finance features a vast array of market information including quotes, financial news, calendars, the latest market news, bulletin boards, chat rooms, SEC filings, earnings estimates, and a custom portfolio feature to keep track of your favorite stocks. I just happen to enjoy Yahoo!'s format, and judging by its popularity, so do millions of other Internet users.

Site Design:	8
User-Friendliness:	9
Real Use:	9
Subscription:	Free

news

ABC News.com
www.abcnews.com
ABC moves from TV to the Net! Scroll down long enough and you'll find plenty of up-to-date business news and a no-frills, global market overview. You can also check out small business information, company and industry sector news, quotes, and technical charts. ABC's site received a 1998 Webby for Best News Site.

Site Design:	7
User-Friendliness:	7
Real Use:	9
Subscription:	Free

Atlantic Broadcasting System
www.abslive.com
General investor program trading from an industry pioneer company with M&A evaluation, custom portfolios, risk analysis, snapshot quotes, technical analysis charts and graphs, plus market alert e-mail, live financial commentary and of course, the latest breaking news complete with sound and video. Their client list in this area includes Bank of America, Soros GE Capital, and Nomura—pretty impressive.

Site Design:	8
User-Friendliness:	7
Real Use:	8
Subscription:	Free

BBC News/Business
news.bbc.co.uk/hi/english/business
British news at its finest. Review international news, download articles from extensive archives, and check out the London stock market. Well-written and thoroughly researched, this site offers a glimpse of how U.S. stocks are viewed from across the pond.

Site Design:	9
User-Friendliness:	7
Real Use:	8
Subscription:	Free

Bloomberg
www.bloomberg.com
Bloomberg's site has a staggering array of free and subscription services including up-to-the-minute headlines and daily news on stocks, bonds, Treasuries, global indexes, IPOs, currencies, and commodities. You can access financial market updates by live video (Bloomberg Television) or audio (Bloomberg News Radio). Bloomberg subscription services integrate a variety of traders' tools including quotes, a chart builder, a portfolio tracker, the Dow 30, and the "Market Monitor" which can be used to hunt down the latest news on up to 10 companies. And just in case you're ready for a break, traders can monitor the latest sports news or check out a recent interview from Charlie Rose's syndicated television series which is housed in the studios at Bloomberg Television News studios and currently airs on 215 PBS affiliate stations.

Site Design:	8
User-Friendliness:	9
Real Use:	9
Subscription:	Free/$24.95 annual magazine subscription

CBS MarketWatch
www.cbsmarketwatch.com
CBS MarketWatch is sure to be on everyone's bookmark list, with comprehensive coverage of news from exceptional journalists, headlines, and market data. Plenty of web sites link to CBS MarketWatch to access the latest breaking and scheduled news. Delayed quotes are supplied by DBC. The discussion page has forums to discuss stocks, mutual funds, futures, options, and global investing.

Site Design:	10
User-Friendliness:	9

Real Use: 9
Subscription: Realtime—$34.95/month
                 or StockEdge Online—$79/month

CNBC
www.cnbc.com
The CNBC television news channel is the leader in business news. Its web site seeks to continue this tradition. The CNBC site offers programming information for CNBC in the United States, Europe, and Asia. Biographies for the CNBC staff are also online. Extensive executive and job search Web listings and phone numbers are available.
Site Design: 9
User-Friendliness: 9
Real Use: 8
Subscription: Free

CNNfn
www.cnnfn.com
The CNN television news channel has created a successful online spin-off featuring the hottest stories of the day, breaking market updates, quotes, extensive company profiles and industry news, plus customized portfolios and daily e-mailed market briefings. The site received a 1997 Webby award as the Best Money Site.
Site Design: 8
User-Friendliness: 8
Real Use: 8
Subscription: Free

DartZ.com
www.dartz.com
DartZ focuses on financial news and daily investment articles and also serves as a multi-service site with custom portfolios and e-mail stock updates, message and chat boards, quotes, and charting search engines. A weekly stock pick is posted 10 hours before the market week opens. You can also compete with friends in a fun market forecast game called the Invisible Hand Electronic Market.
Site Design: 8
User-Friendliness: 8
Real Use: 7
Subscription: Free

Financial Newsletter Network
www.financialnewsletters.net
The beauty of this site is the way it links to hundreds of financial newsletters complete with expert market research guides and online seminars. You can participate in an online market sentiment survey or find out about investment conferences and shows all over the country. There are also charts and graphs and a ticker quote search engine. On the lighter side, there are weekly cartoons and clever animations to download.
Site Design: 8
User-Friendliness: 8
Real Use: 7
Subscription: Free/newsletter prices vary

Financial Times
www.ft.com
Produced by England's *Financial Times*, this sterling site provides a welcome change from the usual slick sites boasting bells and whistles. This site offers superb research tools and resources, exhaustive archives with over 3,000,000 articles from 3,000 different publications and insightful reporting on industry trends and big events of the day. The site also offers personalized share portfolios and an online currency converter to make international trade speculation a lot easier. Free search of archived articles is available. A well-organized site map is the key to finding your way around this unique web site.
Site Design: 8
User-Friendliness: 7
Real Use: 8
Subscription: Free

Fox Market Wire
www.foxmarketwire.com
Sponsored by Fox News, this site offers investor news, tip sheets, multiple quotes, charts, top performer lists, and free screening of stocks and funds. There are custom portfolios with e-mailed updates. You can also register for 50 real-time quotes per day and 50 research quotes per month as well as notifications on major business events.

Site Design:	8
User-Friendliness:	8
Real Use:	8
Subscription:	$19.95/year

Holt Stock Report
www.holtreport.com
The Holt Report is user-friendly and full of interesting investment ideas. Check out the hot stocks reports, stocks up 50%, and the most recent closings reports for stocks and options. There's a "web menu" listing of recommended investment web sites to explore as well as the Holt Report archives to research. Select Surf rated this site as the Best of the Web, although its design is in need of a facelift.

Site Design:	5
User-Friendliness:	7
Real Use:	8
Subscription:	Free

Internet.com
www.internetnews.com/stocks
This site specializes in information about Internet stocks offering stock and news sections with a variety of feature articles and news stories about Internet e-commerce, Web development, and Internet technology. Register for a free subscription to their daily online newsletter or download some unique Web tools. I especially enjoy the "Top Internet News Stories" section for quick referencing hot stocks.

Site Design:	7
User-Friendliness:	7
Real Use:	7
Subscription:	Free

Investors Alley
www.investorsalley.com
This is a massive site featuring daily investment news on stocks, options, bonds, IPOs, mutual funds, earnings reports, and economic calendars. It offers a free daily e-mail newsletter, custom portfolios, and a stock screener, check out the latest upgrading and downgrading, or see what advisers have to say about the next day's marketplace. You can also take a look at global markets or interact at a chat room or street talk forum.

Site Design:	7
User-Friendliness:	8
Real Use:	8
Subscription:	Free

Investor's Business Daily
www.investors.com
The *IBD*'s online spin-off is a great place for novice investors to get their bearings and active investors to keep abreast of market trends and company changes. Featuring topical daily news articles from daily newspaper sections such as Inside Today, Front Page, Computers & Tech, the Economy, the Markets, and Vital Signs, this site is also an excellent educational section with great tips from investment guru William O'Neil.

Site Design:	8
User-Friendliness:	8
Real Use:	7
Subscription:	Free

JagNotes
jagnotes.com
JagNotes is primarily a consolidated investment report on all the stocks that have had newly issued research, analyst opinions, upgrades, downgrades and coverage changes.

The information contained in the morning JagNotes is typically not released to the street until after the start of trading. JagNotes also offers a fax transmission service with stocks and options, daily news, and Wall Street insights.

Site Design:	6
User-Friendliness:	6
Real Use:	6
Subscription:	$500/quarter

Money.com

www.pathfinder.com/money

Primarily a news site, Money.com features upbeat edgy feature articles and columns, investing tools, and market summary. Use the quote search and news search features, or set up custom charts and portfolios. Additional information can be found on real estate, insurance, autos, retirement, and taxes. This site just completed a major design overhaul.

Site Design:	9
User-Friendliness:	8
Real Use:	7
Subscription:	Magazines $29.95/month

MSNBC

www.msnbc.com

This online spin-off of NBC television provides market updates and breaking news, feature articles and commentary plus a major exchanges chart and quote search tools. Lots of breaking news and video clips as well as links and advertisements. This site won a 1998 Webby award for the Best News Site.

Site Design:	8
User-Friendliness:	6
Real Use:	6
Subscription:	Free

News Alert

www.newsalert.com

This site offers customized portfolios with e-mail alerts and a desktop notifier system to keep you instantly informed of how your holdings are moving along and what you don't have but need. There's news and analysis with the "Gainers at a Glance" feature, as well as real-time quotes, market research, charts, graphs, calendars, and indexes.

Site Design:	7
User-Friendliness:	8
Real Use:	8
Subscription.	$9.95 to $20/month

Pathfinder

www.pathfinder.com/welcome

Time Warner's Pathfinder site has links to all the online publications in the Time Warner family, such as *Time, People, Money, Fortune,* and *Entertainment Weekly.* The scrolling news wire is useful, as are the numerous links to prominent financial news sites.

Site Design:	8
User-Friendliness:	7
Real Use:	7
Subscription:	Free

Reuters

www.reuters.com

Reuters news service has an impressive array of financial information. It is renowned for its information on the foreign exchange (ForEx) markets, Euromart, and the world market indexes.

Site Design:	8
User-Friendliness:	8
Real Use:	8
Subscription:	Free

StockSite.com
www.stocksite.com
StockSite.com features the latest news, a "Daily Market Rap" and "U.S. Economy Weekly" from seasoned writers as well as the usual online services including quotes, charts, custom portfolios, market tools, stocks splits, upgrades and downgrades, an IPO monitor, and a daily newsletter.

Site Design:	7
User-Friendliness:	7
Real Use:	7
Subscription:	Free

StreetNet
www.streetnet.com
This site supplies news and research on public companies and global investing, an e-mailed newsletter, and free quotes. There's lots of hype but not much else on this site, and too many distracting ads on every page.

Site Design:	6
User-Friendliness:	5
Real Use:	6
Subscription:	Free

TheStreet.com.
www.thestreet.com
Hosted by controversial analyst Jim Cramer, this extremely popular site offers insightful articles on stocks, options, tech stocks, funds, taxes, and the international finance scene. Register for a free 30-day trial of their premium subscription service and you'll find yourself in the loop encountering the clever commentary of a cadre of bantering journalists three times a day delivered right to your desktop. TheStreet.com's engaging articles and perceptive market analyses no doubt help to shape the mass psychology of the marketplace.

Site Design:	8
User-Friendliness:	9
Real Use:	10
Subscription:	$6.95 to $9.95/month

Thomson Investors Network
www.thomsoninvest.net and www.thomsonresearch.com
This site allows you to access news from their newsroom and retrieve selected articles from the Market Monitor. Research, breaking news, intraday charts, and real-time quotes are well organized. But the real Thomson site is dedicated to providing derivative and commodity reports, as well as newsletters and consulting services that cost bucks.

Site Design:	8
User-Friendliness	9
Real Use:	8
Subscription:	Fee varies with level of service

USA Today Money
www.usatoday.com/money/mfront.htm
America's premiere national newspaper teams up with Bloomberg to create a comprehensive and well-organized web site featuring a bounty of breaking news and feature articles. The "Market Scoreboard" section provides a lengthy list of trading tools including delayed quotes, most active lists, an IPO center, and industry research. One very cool feature—the home page refreshes automatically bringing you up-to-the-minute news flashes.

Site Design:	8
User-Friendliness:	7
Real Use:	7
Subscription:	Free

Wall Street Journal Interactive
interactive.wsj.com
The Wall Street Journal Interactive, with 24-hour news updates and e-mail stock alerts, has lots of information to help you track markets and investments, allow you to follow

the technology sector, get a global perspective, and research your interests, with per-spectives on over 10,000 companies and mailing lists. Wall Street Journal Interactive Edi-tion (WSJIE) provides both subscription and free areas. Some interesting free features include top business news in Spanish and Portuguese, annual reports from selected com-panies, the Small Business Suite, and Shareholder Scorecard. There is also an updated job and career search section with technical, professional, and management positions listed. Subscription services include access to search engines, additional featured sites, e-mail alerts, and chat rooms.

Site Design:	8
User-Friendliness:	7
Real Use:	9
Subscription:	$49/year

research

Active Investment Research
www.stockresearch.com
This investment site offers its own "Investment Philosophy" along with a host of research tools and services. You'll find quotes, graphs, fundamentals, recommendations, bulletin boards, historical quotes, archival resources, a healthy list of links, and a free advisory newsletter.

Site Design:	7
User-Friendliness:	7
Real Use:	5
Subscription:	Free

Briefing.com
www.briefing.com
This site seems to have caught the ear of the market. The Briefing.com site offers two levels of subscription services. Stock Analysis provides live market commentary, stock analysis, quotes and charts, sector ratings, earnings reports and an economic calendar. Premium services include information on indexes, currencies, and bond markets.

Site Design:	8
User-Friendliness:	8
Real Use:	8
Subscription:	$6.95/month—Stock Analysis; $25/month—professional

Buy Sell or Hold
www.buysellorhold.com
Buy Sell or Hold enthusiastically presents analyst opinions, software to download, funda-mental and technical data, investment recommendations, newsletters and company re-ports. It has custom portfolios with a tracking service and message boards, as well as a handy high-technology glossary.

Site Design:	7
User-Friendliness:	6
Real Use:	6
Subscription:	3 reports for $19.95

Companies Online
www.companiesonline.com
This is a completely different type of research site. Companies Online is an online com-pany database where you can browse by industry, or through its picks for company of the week. There are links to more search tools and to Dun & Bradstreet reports and quotes.

Site Design:	8
User-Friendliness:	8
Real Use:	8
Subscription:	Free

Disclosure
www.disclosure-investor.com
To really get the lowdown on companies you may be interested in, you need to access a site like Disclosure. It offers company reports, news, quotes, annual reports, 10Ks, 20Fs, 10Qs, 8Ks, a guide to SEC filings with information on over 12,000 U.S. companies and over 13,000 international companies, and lists of the latest company press releases.

Site Design:	8
User-Friendliness:	8
Real Use:	7
Subscription:	Free; reports vary

Doh! Stock Picks
www.doh.com
Doh! Stock Picks says that it's the web site that "takes the Homer Simpson out of stock picking" and investing. Check out the buy, sell, and hold recommendations, plus the "Dogs of the Dow" feature, three custom portfolio setups, 10 lists of picks, stock advice, and book recommendations. Humor is always welcome in cyberspace.

Site Design:	8
User-Friendliness:	8
Real Use:	7
Subscription:	Free

Dow Jones
www.dowjones.com
The Dow Jones site offers global market updates, economic indicators, quotes, and news. Access to the *Dow Jones Index* pages and other business publications are also available.

Site Design:	8
User-Friendliness:	8
Real Use:	8
Subscription:	$69/year; fees for additional publications vary

Dun & Bradstreet
www.dnb.com
Dun & Bradstreet specializes in press releases and company profiles, focusing on news, views, and trends. Check out its renowned business database for report requests.

Site Design:	9
User-Friendliness:	9
Real Use:	8
Subscription:	Free

FinanceWise
www.financewise.com
This no-frills site will enable you to search financial web sites by allowing you to query it using individual words. Searching by key terms or phrases, company names, or industrial sectors locates special reports and news articles. You have to register and use a personalized postregistration bookmark to access the site again.

Site Design:	8
User-Friendliness:	6
Real Use:	8
Subscription:`	Free

FINweb
www.finweb.com
FINweb is a highly concentrated financial economics web site dedicated to listing Internet resources providing substantive information concerning economics and finance-related topics. Sections include Electronic Publishing (Journals), Working Papers, Databases and Research Tools, and of course extensive links. Very highbrow—check out the jokes about economists, too.

Site Design:	5
User-Friendliness:	6
Real Use:	6
Subscription:	Free

First Call

www.firstcall.com

Available in Spanish, Portuguese, and Chinese, this site is an excellent source for real-time, assimilated research. You'll find access to more than 5,000,000 equity and fixed-income detailed research documents, complete with earnings estimates and corporate information. First Call services also include a market source and estimate monitor, and a stock portfolio manager.

Site Design:	8
User-Friendliness:	7
Real Use:	8
Subscription:	Free

Hoover's Online

www.hoovers.com

A premiere investment research web site, Hoover's Online makes it easy to research a company's financials while exploring historical market data. A small monthly subscription fee gives you access to proprietary profiles on 3,300 stocks. Get the jump on IPO filings, investigate industry overviews, quotes, and price forecasting each trading week. Access stock screeners, breaking news stories, research tools and links, or download reports. This site has received numerous awards including the Dow Jones Business Directory's Select Site, Investor Link's Top Site and is a Yahoo! 98 Winner as well.

Site Design:	9
User-Friendliness:	9
Real Use:	10
Subscription:	$12.95/month

IBES

www.ibes.com

This site originated from the Institutional Brokers Estimate System, started in 1971. The services offered include live earnings forecasting with analysts' earnings expectations, stock charts, alerts, stock selection tools, and daily updates. Check out the basic and premium services.

Site Design:	7
User-Friendliness:	7
Real Use:	7
Subscription:	$9.95 to $99.95/month

InfoBeat

www.infobeat.com

InfoBeat is a one-stop shopping site for information delivered right to your PC. Just click on "Finance" to set up portfolios of stocks and receive daily e-mail messages containing closing prices and pertinent news. Click on "Select" and then "Business and Finance" to browse the extensive selection of free subscriptions to e-mail newsletters and columnists from leading publishers.

Site Design:	8
User-Friendliness:	8
Real Use:	9
Subscription:	Free

Inter@ctive Investor

www.zdii.com

This site is filled with research tools, breaking news, featured articles, and commentary. Use the news search tool to locate information on subjects that interest you. Play the

"Investment Challenge" stock game with $100,000 of play money to win experience and insight as well as some great computer-friendly prizes.

Site Design:	6
User-Friendliness:	6
Real Use:	6
Subscription:	Free

Market Guide Investor

www.marketguide.com

This site offers free real-time quotes, technical charts, an excellent "What's Hot" section, and a market summary complete with headlines, commentary, and a list of upgrades/downgrades. The screening section features three distinct levels of screening: NetScreen, Stock Quest, and the Market Guide database. The Market Guide database is available only on CD-ROM, and provides 550 screening variables on 10,000 companies including a comprehensive 12-page report, earning estimates, annual reports, insider trading activity, business, short interest data, and company to industry, sector, and market comparisons. Lots of advertising must help to keep most of the site free.

Site Design:	8
User-Friendliness:	7
Real Use:	8
Subscription:	Free and subscription areas

MoneyClub

www.moneyclub.com

MoneyClub specializes as a personal finance network of regional and cobranded sites that cover retirement, estate, credit, bankruptcy, insurance, and "Taxweb" tax planning. It also features something called "Netnoir" that is a financial resources organization created especially for African-Americans.

Site Design:	8
User-Friendliness:	8
Real Use:	7
Subscription:	Free

MSN MoneyCentral

investor.msn.com

MSN MoneyCentral has quotes, graphs and charts, news, tutorials and instructional workshops, strategy labs, market updates, news on upcoming stock splits, and advisory FYI alerts. You can also download free investor tools software or screen 16,000 stocks and funds using more than 500 criteria. Receive up to 50 free real-time quotes per day just by registering.

Site Design:	7
User-Friendliness:	8
Real Use:	8
Subscription:	Free

Multex

www.multex.com

This site offers freely accessible professional research and analysis data. It's filled with technical charts, quotes, graphs, e-mail alerts, investors' discussion forums, and online seminars with top Wall Street analysts. In addition, Multex specializes in providing access to comprehensive reports on individual companies that can be produced on a pay-per-view basis for a fee from $4 to $150 a report.

Site Design:	8
User-Friendliness:	9
Real Use:	7
Subscription:	Free

Reuters MoneyNet

www.moneynet.com

Reuters is one of the primary international wire services. Its web site serves up a double dose of global news as well as top-notch investment commentary and market news—

quite different from the main Reuters financial page. Reuters's MoneyNet has a custom portfolio tracker feature, charts, and real-time quotes including options. You can also find hot stocks, company profiles, and headline news.

Site Design:	8
User-Friendliness:	8
Real Use:	8
Subscription:	Free

Small Stock News Network
www.ssnn.com
The Small Stock News Network has the most current news and data on over 10,000 small-cap stocks. News, research, and expanded coverage of small-cap stocks are available, in addition to e-mail alerts on individual companies.

Site Design:	7
User-Friendliness:	7
Real Use:	8
Subscription:	Free

Stock Research Group (SRG)
www.stockgroup.com
The Stock Research Group's site offers feature articles, headlines, and interesting sector reports on tech stocks, petroleum, and diamond stocks. Quotes, custom portfolio managers, indexes, and an analyst corner are well-organized features.

Site Design:	7
User-Friendliness:	6
Real Use:	7
Subscription:	Free

Stock Research Group
www.stockgroup.com
Based in Canada, this practical site is filled with small-cap stock research and investment tools including company profiles and reports, discussion groups, news headlines, market commentary, and portfolio management features including e-mail alerts and a daily Small Cap Express market report. You can customize the design of this web site to show and receive news regarding your preferred markets and stocks of choice. It also provides in-depth analysis of petroleum and mining stocks.

Site Design:	9
User-Friendliness:	8
Real Use:	8
Subscription:	Free

Stocks.com
www.stocks.com
The Stocks.com site acts as a portal to a multitude of featured financial resource links. You can also access quotes, news, and free investment tools to download as well as the "Company Sleuth" feature that e-mails you an account of messages from a variety of chat rooms on the specific stocks of your choice. Check out several new features including the "Hedge Fund Trader" by technical analyst Richard Eakle, "Key Reversals" (their computers screen 11,000 NYSE and Nasdaq stocks searching for those that have changed direction), and the "Wave Theorist" (a graphic assessment of specific industries). Too bad this site moves so slowly.

Site Design:	8
User-Friendliness:	6
Real Use:	7
Subscription:	Free

Stockscreener
www.stockscreener.com
This site is part of Hoover's Online and features an easy-to-use stock screening mega-search engine with more than 20 performance criteria, including company size, margins,

growth size, and rates of return. Your resulting stock picks will link to a Hoover's Company Capsule. You can also search for information on IPOs or look at data on more than 8,000 individual companies.

Site Design:	9
User-Friendliness:	8
Real Use:	8
Subscription:	Free

StockSecrets

www.stocksecrets.com

The Stock Secrets site claims to be *the* most complete financial library on the Internet offering quality research and in-depth information on little-known stocks with amazing profit potential. Use the search engine to scroll through more than 3,000 pages of financial books and sign up for the free "Diamond in the Rough" monthly newsletter. The site also offers a trading course featuring short-term trading strategies.

Site Design:	7
User-Friendliness:	7
Real Use:	7
Subscription:	Free

StockSmart Pro

www.stocksmartpro.com

This subscription site offers its members an escape from sites littered with advertisements. Services include tracking the market, following intraday trading, accessing company profiles and industry fluctuations, custom portfolios, automatic e-mail alerts, search engine tools, limited technical analysis tools, and stock screening. You must be a registered member to use this site.

Site Design:	7
User-Friendliness:	7
Real Use:	7
Subscription:	12.95/month

StockZ

www.stockz.com

Best known for their stock and options picks, StockZ also features extensive research resources, chart and quote search engines, news, daily articles, message boards, an extensive online bookstore, and a feature called the "Day's Charts of Interest."

Site Design:	7
User-Friendliness:	8
Real Use:	5
Subscription:	$49.95/3 months

Telescan Direct

www.telescandirect.com

This site hosts a major quote service that offers wireless news and real-time stock quotes for mobile traders. It offers stock alerts sent via e-mail, pager, or PCS device to handheld units. When market conditions change, it lets you know by sending you high or low price and/or volume alerts. It is an innovative company to watch; its latest is a new feature that helps you create a real-time ticker quote search tool for your own Web page. It also offers a refined search capability that locates stocks and options based on the criteria of choice for a fee.

Site Design:	9
User-Friendliness:	9
Real Use:	7
Subscription:	From $19.95 to $299.95/month

VectorVest

www.vectorvest.com

The VectorVest site provides services that integrate fundamental and technical analysis to sort, screen, rank, graph, and analyze over 6,500 stocks, industry groups, and industry sectors for price, value, safety, timing, and more. All stocks receive buy, sell, hold, and stop order recommendations as well as price and dividend risk assessments of low, high, or medium.If you're not ready for a subscription, you may want to take advantage of the free in-depth stock analysis service—just click on the "Free Stock Analysis" box on the upper left-hand corner of the home page screen.

Site Design: 9
User-Friendliness: 8
Real Use: 9
Subscription: $29 to $49/month; 5-week trial offer $29.95

Wall Street Research Net
www.wsrn.com
The Wall Street Research Net has over 500,000 links to help professional and private investors perform fundamental research on actively traded companies and mutual funds, and locate important economic data that moves markets. It offers access to SEC documents, research reports, baseline reports, spreadsheets, news, charts, and statistical analysis. You can also research what the major technical indicators are signaling for stocks in your portfolio or download up to 10 years of historical stock data.

Site Design: 7
User-Friendliness: 7
Real Use: 9
Subscription: Some services are free and some require payment. Baseline reports— $4.95/month; historical downloads— $5 per report; WSRN Data Center—$9.95/month

WallStreetView.com
www.wallstreetview.com
WallStreetView.com offers four main areas of market monitoring: markets, ideas, trading pits, and research. Well-organized and pleasing to the eye, this site provides access to real-time quotes, top 50 options lists, investment ideas, research SEC filings and IPOs, custom portfolios, custom tickers stock alerts, and an intraday market watch.

Site Design: 9
User-Friendliness: 9
Real Use: 8
Subscription: Free

World Wide Financial Network
www.wwfn.com
The World Wide Financial Network has an excellent variety of investor resources including company profiles, free real-time quotes and charts, upgrades and downgrades, real-time Globex, insider trading, news, extensive research, feature articles, and access to online brokers. Overall a great site.

Site Design: 6
User-Friendliness: 8
Real Use: 9
Subscription: Free

Zacks Investment Research
www.zacks.com
Zacks Investment Research is a very popular financial site that offers a variety of free and subscription services. The site provides access to research produced by over 3,000 analysts at more than 240 brokerage firms as well as a vast array of brokerage and equity research, screening, and advisory tools. Check out the free stock picks, analysis, quotes, and balance sheets, or get a free company report. Register for a free 30-day trial to the get the full Zacks experience including portfolio news and quotes delivered directly to your PC.

Site Design: 8
User-Friendliness: 8
Real Use: 10
Subscription: $295/year

ZDNet
www.zdnet.com
This site offers snapshot quotes and charts, plus free software. You can participate in ZD-Net auctions and enjoy daily news articles like "How to get rich on your stock options!" Shop for investment books and check out over 7,000 software products.
Site Design: 8
User-Friendliness: 9
Real Use: 7
Subscription: Free

education

American Association of Individual Investors
www.aaii.com
This active investor's association boasts more than 70 local chapters across the United States. Dedicated to education, the friendly site offers free and member services. The home page features insightful articles and links to publications, message boards, articles and commentary, quote search tools, custom portfolios with portfolio management services, an extensive archival library, and a calendar of upcoming local events
Site Design: 7
User-Friendliness: 8
Real Use: 6
Subscription: $49/annual membership

Armchair Millionaire
www.armchairmillionaire.com
Ironically enough, the motto at this extremely slow site is "Get Rich Slowly but Surely." The site follows a basic educational theory called the "Five Steps to Financial Freedom." Plenty of nice graphics keep wanna-be investors from falling asleep while climbing the investment learning curve. Check out the host of chat rooms and the topical message board. There is a free e-mail newsletter, plus feature articles and commentary from what's called the "community of investors."
Site Design: 7
User-Friendliness: 4
Real Use: 5
Subscription: Free

Cassandra's Revenge
www.stockscape.com/newsletters/cassandra
This feisty site is a veritable forum for women. Its creator, Ellen McGirt, a self-made investment educator and journalist, is dedicated to educating women in the fields of finance and investment. Perceptive investment articles from the female point of view dominate the site along with an array of educational tools. Sign up for your own stock quote portfolio and news wire service and you'll have daily data delivered to your desktop. Check out Cassandra's concept of "Ultimate Revenge."
Site Design: 9
User-Friendliness: 9
Real Use: 7
Subscription: Free

Dr. Ed Yardeni's Economics Network
www.yardeni.com
Dr. Yardeni's site is an extensive research tool for weekly analysis, including a macroeconomics netbook, as well as a global and U.S. forecast table. There are online chart rooms, economic indicators, Dr. Yardeni's published articles, polls, and an entire section devoted to the Y2K bug dilemma. InvesorLinks rated this site on its Top Ten Financial Sites List and it also made *SmartMoney*'s 10 Most Valuable Sites for Investors.
Site Design: 8
User-Friendliness: 8
Real Use: 9
Subscription: Free

E-Line Financials
www.financials.com
Easy-to-follow step-by-step guides to understanding the basics of financial online investing and how to do research on companies that may be of interest. There are links to investment news groups and investment clubs along with customized portfolios. The layout and design here are a bit busy and some pages are hard to read.

Site Design:	5
User-Friendliness:	6
Real Use:	6
Subscription:	Free

Equity Analytics
www.e-analytics.com
The Equity Analytics site provides comprehensive investing and analysis tutorials, trading systems, as well as an extensive financial glossary. You can also find fundamental research and technical analysis of individual companies and industry sectors, portfolio modeling advisement, IPO assistance, government report forecasts, and financial engineering.

Site Design:	8
User-Friendliness:	8
Real Use:	7
Subscription:	Free

Final Bell
www.sandbox.net/finalbell/pub-doc/home.html
CNN Financial Network hosts the Final Bell, a place where you can master the basics of online investing. Put your metal to the test by participating in free stock trading simulations, compete for great prizes, and learn the art of trading.

Site Design:	8
User-Friendliness:	9
Real Use:	6
Subscription:	Free

Financial Center
www.tfc.com
This site contains many educational offerings including small investors' and beginners' options courses. There's a collection of expert articles and analysis, but only links to their other newsstand web sites for headlines. Set up a junior or senior "partnership" with Financial Center and have investment newsstand and bookstore information linked to your own web site. A good resource for the latest books covering finance and investments.

Site Design:	8
User-Friendliness:	8
Real Use:	8
Subscription:	Free

GreenJungle
www.greenjungle.com
This site specializes in education for beginners with materials on everything from stocks to mutual funds to insurance. Make use of articles, research resources, and valuable links on the Web.

Site Design:	7
User-Friendliness:	8
Real Use:	7
Subscription:	Free tutorials; advisery services vary

Investment FAQ
www.invest-faq.com
This site has free quotes, charts, graphs and research reports. There is a basic tour with educational articles for beginners with info on mutual funds, stocks, bond basics, and P/E ratios with a list of common errors to avoid. You can browse the site by categories or enter your own questions to find answers. This site also provides links to other sites in order to find additional answers to your investment questions.

Site Design:	8
User-Friendliness:	8
Real Use:	9
Subscription:	Free

Max's Investment World

www.maxinvest.com

This site seeks to help the average Joe (and Josephine) get their investment bearings. Offering four main areas—Basics, Research, Ideas, and Investment Picks—Max IW fosters education on investing in a fun, light environment.

Site Design:	5
User-Friendliness:	6
Real Use:	5
Subscription:	Free

Stock Valuation with Sense

www.stocksense.com

This educational site offers a wide variety of investment tutorials and services including Quote TV (a good, low-bandwidth Java Web applet that displays financial data at regular intervals), custom portfolios, ticker quote searchers, free software downloads, and models and spreadsheets geared to help you understand online investing and make sensible choices. This site donates all of its profits to the American Red Cross.

Site Design:	6
User-Friendliness:	7
Real Use:	7
Subscription:	Free

Teachdaq

www.teachdaq.com

Teachdaq calls itself the "School of Stock Market Training." The site offers teaching courses including Introduction to the Stock Market 101, Trading 201, and Day Trading 301, a complete trading package, as well as one-on-one training and seminars.

Site Design:	6
User-Friendliness:	5
Real Use:	3
Subscription:	Up to $1,000 for training course with Teachdaq Trader

Undergrad Investment News

www.uinews.com

This is a peppy little site with news headlines, resource links, custom portfolios, and articles relating to starting out in investment from a college level. It also provides links to online tutorials and other educational materials, plus search tools for charts, graphs, and quotes. Play the stock market game and compete with other members for cash.

Site Design:	8
User-Friendliness:	9
Real Use:	8
Subscription:	Free

Virtual Stock Exchange

www.virtualstockexchange.com

The Virtual Stock Exchange is a simulation web site utilized by over 65 colleges and investment clubs, managing portfolios through free simulations. The investment guide contains a glossary, online resources, and market strategies.

Site Design:	8
User-Friendliness:	9
Real Use:	7
Subscription:	Free

Young Investor Website
www.younginvestor.com
This is a supersite for kids (and fun for grown-ups, too) featuring several sections designed to entertain and educate. It's an outstanding way for kids to learn the fundamentals of money and investing in a comfortable, familiar, and interactive environment. See how your investment knowledge measures up by playing the "Money-Tration" memory game or the "Young Investor Trivia Game."

Site Design:	10
User-Friendliness:	10
Real Use:	8
Subscription:	Free

technical analysis

Ask Research
www.askresearch.com
This well-organized site focuses on providing technical analysis tools using historical and real-time market data to create intraday and daily charts. You can also access option chains (delayed quotes) and take a look at the highest and lowest percentage option leaders. A good, clean site with most of the amenities such as watch lists and customized portfolio tools, and a link to news by CBS MarketWatch. The home page also offers a handy live S&P 500 intraday chart at five-minute intervals.

Site Design:	7
User-Friendliness:	8
Real Use:	7
Subscription:	Free

Barchart.com
www.barchart.com
Barchart.com is a comprehensive site that provides technical information on stocks, futures, and options. Customized charts and quotes are just the tip of the iceberg. Other advantages include options reports, a "trend spotter" feature, indexes, webmaster tools, and a learning center. This no-frills site is worth the small subscription fee.

Site Design:	7
User-Friendliness:	8
Real Use:	8
Subscription:	$20/month

BigCharts
www.bigcharts.com
Bigcharts is sure to become one of your favorite free sites. It features easily customized intraday charts, historical quotes, and snapshot quotes and profiles on more than 34,000 stocks, mutual funds, and indexes. With an excellent design and very user-friendly format, BigCharts.com also offers information on the big movers and losers in the main markets, momentum charts, and other goodies. You'll find links to this site from all over the Net.

Site Design:	10
User-Friendliness:	10
Real Use:	10
Subscription:	Free

ClearStation
www.clearstation.com
This site focuses on technical information including customized charts, graphs, and company profiles. Enjoy custom portfolios, quotes, charts, message boards, and daily e-mail alerts plus recommendations that are actually worthwhile. Check out their "Tag and Bag" feature, which lists stocks that are entering trends or experiencing events. These lists are updated throughout the day. They also offer an excellent section on options trading education and a very useful daily e-mail newsletter.

Site Design:	10
User-Friendliness:	10
Real Use:	10
Subscription:	Free

Daily Graphs Online
www.dailygraphs.com
This comprehensive site is the online market analysis arm of *Investor's Business Daily* (*IBD*) offering more than 70 key technical and fundamental factors with technical analysis and charts with data for over 11,000 companies. You can also access in-depth analysis on 2,800 stocks that have met certain *IBD* criteria. Requires proprietary software to be a subscriber. Options analysis data will be added in the near future.

Site Design:	8
User-Friendliness:	8
Real Use:	9
Subscription:	Software download $189/quarter

Equis International
www.equis.com
This site offers the experience and expertise of its host corporation, Reuters International. Technically it's designed to make full use of Windows programs. You can gain access to Reuters' extensive historical data via the "Downloader" and also download real-time software so you can see your open charts updated as you watch. Multiple securities and indexes can be plotted on the same chart for easy comparison. In 1998, this site received a Readers Choice Award from *Technical Analysis of Stocks and Commodities.*

Site Design:	7
User-Friendliness:	7
Real Use:	8
Subscription:	Free

InfoSpace
quotes.infospace.com
InfoSpace has access to 50 real-time stock quotes per day and unlimited delayed quotes. Company research and market updates such as movers and performers are available. Links to the Yellow and White pages let you search for Financial Advisors. Stock news is available by ticker symbol. Excellent midmorning update and closing bell newsletters (e-mailed directly to your PC).

Site Design:	7
User-Friendliness:	8
Real Use:	8
Subscription:	Site tools free; newsletter—$19.95/year

InSite
www.dbcms.com
Offering professional real-time, market data feeds, automated news, editorials, and analysis, this site requires that you first download programs so you can have access to the DBC data banks. Its quote service interfaces with a variety of different software programs.

Site Design:	7
User-Friendliness:	7
Real Use:	8
Subscription:	$150/month

InvestViews
www.investviews.com
This site offers standard investment services with technical analysis, market data, quick quote ticker symbol search, custom portfolios with choice of brand name strategies, automatic updates and web site "time-stamps" that let you know of changes to your portfolio as soon as you log on. The site also provides archival evidence of profitable past performances as well as real estate and personal finance guidance and assistance.

Site Design:	8
User-Friendliness:	7
Real Use:	8
Subscription:	$29.90/month

IQC.com
www.iqc.com
This site maintains a variety of different news sources and an online investors forum, customized chart settings where you set up your own portfolio and can check on it instantly. There's a full-service educational center with a comprehensive technical analysis glossary of different terms and explanations of how to read the charts and graphs. This site won first place in the 1998 Java Financial Object Xchange software contest.

Site Design:	8
User-Friendliness:	8
Real Use:	7
Subscription:	Free; tech charts $24.95/month

MarketEdge
www.stkwtch.com
This free and subscription Computrade Systems site offers technical analysis tools for more than 5,000 stocks and recommendations based on its own market analysis system. There are custom features, depending on which package you subscribe to, including news links, research and full investment services, custom portfolios, stock alerts, and market mover analysis. Check out the "Pick 6" feature that allows traders to use different combinations of indicators to uncover specific trading opportunities. A subscription to this site is often offered by a handful of online brokerages to their clients at a discounted rate.

Site Design:	8
User-Friendliness:	8
Real Use:	8
Subscription:	$12.95 to $49.95/month

Nordby.com
www.nordby.com
A full-service technical analysis site with free graphs, charts, and tailored stock quotes, marketing lists, investment guides, and a handy glossary of terms. Play an interactive trading game that lets you practice online trading and possibly win up to $250 a month. Unfortunately, this site moves quite slowly.

Site Design:	7
User-Friendliness:	6
Real Use:	7
Subscription:	Free

Pristine
www.pristine.com
This site focuses on supplying day traders with daily stock recommendations, market commentary, technical analysis charts, and unlimited real-time quotes. Check out the Pristine Educational section with seminars and tutorials and recommended readings.

Site Design:	7
User-Friendliness:	8
Real Use:	7
Subscription:	$125/month

StockMaster
www.stockmaster.com
StockMaster claims to have been the first financial site on the World Wide Web. It definitely has all the usual bells and whistles including technical charts and graphs, customized portfolios, search engines, free software downloads, discussion groups and a top 40 list of up-and-coming stocks to put on your watch list. Check out the investor sentiment surveys.

Site Design:	8
User-Friendliness:	7
Real Use:	7
Subscription:	Free

StockTools
www.stocktools.com
The StockTools site has delayed quotes on all the major U.S. and Canadian exchanges and a wide variety of industry groupings for selecting quotes. Customizable graphs and extensive historical quotes are also available.

Site Design:	7
User-Friendliness:	8
Real Use:	7
Subscription:	Free

Timely.com
www.timely.com
Timely.com is a friendly little site with 15-to-20-minute-delayed quotes, charts, and indicators on over 17,000 different securities. Lists most actives, biggest gainers, and losers also.

Site Design:	7
User-Friendliness:	8
Real Use:	7
Subscription:	Free

Value Line
www.valueline.com
Best known for publishing the *Value Line Investment Survey*, this subscription-based investment information center has it all—free quotes, graphs and charts, featured articles, research on mutual funds, stocks, and options. It also offers excellent interactive online investment tutorials. A first-rate site from a first-rate investment publishing and research company.

Site Design:	8
User-Friendliness:	8
Real Use:	9
Subscription:	$50 to $270/month

options

Committee on Options Proposals (COOP)
www.coop-options.com
COOP is comprised of respected options industry professionals and marketing personnel from 40 stock exchange member firms, the four options exchanges, and the OCC. They work toward expanding the use of options in the marketplace through education, public relations, and networking.

Site Design:	3
User-Friendliness:	5
Real Use:	3
Subscription:	Free

CoveredCall.com
www.coveredcall.com
This site offers options strategy advice and education, including information on covered calls, credit spreads, LEAPS, and stock splits. If you're unfamiliar with these terms, the site also offers an options covered calls primer with suggested readings and a tutorial. Take advantage of custom portfolios, a free newsletter, and features like the "War Room" message boards.

Site Design:	7
User-Friendliness:	6
Real Use:	6
Subscription: Monthly:	$29.95—Covered Calls; $49.95—Stock Splits; $69.95—both

CoveredCall Hotline
www.coveredcallhotline.com
This site offers 15 daily picks by an e-mail–based subscription newsletter. Membership includes access to an extensive glossary and training programs.

Site Design:	4
User-Friendliness:	4

Real Use: 4
Subscription: $200/month

INO
www.ino.com
Futures and options are what this simple, well-organized, and free site is all about. You'll find the latest news headlines, discussion and investment support groups, free charts and graphs, a ticker symbol search engine, plus sweepstakes and prizes.

Site Design: 8
User-Friendliness: 8
Real Use: 8
Subscription: Free

Netpicks
www.netpicks.com
Designed for aggressive options traders, Netpicks offers free stock quotes, graphs, and charts, as well as paid services that include real-time paging on hot stocks, a daily updated morning and evening newsletter, investment links, and news headlines. There are quite a few different payment plans and a free two-week trial.

Site Design: 7
User-Friendliness: 6
Real Use: 7
Subscription: $75 to $250 a month

OptionInvestor.com
www.optioninvestor.com
Founded in December 1997, this site has quickly become the fastest growing options advisory site on the Net. It offers a unique tour de force of options services, research, commentary, market analysis, trade recommendations, option quotes, live charts, S&P futures data, and a virtual options community of live chat rooms and message boards. This integrated options site is an excellent resource for novice and seasoned options traders.

Site Design: 9
User-Friendliness: 9
Real Use: 10
Subscription: $39.95/month

Options Industry Association
www.optionscentral.com
The Options Industry Council (OIC) is the educational arm of several exchanges, including the American Stock Exchange (AMEX), Chicago Board Options Exchange (CBOE), Pacific Stock Exchange (PCX), the Philadelphia Stock Exchange (PHLX), and the Options Clearing Corporation (OCC). The site offers free educational material including downloads and videos to help you learn all about trading options.

Site Design: 8
User-Friendliness: 9
Real Use: 6
Subscription: Free

OptionSource.com
www.optionsource.com
This comprehensive web site is the creation of option investment adviser and educator Bernie Schaeffer. Well organized and jam-packed with information, it provides stock and stock options quotes, lists of most active stocks and options, an options calendar and calculator, an excellent selection of options educational resources, as well as information concerning subscription newsletters, recommendation services, and access to his hardback book and options trading course.

Site Design: 8
User-Friendliness: 9
Real Use: 9
Subscription: $119/1 year and $149/2 years to the *Option Advisor* and $295/year for *Schaeffer's Research Review*

Option Strategist
www.optionstrategist.com
A web site that focuses on providing short-term stock and option trading resources developed by author and options educator Lawrence G. McMillan, this site features free op-

tions quotes, historical volatility data, volume alerts, a list of expensive options, chat rooms, and information regarding McMillan's seminars and other education tools.

Site Design:	7
User-Friendliness:	5
Real Use:	7
Subscription:	$250/annual or

$29/6 issues of bimonthly newsletter

Stricknet.com
www.stricknet.com/index.htm

If you're looking for suggestions, Stricknet.com offers options and covered call picks, pure plays, and naked puts. There's daily commentary and screening of over 220,000 options a day, a calculator, plus market alerts. Check out the supplemental educational pages.

Site Design:	6
User-Friendliness:	7
Real Use:	6
Subscription:	$35/month

Strikeprice.com
www.strikeprice.com

This extensive site is one of my favorites for reviewing fundamental data and historical prices of options and stocks. In addition, it offers stock and option quotes and charts as well as a list of the most active options. Take advantage of the new custom portfolio manager system.

Site Design:	8
User-Friendliness:	8
Real Use:	9
Subscription:	Free

webzines

Absolute Investments Web-zine
www.absolute-investments.com

This site offers portfolio research and the "Absolute Twenty" of recommended model portfolios to use as benchmarks against which to measure your own portfolio performance. It has snapshot quotes, news, and commentary along with study courses, recommended readings, and a dose of much-needed market humor.

Site Design:	8
User-Friendliness:	8
Real Use:	7
Subscription:	$14.95/3 months

Barron's Online
www.barrons.com

This outstanding webzine offers breaking and scheduled financial news and commentary from the Wall Street Journal Interactive Edition, plus exclusive weekday coverage from industry giant and pioneer *Barron's* magazine. In addition, subscribers are eligible to receive free annual reports, *Barron's* roundtable, movers, and more.

Site Design:	7
User-Friendliness:	7
Real Use:	7
Subscription:	$59/year or $29/year to print

subscribers of the *Wall Street Journal*

Business Week
www.businessweek.com

This online version of a popular magazine offers a great selection of business news and commentary, quotes, portfolio, and an e-mail newsletter.

Site Design:	8
User-Friendliness:	8
Real Use:	8
Subscription:	$39.95 annual online

subscription; WEBZINES $42.95 w/magazine

Daily Rocket
www.dailyrocket.com
The Daily Rocket is a free investment webzine filled with breaking news, quirky articles, and market commentary. There are IPO reports, weekly market commentary, free annual reports, message boards, a searchable historical archive, a handy glossary of investment jargon, and a quote search tool. They also offer Investment Monitor software, which consistently provides an abundance of investment tools including portfolio management, timely news, and market updates.

Site Design:	7
User-Friendliness:	8
Real Use:	9
Subscription:	Free

Economist
www.economist.com
The online edition of the *Economist*, a British business journal renowned for its excellent analysis of global politics and economic forces, offers thought-provoking articles, technical analysis, as well as access to archived editions.

Site Design:	8
User-Friendliness:	9
Real Use:	8
Subscription:	$48/year

Forbes Digital Toolbox
www.forbes.com
Forbes Digital Toolbox is an intriguing site featuring *Forbes*'s legendary lists, interesting market commentary, downloads, forums, technical analysis and charts, delayed quotes search tools, as well as access to other *Forbes* sites and information.

Site Design:	7
User-Friendliness:	7
Real Use:	7
Subscription:	Free

Fortune
www.fortune.com
Hosted by *Fortune* magazine, this site presents an overview of what you'll receive as a print subscriber and offers lists of top company performers, industry medians, and of course the famous Fortune 500. Top analysts give an inclusive analysis of the unique Fortune 500 macro view of financial events. In 1997, this site received a Webby award for Best Money Site.

Site Design:	8
User-Friendliness:	7
Real Use:	7
Subscription:	$19.95/year

Inc.Online
www.inc.com
Hosted by *Inc.* magazine, this online magazine acts as an electronic consultant for small business owners and entrepreneurs. The site provides hands-on advice, case studies, and big-picture overviews for growing companies. You can also find tutorials, glossaries, recommended readings, news and feature articles, and interactive networking opportunities. Check out the virtual consultant feature, chat rooms and topical message boards. In 1997, Folio named Inc.Online the Best Online Magazine and the Computer Press Association gave it their Best Overall New Publication award.

Site Design:	7
User-Friendliness:	6
Real Use:	8
Subscription:	*Inc.* magazine costs $14/year for 18 issues. Subscription to the online magazine is free for *Inc.* magazine subscribers.

Kiplinger Online
www.kiplinger.com
Kiplinger Online is an excellent source for business forecasts, top business news, topical feature articles, and personal financial advice. Check out the "Toolbox," complete

with portfolio tracker, calculator, forums, delayed quotes, and stock research capabilities.

Site Design:	8
User-Friendliness:	7
Real Use:	8
Subscription:	$48/year

Online Investor
www.onlineinvestor.com

This online spin-off site from Online Investor magazine is almost a supersite. Given time—considering Online Investor's vast resources—it will be. There are free quotes and charts, search engines, a fund and stock screener, online forums, chat rooms, and a custom portfolio feature. Look to this site for the latest reviews of financial web sites as well as snappy news and insightful trading articles. Great writers and unique perspectives keep this relative newcomer a definite up-and-comer.

Site Design:	9
User-Friendliness:	8
Real Use:	9
Subscription:	Free

Red Chip Review
www.redchip.com

This site focuses on undervalued and undiscovered small-cap companies. Over 200 companies in 28 industries are analyzed and evaluated, including company specs, offerings, and timetables.

Site Design:	7
User-Friendliness:	7
Real Use:	7
Subscription:	$199/year

Red Herring Online
www.herring.com

One of the most popular financial webzines, this site offers a multitude of insider news, analysis, and commentary by highly respected journalists as well as an excellent e-mailed newsletter. Look for Wolf picks, option picks, and the "Catch of the Day" column for investment ideas. Check out the search tools and the featured links to hot web sites.

Site Design:	9
User-Friendliness:	9
Real Use:	10
Subscription:	$39.95/year

SmartMoney Interactive
www.smartmoney.com

SmartMoney calls itself the "*Wall Street Journal* Magazine of Personal Business." It has an edgy twentysomething feel with features that include the "Map of the Market" (11 categories with data on all companies on the map), an hourly stock update with custom portfolios, top stories and headlines, and info on bonds, mutual funds, and IPOs.

Site Design:	9
User-Friendliness:	9
Real Use:	8
Subscription:	Free

Technical Analysis of Stocks and Commodities
www.traders.com

The online site of *Technical Analysis of Stocks and Commodities* magazine is designed to foster trader success by offering information on technical trading strategies, charting patterns, indicators, and computerized trading methods through well-researched feature articles and a wide variety of links and resources. Archived articles from the print magazine are also available.

Site Design:	8
User-Friendliness:	8
Real Use:	8
Subscription:	$49.95/year

Traders Digest
www.tradersdigest.com
Traders Digest offers information and resources for traders including feature articles, editorials and commentary, picks of the week, and free educational tutorials. Traders Digest also features a free e-mailed newsletter and invites readers to submit articles for the web site.

Site Design:	4
User-Friendliness:	5
Real Use:	4
Subscription:	Free

Wired.com
www.wired.com
This online version of *Wired* magazine is well-known for its cutting edge style and lively commentary—perhaps a side effect of being based in San Francisco. It has lots of interesting news, articles, commentary, and market analysis, especially regarding the world of high technology. There are custom portfolios, search tools for news or quotes, daily summaries and market indexes, plus IPO reports with an inclination for the online dot-com companies. They also offer a worthwhile daily e-mailed newsletter. Wired.com received a 1998 Webby award for Best News Site.

Site Design:	9
User-Friendliness:	8
Real Use:	9
Subscription:	Site free; magazine $21.95/year

Worth Online
www.worth.com
The online edition of *Worth* magazine offers a variety of investment articles, feature stories, and archived stories from previous editions. There is a link to the complete Peter Lynch archives, a section for investor resources, and Investing 101 for beginners.

Site Design:	7
User-Friendliness:	8
Real Use:	7
Subscription:	$12/year

high technology

CMPnet
www.cmpnet.com
CMPnet is mainly a site about the computer industry with tech news and commentary, product reviews and software downloads, links to information technology networks, and computer industry insider "sneak peak" reports.

Site Design:	6
User-Friendliness:	6
Real Use:	6
Subscription:	Free

Cyberstocks
www.cyberstocks.com
This site offers news and market data focusing on Internet stocks. Check out the well-organized tutorial history of the Internet and the development of the major online companies as well as a glossary to decipher Internet terminology. Cyberstocks is hosted by Hoover's Online with links to CBS MarketWatch.

Site Design:	8
User-Friendliness:	9
Real Use:	8
Subscription:	Free

Dataquest
www.dataquest.com
The Dataquest site is devoted to data, research, analysis, and advice with more than 140 annual strategic research programs, quarterly statistics programs and databases, and

featured articles. Each subscriber receives a specified number of hours of strategic advice in areas including business plan development, user trends, technology developments, and overall industry directions.

Site Design:	8
User-Friendliness:	8
Real Use:	8
Subscription:	Free

Good Morning Silicon Valley
www.gmsv.com
A member of the Knight Ridder Real Cities Network, this colorful site takes a global look at what's happening in technology stocks, with a special column detailing the news from Silicon Valley. Columns written by insightful journalists along with breaking news, special reports, and a convenient tech news archive help to make this site a bookmark for the intelligent Internet investor.

Site Design:	8
User-Friendliness:	8
Real Use:	8
Subscription:	Free

Register
www.hubcom.com/register
This is actually a British site with a different angle on a global view of high-tech stocks. The Register says they tell it like it is. Their symbol is a buzzard and their motto is "Biting the hand that feeds it," so there is no false loyalty to big impressive companies that fail to make the mark. The site is almost all headline news and reports with a few search tools as well.

Site Design:	7
User-Friendliness:	6
Real Use:	8
Subscription:	Free

Silicon Investor
www.techstocks.com or www.siliconinvestor.com
The Silicon Investor site claims to be the largest discussion community on the Web with over 3,500,000 messages in its chat room database. This haven for tech stock investors specializes in computers, software, communication, semiconductors, biotechnology and medical devices, and much more. Quotes and charts are supplied by North American Quotations, Inc., and are delayed 15 to 20 minutes.

Site Design:	8
User-Friendliness:	9
Real Use:	8
Subscription:	$9.95/month

TradeLogic Financial Suite
www.tradelogic.com
This site specializes in downloadable personal finance software complete with clear instructions on how to set it up and use it. You can custom-design visual pages containing intraday and end-of-day price information, company news headlines and stories, fundamental data, and point-and-click access to financial research and recommendations, quotes, historical price/volume, and customized portfolios.

Site Design:	8
User-Friendliness:	8
Real Use:	8
Subscription:	$89/onetime fee

exchanges

Chicago Board of Trade
www.cbot.com
The Chicago Board of Trade is primarily a futures and options exchange, where the Dow Jones Industrial Average (DJIA) futures trade. The CBOT also has a trading simulation through the Auditrade system. There is a charge of $10/month to participate in Audi-

trade's simulated trading. This will allow you to practice trading using a fake account and real prices, until you get comfortable with the strategies and their results.

Site Design: 7
User-Friendliness: 8
Real Use: 8
Subscription: Free—Market Plex: premium services vary

Chicago Board Options Exchange
www.cboe.com
The Chicago Board Options Exchange is the largest options exchange in the United States. Its web site offers news, new option listings, and exchange information on equities, options, and LEAPS. Specialization includes calls and puts on NYSE stocks, the S&P 500, U.S. Treasury bonds, and other indexes.

Site Design: 7
User-Friendliness: 8
Real Use: 9
Subscription: Free

Nasdaq-AMEX
www.nasdaq-amex.com or www.amex.com or www.nasdaq.com
Nasdaq and the American Stock Exchange (AMEX) have united to create the Nasdaq-AMEX Market Group, an innovative securities market that combines extensive information on Nasdaq's computerized markets with the stocks available through AMEX's auction-style exchange. Receiving more than 20 million hits a day, this comprehensive site features the internationally acclaimed Nasdaq overview and the worldwide Nasdaq network of performance data as well as quotes, charts, graphs, ticker search services, and features such as the 10 most active share volumes, polling volumes, and most active advanced performances. A good site to set up portfolio tracking and stock screening. An excellent site tour helps you get started.

Site Design: 9
User-Friendliness: 9
Real Use: 9
Subscription: Free

New York Stock Exchange
www.nyse.com
The New York Stock Exchange (NYSE)—the Big Board—is the world's largest equities market with a capitalization of over $12 trillion. The NYSE web site offers a tremendous amount of information about new and previously listed companies, with annual reports, research, publications, and news.

Site Design: 9
User-Friendliness: 8
Real Use: 9
Subscription: Free

Pacific Stock Exchange
www.pacificex.com
The Pacific Stock Exchange (PCX) is the third most active stock exchange in the country and the third largest stock options exchange in the world. More than 2,600 stocks, bonds, and other securities issued by publicly traded companies, as well as options on more than 550 stocks, are traded on the PCX, along with a variety of indexes. Quotes on equities and options are delayed 20 minutes.

Site Design: 10
User-Friendliness: 9
Real Use: 9
Subscription: Free

Philadelphia Stock Exchange
www.phlx.com
The Philadelphia Stock Exchange (PHLX) was founded in 1790 as the first organized stock exchange in the United States. The PHLX trades more than 2,800 stocks, 700 equity options, 12 index options, and 100 currency options. Fifteen-minute-delayed quotes and volatility charts are available, along with news, research, and daily market analysis.

Site Design:	7
User-Friendliness:	9
Real Use:	9
Subscription:	Free

Securities and Exchange Commission
www.sec.gov
The Securities and Exchange Commission (SEC) site has a lot of detailed securities-related information—SEC reports of listed companies, investor guides, and EDGAR. The database EDGAR performs automated collection of corporate information and reports required to be filed with the SEC. In 1998, the SEC's web site received a Webby award for Best Money/Business Site.

Site Design:	10
User-Friendliness:	10
Real Use:	10
Subscription:	Free

advisory sites

Avid Trading Company
www.avidtrader.com
Avid Trading breaks up its offerings into four main categories: Trading Ideas, Interactive, Market Monitor, and Recreation. The Trading Ideas area offers short-term picks, probable support and resistance levels for several popular stocks, a "Heads-Up" column filled with intraday market commentary, and short-selling stock picks. The Interactive area contains chat rooms and topical message boards. The Market Monitor offers a few tools but mainly links to other sites for charts, daily investment articles, and commentary. The Recreation area is filled with additional links and a few fun market-oriented diversions including Wall Street Sports, an online game in which you buy and sell sports figures.

Site Design:	8
User-Friendliness:	8
Real Use:	6
Subscription:	Free

Buttonwood Financial Resources
www.buttonwood.net
The Buttonwood site offers investment ideas with the "Acclaimed Blue Star List," market reports, links to charts, quotes, newsletter, education, long-term investment strategies, and mutual funds. Buttonwood says it'll do the "dirty work" that most investors never get around to.

Site Design:	8
User-Friendliness:	8
Real Use:	8
Subscription:	Free

Crash Proof Advisors Services
www.crashproofadvisors.com
Crash Proof Advisors Services is an index option trading service with an optimistic name. They have a real-time trading room, a newsletter called the "Bullseye Perspective," plus e-mailed alerts, custom portfolios, and hedge recommendations.

Site Design:	5
User-Friendliness:	5
Real Use:	5
Subscription:	$119.95/month or $139.95 pager/month

Daily Picks
www.dailypicks.com
This is a stock picks and analyses site with, just as they say, daily picks based on the opinions of the Daily Picks staff. Educate yourself regarding the latest stock behavior analysis methodologies in the weekly newsletter's trading tips on short-term picks, quotes, and more. This site garnered WildFROG's Top Honor for Financial Newsletters and made Starting Point's Hot Site List.

Site Design:	8
User-Friendliness:	8
Real Use:	7
Subscription:	$108/month or $840/year

Elliott Wave International

www.elliottwave.com

This site is mostly about forecasting, with interactive billboards and discussion forums. Its host is master predictor Robert Prechter who foretold of the big Clinton win in 1992. There's expert international analysis with links to full time analysis services. There are global market reports and a market watch as well as specialized forecasting services to subscribe to.

Site Design:	6
User-Friendliness:	5
Real Use:	7
Subscription:	Free

FundTrader.com

www.fundtrader.com

FundTrader bills itself as a free mutual funds, short-term mutual funds, and trading service. The site provides several short-term trading strategies to trade the "ProFunds" "UltraOTC" no-load Nasdaq 100 index fund. Use the "Model Performance" tools to practice trading and learn what to avoid.

Site Design:	4
User-Friendliness:	4
Real Use:	5
Subscription:	Free

Galateia Corp.

www.voicenet.com/~mitochon

This site itself is pretty much nothing but an advertisement for its subscription service that offers price pattern projection for a variety of artificial neural networks, genetic algorithms, nearest-neighbor modeling, and other pattern classification techniques on stocks, mutual funds, stocks, indexes, commodities, and currencies. You also get access to an analysis hot line offering predictions and expert market updates.

Site Design:	6
User-Friendliness:	6
Real Use:	5
Subscription:	$60/3 months

Hedgehog

www.hedge-hog.com

Created by a former Naval officer with a talent for trading, this site offers his straightforward evaluations of a long list of companies as well as IPO reports, featured articles, stock quotes, a portfolio tracker, and discussion forums.

Site Design:	6
User-Friendliness:	7
Real Use:	7
Subscription:	Free

Investor's Forecast.com

www.investorsforecast.com

Featuring forecast reports and charts as well as message boards and contests, Investor's Forecast is a free advisory site that offers collective and personal stock forecasts and the 14C Index (based on 140 current forecasts).

Site Design:	6
User-Friendliness:	8
Real Use:	6
Subscription:	Free

Smart Portfolio.com

www.smartportfolio.com

This is really just two newsletter services at a small site designed to be an in-between stop. There are stock picks, technical analysis, and charts and graphs. But the real point of this site is to link you to the advisory services offered by the company.

Site Design:	7
User-Friendliness:	6
Real Use:	5
Subscription:	$9.95/month

StockPicks

www.stockpicks.com

This site focuses on providing stock picks to members within an hour after the market opens with 1-, 3-, 5-, 30-, and 50-day horizons posted daily. It also provides links to research tools, technical charts, real-time quotes, and SEC filings. StockPicks says they are getting ready to relaunch the site soon. Let's hope the new design is less busy.

Site Design:	4
User-Friendliness:	5
Real Use:	4
Subscription:	Free

StockRumors

www.stockrumors.com

Rumors, rumors, and rumors; they say 106 of their rumors became facts in 1998. There are also options alerts with real-time market news, personalized stock and commodities alerts to your pager, and sports scores.

Site Design:	6
User-Friendliness:	7
Real Use:	6
Subscription:	$19.99 to $99/month

SuperStockPicks.com

www.superstockpick.com

SuperStockPicks has long- and short-term stock picks and a pick of the day feature, as well as message boards. Companies profiled by SSP are typically small or micro-cap stocks that have not yet attracted the attention of Wall Street. There are research and educational articles as well as free stock analysis and reports.

Site Design:	6
User-Friendliness:	7
Real Use:	5
Subscription:	Free (donations accepted)

TradInvestors.com

pages.prodigy.net/xliu

This site has stock and option and intraday picks, message boards and chat rooms, buy and sell alerts, plus links to quotes, graphs, charts, and news. It also offers combination strategies for day traders, short-and long-term investors, and options investors. Parts of the service are free.

Site Design:	6
User-Friendliness:	6
Real Use:	5
Subscription:	$50 to $270/month

Wall Street SOS Forum

www.sosadvisors.com

The Wall Street SOS Forum is a presentation of Security Objective Services, an investment advisory publishing company. The site offers a free newsletter, a bull/bear index, options and stock alerts, up-to-the-minute domestic and foreign market news, and indexes.

Site Design:	7
User-Friendliness:	7
Real Use:	5
Subscription:	Free

Wolf

www.netword2000.com/wolf

The Wolf is basically an advisory-based analysis site with a daily service that uses option volume open interest to find options under accumulation. The Wolf filters out volume caused by other factors such as takeover rumors, hedges, and spreads.

Site Design:	8
User-Friendliness:	5
Real Use:	5
Subscription:	$129/month

World Mergers and Acquisitions Network
www.worldm-anetwork.com

World Mergers and Acquisitions Network has more than 2,000 active merger and acquisition leads annually. These are companies for sale, merger candidates, corporate and strategic buyers, and sources of financing in the United States and worldwide. Clients are encouraged to network through chat rooms and message boards.

Site Design:	7
User-Friendliness:	7
Real Use:	7
Subscription:	$345 to $495/year

specialty sites

Biofind
www.biofind.com

At Biofind, you'll find news and commentary on the biotech industry and biotech companies and timely reports on new innovations. There is an interesting feature called the "rumor mill" that allows free anonymous public postings of events in the biotech arena. Check out the message boards, and biotech industry e-mail updates from hot cutting-edge companies.

Site Design:	7
User-Friendliness:	8
Real Use:	8
Subscription:	Free

Coalition of Black Investors
www.cobinvest.com

The Coalition of Black Investors' site is described as the "place where black investors communicate." It offers "The Plan," which promotes financial and investment literacy, and links black investors and black investment clubs together to exchange ideas and investment strategies. This site offers up-to-date news and commentary on the "black dollar" and a calendar of upcoming local events.

Site Design:	7
User-Friendliness:	8
Real Use:	8
Subscription:	$10/month

Direct Stock Market
www.dsm.com

Direct Stock Market provides investors and securities professionals with all there is to know about public and private offerings. In return, DSM also enables companies issuing stock in a public offering or completing a private placement to distribute their reports and company profiles to prospective investors. They offer a monstrous variety of services on both sides of the fence including a "Virtual Roadshow" composed of live, interactive video presentations that provide exposure for the company's potentials to a wide range of web-surfing investors.

Site Design:	7
User-Friendliness:	6
Real Use:	6
Subscription:	Free

Equity Web
www.equityweb.com

This site provides recommendations and commentary from a vast selection of investment news sources. Just enter a stock symbol in the ticker window and you'll have instantaneous access to quotes, charts, news, earnings, filings, profiles, financials, and more from the Net's best sites.

Site Design:	8
User-Friendliness:	8
Real Use:	9
Subscription:	Free

FreeRealtime.com

www.freerealtime.com

FreeRealtime specializes in giving investors access to real-time quotes direct from the NYSE, Nasdaq, and AMEX. You can also access the latest breaking news, monitor your stocks and holdings, utilize research market indexes and stocks, and review featured articles. Links to charts, index updates, news, and commentary round out this site.

Site Design:	7
User-Friendliness:	8
Real Use:	7
Subscription:	Free

Gomez Advisors

www.gomez.com

Founded by Juan Gomez, a senior analyst from Forrester Research, this well-researched site has become an Internet favorite and is widely referenced as the premiere online brokerage watchdog. Cyberfinance scorecards for bankers and brokerages are ranked by overall score, categories, and consumer profiles. There's a booksellers' scorecard, tutorials, performance monitors, and a ticker symbol quote search engine, plus news, columns, essays, and expert news analysis. You can also subscribe to the Gomez alert that keeps you up-to-date on the latest news from the brokerage community.

Site Design:	9
User-Friendliness:	8
Real Use:	9
Subscription:	Free

Good Money

www.goodmoney.com

This web site evolved from the original "Good Money" newsletter that goes back to 1982. They are experts at helping people to invest in socially and environmentally responsible companies with stock averages, company profiles, articles, and studies. There are stock advisers and online tutorials as well as information about teach-ins, conferences, and even demonstrations.

Site Design:	8
User-Friendliness:	9
Real Use:	8
Subscription:	Free

Green Money Online Guide

www.greenmoney.com

The Green Money Online Guide specializes in socially and environmentally responsible business, investing, and consumer resources. Its motto is "Responsibility from the supermarket to the stock market." There is a Web resource guide, a Green Money bookstore with recommended readings, and a calendar of upcoming events.

Site Design:	9
User-Friendliness:	9
Real Use:	9
Subscription:	Free

InterQuote

www.interquote.com

InterQuote is a real-time quote service that provides information on stocks, options, indexes, mutual funds, bonds, and futures from most U.S. exchanges, portfolios, spreadsheets, snapshots, free software to download, data on stocks, options, mutual funds, and indexes.

Site Design:	6
User-Friendliness:	8
Real Use:	7
Subscription:	5 packages $9.95 to $69.95/month

Investor Home
www.investorhome.com
The Investor Home page is a treasure trove of links, quotes, charts, research, profiles, and earnings estimates. The sites are coded to denote if registration or payments are necessary, and each site is judged for market data, stock charts and charting tools, and fund-specific info-gatherers. This site has won five awards the last time we checked and was nominated for a 1999 Webbie.

Site Design:	9
User-Friendliness:	8
Real Use:	8
Subscription:	Free

Investor Words
www.investorwords.com
This is a consummate educational site with a full investment glossary containing more than 5,000 terms and 15,000 links between related terms. Need to know the difference between a "margin account" and a "margin agreement" or a "death benefit" and a "dead cat bounce"? This is the place. There are charts, quotes, investors forums, and a comprehensive investor's guide all laid out in an understandable, easy-to-use format.

Site Design:	9
User-Friendliness:	10
Real Use:	9
Subscription:	Free

Investors Free Forum
www.gate.net/~matt5150/chat.html
Popular stock market chat room with links to others plus a stock symbol quote search engine, links to market quotes, news, charts and market research data. You can download real-time software and an auto update news service. There are instructions for Net "Newbies" and "Download Dummies" and other fun links.

Site Design:	8
User-Friendliness:	4
Real Use:	5
Subscription:	Free

Investor's Galleria
www.centrex.com
As "Galleria" implies, this site is basically an online shopping center. You'll find all kinds of online trading software, new or discounted, plus multiple referrals to various resources. It also has a ticker symbol quote search and custom portfolios. The Investor's Galleria also invites you to buy into the site itself.

Site Design:	8
User-Friendliness:	6
Real Use:	5
Subscription:	$150/month

InvestorSoftware.com
www.invest-soft.com
This site is basically an investor's software showroom: the latest online investment software offered, with additional demo pages, for educational, options, and many more; also, various discussion groups and Q and A pages, from beginning investors' software problems to real estate and personal financial planning.

Site Design:	7
User-Friendliness:	7
Real Use:	7
Subscription:	Free

Moby Data
www.mobydata.com
Install the free Moby Data utility software, and you're ready to access end-of-the-day market index and breadth indicator data, along with charts, graphs, and ticker symbol searches. Moby Data also allows you to maintain three automatically updated historical files on the companies of your choice.

Site Design: 7
User-Friendliness: 6
Real Use: 8
Subscription: $6.25/month

MoneyMinded

www.moneyminded.com

This site focuses on financial information in a female context geared to women's financial independence. There are interactive polls, calculators, news, essays, articles, and advice columns for figuring out personal and investment finances as well as college aid and prenuptial agreements. This site has also garnered a few awards, including a 1997 Webby award for design, a 1998 DX Design Excellence Award, and a Five-Star 1998 Lockman Award.

Site Design: 9
User-Friendliness: 10
Real Use: 9
Subscription: Free

Moody's Investors Service

www.moodys.com

Moody's Investors Service is the leading provider of credit ratings, research, and financial information to the capital markets and has set the standard for rating parameters since 1909. Different companies, from industries to medical research to banking, are investigated and rated to assess investment risks. You can also access continuous information gathering and an updating of all the ratings.

Site Design: 8
User-Friendliness: 9
Real Use: 8
Subscription: Free

Morningstar

www.morningstar.net

Mutual fund analyses and reports are the cornerstone of this well-known mega-site. The site also offers midday market reports, daily news, and an instructional section with educational articles and recommended readings. Check out the edgy and even daring featured articles and analyst commentary. The usual custom portfolios, stock selectors, research tools, monitors, charts, and quotes help to make this site a welcome addition to the research tools offered by many online brokerages.

Site Design: 8
User-Friendliness: 9
Real Use: 9
Subscription: Free; premium membership at $9.95/month

Netquote

www.netquote.com.au

This technical analysis site is geared to the Australian market offering free quotes and portfolio management. For-pay services include live ASX data, real-time AAP news and quotes, and e-mailed hot stock updates.

Site Design: 7
User-Friendliness: 6
Real Use: 7
Subscription: $9.95 to $295/month

North American Quotation

www.naq.com

This quote site offers a daily stock pick, lists of splits, and real-time software downloads. There are custom portfolio services and history files plus mutual funds, corporate quotes, and stock, options, and futures market support groups.

Site Design: 8
User-Friendliness: 9
Real Use: 8
Subscription: Free

Online Investment Services
www.sonic.net/donaldj
This free site is dedicated to researching and collecting comments on online brokerages. Compare high, middle, and deep-discount brokerages by service, commission rates, and customer service. If you have an experience with a brokerage that you want to share with the public at large, this is the place to post it. Comprehensive and regularly updated, this is a site you'll definitely want to bookmark.

Site Design:	9
User-Friendliness:	9
Real Use:	10
Subscription:	Free

PC Quote
www.pcquote.com
PC is an excellent quote service with a wide range of ticker symbol services including stock analysis, profiles, and access to real-time quotes and delayed quotes on commodities.

Site Design:	8
User-Friendliness:	9
Real Use:	8
Subscription:	Free

Securities and Industry Association
www.sia.com
The "Investor's Checklist" on this site is alone worth the visit, with an easy-to-follow on-line investment wisdom. There are research resources, an online newsletter service, quizzes, ongoing investor surveys, and an educational interactive investment game.

Site Design:	8
User-Friendliness:	5
Real Use:	8
Subscription:	Dues rated by profit

Small Cap Investor
www.smallcapinvestor.com
This site specializes in small-cap stocks with a lot of potential considered to be undervalued and overlooked. There are the standard services including quotes, stock screeners, custom portfolios, news, humor, educational programs, and a free newsletter.

Site Design:	9
User-Friendliness:	9
Real Use:	8
Subscription:	Free

Social Investment Forum
www.socialinvest.org
The SIF is a nonprofit organization that promotes socially responsible investing. Members receive special reports on news-making issues, monthly reports, and a quarterly newsletter. There is stock screening, shareholder advocacy, and links to other socially responsible investment products and services.

Site Design:	9
User-Friendliness:	8
Real Use:	8
Subscription:	$135/year; $65 for nonprofits

Stock City
www.stockcity.com
This nonprofit site is dedicated to helping the individual investor get a share in the global market. The site has a world of ADR listings listed by countries and sector industries. There are graphs, charts, and technical analysis of the global market, with international indexes and foreign hot stocks.

Site Design:	9
User-Friendliness:	8
Real Use:	8
Subscription:	Free

Stock Club
www.stockclub.com
The stock club really works like a club with investment information and research with general investment online discussion groups and forums on specific stocks. There are e-mail stock alerts and links to many different investment sites.

Site Design:	8
User-Friendliness:	8
Real Use:	6
Subscription:	Free

Stock Detective
www.stockdetective.com
The Stock Detective shows you how to avoid becoming a victim of stock scams and schemes in the bowels of Wall Street. It's designed with links to every state's securities departments and the SEC to help with online investment problems and fraud. There is also news, charts, stock screening, e-mail stock alerts, a ticker quote searcher, and a feature called "Stinky Stocks" to tell investors what stocks to avoid.

Site Design:	10
User-Friendliness:	9
Real Use:	9
Subscription:	Free

Stockpage
www.thestockpage.com
Specializing in small and micro-cap stocks, this site has market index charts, up-to-date market analysis, news and articles, real-time stocks and options quote searches, detailed company profiles, SEC filings, and research on public companies.

Site Design:	6
User-Friendliness:	6
Real Use:	6
Subscription:	Free

StockTalk
www.stock-talk.com
StockTalk has more than 7,800 stocks, hot picks, IPOs, and over 7,000 discussion boards, plus stock quotes and research. Search for the forum you want alphabetically or by industry sector. There are also live chat sites for stocks, community issues, and college students.

Site Design:	7
User-Friendliness:	8
Real Use:	7
Subscription:	Free

StreetForce.com
www.streetforce.com
StreetForce.com is actually an ongoing research project conducted by Intel. There are research sources, articles, and links pages all geared to filter out the real deals from the losers in stocks, options, and IPOs. They offer no "picks of the week" type features because they say that honestly sometimes there are no picks.

Site Design:	7
User-Friendliness:	7
Real Use:	6
Subscription:	Free

Trader's Bookstore.com
www.booksfortraders.com
This site features a comprehensive online library of investment books for beginners and professional traders, with subjects including astro-finance biographies, candlesticks, El-liot Wave trading tactics, and technical analysis. There are reviews and comments from other readers to go by as well as seven different ways to search for the book you need in its massive database.

Site Design:	7
User-Friendliness:	8
Real Use:	6
Subscription:	Free

TradingTactics.com

www.tradingtactics.com

This interactive site offers a variety of articles and commentaries on trading systems, as well as insights on technical analysis, free historical data, and competitions. They also invite traders to contribute systems/indicators/technical analysis information to be published on the site.

Site Design:	6
User-Friendliness:	6
Real Use:	6
Subscription:	Free

Value Point Analysis Financial Forum

www.eduvest.com

Value Point Analysis Financial Forum is a community of investors who have been sharing their stock picks and analysis by using a common valuation model. By visiting the site, you can evaluate your stocks using a 13-field fundamental analysis model and then post the results, with additional message boards and chat rooms.

Site Design:	8
User-Friendliness:	8
Real Use:	7
Subscription:	Free

Women's Wire

womenswire.com/money

This is really a supersite for women with free quotes, charts and graphs, custom portfolios, message boards, chat rooms, news, investment clubs, educational investment materials, and recommended readings. Personal financial advice and market commentary are offered from a women's point of view.

Site Design:	9
User-Friendliness:	9
Real Use:	6
Subscription:	Free

XOLIA Expert Online Investment Advocates

www.xolia.com/public

Independent cyberfinance specialists focus on helping self-directed investors find the most suitable online brokerage. XOLIA operates by educating motivated investors and connecting their fundamental requirements and personal choices with the best online brokerage to fit their individual needs. They offer in-depth broker profiles and XOLIA experts keep the files updated twice a month with additional comments drawn from postings on various Internet news and chat groups. They also offer a short educational page to help with the basics of online trading and an extensive technical analysis section.

Site Design:	8
User-Friendliness:	8
Real Use:	7
Subscription:	Free

fun & games

Hey Idiot.com

www.heyidiot.com

When it all gets too serious, check out a marketing program devoted to buzz, buzz creation, buzz building, and buzz management, plus the orgy of greed and cash portal creating.

Site Design:	10
User-Friendliness:	9
Real Use:	6
Subscription:	Free

Kids' Money
pages.prodigy.com/kidsmoney
Kids' Money is an interactive online resource for parents interested in helping their children develop successful money management habits and financial responsibility. Kids and parents can learn a lot about investing and the ins and outs of giving kids an allowance and helping them to invest it. Plus they can post pictures of themselves with their piggy banks in the "That's My Piggy" feature.

Site Design:	9
User-Friendliness:	9
Real Use:	7
Subscription:	Free

Stock Track
www.stocktrak.com
This site is a huge educational exercise/game used by over 600 professors at over 500 schools. You start with a portfolio simulation worth $100,000 and trade away. There's lots of information and explanations. The rules are very specific but this can be a great place for beginners to test strategies, place trades, and learn about the financial markets before using real money. This site also provides links to trading guides on options and technical analysis, as well as stock splits, upgrades and downgrades, historical prices, annual reports, and more.

Site Design:	10
User-Friendliness:	8
Real Use:	8
Subscription:	Free

Wall Street Sports
www.wallstreetsports.com
This is definitely a twist! Wall Street Sports looks a lot like a well-designed investment web site, but it's actually a sports stock market where you can buy and sell fantasy shares of your favorite athletes from all your favorite sports. It's free to play and you can win cash prizes. Create a custom portfolio to play along and get news analysis and commentary on your favorite stars, plus chat rooms and message boards.

Site Design:	9
User-Friendliness:	9
Real Use:	4
Subscription:	Free

search engines

AltaVista Connections
www.altavista.com
This search engine's home site offers a variety of investment-related information. Just click on "Business & Finance" or go to AltaVista Finance to create a portfolio, receive stock quotes, or get the latest market news.

Site Design:	7
User-Friendliness:	7
Real Use:	7
Subscription:	Free

Excite
www.excite.com
Excite's Money and Investing page has news articles, customized portfolios, quotes and charts, and links to some of the best investment sites on the Net. You'll also find plenty of personal finance information as well as new tax assistance features.

Site Design:	8
User-Friendliness:	7
Real Use:	7
Subscription:	Free

HotBot
www.hotbot.com
HotBot is a superb search engine with fast access to business and financial information, discussion groups and games, and free downloads.

Site Design:	8
User-Friendliness:	8
Real Use:	8
Subscription:	Free

Infoseek
www.infoseek.com
Infoseek has both business and personal finance sections, with quotes, charts, market research, DRIPs, shareholder reports, and a section on stock market basics.

Site Design:	9
User-Friendliness:	9
Real Use:	8
Subscription:	Free

Lycos and Lycos Stockfind
www.lycos.com/money, www.lycos.com/business, and stockfind.lycos.com
Besides being a top news source, the Lycos site is an excellent source for stock and other financial information. It offers access to charts and quotes, market analysis, custom portfolios, stock alerts, and a link to the top 10 investment sites.

Site Design:	8
User-Friendliness:	7
Real Use:	8
Subscription:	Free

Yahoo!
www.yahoo.com
The premier search engine hosts an excellent variety of news, articles, and investment tools. Expansive search engine and great graphics make this site a surefire bookmark.

Site Design:	9
User-Friendliness:	9
Real Use:	10
Subscription:	Free

sites from george fontanills

MarketScoreboard
www.marketscoreboard.com
The MarketScoreboard site offers an extensive array of stock, options, and futures data. Check out the most active lists by volume, and the biggest percentage gainers and losers on the NYSE, AMEX, and Nasdaq as well as stock options. Check out the quotes, analysis tools, research, education, international investments, news, stock option quotes, and trading game sections.

Subscription:	Free

Optionetics
www.optionetics.com
The Optionetics site provides comprehensive information on all financial markets. Not only does it have a customized portfolio feature but it also features delayed quotes, lists of most active gainers and losers, market analysis, index charts, company research, bond quotes, and a large selection of market reports; you can also access updates on all major markets. Check out the link to an in-house section called "Options Analysis." Comprehen-

sive options, educational materials, and a calendar of upcoming Optionetics Seminars are available. This site also offers updates and additions to the financial webguide and online brokerages reviewed in this book.

Subscription: Free

OptionsAnalysis.com
www.optionsanalysis.com
Once you start looking at the volatility of options and stocks, this site is a must-have bookmark! The OptionsAnalysis.com site is dedicated to providing an immense amount of information on both stock and futures options information, such as call and put prices, implied volatility (IV), skew charts and the Greeks (delta, vega, gamma, and theta) as well as open interest ratios. If you understand what all of these are, then you have become a serious trader!

Subscription: $49.95/month

appendix e

online brokerage directory

Name of Online Brokerage	Web Site	Phone
A. B. Watley	www.abwatley.com	888-229-2853
Accutrade	www.accutrade.com	800-494-8949
America First Associates	www.aftrader.com	888-682-6973
American Express Financial Direct	www.americanexpress.com/direct	800-658-4677
Ameritrade	www.ameritrade.com	800-669-3900
Andrew Peck	www.andrewpeck.com	800-221-5873
A-1 Financial	www.a1financial.com	877-213-4626
Atlantic Financial	www.af.com/af.html	781-235-5777
BCL Online	www.bclnet.com	800-621-0392
Benjamin & Jerold Discount Brokerage	www.stockoptions.com	800-446-5112
Bidwell	www.bidwell.com	800-547-6337
BOSC Online Brokerage	www.oneinvest.com	888-843-6382
Brown & Co.	www.brownco.com	800-357-4410
Bull & Bear Online	www.bullbear.com	212-785-0900
Bush Burns Securities	www.bushburns.com	800-821-4803
Castle Securities	www.castleonline.com	800-891-1003
Charles Schwab Online	www.eschwab.com	800-540-9874
Citicorp Investment Services	www.citicorp.com/us/investments	212-559-4285
CompuTEL Securities	www.computel.com	800-432-0327
CyBerBroker, Inc.	www.cybercorp.com	512-320-0833
Datek Online	www.datek.com	212-231-5400
Discover Direct	www.discoverbrokerage.com	415-537-8616
DLJdirect	www.dljdirect.com	800-825-5723
Dreyfus Brokerage Services	www.edreyfus.com	800-421-8395
Empire Financial Group	www.lowfees.com	800-900-8101
E*Trade	www.etrade.com	650-842-8766
FarSight Financial	www.farsight.com	800-830-7483
Fidelity Web Xpress	www.fidelity.com	617-563-7000
Firstrade.com	www.firstrade.com	800-869-8800
ForbesNet	www.forbesnet.com	800-488-0090
Freedom Investments	www.freedominvestments.com	800-381-1481
Freeman Welwood	www.freemanwelwood.com	800-729-7585
Frontier	www.ffutures.com	800-777-2438

Name of Online Brokerage	Web Site	Phone
InternetTrading.Com	www.internettrading.com	800-696-2811
InvestEXpress Online	www.investexpress.com	800-822-2050
InvestIN.com Securities	www.investinsecs.com	800-327-1883
InvesTrade	www.investrade.com	847-375-6051
J. B. Oxford & Company	www.jboxford.com	800-782-1876
Main Street Market	www.mainstmarket.com	800-710-7160
MB Trading	www.mbtrading.com	888-790-4800
Mr. Stock	www.mrstock.com	800-467-7865
Muriel Siebert & Co.	www.siebertnet.com	800-872-0711
MyDiscountBroker.com	www.mydiscountbroker.com	888-882-5600
National Discount Brokers	www.ndb.com	800-888-3999
Net Investor	www.netinvestor.com	800-NET-4250
Newport Discount Brokerage	www.newport-discount.com	800-999-3278
Olde Discount Corp.	www.olde.com	800-235-3100
Peremel Online	www.peremel.com	800-666-1440
Preferred Trade	www.preferredtrade.com	800-949-3504
Quick & Reilly	www.quick-reilly.com	800-221-5220
Regal Securities	www.regaldiscount.com	800-786-9000
Scottsdale Securities	www.scottrade.com	314-965-1555
Sunlogic Securities	www.sunlogic.com	800-556-4600
Suretrade	www.suretrade.com	401-642-6900
Trade4Less	www.trade4less.com	800-780-3543
TradeStar Investments	www.4tradestar.com	800-993-2014
Tradewell Discount Investing	www.trade-well.com	888-907-9797
Trading Direct	www.tradingdirect.com	212-766-0241
TruTrade	www.trutrade.com	800-671-8505
		800-328-8600
Vision Trade	www.visiontrade.com	516-374-2184
Wall Street Access	www.wsaccess.com	800-925-5781
Wall Street Discount Corporation	www.wsdc.com	888-4-WALLS
WallStreet Electronica	www.wallstreete.com	888-925-5783
Wang Investments	www.wangvest.com	800-353-9264
Waterhouse Webroker	www.waterhouse.com	800-934-4410
Web Street Securities	www.webstreetsecurities.com	800-932-8723
Wilshire Capital	www.wilshirecm.com	800-926-9991
Wit Capital Corporation	www.witcapital.com	888-494-8227
Wyse Securities	www.wyse-sec.com	800-640-8668
Ziegler Thrift	www.ziegler-thrift.com	800-328-4854

online brokerages

A. B. Watley
www.abwatley.com
Address: 33 West 17th Street, New York, NY 10003
Toll-Free: 888-229-2853
Fax: 212-509-1672
E-mail: info@abwatley.com
Category: Deep discount brokerage
Slogan: "Wired to Wall Street"
Site Design: 9
User-Friendliness: 7
Options Usefulness: 6
General Comments: Several levels of trading service available (Watley Trader—basic on-line service; Ultimate Trader—premium software-based service).

Account Minimum: $3,000
Option Commission: $30 + $1.75 per contract (minimum $35).
Spread Trades: No naked options allowed in any service. Ultimate Trader includes "Turbo Options"—an advanced options quote screen that displays up to 44 different values for a given underlying symbol and, when eligible, routes orders directly into the RAES system (Retail Automated Execution System). This system enhances options executions.
Stock Commission: Market and limit orders—$9.95 for up to 5,000 shares and $.01 per share for any additional shares.
Real-Time Quotes: $50 to $300 month for unlimited real-time quotes (RealTick III).

Accutrade
www.accutrade.com
Address: 4211 South 102d, Omaha, NE 68127
Toll-Free: 800-882-4887 or 800-494-8949
Fax: 800-821-0743
E-mail: info@accutrade.com
Category: Middle-cost discount brokerage
Slogan: "Making Investors Smarter One by One"
Site Design: 9
User-Friendliness: 8
Options Usefulness: 8
General Comments: Accutrade is part of the Ameritrade Holding Corporation and has recently added spread trading capabilities to its lineup of options services. It is included in our top 10 list because it provides a multitude of services that benefit options traders. Accutrade allows trading through both a browser and proprietary software and you get three free trades when you open an account. Although commissions tend to be a little high, customer commentary reflects an excellent track record for customer service and reliability.
Account Minimum: $5,000
Option Commission: Minimum commission $35; $1.50 to $8 per contract.
Spread Trades: Complex option orders can be placed online. Minimum equity for short equity options $10,000. Stop limits on options are available.
Stock Commission: Market and limit orders—$29.95 up to 1,000 shares, and $.02/share over 1,000.
Real-Time Quotes: $20/month unlimited dynamic quote service; 100 free quotes per trade.

AFTrader (America First Associates)
www.aftrader.com
Address: 415 Madison Avenue, 3d floor, New York, NY 10017
Tel: 212-644-8520
Toll-Free: 888-OTC-NYSE
Fax: 212-644-3515
E-mail: support@aftrader.com
Category: Deep discount brokerage
Site Design: 3
User-Friendliness: 5
Options Usefulness: 4
General Comments: This deep-discount brokerage provides a wide variety of trading tools and services at a low cost. Comments on customer service are relatively good, but the brokerage does not have many services specific to the options trader. High marks for reliability.
Account Minimum: No minimum balance to open an account.
Option Commission: $25 + $1.75 per contract.
Spread Trades: Broker-assisted $50 + $1.75 per contract
Stock Commission: $14.95; trades over 5,000 shares add 1 cent per share
Real-Time Quotes: $29.95 per month for unlimited real-time quotes

American Express Financial Direct
www.americanexpress.com/direct
Address: IDS Tower 10, Minneapolis, MN 55440
Toll-Free: 800-658-4677
E-mail: Located on the web site

Category: High-cost discount brokerage
Slogan: "Everything you need for Smart Investing."
Site Design: 6
User-Friendliness: 6
Options Usefulness: 5
General Comments: The online service is referred to as InvestDirect and it allows you to place equity orders online, get quotes and account information. They provide comprehensive research tools; news, company research, and sophisticated stock and mutual fund searches for a medium cost. Customer comments are not too favorable when it comes to service reliability.
Account Minimum: $2,000
Option Commission: No minimum–$2,500 is $32 + 1.60% of principal amount; $2,500 – $10,000 is $49.50 + 0.90% of principal amount; minimum $48 + $2 per contract.
Spread Trades: Complex option orders are allowed but only through a live broker. Phone representatives were not very knowledgeable about specific option services.
Stock Commission: Market and limit orders—$24.95 per equity trade; trades more than 4,000 shares add 2 cents per share.
Real-Time Quotes: No. Real-time quotes are available only by phone.

Ameritrade
www.ameritrade.com
Address: 4211 South 102d St., Omaha, NE 68127
Toll-Free: 800-400-3603 or 800-454-9272
E-mail: starting@ameritrade.com
Category: Deep discount brokerage
Slogan: "The way to trade. Period."
Site Design: 8
User-Friendliness: 7
Options Usefulness: 8
General Comments: Ameritrade is a large online brokerage that made our top 10 list primarily because it allows spread orders to be placed online. Although it has a long list of excellent services, it is definitely experiencing growing pains. Customer comments go from mediocre to poor. Reliability and availability need definite improvement.
Account Minimum: $2,000
Option Commission: $25 + 1.75 per contract ($29 minimum); 10% discount for online orders.
Spread Trades: Complex option trades can be placed online.
Stock Commission: Market orders—$8 for any number of shares; Touch-Tone phone orders—$12; broker-assisted orders—$18; all limit orders are an additional $5.
Real-Time Quotes: 100 free quotes upon account opening, and 100 additional quotes with each trade execution. Unlimited real-time quotes are available for $20 per month.

Andrew Peck
www.andrewpeck.com
Address: 111 Pavonia, Suite 310, Jersey City, NJ 07310
Tel: 201-217-9500
Toll-Free: 800-221-5873
Fax: 201-217-1919
E-mail: andrewpeck@smartserv.com
Category: High-cost discount brokerage
Site Design: 8
User-Friendliness: 7
Options Usefulness: 6
General Comments: I like this firm. Their registered personnel average over 10 years' experience and each one is a registered options principal and margin expert. They are all able to calculate the margin requirements for complex option strategies over the telephone. But my favorite part is that you actually get a live person on the phone when you call them. They make every attempt to work toward prompt personal communication by providing their associates, not computers, to answer your toll-free calls and e-mails.
Account Minimum: No minimum
Option Commission: $1.90–$6 per contract ($50 minimum).
Stock Commission: $24 for 100–2,400 shares; and $.01 per share up to 5,000 shares
Real-Time Quotes: $49.95/month for dynamic quote system.

A-1 Financial
www.a1financial.com
Address: 10401 NW 21 Street, Sunrise, FL 33322
Tel: 954-253-0970
Toll-Free: 1-877-A1-FINANCIAL
E-mail: info@a1financial.com
Category: Middle-cost discount brokerage
Site Design: 7
User-Friendliness: 6
Options Usefulness: 7
General Comments: Specializing in day trading for stocks and options, A-1 has an excellent reputation for fast executions and reliability.
Account Minimum: $1,000
Option Commission: $23 + $2.50 per contract.
Spread Trades: Combination and spread orders are allowed, but must be placed through a broker. Stop orders on options are also allowed. The margin required for a naked short option is 25% of underlying security plus the premium received minus the out-of-the-money amount.
Stock Commission: Market orders—$15.95 plus $.01/share for more than 2,000 shares; limit orders—$19.95 plus $.01/share for more than 2,000 shares.
Real-Time Quotes: $29.95 a month for dynamic real-time quotes.

Atlantic Financial
www.af.com/af.html
Address: 9 Crest Road, Suite 9, Wellesley, MA 02432
Tel: 781-235-5777
Toll-Free: 800-559-2900 or 781-235-5777
Fax: 781-235-9222
E-mail: info@af.com
Category: Middle-cost discount brokerage
Slogan: "Service, Selection, and Value"
Site Design: 8
User-Friendliness: 7
Options Usefulness: 5
General Comments: Atlantic Financial is an independent firm offering stocks, bonds, CDs, and over 7,000 mutual funds. Atlantic Financial also offers offshore accounts and 401(k) plans. Although this middle-cost brokerage offers only basic option services, I still like them because it is the only firm we found that has a firm commitment to charities and social causes. A portion of Atlantic Financial's profits from every transaction goes to charitable causes. They also have a whole section devoted to socially responsible investing to help investors find companies that meet the investor's standards of ethics and operational habits. Socially conscious investors support companies that are environmentally friendly and not involved in businesses that are perceived to harm the general population.
Account Minimum: $10,000 regular accounts. Their services are suited to investors with over $200,000.
Option Commission: $39 + $2 per contract.
Spread Trades: No complex option strategies or naked calls online. Spread orders are accepted if called into a live broker and they do not charge an extra fee. Options cannot be traded on margin. Stop orders on options are allowed.
Stock Commission: Market and limit orders—$39 flat fee
Real-Time Quotes: None

BCL Online
www.bclnet.com
Address: 303 W. Madison, 4th Floor, Chicago, IL 60606
Toll-Free: 800-621-0392
E-mail: Located on the web site
Category: Middle-cost discount brokerage
Slogan: "Experience You Can Depend On . . . Peace of Mind You Deserve"
Site Design: 5
User-Friendliness: 6

Options Usefulness: 6
General Comments: This firm seems a little uptight. They are not in the business of making the option trader feel welcome. Comments range from good to fair regarding reliability and service.
Account Minimum: No minimum
Option Commission: Online commissions are discounted 10% from the standard option commission rate of $27 + .0035 of principal + $1.50 per contract ($34 minimum)
Spread Trades: BCL requires $25,000 initially in equity for naked options plus the house requirements. Stop orders on options are available. BCL requires that potential options traders provide certain financial information on their account application. Option trades must meet specific equity requirements.
Stock Commission: $13 per market order and $18 for limit or stop orders up to 5,000 shares on NYSE, AMEX, and Nasdaq for stocks trading over $1; for more than 5,000 shares, add $.01 per share.
Real-Time Quotes: 100 free real-time quotes to start and 100 more for each executed trade.

Benjamin & Jerold Discount Brokerage
www.stockoptions.com
Address: Suite 3550, 141 West Jackson Blvd., Chicago, IL 60604
Tel: 312-554-0202
Toll-Free: 800-446-5112
Fax: 312-554-0268
E-mail: info@stockoptions.com or jkopf@sellingputs.com
Category: Middle-cost discount brokerage
Slogan: "Your Best Option"
Site Design: 7
User-Friendliness: 7
Options Usefulness: 8
General Comments: This company exclusively handles stocks and options—no mutual funds, bonds, and so on. Rates are negotiable for very active accounts and they do not charge extra for stops, contingent or spread orders held day or GTC. Naked short index options and naked short call stock options are not permitted, but short equity put options are allowed if 100% cash-secured. In addition, they'll let you trade options out of your IRA account ($15,000 minimum). Look for this firm to become a dynamic trading firm for options traders in the future.
Account Minimum: $5,000 account minimum.
Option Commission: $1.50 to $5.90 per contract for stock or index options ($36 minimum).
Spread Trades: Spread trades can be entered directly through their "BBS Direct Trade" sytem—a bulletin board accessed through a hyper terminal. Increased Internet access is in the works.
Stock Commission: Market and limit orders—$29 flat fee via the Internet; $36 for 200 shares; $66 for 1,000 to 2,000 shares. Exchange fees included. $2 ticket charge per transaction.
Real-Time Quotes: Free real-time and delayed quotes.

Bidwell
www.bidwell.com
Address: 209 SW Oak Street, Portland, OR 97219
Tel: 503-790-9000
Toll-Free: 800-547-6337
E-mail: info@bidwell.com
Category: Middle-cost discount brokerage
Site Design: 8
User-Friendliness: 7
Options Usefulness: 5
General Comments: Option commissions are high and so are the margin rates. Customer comments vary from excellent to frustrated. Option traders are not really catered to.
Account Minimum: No minimum
Option Commission: $27 plus $3 per contract regardless of how the order is placed.
Spread Trades: To become eligible for option trading, Bidwell requires customers to fill out an option application which is separate from their standard account application. All option spread orders have to be placed over the phone as Bidwell does not yet offer an auto-

mated interface for option spread orders. Spread orders must be placed in a margin account with a minimum equity on the account of $2,000. Due to the use of the margin requirements, they do not restrict option strategies. The margin requirement will be greater for the strategies which have less protection. You can pick the exchange; Bidwell will default to the American exchange (ASE) when the option is traded on the ASE. No stop orders on options.

Stock Commission: Market orders are a $12 flat fee for up to 1,500 shares and then it's an additional $.01 per share. For limit orders, add $3 per order.

Real-Time Quotes: 100 free real-time quotes when you open an account and subsequently 100 free quotes per trade.

BOSC (Banc One Securities Corp.) Online Brokerage

www.oneinvest.com

Address: 300 S. Riverside Plaza, MS 0860, Chicago, IL 60670-0860

Toll-Free: 888-843-6382

E-mail: Located on the web site

Category: Middle-cost discount brokerage

Site Design: 6

User-Friendliness: 5

Options Usefulness: 4

General Comments: This brokerage firm has slightly higher commission rates, but comments reflect excellent customer service and order execution.

Account Minimum: No minimum

Option Commission: Pro-rated according to the total cost of the order. $3,000 and less is $35 + 1.5%; $3,000 to $10,000 is $50 + .85%; and more than $10,000 is $60 + .7%.

Spread Trades: Depending on the type of option trading you select, you may be required to have a $10,000 cash minimum balance in your margin account. Spread orders must be placed through a live broker.

Stock Commission: Market and limit orders—1000 shares or less are $19.95; more than 1,000 shares add $.02 per share.

Real-Time Quotes: 100 free real-time stock and option quotes when you open your account plus you accumulate 100 real-time quotes each time you execute an online trade.

Brown & Co.

www.brownco.com

Address: 1 Beacon Street, 18th Floor, Boston, MA 02108

Toll-free: 800-357-4410

E-mail: Located on the web site

Category: Deep discount brokerage

Slogan: "Where your experience pays off."

Site Design: 8

User-Friendliness: 7

Options Usefulness: 6

General Comments: This is an exclusive firm that accepts only clients with an income of $40,000 or more and a net worth (exclusive of real estate) of $50,000, and five years of market experience. We placed this firm on our top 10 list because it has an excellent reputation for executions and reliability in a no frills-atmosphere and low commissions.

Account Minimum: $15,000

Option Commission: Market orders—$15 + $1.50 per contract ($25 minimum) for up to 30 contracts, then $1.75 per contract; limit orders—$15 + $1.75 per contract ($25 minimum).

Spread Trades: Spread orders are welcomed but must be placed through a live broker.

Stock Commission: Market orders (online and Touch-Tone)—$5 up to 5,000 shares, then add $.01 per share. Limit orders—$10 up to 5,000 shares, then add $.01 per share.

Real-Time Quotes: 100 free real-time quotes per executed trade.

Bull & Bear Online

www.bullbear.com

Address: 11 Hanover Square, 12th Floor, New York, NY 10005

Tel: 212-785-0900

Toll-Free: 800-262-5800

E-mail: info@bullbear.com
Category: Middle-cost discount brokerage
Site Design: 8
User-Friendliness: 6
Options Usefulness: 5
General Comments: This site is quite attractive and has won numerous awards for design. Option commissions are quite high and spread orders must be made through a live broker. Customer comments are fair to partly cloudy when it comes to site efficiency and executions.
Account Minimum: There is no account minimum but in order to receive the $19.95 commission rate you must maintain a minimum of $5,000 in your account
Option Commission: $37.25 + $1.75 per contract plus.
Spread Trades: Spreads and complex option orders must be placed through live broker and have the following minimum requirements: credit spreads—the lesser of the naked requirement or the difference in the strike price; debit spreads—100% of the debit with a minimum of $2,000. For naked options the minimum is $100,000. You cannot pick the exchange. No stop orders on options are allowed.
Stock Commission: Market and limit orders—$19.95 for up to 1,000 shares and $.02 per share or $29 plus 1.6% of principal additional shares (for up to 2,500 shares). Minimum charge: $40 per contract on the first two contracts, plus $4 per contract thereafter.
Real-Time Quotes: 100 quotes to start and 50 quotes per executed trade.

Bush Burns Securities
www.bushburns.com
Address: 4111-W Andover, Bloomfield, MI 48302
Toll-Free: 800-821-4803
Fax: 810-540-2968
E-mail: service@bushburns.com
Category: High-cost discount brokerage
Site Design: 6
User-Friendliness: 6
Options Usefulness: 3
General Comments: This firm offers a wide array of online investment products including stocks, options, bonds, mutual funds, corporate and municipal bonds, Treasuries, agencies, and Canadian stocks.
Account Minimum: No minimum.
Option Commission: Option price below $1—$15 per trade plus $3 per contract; option price $1 and over—$15 per trade plus $4 per contract (minimum $35).
Spread Trades: Spreads, straddles, or uncovered call writing are not allowed. Put writing is allowed with specific approval and limitations.
Stock Commission: Market orders—$20 up to 5,000 shares, then add $.015 per share; limit orders—$25 up to 5,000 shares, then add $.015 per share.
Real-Time Quotes: Real-time quotes available for a small fee.

Castle Securities
www.castleonline.com
Address: 45 Church Street, Freeport, MA 11520
Tel: 516-868-8812
Toll-Free: 800-891-1003 or 800-661-5133
Fax: 516-868-5131 or 516-868-0228
E-mail: paul@castleonline.com or tony@castleonline.com
Category: High-cost discount brokerage
Site Design: 6
User-Friendliness: 6
Options Usefulness: 0
General Comments: Customer commentary continually sings this firm's praises. It has two kinds of service available with its own software: Prince Package—Nasdaq Level II and My-track Data Package: $150 per month or free for customers that execute 100 trades or more per month (50 round turns); King Package—Nasdaq Level II and the AT Financial Major Attitude Package—$300 per month. Free for customers that execute 150 trades or more per month (75 round turns)—$150/month if client executes 100 tickets/month.
Account Minimum: $10,000

Option Commission: Not yet available but coming soon.
Spread Trades: None
Stock Commission: Market and limit orders (listed)—$19.95 plus $.01 per share; market and limit orders (Nasdaq)—$19.95 up to 10,000 shares.
Real-Time Quotes: Real time level one quotes are free to all account holders.

Charles Schwab Online
www.eschwab.com
Address: 101 Montgomery MS120-12, San Francisco, CA 94104
Toll-Free: 800-435-4000
E-mail: Located on the web site
Category: High-cost discount brokerage
Slogan: "The online leader. The service you expect, the value you want."
Site Design: 8
User-Friendliness: 6
Options Usefulness: 7
General Comments: As the number one online brokerage, Charles Schwab has the lion's share of clients and boasts more than 450 offices nationwide. Schwab has it all: stock, stock options, mutual funds, bonds, Treasuries, stock screening, and portfolio management. It makes our top 10 list because of its extensive products and services that help options traders to compete in the marketplace. Commissions tend to run a little high but that hasn't stopped the firm from leading the online trading market with a 33% share. Some of its success can be attributed to their dedication to providing excellent customer service.
Account Minimum: $2,500
Option Commission: $35 plus $1.75 per contract (this varies due to the quantity of the order and the option premium).
Spread Trades: Complex spread orders are welcomed. Schwab even offers access to a dedicated team of expert options specialists. You must place complex options orders through a live broker (however, this will be changing by the end of 1999). They do require a special account minimum for spread trades: Equity options—$5,000; index options—$25,000.
Stock Commission: $29.95 up to 1,000 shares, then add $.03 per share.
Real-Time Quotes: 100 free for opening an account and 100 free for each executed trade.

Citicorp Investment Services
www.citicorp.com/us/investments
Address: 701 East 60th Street North, Suite 3280, Sioux Falls, SD 57117
Toll-Free: 800-275-2484 ext. 0263
Fax: 212-559-4285 or 212-527-1181
E-mail: Located on the web site
Category: Middle-cost discount brokerage
Site Design: 6
User-Friendliness: 4
Options Usefulness: 0
General Comments: So far, Citicorp only allows traders to buy and sell stocks, bonds, and mutual funds. The web site is not easy to navigate around but they do allow option trading at their New York office (by phone). Citicorp may be an excellent bank, but it seems to be just starting to get its feet wet as an online brokerage.
Account Minimum: No minimum
Option Commission: No options.
Spread Trades: No options.
Stock Commission: Limit and market orders—$19.95 for up to 10,000 shares or $100,000.
Real-Time Quotes: 100 real-time quotes every day.

CompuTEL Securities
www.computel.com
Address: 301 Mission Street, 5th Floor, San Francisco, CA 94105
To Open an Account: 800-432-0327
Account Holder Support: 888-597-6840
Trading Desk: 888-240-2835
Fax: 415-543-3714

E-mail: support@computel.com
Category: High-cost discount brokerage
Site Design: 7
User-Friendliness: 8
Options Usefulness: 7
General Comments: CompuTEL was one of the first brokerages to offer Internet trading. We placed this firm on our top 10 list because of their commitment to options services, excellent record for executions, and reliability.
Account Minimum: $5,000
Option Commission: $24.00 plus $1 per contract.
Spread Trades: Comprehensive option services. Easy and cheap commission schedule. No hidden costs. Spread orders welcomed although they do not offer online spread services. No stop orders on options.
Stock Commission: Market orders—$16.50 (less than 1,000 shares) and $11.50 (1,000 to 5,000 shares), then add $.01 per share; limit orders—$21.50 up to 5,000 shares, then add $.01 per share.
Real-Time Quotes: $62.95/month for dynamic update quote system; 100 free real-time quotes per trade; 25 free real-time quotes provided each day.

CyBerBroker, Inc.
www.cybercorp.com
Address: 1601 Rio Grande #456, Austin, Texas 78701
Tel: 512-320-0833
Fax: 512-320-9921 or 512-320-5444
E-mail: correspondence@cybercorp.com
Category: Deep discount brokerage
Slogan: "The Next Generation in Electronic Trading"
Site Design: 7
User-Friendliness: 7
Options Usefulness: 0
General Comments: CyBerBroker provides online brokerage services and trading technology—specifically CyBerTrader and CyBerX—to day traders and active investors. The difference between this firm and traditional online brokers is these brokers are part of CyBerCorp, an electronic trading technology group, which develops high-end, real-time electronic stock trading and execution systems. CyBerBroker sends orders electronically to whichever market maker or ECN is offering the best price and the required volume. Cy-BerCenter Inc. is the data, server, and networking and technical support group that acts as the "central nervous system" for Internet and online trading. These systems require the use of special software for online trading.
Account Minimum: CyBerTrader—15,000 initial trading capital. Income of at least $50,000/year and a net worth of at least $100,000. Account must maintain a minimum daily equity balance of $7,500. CyBerX—$10,000 initial trading capital. Income of at least $35,000/year and net worth of at least $60,000 (exclusive of farm and home).
Option Commission: No options.
Spread Trades: No options.
Stock Commission: $19.95 per trade
Real-Time Quotes: CyBerTrader and CyBerT—$250 per month or free if you place more than 100 trades per month. CyBerX—$49 per month or free if you place more than 50 trades a month.

Datek Online
www.datek.com
Address: 100 Wood Avenue South, Iselin, NJ 08830-2716
Tel: 212-231-5400 or 732-635-8800
Toll-Free: 888-Go-Datek (888-463-2835)
Fax: 732-744-9144 or 732-744-9150
E-mail: support@datek.com
Category: Deep discount brokerage
Slogan: "Trade Now"
Site Design: 8
User-Friendliness: 8
Options Usefulness: 0

General Comments: An early pioneer of online investing, Datek Online, established in 1996, is ranked the fourth largest broker based on volume by Piper Jaffray and was recently named the number one online brokerage by TheStreet.com and number two by *SmartMoney* magazine. Datek has developed an excellent reputation in the day trading industry and offers low commissions ($9.99/trade). This firm also emphasizes fast executions—if a marketable order takes longer than 60 seconds, the trade is commission-free. Unfortunately, Datek also appears to be experiencing growing pains as customers complain of long phone waits, poor web access, and unavailable servers.
Account Minimum: $2,000
Option Commission: No options.
Spread Trades: No options at this time (they keep saying they will be adding options to their line of products).
Stock Commission: Market and limit orders are $9.99 up to 5,000 shares, then add $.01 per share.
Real-Time Quotes: Free dynamic quote service.

Discover Direct
www.discoverbrokerage.com
Address: 333 Market Street, 25th Floor, San Francisco, CA 94105
Tel: 415-537-8616
Toll-Free: 800-584-6837
E-mail: support@discoverbrokerage.com
Category: Middle-cost discount brokerage
Site Design: 8
User-Friendliness: 6
Options Usefulness: 5
General Comments: Discover's option commissions are a little high, but they do offer a host of excellent online services that will help option traders to get their piece of the pie. Discover's real-time account updates are also a big plus and they reportedly have excellent trade execution. Customer comments run from excellent to frustrating regarding the system being down and the backup systems (Touch-Tone and live brokers) without the capacity to deal with the overload. Their commercials border on ludicrous and have been the focus of some controversy due to their misleading edge (i.e., truck drivers owning islands thanks to their online Discover accounts).
Account Minimum: $2,000
Option Commission: Options less than $1 per contract are $1.75 per contract with a minimum commission of $27.50; options of $1–$3$^7/_8$ per contract are $3 per contract with a minimum commission of $27.50; options of $4 and up per contract are $3 per contract with a minimum commission of $30; options exercises and assignments 1 to 4,999 shares are $34 per exercise/assignment.
Spread Trades: Option spread orders must be placed by telephone. To place a naked option, you need options approval and at least $10,000 equity/+ greater of 35% market value of stock plus premium minus out-of-the-money or 20% market value stock plus premium. Naked call writing, uncovered sell straddles, call spread orders in which the long position expires before the short leg, naked index options, and index option spreads are not permitted. Option orders may be routed to a specific exchange if placed with a live broker; the routing commission is $25 plus $3 per contract. Stop orders on options are not permitted.
Stock Commission: Market orders—$14.95; limit orders—$19.95; listed stocks—add $.01 per share for more than 5,000 shares; Nasdaq stocks—1$^1/_2$ cents per share (minimum commission per order $34)
Real-Time Quotes: Free, unlimited real-time quotes and graphs.

DLJdirect
www.dljdirect.com
Address: 1 Persian Plaza, 11th Floor, Jersey City, NJ 07399
Tel: 201-332-4965
Toll-Free: 800-825-5723
E-mail: Located on the web site
Category: High-cost discount brokerage
Slogan: "A Great Place to Start"
Site Design: 7

User-Friendliness: 6
Options Usefulness: 3
General Comments: One of the original online brokerages, DLJ is a big firm with branch offices in 12 U.S. cities and 12 foreign cities. Their order screens are easy to use and they offer a wide range of services, including access to IPOs. DLJ is rated as the number one online brokerage by Gomez, but customer complaints are on the rise. Growing pains abound, including lengthy phone waits and frequent server problems.
Account Minimum: No minimum
Option Commission: $35 + 1.75 per contract (minimum $40).
Spread Trades: Covered call and buying or selling or options only. No naked option writing or stop-sell orders on options.
Stock Commission: $20 for up to 1,000 shares, and then $.02 per share.
Real-Time Quotes: 100 free real-time quotes for each executed trade.

Dreyfus Brokerage Services
www.edreyfus.com
Address: 401 N. Maple Drive, Beverly Hills, CA 90210
Toll-Free: 800-421-8395 or 800-416-7113
E-mail: support@edreyfus.com
Category: Middle-cost discount brokerage
Site Design: 8
User-Friendliness: 7
Options Usefulness: 7
General Comments: This one made our top 10 list! A good site for options traders due to low option commissions and an easy options quotation system. Unfortunately, spread orders require a hefty $20,000 minimum which may be too rich for many new traders just starting out. Relatively good client comments regarding reliability. Even better comments for executions and customer service.
Account Minimum: $1,000 (cash), $2,000 (options), and $2,000 (margin).
Option Commission: $15 plus $1.75 per contract.
Spread Trades: Spread orders require a live broker which is an additional $25 commission fee plus $1.75 per contract for options priced below $1 and $2.25 per contract for options priced at or above $1 per contract. There is a $20,000 minimum for option spreads or to write naked options (plus 50% of value of the underlying stock). No index option cross spreads or straddles—OEX versus SPX. Uncovered equity and index options and spreads (except for covered writes) must be approved by their designated "option principal." Stop orders on options are allowed if phoned in to a live broker.
Stock Commission: $15 flat fee applies to all market and limit orders.
Real-Time Quotes: Dreyfus does not offer real-time option quotes. However, you may subscribe to eSignal Online for $130–$155 per month or receive five free StockEdge quotes per month or pay $59–$79 per month.

Empire Financial Group
www.lowfees.com
Address: 2170 W. State Road 434 Suite 150, Longwood, FL 32779
Tel: 407-774-1300
Toll-Free: 800-900-8101
Fax: 407-774-2275
E-mail: empire1@sprintmail.com
Category: Deep discount brokerage
Site Design: 7
User-Friendliness: 6
Options Usefulness: 3
General Comments: Perhaps Empire's greatest claim to fame is its commission-free trading system. They also offer a pager service on 25 trades per month to notify clients of splits, news, quotes, filings, and so on. Customer comments reflect good to fair service.
Account Minimum: No minimum.
Option Commission: $25 + $1.95 per contract.
Spread Trades: Agents not very knowledgeable about option trading. Spread orders are allowed but you have to call them in (good luck finding a trading rep who knows what you're talking about). Stop orders on options are also allowed.
Stock Commission: Commission free on all Nasdaq orders of 1,000 shares or more or all

listed stock orders of 1,000 to 5,000 shares valued at $5 or more per share (market orders only). All market stock transactions that do not qualify for commission-free trading are executed at a flat rate of $6.95 for market orders up to 5,000 shares, and then $.01 per share and $11.95 on limit orders up to 5,000 shares, and then $.01 per share. A $3 postage fee is applied to all transactions. Short sales do not qualify for commission-free trading.
Real-Time Quotes: A fee of $14.95, plus. No minimum $.05 per quote, minus 250 free quotes, minus 25 free quotes per executed online transaction will be debited to your account on the first of every month.

E*Trade
www.etrade.com
Address: 66 Brooks Drive, Braintree, MA 02184-8160
Tel: 650-842-8910
Toll-Free: 800-786-2575
E-mail: service@etrade.com
Category: Middle-cost discount brokerage
Slogan: "Someday, we'll all invest this way."
Site Design: 9
User-Friendliness: 5
Options Usefulness: 6
General Comments: E*Trade has a multitude of online services, charts, and products. Their web site has a customizable welcome screen and alerts that should make trading there even more agreeable. They offer the usual stocks, options, bonds, and mutual funds as well as penny stocks, Canadian and foreign stocks, and IPOs.
Note: E*Trade may have been a pioneer in the online brokerage industry, but its recent system failures have been making national headlines. Customer comments range from slightly negative to outrage. Waiting for customer service by phone can take as long as two to five hours and the web site is slow and laborious. They say that they are experiencing growing pains and it remains to be seen just how long it will take to straighten out their vast medley of problems. Even calling the customer service department to ask questions was a Touch-Tone nightmare that led us from one robot to the next and finally to a dead end and a dial tone.
Account Minimum: $2,000
Option Commission: $20 + $1.75 per contract (minimum $29).
Spread Trades: There is not an account minimum for options trading. Your account must be approved to trade options and this cannot be done on margin so you must have the funds available in your account at the time of the order. Spreads and most other complex options trades must be placed through a broker. E*Trade does not allow short straddles or naked calls. Stop orders and stop limit orders must be entered at least $1/4$ point different than the current price and can be entered only as day orders. All E*Trade option orders are routed to the principal exchange where that option trades. Check out the options analysis web area for checking volatility and so on. $10,000 minimum account requirement for naked puts; $25,000 minimum account requirement for naked calls.
Stock Commission: Market orders—$14.95 (for all listed stocks) or $19.95 (for all Nasdaq stocks) for up to 5,000 shares, plus $.01 per share for entire order; limit orders—$19.95 for up to 5,000 shares, then $.01 per share for entire order.
Real-Time Quotes: When you view an option quote, it will tell you if it is a 20-minute-delay or a real-time quote. Free unlimited real-time quotes.

FarSight Financial
www.farsight.com
Address: 201 Broadway, 5th Floor, Cambridge, MA 02139
Toll-Free: 800-830-7483
E-mail: service@farsight.com
Category: High-cost discount brokerage
Slogan: "Integrated Online Personal Service"
Site Design: 7
User-Friendliness: 5
Options Usefulness: 0
General Comments: This firm's medium-priced commissions and high margin rates are balanced out by fast executions and excellent customer service. Customers tend to complain that the web site moves slowly and of not getting the best prices on trades. To their

credit, FarSight conducts a pilot program for online investors who are interested in helping them improve the design of their online services.

Account Minimum: No minimum
Option Commission: No options yet. Supposedly coming in the near future.
Spread Trades: No options.
Stock Commission: Market and limit orders—$20 up to 1,000 shares, and then $.02/share.
Real-Time Quotes: 100 free real-time quotes per trade plus 200 free to start.

Fidelity Web Xpress

www.fidelity.com
Address: 2300 Litton Lane, Mailzone KH1A, Hebron, KY 41048
Tel: 617-563-7000
Toll-Free: 800-544-6666
E-mail: Located on the web site
Category: High-cost discount brokerage
Slogan: ". . . every second counts . . ."
Site Design: 5
User-Friendliness: 3
Options Usefulness: 3
General Comments: Fidelity does not make it easy to find out what you need to know by consulting their web site. Each screen opens unto another one with more questions to be asked. It took seven screens just to get to where we could e-mail a few questions of our own. This is partly because Fidelity is a large national brokerage and the online part of the firm is just a small contingent of Fidelity's overall services. After spending way too much time, we discovered that Fidelity has very little in the way of services for option traders, anyway! They also have a very confusing commission schedule based on the number of trades you place per year and the amount of the trade. They don't even offer a commission schedule on their web site (although a customer service rep did offer to send me one by snail mail).
Account Minimum: $5,000
Option Commission: Actually based on the amount of the trade and a 25% discount for online. $5 extra for Touch-Tone; $15 extra for broker-assisted. Minimum of $27.
Spread Trades: Spread trades are allowed but they must be called in through a live broker.
Stock Commission: Market orders—$25 up to 1,000 shares, then add $.02 per share; limit orders—$30 up to 1,000 shares, then add $.02 per share.
Real-Time Quotes: Free snapshot real-time quotes of stocks and options.

Firstrade.com

www.firstrade.com
Address: 136-21 Roosevelt Avenue, 3d Floor, Flushing, NY 11354
Tel: 718-961-6600
Toll-Free: 800-869-8800
Fax: 718-961-6202
E-mail: service@firstrade.net
Category: Deep discount brokerage
Slogan: "The easiest way to trade."
Site Design: 6
User-Friendliness: 8
Options Usefulness: 6
General Comments: Customer comments vary, but lean towards the negative regarding executions and customer service. Not recommended for day traders since approval is required for online trades, which can slow down the process considerably.
Account Minimum: $2,000 for margin accounts
Option Commission: $20 plus $1.75 per contract ($29 minimum); $30 plus $1.75 per contract for phone trades ($35 minimum).
Spread Trades: Regrettably, spread orders and naked option orders are not accepted via the Internet. All broker-assisted option transactions are charged $30 + $1.75 per contract (minimum charge per order is $35). Cleared funds must be in the account prior to accepting orders. No stop orders on options. You may choose the exchange if you place your order with a live broker. In order to be eligible for option trading, you need to complete an option agreement which will then be reviewed for option trading eligibility. In other words, you have to have some bucks if you want to play in their playground.

Stock Commission: Market and limit orders have a $9.95 flat fee; market orders for 1,000 shares or more of any Nasdaq stock are only $4.95 each.
Real-Time Quotes: Real-time quotes are provided on a quote bank basis; 100 quotes are provided initially, and 100 quotes are added for every trade executed.

ForbesNet
www.forbesnet.com
Address: 8 Fletcher Place, Melville, NY 11717
Tel: 516-549-7000
Toll-Free: 800-488-0090
Fax: 516-549-7004
E-mail: webmaster@rjforbes.com
Category: Deep discount brokerage
Slogan: "Speculate on your investment. Not your broker."
Site Design: 8
User-Friendliness: 6
Options Usefulness: 5
General Comments: This site does very little for the options investor and has expensive options commissions. The site is quite attractive, although the graphics do take a while. Perhaps that's the reason that customers complain that the site moves slowly. Other comments vary from excellent to slow when it comes to executions.
Account Minimum: $5,000
Option Commission: $40 plus $1–$4 per contract depending on option premium.
Spread Trades: You must call their trading desk to place spread orders. There is a $25,000 minimum for spread trades plus the margin requirements. Traders cannot pick the exchange, but stop orders on options are allowed.
Stock Commission: $9.95 up to 5,000 shares, then add $.01 per share for each additional share.
Real-Time Quotes: $29.95 per month for unlimited real-time quotes.

Freedom Investments
www.freedominvestments.com
Address: 11422 Miracle Hills Drive, Suite 501, Omaha, Nebraska 68154
Tel: 402-431-8500
Toll-Free: 800-381-1481
E-mail: support@freedominvestments.com
Category: Middle-cost discount brokerage
Site Design: 7
User-Friendliness: 6
Options Usefulness: 6
General Comments: Founded in 1994, this brokerage is small enough to be reliable and clients appear happy with executions and service. Option trading is not the main focus, but they do have a variety of services for active stock traders.
Account Minimum: $2,000
Option Commission: $40 + $2 per contract ($50 + $3.50 per contract by phone).
Spread Trades: Freedom does allow spread orders to be placed online, but they can be placed with a live broker. Your account must be approved for spreads before an order can be placed. Stop orders on options are accepted, but only for the day.
Stock Commission: $15 flat fee for market and limit orders; Touch-Tone: $25; Broker-assisted: $45 plus $.03 per share.
Real-Time Quotes: 15 minutes free; 4 additional minutes free for each trade, then $.25 per minute or $25 per month for unlimited real-time quotes.

Freeman Welwood
www.freemanwelwood.com/
Address: P.O. Box 21886, Seattle, WA 98111
Tel: 206-382-5353
Toll-Free: 800-729-7585
E-mail: service@freemanwelwood.com
Category: Middle-cost discount brokerage
Site Design: 8
User-Friendliness: 6

Options Usefulness: 6
General Comments: This site is well laid out and although it doesn't cater to options traders, you can do complex spread orders by phone. Although some customers complain about the site being slow, they seem generally pleased by executions and customer service. No complaints of system failures either, even during heavy Internet stock mania.
Account Minimum: No minimum.
Option Commission: $34 plus $2.50 per contract; 10% off for online orders.
Spread Trades: Spread trades must be entered through a live broker. Stop orders on options are allowed. No account minimum for spread trades.
Stock Commission: Market orders—$14.95 up to 1,000 shares and $.01 per share for additional shares; limit orders—$19.95 up to 1,000 shares and $.01 per share for additional shares.
Real-Time Quotes: 100 free per trade execution.

Frontier
www.ffutures.com
Address: 4000 River Ridge Drive NE, Cedar Rapids, IA 52402
Toll-Free: 800-278-6257—Stocks / 800-777-2438—Futures
Email: request@ffutures.com
Category: High-cost discount brokerage
Site Design: 6
User-Friendliness: 6
Options Usefulness: 5
General Comments: Although this firm has relatively high commissions, it is one of the few firms where you can trade stocks, options, and commodities. They also offer access to company reports. All research is sent to a member's PC or fax machine within five minutes of ordering, or the report is free.
Account Minimum: No minimum
Option Commission: $29 plus $2.50 per contract, plus a $4 confirmation of execution fee.
Spread Trades: Spread orders are allowed on equity and futures options. No stop orders on options. No account minimums for placing spread trades beyond the margin requirement.
Stock Commission: For listed stocks $2 per share or higher—up to 2,999 shares costs $29 and 3,000 shares or more the commission is free. A $4 confirmation fee is added to all executed transactions.
Commodity Commission: Ranges from $29 per round turn contract to as low as $9 per contract for exceptionally active traders (5,000+ shares).
Real-Time Quotes: $15 month for unlimited real-time snapshot quotes.

InternetTrading.Com
www.internettrading.com
Address: 100 Bush Street 10th Floor, San Francisco, CA 94104
Toll-Free: 800-696-2811
Fax: 415-362-0671
E-mail: webmaster@internettrading.com
Category: Middle-cost discount brokerage
Site Design: 6
User-Friendliness: 6
Options Usefulness: 5
General Comments: This firm has a few carrots for the options trader, but nothing that makes us jump up and down. Comments complain about high margin rates, executions, and reliability.
Account Minimum: $10,000
Option Commission: $17.50 plus $2 per contract.
Spread Trades: Spread trades are accepted through a live broker at a minimum ticket of $20 plus $2 per contract. No stop orders on options allowed.
Stock Commission: $14 per trade; over 5,000 shares add $1^3/_4$ cents per share.
Real-Time Quotes: Unlimited free real-time snapshot quotes.

InvestEXpress Online
www.investexpress.com
Address: 50 Broad Street, New York, NY 10004
Toll-Free: 800-822-2050

E-mail: aschrott@entelechy-inc.com
Category: Middle-cost discount brokerage
Site Design: 7
User-Friendliness: 6
Options Usefulness: 5
General Comments: Comments are very high from customers, especially concerning relia-bility, execution, and customer service. Not a lot of perks for options traders—no quotes for options at all.
Account Minimum: No minimum to open. A margin account for stocks or options must maintain a $5,000 minimum equity.
Option Commission: $20 + $1.75 per contract; broker-assisted: $25 + $2.50 per contract.
Spread Trades: Spreads are allowed, but they have certain requirements (call 800-392-7192 for requirements).
Stock Commission: Market orders—$13.95 plus $.005 per share for up to 4,999 shares; $17.95 for limit orders.
Real-Time Quotes: $14 per month for unlimited real-time quotes. Quotes for options are not yet available.

InvestIN.com Securities
www.investinsecs.com
Address: Infomart—Suite 2016, 1950 Stemmons Freeway, Dallas, TX 75207
Toll-Free: 800-327-1883
E-mail: newaccounts@investin.com
Category: Middle-cost discount brokerage
Site Design: 5
User-Friendliness: 5
Options Usefulness: 0
General Comments: This firm has wholly owned subsidiaries in Great Britain. It does not handle options at all.
Account Minimum: $2,000
Option Commission: No options.
Spread Trades: No options.
Stock Commission: $14.95 listed stocks plus $.01 per share; $19.95 Nasdaq up to 5,000 shares; limit and stop orders are $19.95. Add $10 for broker-assisted trades.
Real-Time Quotes: 100 free real-time quotes per month and 50 additional quotes per trade.

InvesTrade
www.investrade.com
Address: 950 Milwaukee Avenue, Suite 102, Glenview, IL 60025
Tel: 847-375-6051
Toll-Free: 800-498-7120
Fax: 847-298-6165
E-mail: support@investrade.com
Category: Deep discount brokerage
Site Design: 8
User-Friendliness: 7
Options Usefulness: 2
General Comments: InvesTrade is a small deep discount online brokerage that charges one flat rate for electronic stock trade executions, with no limit on size. They also offer a wide range of products including high-yield bonds, T-bill rollovers, and CDs. Customer comments reflect a slow web site and slow execution confirmations, lengthy phone waits, and inaccurate real-time option quotes.
Account Minimum: $2,000
Option Commission: $1.75 per contract ($14.95 minimum).
Spread Trades: No naked calls; no buy writes, spreads, or straddles spreads. Offers hand-held wireless quote and news and ordering system (w-Trade System) for options traders. Naked puts are allowed with a $50,000 margin account. You have to use their sister firm—Regal—to do spreads.
Stock Commission: Market orders—$7.95 per trade; limit orders—$11.95 for any trade.
Real-Time Quotes: 50 free real-time quotes per trade.

J. B. Oxford & Company
www.jboxford.com/
Address: 9665 Wilshire, Suite 300, Beverly Hills, CA 90212
Tel: 310-777-8888
Toll-Free: 800-782-1876
Fax: 310-777-8820
E-mail: sales@jboc.com
Category: Middle-cost discount brokerage
Site Design: 8
User-Friendliness: 6
Options Usefulness: 5
General Comments: J.B. Oxford updates account information in real time, and offers a full year's worth of account history. J.B. Oxford is also known for having a lot of additional fees and charges as well as a higher-than-average margin rate—8.5% for an account balance of $10,000. Commentary on this brokerage has been quite negative, especially when it comes to customer service.
Account Minimum: $2,000
Option Commission: $28, plus $2.50 per contract; $8 extra for broker assistance by phone.
Spread Trades: Account must be approved for options trading. No naked option writing.
Stock Commission: Market orders—$13 for up to 3,000 shares, then $.01/share for entire order; $100 for 10,000 shares; limit orders—$18 for up to 3,000 shares, then $.01/share for entire order; $50 for 5,000 shares.
Real-Time Quotes: 100 free for each order or $75 per month for dynamic real-time quotes.

Main Street Market
www.mainstmarket.com
Address: 26 Broadway, 13th Floor, New York, NY 10004
Toll-Free: 800-710-7160
Fax: 212-747-4850
E-mail: acuccuru@usclearing.com
Category: Middle-cost discount brokerage
Slogan: "Where Wall St. Meets Main St."
Site Design: 8
User-Friendliness: 7
Options Usefulness: 6
General Comments: Main Street Market, the online brokerage section of Independent Bankers Association, is primarily suited for day traders. Customer comments are relatively positive regarding customer service and executions. Option commissions are value-based, which can be a hassle to calculate. Customer representatives were very uneducated regarding options spreads when contacted by phone.
Account Minimum: No
Option Commission: $3,000 and under—$35 + .009 of principal; $3,001 to $10,000—$35 + .008 of principal; and $10,001 and over—$35 + .007 of principal.
Spread Trades: Spread trades are allowed. Stop orders on options are not permitted. There is no account minimum for spread trading—you just have to be able to cover the cost of the spread.
Stock Commission: Market orders—$14.95 up to 1,000 shares and $.02 per share for any additional shares; limit orders—$19.95 up to 1,000 shares and $.02 per share for any additional shares.
Real-Time Quotes: $30 per month (Reuters).

MB Trading
www.mbtrading.com
Address: 840 Apollo Street, Suite 251, El Segundo, CA 90245
Toll-Free: 888-790-4800 / 800-452-6294—options desk
Fax: 310 414-0567
E-mail: clients@mbtrading.com
Category: High-cost discount brokerage
Site Design: 4
User-Friendliness: 3
Options Usefulness: 2

General Comments: MB Trading attracts primarily day traders offering Real Tick III, Level II dynamic real-time quotes as well as real-time updates. Customer comments raved about profitable executions.
Account Minimum: $5,000
Option Commission: $20 minimum; $3 to $7 per contract.
Spread Trades: No spread trading. Only covered calls or buy and sell options. No stop orders on options.
Stock Commission: Market and limit orders—$22.95 up to 2,000 shares, then add $.01 per share for each additional share.
Real-Time Quotes: Free unlimited real-time snapshot stock quotes; or get RealTick III with Level II quotes for $300/month; or $100/month with 20–49 trades/month; or free with 50+ trades/month.

Mr. Stock
www.mrstock.com
Address: 220 Bush Street, Suite 360, San Francisco, CA 94104
Tel: 415-249-4384
Toll-Free: 800-470-1896 or 800-467-7865
Fax: 415-986-8380
E-mail: info@mrstock.com
Category: Middle-cost discount brokerage
Slogan: "Reliable, accessible, fast & cheap."
Site Design: 9
User-Friendliness: 8
Options Usefulness: 9
General Comments: This firm rated #3 on our 10 best online brokerages for options traders. The site is well-designed and fast. They have a myriad of services to help options traders find and place all kinds of complex option combination and spread trades. Customer service is very knowledgeable about options trading and confirms executions by e-mail. They are quick to return e-mails and solve account problems and offer 45-day history real-time updates for trades. All in all, one of the very best online brokerages when it comes to trading options online.
Account Minimum: $2,000 minimum balance for spread trades.
Option Commission: $19.95 + $1.75 per contract.
Spread Trades: All kinds of complex options combinations and spread orders can be processed online. Mr. Stock then directly routes them to the exchange floor to be traded as spreads, not legged into. Stop orders on options are allowed.
Stock Commission: Market orders—$14.95 for up to 5,000 shares, add $.015 per share for over 5,000; limit orders—$19.95 for up to 5,000 shares, add $.015 per share for over 5,000.
Real-Time Quotes. 100 free per trade.

Muriel Siebert & Co.
www.siebertnet.com
Address: 885 Third Avenue, 17th Floor, New York, NY 10022
Toll-Free: 800-872-0711
E-mail: service@siebertnet.com
Category: Middle-cost discount brokerage
Site Design: 7
User-Friendliness: 5
Options Usefulness: 5
General Comments: This brokerage went online early in 1996 and has had more time than most to develop its infrastucture. Their online services have garnered more than a few kudos from *Barron's* and *SmartMoney*. Although their live broker rates are a little pricey, they are rated as a middle-cost discount online brokerage. They have a reputation for excellent customer service and prompt executions. There are, however, a few complaints about high prices and the firm's complex accounting system.
Account Minimum: No minimum. But the minimum margin balance is $2,000.
Option Commission: $34 plus, depending on the number of contracts and the option's premium.
Spread Trades: Spread orders on stocks are accepted through a live broker. No index option spreads or stop orders. $25,000 minimum requirement to place spreads.

Stock Commission: Market and limit orders—$14.95 up to 1,000 shares and then $.02 for each additional share.
Real-Time Quotes: Unlimited real-time snapshot quotes.

MyDiscountBroker.com (Sovereign Securities)
www.mydiscountbroker.com
Address: 1201 Elm Street, Suite 121, Dallas, TX 75270
Tel: 214-672-6400
Toll-Free: 888-882-5600
Fax: 214-672-6440
E-mail: info@mydiscountbroker.com
Category: Deep discount brokerage
Slogan: "Where Low Commissions and Quality Service Reign"
Site Design: 7
User-Friendliness: 7
Options Usefulness: 6
General Comments: This firm's web site features a wide variety of investment resources and tools but gets mixed reviews from customers—some say the service is the pits and others say they've never seen better. People praise Sovereign's research capacities while others complain of stock availability limitations and technical problems. The web site is fast, but there can be lengthy phone waits for a live broker.
Account Minimum: Cash account—no minimum; margin account—$2,000.
Option Commission: $12 per trade plus $2 per contract (options $1+) or $1 per contract (options $.50–$.99) or $.50 per contract (options less than $.50); broker-assisted—$25 per trade plus $2 per contract.
Spread Trades: Spread orders are allowed but must be placed through a live broker, but will receive the Internet commission rate. Stop orders are allowed. Naked options are allowed also.
Stock Commission: $12 for up to 5,000 shares, then $.01 per share for the entire order.
Real-Time Quotes: Free unlimited real-time snapshot quotes.

National Discount Brokers
www.ndb.com
Address: 7 Hanover Square, 4th floor, New York, NY 10004
Tel: 212-863-4200
Toll-Free: 800-888-3999
Fax: 212-863-4400
E-mail: help@ndb.com
Category: Middle-cost discount brokerage
Site Design: 7
User-Friendliness: 5
Options Usefulness: 3
General Comments: Comments reflect that the firm is experiencing growing pains. NDB may have gotten too big too fast and therefore the web site is routinely down 10 or more minutes during high-volume periods. Nice touch: Brokers who speak Chinese (Mandarin and Cantonese), Spanish, and English are provided. No short sales online.
Account Minimum: $2,000
Option Commission: $35 plus $2.50 per contract (if the order is placed online or through the Touch-Tone phone system, you will get a 10% discount).
Spread Trades: NDB does not allow option spreads, stops on options, or naked options.
Stock Commission: Market orders—$14.75 plus $.01 per share for more than 5,000 shares; limit orders—$19.75 plus $.01 per share for more than 5,000 shares.
Real-Time Quotes: Free unlimited real-time snapshot quotes.

Net Investor
www.netinvestor.com
Address: 300 Route 38, West Moorestown, NJ 08057
Tel: 312-655-2650
Toll-Free: 1-800-NET-4250
E-mail: info@netinvestor.com
Category: High-cost discount brokerage
Slogan: "Personal Service, Professional Results"

Site Design: 6
User-Friendliness: 5
Options Usefulness: 5
General Comments: Created in 1994 by Wall Street prime mover Howe-Barnes, the Net Investor provides a variety of online services. Customer feedback is generally good with some reportage of slight technical problems and slowdowns. But *Barron's* called it the "Most Improved Website" in 1998, which shows a dramatic improvement. In addition, I got a knowledgeable live broker the very first time I called!
Account Minimum: $5,000
Option Commission: $35 plus $2.50 to $3 per contract.
Spread Trades: Spread orders must be placed through a live broker. Naked puts must be completely cash covered. No naked calls.
Stock Commission: Market and limit orders—$19.95 and $.01 per share. All stop orders must add $.01/share.
Real-Time Quotes: Free for active traders who place at least six trades per month; or $12.50 to $25 per month.

Newport Discount Brokerage
www.newport-discount.com
Address: 5499 North Federal Highway, Suite N, Boca Raton, FL 33487
Tel: 561-997-0471
Toll-Free: 800-999-3278
Fax: 561-997-0647
E-mail: newport@newport-discount.com
Category: Middle-cost discount brokerage
Site Design: 5
User-Friendliness: 4
Options Usefulness: 4
General Comments: Customer comments tend to be negative concerning the efficiency of Newport's trading process. The site definitely has some glitches, even for visitors.
Account Minimum: No minimum.
Option Commission: $40 minimum plus $3 per contract for options $1 and under; $4 per contract for options under $3.99; $5 per contract for options $4 and over.
Spread Trades: Spreads are allowed through a live broker. No stop orders on options. You must maintain an account minimum of $25,000 to be eligible to trade spreads and naked options.
Stock Commission: $19 for any trade (20,000 share online limit).
Real-Time Quotes: $29.95 per month for unlimited real-time quotes; free by Touch-Tone phone.

Olde Discount Corp.
www.olde.com
Address: 751 Grizwald, FMS, Detroit, MI 48226
Toll-Free: 800-235-3100
E-mail: Located on the web site
Category: High-cost discount brokerage
Site Design: 5
User-Friendliness: 3
Options Usefulness: 2
General Comments: Unfortunately, the word on Olde is not good. Customers have done more than complain; some are even taking the firm to court. They say they lost money while Olde brokers reap in the high commissions. There are also complaints of having nowhere stocks substituted for others more preferred. It's reported that they've been given the biggest fine in SEC history. Some people say they just spend too much for incompetent service and inadequate research. Perhaps the only way around it is to have a SmartTrade account—with a minimum of half a million dollars, you'll get free commissions on trades of 1,000 shares or more.
Account Minimum: $1,000.
Option Commission: Minimum of $40—1–5; $45—6–10; depends on how many contracts.
Spread Trades: Spreads are allowed, but only through a live broker. Stop orders on options are not allowed. You must have a minimum of $5,000 to trade options and a net worth of $40,000 (liquid assets, no real estate).

Stock Commission: 100 shares—$20 to $40; 500 shares is $40 to $100; 1,000 shares is $62.50 to $126; 2,000 shares is $77.50 to $175; 5,000 shares + is $152.50 to $325.
Real-Time Quotes: Delayed quotes only.

Peremel Online
www.peremel.com
Address: 1829 Reisterstown Road, Suite 120, Baltimore, MD 21208
Tel: 410-486-4700
Toll-Free: 800-PEREMEL
Fax: 410-486-4728
E-mail: info@peremel.com
Category: High-cost discount brokerage
Slogan: "The New Class of Discount Broker"
Site Design: 8
User-Friendliness: 6
Options Usefulness: 5
General Comments: Peremel is a relatively small firm with a few basic online services. They offer three levels of trading services: Peremel Personal, Peremel Direct, and Managed and Fee-Based Accounts. Peremel Personal gives you access to a licensed adviser; with Peremel Direct, you're on your own. Their site moves a little slowly, but it was easy to reach a live broker by phone. Company reports from Standard & Poor's or Morningstar are available for free.
Account Minimum: $1,000
Option Commission: $25 plus $1.50 to $2 per contract; $35 minimum commission.
Spread Trades: Spreads are allowed but must be placed through a live broker. Naked options require a $10,000 minimum. Must go through a review process prior to being allowed to trade options.
Stock Commission: Market orders—$18; limit orders—$20; Touch-Tone—$34; broker-assisted—$38; up to 2,000 shares, then $.01 per share on the entire order.
Real-Time Quotes: Delayed quotes only. Must call a live broker for real-time quotes.

Preferred Trade
www.preferredtrade.com or www.preftech.com
Address: 220 Montgomery, Suite 777, San Francisco, CA 94104
Tel: 415-781-0205
Toll-Free: 800-949-3504 or 888-781-0283
Fax: 415-781-0292
E-mail: info@preftech.com
Category: Middle-cost discount brokerage
Slogan: "Anything else is too slow."
Site Design: 9
User-Friendliness: 8
Options Usefulness: 7
General Comments: This firm made our top 10 list. They work hard to satisfy an options trader's needs. Customer comments report this site as helpful and responsive. Extra charges are not required for phone orders. Their RAES interface speeds up the execution process considerably.
Account Minimum: Cash account—$1,000; margin account—$5,000
Option Commission: $19.95 or $2.50 per contract (under 10) and $3 per contract (10 +).
Spread Trades: Spread trades are welcomed, but must be placed through a live broker. You must have a $10,000 minimum to place spread trades and a $100,000 minimum to place naked options.
Stock Commission: Market orders—$15 per trade (minimum) routed through direct access or ECNs; limit orders—$22.50 or $7.75 flat fee for eligible OTC routed to a third party.
Real-Time Quotes: Free unlimited real-time snapshot quotes.

Quick & Reilly
www.quick-reilly.com
Address: 26 Broadway, 13th Floor, New York, NY 10004
Toll-Free: 800-221-7220 or 800-533-8161
E-mail: help@quick-reilly.com
Category: Middle-cost discount brokerage

Site Design: 8
User-Friendliness: 7
Options Usefulness: 6
General Comments: Q&R almost made our top 10 list. It is working toward being a fully functional firm for the online options trader. Customer comments on the whole are very positive and tend to praise Q&R's execution capabilities and customer service responsiveness. System failures have been kept to a minimum.
Account Minimum: No minimum.
Option Commission: $37.50 and up plus $1.75 per contract.
Spread Trades: Currently, traders must call in option spread orders to a live broker. However, Q&R hopes to have the simultaneous placing of spread orders and other combination strategies available through online services by late 1999. Stop orders on options are not allowed and you cannot pick the exchange where your order will be processed. The minimum account requirement for naked orders depends on the equity in your account, option approval, and option experience—it's usually around $25,000.
Stock Commission: Market orders—$14.95 up to 5,000 shares and $.02 per share above 5,000 shares; limit orders—$19.95 up to 5,000 shares and $.02 per share above 5,000 shares.
Real-Time Quotes: 100 free real-time quotes upon opening an account and 100 free real-time quotes with every executed trade; 29.95 per month for unlimited free real-time quotes.

Regal Securities
www.regaldiscount.com
Address: 209 W. Jackson Street, Suite 404, Chicago, IL 60606
Toll-Free: 800-786-9000
E-mail: Located on the site
Category: High-cost discount brokerage
Site Design: 7
User-Friendliness: 6
Options Usefulness: 5
General Comments: Regal has been receiving some very positive reviews. Commissions are high, but margin rates are relatively low. Staff was very friendly and knowledgeable and easy to reach by phone. They are currently beta testing a brand-new, greatly expanded online trading system that should be available to customers very soon.
Account Minimum: $2,000 (margin account)
Option Commission: $29 for up to five contracts, then add $1.50 per additional contract.
Spread Trades: Spread trades must be placed through a live broker. You must have a minimum of $2,000 per spread trade. Naked put options require a minimum account balance of 50,000 and naked calls require $250,000. Stop orders must be called in each morning for they are only good for the day.
Stock Commission: Listed stocks—$26.50 up to 5,000 shares, then add $.01 per share for each additional share; Nasdaq stocks—$20 up to 999 shares; then a flat fee of $18 per order.
Real-Time Quotes: 50 real-time snapshot quotes per executed trade. Basically free to active investors.

Scottsdale Securities
www.scottrade.com
Address: 12855 Flushing Meadows Drive, St. Louis, MO 63131
Tel: 314-965-1555
Toll-Free: 800-619-7283
E-mail: support@mail1.scottsave.com
Category: Deep discount brokerage
Site Design: 6
User-Friendliness: 6
Options Usefulness: 2
General Comments: Scottrade, the online trading division of Scottsdale Securities, Inc., requires that 75% of all trades must be done on the Internet. They offer access to news, charts, research and local offices (90 across the nation) where you can develop a strong relationship with one individual broker. Customer comments report that the Scottsdale site has had more than its share of problems with intermittent luck in solving them. Some

people have found services to be very good and the site itself to be well designed and easy to use, but still complain of log-in problems almost daily.
Account Minimum: $2,000
Option Commission: $20 and up $1.60 per contract.
Spread Trades: Not available yet. Only basic services (buy or sell puts and calls or sell covered calls).
Stock Commission: Market orders—$7 flat fee; limit orders—$12 flat fee.
Real-Time Quotes: 100 real-time snapshot quotes. Unlimited real-time snapshot quotes are available from RT for $20 per month.

Sunlogic Securities
www.sunlogic.com
Address: 5333 Thornton Avenue, Newark, CA 94560
Toll-Free: 800-556-4600
Fax: 310-450-8340
E-mail: members@sunlogic.com
Category: High-cost discount broker
Site Design: 8
User-Friendliness: 6
Options Usefulness: 5
General Comments: Sunlogic is limited to providing service in the following states: New York, California, Arizona, Nevada, Virginia, Washington, and Georgia. It is one of the rare sites that lets customers transact in either English or Chinese. Its complex commission schedule can be confusing but the customer service staff gets high ratings.
Account Minimum: $2,000
Option Commission: Minimum $34 per trade; no minimum–$2,000—$18 plus 1.6% of principal; $2,001–$10,000—$39 plus 0.7% of principal; $10,000 and up—$76 plus 0.3% of principal; $6 per contract for the first five contracts; $2.50 per contract thereafter.
Spread Trades: Spread orders are allowed, but must be placed through a live broker. There is a minimum account balance of $5,000 to place spread orders. No naked options or stop orders on options are allowed.
Stock Commission: $18.99 up to 800 shares, then $.02 per share for each additional share. Limit orders—$35 up to 1,600 shares, then add $.02 per share.
Real-Time Quotes: Unlimited real-time quotes are $29.95 per month.

Suretrade
www.suretrade.com
Address: 670 George Washington Highway, Lincoln, RI 02865
Tel: 401-642-6900
Toll-Free: 800-909-6827
Fax: 401-642-5262
E-mail: service@suretrade.com
Category: Deep discount brokerage
Site Design: 7
User-Friendliness: 5
Options Usefulness: 6
General Comments: Suretrade is the deep discount arm of Quick & Reilly. Although Suretrade allows traders to place complicated option orders, it does not focus enough attention on providing option services. In addition, it has a reputation for poor customer service and inconsistent executions. More recent comments show they must be working to improve customer relations.
Account Minimum: $2,000 (margin account)
Option Commission: $20 + $1.70 per contract ($28.95 minimum). Add $25 for broker-assisted trades.
Spread Trades: Simple procedures such as buying calls and puts to open, selling calls and puts to close, selling covered calls, or buying calls to cover are allowed over the Internet. All other spreads and straddles must be placed with a live broker by phone for an additional $25 fee.
Stock Commission: Market and limit orders—$7.95 up to 5,000 shares plus $.01 per share for any additional shares; limit orders—$9.95 up to 5,000 shares plus $.01 per share for any additional shares.
Real-Time Quotes: 100 free per day.

Trade4Less (Downstate Discount)
www.trade4less.com
Address: 259 Indian Rocks Road North, Belleair Bluffs, Florida 33770
Tel: 727-586-3541
Toll-Free: 800-780-3543
E-mail: trade4less@downstate.com
Category: Middle-cost discount broker
Site Design: 6
User-Friendliness: 6
Options Usefulness: 5
General Comments: This firm offers before- and after-hours trading via Instinet. They were easy to reach and quite knowledgeable about options trading.
Account Minimum: $2,000
Option Commission: Under $1—$30 + $1.70/contract; $1 to $2.99—$35 + $2.50/contract; $3 and up—$35 plus $3 per contract.
Spread Trades: Spread trading is allowed with preapproval. Stop orders on options are not allowed. $25,000 minimum requirement for naked calls and $10,000 requirement for naked puts.
Stock Commission: $19.95 flat fee.
Real-Time Quotes: $29.95 per month for unlimited real-time quotes.

TradeStar Investments
www.4tradestar.com
Address: 5599 San Felipe, Suite 1400, Houston, TX 77056
Toll-Free: 800-961-1500 or 800-231-1058
Fax: 713-350-3773
E-mail: info@4tradestar.com or info@investorservices.net
Category: Middle-cost discount broker
Slogan: "Express Trading on the Net"
Site Design: 7
User-Friendliness: 6
Options Usefulness: 6
General Comments: TradeStar offers low flat-rate commissions and a number of special services including the Daily Rocket—a list of companies expected to be the highfliers and outperform the market over the next six months (courtesy of ACME Analytics).
Option Commission: $20 + $1.50 per contract.
Spread Trades: Spread trading is allowed through a live broker at Internet rates. You must maintain a $2,000 minimum account balance to place spread orders. Naked options require a $20,000 account minimum. Stop orders on options are allowed but are day orders only.
Stock Commission: Market orders—$14 for any number of shares; limit orders—$19 for any number of shares.
Real-Time Quotes: Unlimited free real-time snapshot quotes.

Tradewell Discount Investing
www.trade-well.com
Address: 25 Broadway, 7th Floor, New York, NY 10004
Tel: 212-888-8500
Toll-Free: 888-907-9797
Fax: 212-755-6312
E-mail: clientservice@trade-well.com
Category: High-cost discount broker
Slogan: "Same day, same side, same stock = 1 commission."
Site Design: 7
User-Friendliness: 5
Options Usefulness: 6
General Comments: Tradewell's "Priority Select Account" comes with a wide variety of on-line services products. Some of the pluses here are the free checking and free debit cards with no charges for multiple executions, and their research services are rated as excellent. The site is well-organized and attractive to the eye. Customers report effortless trading and fast service. In addition, Tradewell's staff appear to be quite knowledgeable, efficient, and very helpful.

Account Minimum: $500
Option Commission: $24.50 plus $1.50 to $3.50 per contract.
Spread Trades: Spreads orders are allowed but only through a live broker. Spread trading is a Level III account which requires a $5,000 account minimum. Naked options require a $50,000 account minimum. No stop orders on options are allowed.
Stock Commission: Market and limit orders (online and Touch-Tone)—$25.50 up to 3,000 shares, then $.01 per share for entire order.
Real-Time Quotes: Unlimited free real-time snapshot quotes or $75 plus exchange fees per month for Polaris RealTime Level II quotes (free after 25 trades per month except for exchange fees).

Trading Direct
www.tradingdirect.com
Address: 160 Broadway East Building, 10th Floor, New York, NY 10038
Tel: 212-766-0241
Toll-Free: 800-925-8566
Fax: 212-766-0914
E-mail: info@tradingdirect.com
Category: Deep discount broker
Slogan: "Cut out the Middleman. Trade Direct."
Site Design: 8
User-Friendliness: 7
Options Usefulness: 3
General Comments: Trading Direct has almost no additional fees and great rates on margin accounts that are actually below broker call, even when your balance is just $10,000. Limited options trading is available. Online orders require approval, which can delay order execution—not recommended for serious day traders. Customer comments are mixed regarding customer service and efficiency, although we had no problem getting through to a live person who was helpful and friendly.
Account Minimum: $2,000
Option Commission: $20 plus $1.75 per contract ($25 minimum); an additional $10 for broker-assisted transactions.
Spread Trades: TD allows the selling of covered calls and buying options only, and does not permit naked positions, spreads, and so on.
Stock Commission: $9.95 flat fee.
Real-Time Quotes: 50 free daily or $29.95 per month for unlimited real-time quotes.

TruTrade
www.trutrade.com
For ReCom Securities:
Address: 619 Marquette Avenue S., Minneapolis, MN 55402-1701
Toll-Free: 800-671-8505
For Levitt & Levitt:
Address: 39 S. LaSalle Street #1415, Chicago, IL 60603
Toll-Free: 800-328-8600
E-mail: info@levitt-levitt.com
Category: Deep discount broker
Site Design: 6
User-Friendliness: 5
Options Usefulness: 5
*General Comments:*TruTrade is the umbrella brokerage for Levitt & Levitt and ReCom Securities, Inc. (each at their separate rates).
Account Minimum: $5,000
Option Commission: $29 minimum commission; $2 to $4 per contract.
Spread Trades: Spread trades must be placed through a live broker. No stop orders on options are allowed. Spread trading and/or naked options require a $10,000 account minimum.
Stock Commission: Market and limit orders—$12.95 up to 1,999 shares, then $.01 per share.
Real-Time Quotes: Unlimited real-time snapshot quotes are available for $30 per month.

Vision Trade
www.visiontrade.com
Address: 310 Central Avenue, Lawrence, NY 11559
Tel: 516-374-2184
Toll-Free: 800-374-1940
Fax: 516-374-8443
E-mail: info@visiontrade.com
Category: Middle-cost discount broker
Site Design: 8
User-Friendliness: 7
Options Usefulness: 5
General Comments: This site is attractive, but lacks many of the basic amenities required by options traders. Comments reflect high reliability and good executions. Vision has a reputation for having the lowest margin rates around (no minimum–$49,999–$1/_2$% below broker call).
Account Minimum: Cash—no minimum; margin—$2,000
Option Commission: Under $1—$20 plus $1.50 per contract with a $25 minimum. $1 and over—$20 plus $2 per contract with a $25 minimum.
Spread Trades: Debit and credit option spreads must be called in for an additional fee of $20. Potential option traders must fill out an option agreement to properly assess their suitability. No stop loss orders on options. Real-time quotes are offered on options. To sell naked calls, minimum $25,000 account requirement. To sell naked puts, minimum $10,000 account requirement.
Stock Commission: 0–49 trades/mo—$16/trade (market or limit); 50–99 trades/mo.—$12.95/trade (market or limit); 100+ trades/mo.—$10.95/trade (market or limit).
Real-Time Quotes: $29.95 per month for unlimited real-time quotes. You get an initial bank of 100 quotes, and 20 additional real-time quotes for each trade.

Wall Street Access
www.wsaccess.com
Address: 17 Battery Place, New York, NY 10004
Tel: 212-709-9400
Toll-Free: 800-925-5781
Fax: 212-709-9522
E-mail: info@wsaccess.com
Category: High-cost discount broker
Slogan: "Where serious traders trade."
Site Design: 9
User-Friendliness: 9
Options Usefulness: 9
General Comments: Wall Street Access (WSA) easily made our top 10 list. Originally founded in 1981, WSA debuted its premium online brokerage services in 1993 including a wide variety of useful amenities for option traders. Perhaps its biggest claim to fame is that it was the first online brokerage to allow complex option spreads to be electronically placed. They are very proud of being independently owned and operated and provide direct representation on every exchange floor. You can also choose the exchange that you want your trade executed in. Customer comments, although mixed, remain mostly positive.
Account Minimum: $10,000
Option Commission: Less than $1—$25 + $1.50/contract; $1 or above—$25 + $2/contract.
Spread Trades: Spreads can be placed directly online. Naked options require a $50,000 minimum account balance. Stop orders on options are allowed.
Stock Commission: $25 for up to 5,000 shares, then $.02 per share for entire order.
Real-Time Quotes: 100 free quotes for every executed trade.

Wall Street Discount Corporation
www.wsdc.com
Address: 100 Wall Street, 7th Floor, New York, NY 10005
Toll-Free: 888-4-WALLST or 800-221-4034
Fax: 212-809-3899
E-mail: info@wsdc.com
Category: Middle-cost discount brokerage

Site Design: 6
User-Friendliness: 5
Options Usefulness: 4
General Comments: Some option perks, but not many. Customer comments are quite positive regarding executions. The web site is currently being overhauled, which may increase our site design rating in the future.
Account Minimum: No minimum
Option Commission: $29.95 minimum and between $1.50 and $5.75 per contract depending on option premium.
Spread Trades: Spread trades are allowed through a live broker. You must have a $100,000 account minimum for spread trading or naked options. Stop orders on option are allowed. Basic option trades placed on the Internet may not exceed 10 contracts.
Stock Commission: Market and limit orders are $19.95 for up to 2,500 shares and $.015 per share above 2,500 shares.
Real-Time Quotes: 100 free real-time quotes when you get an account and 100 free real-time snapshot quotes per executed trade.

WallStreet Electronica

www.wallstreete.com
Address: 5900 SW 41st Street, Miami, FL 33155
Tel: 305-669-3026
Toll-Free: 888-925-5783
Fax: 305-661-7402
E-mail: info@wallstreete.com
Category: Middle-cost discount brokerage
Slogan: "WallStreetE . . . Where Money Meets Technology"
Site Design: 9
User-Friendliness: 10
Options Usefulness: 9
General Comments: WallStreetE is #1 on our top 10 list because it offers a variety of tools for options traders including online spread trading. The commissions are relatively inexpensive (you pay an additional 1.5 cents per share over the $14.95 base rate on all trades over 1,000 shares), and they offer commission breaks for frequent traders. They are also highly respected for their research tools, offering screening tools for both mutual funds and stocks as well as analyst recommendations and charting. The site is bilingual, offering Spanish and English translations.
Account Minimum: $2,500; $10,000 minimum for spread trades
Option Commission: $25 plus $2.50 per contract (plus frequent trader bonuses).
Spread Trades: Spread trades can be initiated directly online. Stop orders on options are sometimes allowed, depending on market performance.
Stock Commission: Market orders—$14.95 per trade; limit orders—$19.95 per trade; frequent trader bonuses—10 trades in one week entitle you to a complimentary ticket charge.
Real-Time Quotes: 100 free real-time quotes per day.

Wang Investments

www.wangvest.com
Address: 41-60 Main Street, Suite 209, Flushing, NY 11355
Tel: 718-353-9264
Toll-Free: 800-353-9264
Fax: 718.353.9711
E-mail: info@wangvest.com
Category: Middle-cost discount brokerage
Site Design: 7
User-Friendliness: 6
Options Usefulness: 5
General Comments: Wang offers low option commissions and you can choose the exchange at which your options are traded. They also offer the entire online process in Chinese. Comments range from excellent ratings on reliability and execution to complaints about customer service reps with strong accents making it hard to communicate effectively.

Account Minimum: $2,000 (options); $5,000 (margin); $20 fee if less than $5,000 to open.
Option Commission: $23 base charge plus $2 per contract ($25 minimum).
Spread Trades: For a spread order account minimum is $30,000 for equity spread and $100,000 for index spread. Spread orders must be entered through a broker. Stops on options are available, but not a spread order.
Stock Commission: $8 for market and limit orders for stock price over $5; $15 Touch-Tone orders.
Real-Time Quotes: $10 per month unlimited real-time quotes or 100 free quotes per trade.

Waterhouse Webbroker
www.waterhouse.com
Address: 100 Wall Street, 24th Floor, New York, NY 10005
Toll-Free: 800-934-4410
E-mail: custserv@waterhouse.com
Category: Deep discount brokerage
Slogan: "Online trading for the individual investor"
Site Design: 7
User-Friendliness: 6
Options Usefulness: 6
General Comments: This is one of the bigger firms—most recently merging with Jack White and Kennedy-Chabot. Unfortunately, customer comments are not exactly positive about the effect the merger has had on any of these brokerages. They have fair to poor ratings for reliability, web site, and execution speed, and lengthy phone waits. On the bright side, they do offer a lot of services including stock screening, market commentary by Briefing.com, news, charts, portfolio tracking, investment reports, free checking, free debit card, and more.
Account Minimum: $1,000
Option Commission: Prices depend on how many contracts and the respective premium. Prices start at $28.13 and rise all the way to $252.90.
Spread Trades: Option chain quotes are available. Online spread trading should be available in the very near future.
Stock Commission: $12 flat fee for up to 5,000 shares of any stock, then $.01 per share for entire order; $100 for 10,000 shares.
Real-Time Quotes: 100 free real-time quotes on opening an account and 100 free per executed trade; or $5 per 100 quotes.

Web Street Securities
www.webstreetsecurities.com
Address: 510 Lake Cook, 4th Floor, Deerfield, IL 60015
Tel: 847-267-1800
Toll-Free: 800-932-8723
E-mail: CustomerService@WebStreetSecurities.com
Category: Deep discount brokerage
Site Design: 6
User-Friendliness: 7
Options Usefulness: 3
General Comments: Excellent commission costs and some great features have garnered a lot of awards for this firm. Unfortunately, it does not allow spread trades. But for the active stock trader, it does offer automatic live quote updating, and plenty of free research tools, and a "Trading Pit" that resembles Net-based professional trading station. You can also speak to a live broker 24 hours a day—a real plus. Web Street does not charge a commission on stock orders of 1,000 shares or more. They offset whatever loss in profits this may create by routing orders to specific market makers who, in turn, make payments to Web Street for the additional business.
Account Minimum: No minimum.
Option Commission: $14.95 plus $1.75 per contract.
Spread Trades: No spreads allowed.
Stock Commission: Any listed stock trade, any size—$14.95; Nasdaq stock trades under 1,000 shares $14.95 and Nasdaq stock trades 1,000 shares or more FREE.
Real-Time Quotes: Free unlimited real-time quotes. Web Street Securities has developed the Internet's first Java applet which updates your watch list automatically as the market moves. This service is available to account holders for $29.95.

Wilshire Capital
www.wilshirecm.com
Address: 120 Broadway, Suite 960, New York, NY 10271
Toll-Free: 800-926-9991
Fax: 212-433-6024
E-mail: wilshire@pipeline.com
Category: High-cost discount brokerage
Site Design: 5
User-Friendliness: 4
Options Usefulness: 4
General Comments: Wilshire presents immediate executions and price improvement, with rebates on short balances that are over $250,000. Wilshire has order flow sales.
Account Minimum: No minimum. $25,000 option minimum
Option Commission: $3 per contract plus exchange fees (minimum $30).
Spread Trades: Spread trades must be placed through a live broker (you must have a $10,000 minimum balance to place a spread and a $25,000 minimum plus margin requirements for naked options).
Stock Commission: $25 minimum commission; $15 for 100 shares; $17.50 for 200 shares; $20 for 300 shares; $22.50 for 400 shares; and $.03 per share with $150 for 5,000 shares.
Real-Time Quotes: Delayed only. Real-time quotes will be available soon.

Wit Capital Corporation
www.witcapital.com
Address: 826 Broadway, 6th Floor, New York, NY 10003
Tel: 212-253-4400
Toll-Free: 888-394-8227 or 888-474-8241
E-mail: mail@witcapital.com
Category: Middle-cost discount brokerage
Slogan: "The Market Is Now Open"
Site Design: 6
User-Friendliness: 4
Options Usefulness: 4
General Comments: Wit's claim to fame is in regard to IPOs where customers can purchase new-issue shares online. Unfortunately, there are a few customer comments that reflect an inability to get the promised shares. Other than that they seem to be a well-established firm with all the online bells and whistles, but not much of a focus on options. However, in trying to gain more information about this company, I dialed the main number and was referred to a list of numbers that I should call depending on what kind of information or service I was attempting to find. After a few more recordings, I finally reached an operator who turned out to be an operator in a message service. She told me to consult the web site for any questions I may have or fill out an e-mail form for any additional questions. This time-consuming runaround speaks volumes regarding this firm's ability to service their customers. I finally managed to get through and speak with a live broker (quite friendly and helpful) on what I guess was a much less busy day.
Account Minimum: $1,000
Option Commission: Premium under $1—$27 plus $1.50 per contract; premium over $1—$27 plus $3 per contract.
Spread Trades: Spreads are allowed, but must be placed through a live broker. You must be preapproved in order to do spreads and naked options, but they were vague as to any specific requirements.
Stock Commission: Market orders—$14.95 up to 5,000 shares and then $.01 per share for the entire order; limit orders—$19.95 up to 5,000 shares and then $.01 per share for the entire order. If you access Wit by Touch-Tone, you pay 27 cents per minute and are credited 12 free minutes for each executed trade.
Real-Time Quotes: Delayed quotes only.

Wyse Securities
www.wyse-sec.com
Address: 20735 Stevens Creek Boulevard, Suite C, Cupertino, CA 95014
Tel: 408-343-2900
Toll-Free: 800-640-8668
E-mail: johnh@hooked.net

Category: Middle-cost discount brokerage
Slogan: "A Professional Discount Broker You Can Trust"
Site Design: 8
User-Friendliness: 5
Options Usefulness: 3
General Comments: We like the design of this site, but it lacks many of the amenities that options traders really need. Comments reflect reliability and good executions.
Account Minimum: $2,000
Option Commission: $21.50 ($17 + $4.50 fee); $5.75 per option for first five options with $38.50 ($34 + $4.50) minimum; $3.50 minimum for next three, then $1.95 per option thereafter.
Spread Trades: No spread trades. Basic options services only.
Stock Commission: $7.95 flat fee on market and limit orders; live broker trades $19.95.
Real-Time Quotes: 100 quotes per executed trade.

Ziegler Thrift
www.ziegler-thrift.com
Address: 733 Marquette Avenue, Suite 106, Minneapolis, MN 55402
Tel: 612-333-4206
Toll-Free: 800-328-4854
E-mail: ziegler@primenet.com
Category: Middle-cost discount brokerage
Slogan: "A Reduced Commission Brokerage Firm"
Site Design: 7
User-Friendliness: 7
Options Usefulness: 4
General Comments: For what it's worth, I like this company. They respond quickly to inquiries and seem to have a competent customer service department. Comments from customers reflect excellent execution of simple option market orders. Unfortunately, Ziegler does not promote options trading, and is not yet equipped to handle spread orders. Traders are required to fill out a special option application if they wish to trade options.
Account Minimum: No minimum
Option Commission: $27 + $1.50 per contract.
Spread Trades: No naked options or spreads. Stop orders on option trades are not accepted. They do offer free real-time quotes on options.
Stock Commission: Market and limit orders—$19.73 for up to 1,973 shares and then $.01 per share over; $50 for 5,000 shares.
Real-Time Quotes: 100 free real-time quotes per executed trade.

index

about the author

george a. fontanills

Having struggled to overcome a life-threatening illness as a young man, George Fontanills is a true believer in the idea that pursuing your dreams is something that should never be put off until tomorrow. Like many people, George followed the typical educational and work-related path. From high school, he went to college, from college to an accounting job at the prestigious firm of Deloitte, Haskins Sells. Upon receiving his CPA license, George started work with Anderson Consulting. Not quite satisfied with where his life was headed, he left this job to attend Harvard Business School's MBA program.

After receiving his MBA, George decided to get off the treadmill of unsatisfying jobs. In the face of several high-paying job opportunities, George decided that he needed to start his own business. His first business failed. Undaunted, he started a second business that never left the starting gate. A survivor, he kept going. Running low on money, George became a real estate investor buying property with no money down. Finding a business he enjoyed, he quickly began to build a successful track record and increase his net worth. Just as he began to feel that he had found his lifelong career, the bottom fell out of the real estate market—strike three.

As George pondered his next move, he received a brochure on making money in the markets. After ordering the book, he began trading . . . and losing money. Rather than concentrating on his own losses, he began studying successful traders to see what they were doing differently. Using the analysis skills he developed at Harvard, George conducted a comprehensive investigation to determine what differentiated the winners from the losers. Risking the money he made in real estate, George tested his conclusions and eventually learned to use managed risk strategies. This innovative approach uses options to mathematically control risk every time a trade is placed, thereby consistently producing income without the stress of unbridled losses. He called this trading style "Optionetics." As his net worth soared, George gained a reputation as one of the world's most respected traders. As an expert in nondirectional, managed risk trading, George Fontanills became a regular speaker at trading conferences and investment summits.

Today, Mr. Fontanills is the president of Global Investment Research Corp. and remains an active equity options and stock investor. Mr. Fontanills currently teaches this strategic approach through his study program, *Optionetics: The Science of High Profit and Low Stress Trading*. Specializing in delta neutral trading using stocks, options on indexes, and options on stocks, George Fontanills has instructed thousands of traders nationally and around the world.

As President of Pinnacle Investments of America, Inc. (www. piafunds.com), Mr. Fontanills is a registered investment adviser and hedge fund manager in Boston, as well as a consultant to a number of offshore trading organizations, professional trading firms, and large financial institutions. His unique approach to trading and phenomenal success has made him a sought-after speaker at a variety of conferences. His reputation as a pioneer in teaching delta neutral trading has led to numerous guest appearances on television and radio shows across the country. George Fontanills is also the author of numerous articles, publications, and books (including *Interactive Trading*, *Triple Your Money*, *Can't Lose Strategies*, *Vacation Trades Manual*, and the *Wealth Without Worry Newsletter*.) His first hardback release—*The Options Course*, published by John Wiley & Sons—has added to his critical acclaim as one of the best options instructors in the country.

free trading package
from george fontanills

Now that you've read George's book, wouldn't you like to keep up with his day-to-day trading strategies? We're going to make it easy to do by sending you a FREE Trading Package worth $100.

George's company, Global Investment Research Corp., is one of the leading investment publishing companies in the trading industry today. Global has grown to provide dozens of vital resources for stock and stock options traders. Using a simple yet effective philosophy of continued education and personal attention, George and his team of traders strive for excellence in all their trading products and services.

To receive your free trading package, complete and mail the coupon below to:

> Global Investment Research Corp.
> P.O. Box 620238
> Woodside, CA 94062-0238
> or Fax to: 650-378-8320.

You can also reach us by phone at 888-366-8264, or 650-378-8333 outside the U.S, e-mail us at george@global investcorp.com, or visit our web site at www.optionetics.com.

George Fontanills' Trading Package

☐   I would like to learn more about George's trading secrets and strategies. Please send me the FREE trading package mentioned in *Trade Options Online*.

Name: _____

Address: _____

City, State, ZIP: _____

Phone: _____ Fax: _____

E-Mail: _____

I purchased this book from: _____